The **Rough Guide** to

Copenhagen

written and researched by

Lone Mouritsen & Caroline Osborne

ROUGH
GUIDES

NEW YORK · LONDON · DELHI

www.roughguides.com

Contents

Danish design colour section following p.80

Food and drink colour section following p.176

Color maps following p.288

3

◄◄ View across Sortedams Sø ◄ Nyhavn harbour

Introduction to

Copenhagen

Copenhagen (København) is Scandinavia's most vibrant and affordable capital, and one of Europe's most user-friendly cities. Small and welcoming, it's a place where people rather than cars set the pace, with a multitude of pavement cafés, pedestrianized thoroughfares and cycle lanes. It also offers a range of entertainment that belies its relatively modest size: by day, there's a cornucopia of historic royal palaces, national museums, art galleries, lovely parks and excellent shopping; by night, there are plenty of cosy bars and an intimate club and live music network that could hardly be bettered. It's a city that comes into its own in summer – cafés spill out onto the streets, live music (especially jazz) is around every corner, and the harbourfront, currently in the grip of a wave of renovations and exciting building projects, including the new play house, comes to life with plentiful tour boats, open-air swimming pools and events.

The wave of modern buildings along the harbourfront aside, architecturally, much of the city dates from the seventeenth and eighteenth centuries, a cultured ensemble of handsome Renaissance palaces, parks and merchant houses laid out around the waterways and canals that give the city, in places, a pronounced Dutch flavour. Successive Danish monarchs left their mark, in particular Christian IV, creator of many of the city's most striking landmarks – including Rosenborg Slot and the district of Christianshavn – and Frederik V, who graced the capital with the palaces of Amalienborg and the grandiose Marmorkirken. These landmarks remain the highest points in a refreshingly low and undeveloped skyline.

Historically, Copenhagen owes its existence to its position on the narrow Øresund strait separating Denmark from Sweden and commanding the entrance to the Baltic – one of the great trading routes of medieval Europe and now the site of the region's grandest engineering feat, the massive Øresunds Bridge. It's this location, poised between Scandinavia and the rest of Europe, which continues to give Copenhagen its distinctive character. Compared to the relatively staid capitals further north, the city has a more laid-back, European flavour; the freedom with which its most famous export, Carlsberg, flows in the city's hundreds of bars is in stark contrast to the puritanical licensing laws found elsewhere in Scandinavia. Yet Copenhagen is also a flagship example of the Scandinavian commitment to liberal social values – exemplified by its laid-back attitudes to everything from gay marriage to pornography – and its continued (if precarious) respect for the unique "Free City" of Christiania.

For all its success, however, the new millennium finds Copenhagen facing changes and challenges. On the one hand, the magnificent Øresunds Bridge has given the city the infrastructure to become the western Baltic's leading urban centre, and there are many who would like to see it take full advantage of this and develop into a truly internationalist, forward-looking metropolis. On the other, there are some who regard the bridge as, at best, an irrelevance, and at worst, a symbol of all those foreign influences – typified by Copenhagen's burgeoning immigrant community – that threaten to undermine traditional Danish values; simmering racial tensions, and the resulting rise of right-wing politicians, pose increasing challenges to the city's tolerant image. For all that, it's worth remembering that the city's occasional smugness and resistance to change is the result of its citizens' pride in their capital – as a visitor, you'll be made to feel welcome wherever you go, especially since absolutely everybody speaks English.

What to see

Copenhagen is a very manageable city; it takes just thirty minutes to walk across the compact centre and the wealth of green spaces and pedestrianized areas make exploring a relaxed and thoroughly civilized experience. The historic core of the city is **Slotsholmen**, originally the site of the twelfth-century castle and now home to the huge royal and governmental complex of Christiansborg. Facing Slotsholmen over the Slotsholmen Kanal is the medieval maze of **Indre By**, the bustling heart of the city, traversed by Strøget, the world's longest pedestrianized street, and packed with an abundance of shops, cafés and bars, as well as an eclectic clutch of museums and churches. On the opposite side of Slotsholmen from Indre By, the island of **Christianshavn** is one of the inner city's most relaxed and bohemian areas, and home to the "Free City" of Chris-

▲ Kongens Have

tiania, Copenhagen's famous alternative-lifestyle community. Northeast of Indre By, the fairy-tale castle of **Rosenborg**, one of several royal residences in the city, sits at the heart of the inner city's greenest area – Kongens Have and the lush gardens of Botanisk Have – and within striking distance of two excellent art museums. Abutting Kongens Have, **Frederikstad**, Frederik V's royal quarter, is dominated by the huge dome of the Marmorkirken and centred on the royal palaces of Amalienborg. South of Indre By, close to the town hall and main square, Rådhuspladsen, you'll find the more earthy pleasures of the delightful **Tivoli** amusement park, as well as the excellent **Nationalmuseet** and **Glyptotek** art and sculpture gallery.

If you're willing to venture a little out of the centre, you'll discover a variety of distinctive and contrasting districts. To the west, multicultural **Vesterbro**, with its ethnic eateries and trendy nightlife, rubs shoulders with the genteel, villa-lined streets of **Frederiksberg**, where you'll find the tranquil Frederiksberg Have, the city's zoo, and the delights of the Carlsberg brewery visitor centre. To the west lies the rapidly developing island of **Amager** with its beaches and

▲ Cycling in the city

nature reserve. To the north of the centre, the formerly working-class but increasingly gentrified district of **Nørrebro** is centred on the fashionable bars and restaurants of Sankt Hans Torv and Blågårdsgade; to its east, snooty **Østerbro** is home to Copenhagen's old money, as well as the city centre's largest open space, Fælledparken.

Copenhagen, though, as any Dane will tell you, is by no means an accurate reflection of Denmark – indeed, a greater contrast with the sleepy provincialism of the rest of the country would be hard to find. Thanks to rapid transport links that connect the capital with its surrounding countryside, however, you can enjoy all the pleasures of rural Zealand without ever being much more than an hour away from the capital. Amongst the many attractions that ring the city are the stunning modern art museums of **Louisiana** and **Arken**, and the great castles of **Kronborg** (the "Elsinore Castle" of Shakespeare's *Hamlet*) and Frederiksborg, while the ancient Danish capital of **Roskilde**, with its magnificent cathedral and museum of Viking ships, offers another enticing day-trip. A little over an hour away, **Odense**, on the picturesque island of Funen, is birthplace of the country's most famous son, Hans Christian Andersen, and houses a number of fairy tale-themed museums and sights in his name. Thanks to the new bridge, **Malmö**, in southern Sweden, is now

In summer, cafés spill out onto the streets, live music is around every corner and the harbourfront comes to life

also within easy reach of Copenhagen, offering an historic centre as well as many good shops and a variety of restaurants.

Furthermore, if you're here in summer, it's worth bearing in mind that you're just a short train ride away from the **beaches** of the Øresund coast, and – if you fancy making an overnight stop in Helsingør – the even more beautiful sandy stretches and pretty fishing villages of the North Zealand coast make for a very rewarding side-trip.

▼ Storkespringvandet, Indre By

When to go

Copenhagen is on the same latitude as Edinburgh and Moscow, and **winters**, as you'd expect, are wet, windy and cold, with temperatures regularly falling below zero, though if you're prepared to brave the weather, there's the chance to go skating on frozen city lakes before retreating indoors for a comfortable glass of *gløgg*. The city is prettiest in **spring**, when the trees come into leaf and the locals are in high spirits as they emerge from their layers of winter clothing. **Summer** weather can be variable: rain is a common occurrence, though when the sun appears the locals

▲ Børsen's spire

turn out in force, occupying every last corner of every park and pavement café, while the long summer evenings see the city at its liveliest. **Autumn** can also be a pleasant time to visit, with periods of rain interspersed with beautiful sunny days when the seasonal colours can best be appreciated.

Average maximum and minimum daily temperatures, and average monthly rainfall

	Jan	Feb	Mar	Apr	May	June	July	Aug	Sept	Oct	Nov	Dec
Max°C	2	2	5	10	16	19	22	21	18	12	7	4
Min°C	-2	-3	-1	3	8	11	14	14	11	7	3	1
Max°F	36	36	41	50	61	66	72	70	64	54	45	39
Min°F	28	26	30	37	46	52	57	57	52	45	37	34
Rain (In.)	1.9	1.5	1.3	1.5	1.7	1.9	2.8	2.6	2.4	2.3	1.9	1.9

things not to miss

It's not possible to see everything that Copenhagen has to offer in one trip – and we don't suggest you try. What follows is a selective taste of the city's highlights, from atmospheric castles and superb museums to hippie hangouts and beautiful parks. They're arranged in five colour-coded categories to help you find the very best things to see, do, eat and experience. All highlights have a page reference to take you straight into the guide, where you can find out more.

01 Nyhavn Page **64** • Day or night, picture-postcard Nyhavn, with its canalside stretch of lively bars and cafés, is a great spot for a beer and herring platter.

02 **Smørrebrød** See *Food and drink* **colour section** • This quintessentially Danish lunch is best washed down with a snaps or a cold beer.

DIGTEREN

HANS CHRISTIAN

ANDERSEN

F. 2DEN APRIL 1805

D. 4DE AUGUST 1875

DEN SJÆL GUD I SIT BILLEDE HAR SKABT

ER UFORKRÆNKELIG, KAN EI GAAE TABT

04 **Assistens Kirkegård** Page **114** • Search for Hans Christian Andersen's grave or take a picnic and relax in this atmospheric cemetery.

05 **Louisiana** Page **130** • An outstanding collection of modern art in spectacular surroundings, with a fabulous sculpture garden overlooking the Øresund.

03 **Bird's-eye view of the city** Page **70** • Climb one of Copenhagen's spires or towers for a fantastic view of the city.

06 **Cycling** Page **30** • Cycling is the omnipresent mode of transport that puts any destination in the city within quick and easy reach.

08 **Exploring the harbour/ canals** Page **28** • Cruise the city's waterways for a revealing glimpse of its merchant past and stunning views of its modern harbourfront architecture.

07 **Glyptotek** Page **94** • Top off your tour of the Egyptian and Roman artefacts, Rodin sculptures, Danish Golden Age painting and Impressionist wing with lunch among the foliage of the Vinter Have café.

09 **Kronborg Slot** Page **133** • Tactically positioned on a sandy curl of land looking out over the Øresund, for centuries Kronborg collected the Sound Tolls from passing ships, though it's more famous as the moody setting for Shakespeare's *Hamlet*.

10 **Christiania** Page **71** • The hippie city within a city has its own quirky restaurants, cafés, arts venues, shops and galleries, as well as funky, colourful houses in a peaceful waterfront setting.

11 Nightlife Page **200** •
Copenhagen's plethora of nightspots means that there's always somewhere else to head to as the night moves on.

13 Outdoor cafés Page **195** •
Considering its northern latitude, Copenhagen houses an astounding number of outdoor cafés, made cosy with blankets and heaters when it gets cold.

12 Danish pastries See *Food and drink* **colour section** • Lighter, flakier and infinitely more delicious than the ones back home.

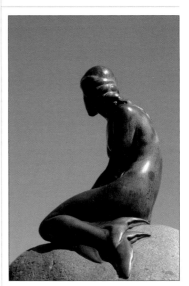

14 The Little Mermaid Page **87** • Despite its modest dimensions, the mermaid is Copenhagen's most famous symbol and the city's de facto emblem.

15 **Brunch by the lakes** Page 179 • Ranging from protein-packed fry-ups to light and refreshing platters of fruit and cheese served with fresh, warm bread, brunch is a culinary treat, best enjoyed at one of the lakeside cafés.

16 **Marmorkirken** Page 82 • Built by Frederick V for his new royal quarter, Marmorkirken was northern Europe's answer to St Peter's in Rome.

17 **Frederiksberg Have** Page 107 • The rolling lawns, lime groves, lakes and follies of this beautiful park are enough to tempt you here, and with visits to the nearby zoo, porcelain factory and Carslberg brewery, it could easily turn into a day-trip.

18 **Tivoli** Page 92 • The city's pleasure gardens still pull in punters by the thousands for the magical mix of funfair, food, festivities and fireworks.

19 Illums Bolighus Page **219** • In the heart of the city's shopping district, Illums is an institution selling the best in Danish design from Arne Jacobsen chairs to Bodum coffeeware.

21 The Queen's Tapestries Page **44** • The royal family may no longer live in Christiansborg Slot, but the colourful, modern tapestries there, depicting Danish history, provide a stunning backdrop to royal functions.

20 Vikingeskibs Museet Page **143** • On the banks of scenic Roskilde Fjord – once home of Viking settlements – this collection of wooden hulls provides an engrossing introduction to Viking boat building and nautical skills.

22 Jazz Page **232** • You're never far from jazz in Copenhagen; in summer, the city's streets and squares come alive with buskers and bands, especially during the Copenhagen Jazz Festival.

23 Swimming in the harbour
Page **227** • In summer, do like the Danes and take a refreshing dip in one of the open-air harbour pools, with the city skyline as a backdrop.

24 Rosenborg Slot
Page **78** • This fairytale-like castle, positioned in the carefully manicured Kongens Have, calls to mind Hans Christian Andersen's more romantic tales.

25 Pølser
Page **177** • The city's ubiquitous fast food of choice goes further than the average hot dog, with a wider range of sausages and sauces.

26 Nationalmuseet
Page **96** • A treasure trove of the nation's history from Stone Age skeletons to dazzling Viking silver to Christian IV's dagger, as well as fascinating ethnological collections from around the world.

Basics

Basics

Getting there

From the UK and Ireland, the most convenient way of getting to Copenhagen is to fly to Copenhagen Airport – there's a good selection of flights, and the cheapest fares are often less expensive than the long and arduous journey by train or bus. An alternative airport, for cheap tickets with discount airlines, is the small Sturup airport in Malmö, Sweden, a short bus journey from the centre of Copenhagen. From North America, a handful of airlines fly direct to Copenhagen, though it may be cheaper to route via London, picking up a budget flight onwards from there. Going via London or another European hub is the only option open for those coming from Australia, New Zealand and South Africa, from where there are no direct flights.

Airfares depend on the **season**, with the highest from (roughly) early June to mid-September, when the weather is best; you'll get the best prices during the low season, November through to April (excluding Christmas and New Year, when prices are hiked up and seats are at a premium). Bear in mind, though, that ticket prices from the UK are not subject to seasonal changes to the extent that they are in North America. Note also that flying on weekends is generally more expensive; price ranges quoted below assume midweek travel.

Flights from the UK and Ireland

Airfares **from the UK** to Copenhagen continue to drop as new operators join the fray. Special offers and discounted tickets apart, the **scheduled fares** of the major airlines are pretty well matched; the cheaper seats tend to be found on smaller carriers such as Sterling and British Midland. Low-cost carriers such as easyJet and Ryanair-to Malmö (Sturup)-offer the best deals.

There are a great number of flights, with direct services from **London** to Copenhagen (1hr 45min) with SAS, British Airways, easyJet, Sterling and Varig. Copenhagen is also well served by regional airports in the UK, including **Aberdeen** (SAS), **Birmingham** (SAS), **Edinburgh** (British Midland, Sterling and SAS), **Glasgow** (British Midland), **Manchester** (SAS) and **Newcastle** (SAS). All these carriers operate at least one flight a day, though services may be reduced at weekends.

The lowest regular **fares** to Copenhagen at the time of writing were with easyJet and Sterling at around £80 return (with limited numbers of seats at discount fares of around £60). Ryanair often has special offers for around £50 or lower on its flights to Malmö (Sturup) in Sweden, from where it's a short bus journey to Copenhagen via the Øresunds Bridge (see p.25). Otherwise, expect to pay in the region of £125 for a discounted return ticket from Britain to Denmark bought directly from SAS, British Midland, Varig or British Airways.

The easiest route to Copenhagen **from Ireland** is on one of the twice-daily SAS flights from **Dublin**. You can also fly with Ryanair from Dublin to Malmö (Sturup) in Sweden, or with Aer Lingus via London Heathrow from Dublin, **Cork** and **Shannon** to Copenhagen.

Official **fares** to Copenhagen are around €174 for a midweek, rock-bottom economy fare; flights with Ryanair from Dublin to Malmö (Sturup) in Sweden start at €85. If you're flying from one of the regional airports, it may be cheaper to find one of the numerous special deals to London and then take advantage of the more competitive airfares available from there (see p.22).

From **Belfast**, there are no direct flights to Copenhagen, and your best bet is probably to fly via London, Glasgow or Edinburgh with British Midland or SAS. **Fares** usually start at £270 for an economy return. Failing that, you should be able to get a reasonable deal through a discount agent, either in Northern Ireland or in mainland Britain.

Flights from the US and Canada

From the US and Canada, the majority of flights to Copenhagen involve **changing planes** in a European hub – and if you don't live in one of North America's gateway cities, you might have to change more than once. **Direct flights** are only available from the US, with SAS, Continental and Delta Air Lines, and if you can be fairly flexible with your departure dates, you should be able to take advantage of the special promotional fares regularly offered by the airlines.

Fares are fairly similar, whichever carrier you choose, though it's still worth shopping around. SAS daily direct flights from Newark (7hr 35min) cost $1100–1200 in the high season and $550–800 in the low. Tickets from **Chicago** (8hr 15min) and **Washington** (8hr) cost $1200–1300 high season, $600–850 low season; from **Seattle** (9hr 30min) $1650–1750 high, $650–950 low. Continental's daily direct flight from Newark (7hr 55min) costs $950–1050 high season and $500–600 low season, while Delta Air Lines fly daily from **Atlanta** (9hr) for $1100–1200 high season, $600–700 low season.

If fares seem high, you might want to consider flying to **London**, one of the cheapest European cities to get to, and taking a flight, train or bus from there (see p.22).

Fly less – stay longer! Travel and climate change

Climate change is a serious threat to the ecosystems that humans rely upon, and air travel is among the fastest-growing contributors to the problem. Rough Guides regard travel, overall, as a global benefit, and feel strongly that the advantages to developing economies are important, as is the opportunity of greater contact and awareness among peoples. But we all have a responsibility to limit our personal impact on global warming, and that means giving thought to how often we fly, and what we can do to redress the harm that our trips create.

Flying and climate change

Pretty much every form of motorized travel generates CO_2 – the main cause of human-induced climate change – but planes also generate climate-warming contrails and cirrus clouds and emit oxides of nitrogen, which create ozone (another greenhouse gas) at flight levels. Furthermore, flying simply allows us to travel much further than we otherwise would do. The figures are frightening: one person taking a return flight between Europe and California produces the equivalent impact of 2.5 tonnes of CO_2 – similar to the yearly output of the average UK car.

Fuel-cell and other less harmful types of plane may emerge eventually. But until then, there are really just two options for concerned travellers: to reduce the amount we travel by air (take fewer trips – stay for longer!), and to make the trips we do take "climate neutral" via a carbon-offset scheme.

Carbon-offset schemes

Offset schemes run by ⓦwww.climatecare.org, ⓦwww.carbonneutral.com and others allow you to make up for some or all of the greenhouse gases that you are responsible for releasing. To do this, they provide "carbon calculators" for working out the global-warming contribution of a specific flight (or even your entire existence), and then let you contribute an appropriate amount of money to fund offsetting measures. These include rainforest reforestation and initiatives to reduce future energy demand – often run in conjunction with sustainable development schemes.

Rough Guides, together with Lonely Planet and other concerned partners in the travel industry, are supporting a **carbon-offset scheme** run by climatecare.org. Please take the time to view our website and see how you can help to make your trip climate neutral.

ⓦwww.roughguides.com/climatechange

Flights from Australia, New Zealand and South Africa

There are **no direct flights** from Australia, New Zealand or South Africa to Scandinavia; instead, you'll have to fly to either a European or Asian gateway city – or both – from where you can get a connecting flight or other onward transport. Fares are pretty steep, so if you're on a tight budget it's worth flying to London, Amsterdam or Frankfurt first, and picking up a cheap flight from there.

Airfares to Europe vary significantly with the **season**: low season runs from mid-January to the end of February and during October and November; high season runs from mid-May to the end of August and from December to mid-January; the rest of the year is counted as shoulder season.

Airlines flying out of **Australia** and **New Zealand** often use SAS for connecting services on to Copenhagen. The most direct routes involve a minimum of two stops en route, one Asian – Singapore, Kuala Lumpur, Hong Kong or Bangkok – and one European – Amsterdam, Vienna or London. The best connections are with airlines such as KLM, British Airways, Qantas and Austrian Airlines. For tickets from **Sydney**, **Melbourne**, **Perth** or **Auckland** expect to pay AUS$2450–2750/ NZ$2900–3300 high season and AUS$1700–2000/NZ$2100–2400 low season. Flights from **Christchurch** and **Wellington** tend to go via Sydney or Auckland and cost around NZ$150–300 more.

The best deals from **South Africa** are from **Johannesburg** with KLM via Amsterdam at R7500–8500 high season and R6500–7500 low season, followed by British Airways via London at R8000–9000 high and R7000–8000 low, and Lufthansa via Frankfurt for R10,000–11,000 high and R8000–9000 low.

Trains

Taking a **train** can be a relaxed way of getting to Copenhagen from the UK, though it's likely to work out considerably more expensive than flying, especially if you're over 26.

You can either cross over to the continent by boat and pick up a train from there or, with the **Channel Tunnel**, take the Euros-tar from Waterloo International in London. Almost all ticketing for train travel within Europe is now handled by **Rail Europe** (see p.23), which provides the fastest and most convenient routings via the Eurostar to Brussels and then on to Copenhagen via Hamburg. Rail Europe can sell you through-tickets from most UK starting points; always, check for special offers. Through-tickets for the train/cross-channel ferry option are only available from a few agents and larger train stations. You could, with careful planning, organize your own train and ferry tickets – a cheaper if more complicated process.

To get the **cheapest fares** on Rail Europe you'll need to book a round-trip fourteen days in advance with one Saturday night away. With this type of ticket, the fare to Copenhagen is currently £300–500, and the journey takes around 20 hours, via Brussels and Hamburg or Cologne.

Buses

Taking the **bus** to Copenhagen can be an endurance test, and with airfares falling it can actually prove more expensive than flying. It's only worth taking the bus if time is no object and price all-important, or if you specifically do not want to fly.

The major UK operator of international bus routes is **Eurolines** (see p.23); tickets are bookable on the Internet, through most major travel agents (see p.22), and through any Eurolines agent.

Eurolines run up to nine services weekly to **Copenhagen** either via Brussels (20hr) or Amsterdam (25hr). **Fares** to Copenhagen start at £102 return, though the Euro-Apex fare (must be booked thirty days in advance; return within one month) reduces this to £92. There's a ten percent discount if you're **under 26**. Note that in the peak summer months, all fares increase slightly.

There are no through-services from anywhere in the UK outside London, though **National Express** connect with Eurolines buses in London from all over the British Isles.

Airlines, agents and operators

Online booking

Ⓦ www.expedia.co.uk (in UK), Ⓦ www.expedia .com (in US), Ⓦ www.expedia.ca (in Canada)

ⓦ www.lastminute.com (in UK)
ⓦ www.opodo.co.uk (in UK)
ⓦ www.orbitz.com (in US)
ⓦ www.travelocity.co.uk (in UK), ⓦ www
.travelocity.com (in US), ⓦ www.travelocity
.ca (in Canada)
ⓦ www.zuji.com.au (in Australia), ⓦ www.zuji
.co.nz (in New Zealand)

Airlines

Aer Lingus UK ☏ 0870/876 5000, Ireland
☏ 0818/365 000, US and Canada ☏ 1-800/IRISH
AIR, Denmark ☏ 33 12 70 55, ⓦ www.aerlingus
.com.
Air New Zealand UK ☏ 0800/0284 149, Ireland
☏ 1800/551447, US ☏ 1-800/262-1234, Canada
☏ 1-800/663-5494, New Zealand ☏ 0800/737 000,
ⓦ www.airnewzealand.com.
Austrian Airlines UK ☏ 0870/124 2625, Ireland
☏ 1800/509 142, US ☏ 1-800/843-0002, Australia
☏ 1800/642 438 or 02/9251 6155, Denmark ☏ 70
11 30 00, ⓦ www.aua.com.
Australian Airlines Australia ☏ 1300/799 798,
ⓦ www.australianairlines.com.au.
bmi UK ☏ 0870/607 0555, Ireland ☏ 01/407 3036,
US ☏ 1-800/788-0555, ⓦ www.flybmi.com.
British Airways UK ☏ 0870/850 9850, Ireland
☏ 1890/626 747, US and Canada ☏ 1-800/
AIRWAYS, Australia ☏ 1300/767 177, New Zealand
☏ 09/966 9777, Denmark ☏ 70 12 80 22, ⓦ www
.ba.com.
Continental Airlines UK ☏ 0845/607 6760,
Ireland ☏ 1890/925 252, US and Canada ☏ 1-
800/523-3273, Australia ☏ 2/9244 2242, NZ
☏ 9/308 3350, Denmark ☏ 70 12 62 33, ⓦ www
.continental.com.
Delta UK ☏ 0845/600 0950, Ireland ☏ 1850/882
031 or 01/407 3165, US and Canada ☏ 1-800/221-
1212, Australia ☏ 1300/302/849, New Zealand
☏ 09/379 3370, Denmark ☏ 33 32 45 59, ⓦ www
.delta.com.
easyJet UK ☏ 0905/821 0905, Denmark ☏ 70 12
43 21, ⓦ www.easyjet.com.
KLM (Royal Dutch Airlines) UK ☏ 0870/507
4074, Australia ☏ 1300/303 747, New Zealand
☏ 09/309 1782, Denmark ☏ 70 10 07 47, ⓦ www
.klm.com.
Lufthansa UK ☏ 0870/837 7747, Ireland
☏ 01/844 5544, US ☏ 1-800/645-3880, Canada
☏ 1-800/563-5954, Australia ☏ 1300/655 727,
New Zealand ☏ 09/303 1529, Denmark ☏ 70 10 20
00, ⓦ www.lufthansa.com.
Qantas Airways UK ☏ 0845/774 7767, Ireland
☏ 01/407 3278, US and Canada ☏ 1-800/227-
4500, Australia ☏ 13 13 13, New Zealand

☏ 0800/808 767 or 09/357 8900, ⓦ www.qantas
.com.
Ryanair UK ☏ 0871/246 0000, ⓦ www.ryanair
.com.
SAS (Scandinavian Airlines) UK ☏ 0870/6072
7727, Ireland ☏ 01/844 5440, US ☏ 1-800/221-
2350, Canada ☏ 1800/221-2350, Australia
☏ 1300/727 707, SA ☏ 011 484-4711, Denmark
☏ 70 10 20 00, ⓦ www.scandinavian.net.
South African Airways UK ☏ 0870/747 1111,
US and Canada ☏ 1-800/722-9675, Australia
☏ 1800/221 699, New Zealand ☏ 09/977 2237, SA
☏ 011 978-1111, ⓦ www.flysaa.com.
Varig UK ☏ 0870/120 3020, US and Canada
☏ 1-800/GO-VARIG, Denmark ☏ 33 45 55 00,
ⓦ www.varig.com.

Agents and operators

ebookers UK ☏ 0800/082 3000, Ireland ☏ 01/488
3507, ⓦ www.ebookers.com. Low fares on an
extensive selection of scheduled flights and package
deals.
North South Travel UK ☏ 01245/608 291,
ⓦ www.northsouthtravel.co.uk. Friendly, competitive
travel agency, offering discounted fares worldwide.
Profits are used to support projects in the developing
world, especially the promotion of sustainable tourism.
Scanmeridian UK ☏ 020/7431 5322, ⓦ www
.scanmeridian.co.uk. Scandinavia specialist offering
city breaks and tailor-made trips.
Scantours UK ☏ 020/7839 2927, ⓦ www
.scantoursuk.com, US ☏ 1-800/223-7226, ⓦ www
.scantours.com. Huge range of package deals, hotel
booking, customized itineraries, and city sightseeing
tours.
STA Travel UK ☏ 0870/163 0026, US ☏ 1-
800/781-4040, Canada ☏ 1-888/427-5639,
Australia ☏ 1300/733 035, New Zealand
☏ 0508/782 872, ⓦ www.statravel.com. Worldwide
specialists in independent travel; also student IDs,
travel insurance, car rental, rail passes, and more.
Good discounts for students and under-26s.
Trailfinders UK ☏ 0845/058 5858, Ireland
☏ 01/677 7888, Australia ☏ 1300/780 212,
ⓦ www.trailfinders.com. One of the best-
informed and most efficient agents for independent
travellers.

Rail contacts

DSB Denmark ☏ 70 13 14 15, ⓦ www.dsb.dk.
Europrail International Canada ☏ 1-888/667-
9734, ⓦ www.europrail.net.
Eurostar UK ☏ 0870/518 6186,
ⓦ www.eurostar.com.

Rail Europe UK ℡0870/837 1371, US ℡1-877/257-2887, Canada ℡1-800/361-RAIL, ⓦwww.raileurope.co.uk. STA Travel UK ℡0870/163 0026, US ℡1-800/781-4040, Canada ℡1-888/427-5639, Australia ℡1300/733 035, New Zealand ℡0508/782 872 ⓦwww.statravel.com.

STA Travel UK ℡0870/163 0026, US ℡1-800/781-4040, Canada ℡1-888/427-5639, Australia ℡1300/733 035, New Zealand ℡0508/782 872, ⓦwww.statravel.com. Trailfinders UK ℡0845/058 5858, Ireland ℡01/677 7888, Australia ℡1300/780 212, ⓦwww.trailfinders.com.

Bus contacts

Eurolines UK ℡0870/580 8080, Ireland ℡01/836 6111, Denmark ℡70 10 00 30, ⓦwww.nationalexpress.com/eurolines.

Channel Tunnel

Eurotunnel UK ℡0870/535 3535, ⓦwww.eurotunnel.com.

Arrival

However you arrive in Copenhagen you'll find yourself within easy reach of the city centre. Copenhagen airport is just a few kilometres to the southeast, on the edge of the island of Amager, while almost all trains and buses deposit you near the city's main transport hub, Central Station.

By air

Copenhagen **airport** (ⓦwww.cph.dk), 11km from the city in the suburb of Kastrup, is the air hub of Scandinavia and your most likely point of arrival. Getting into the city from here couldn't be easier: a rail line – one of the fastest airport-to-city links in Europe – runs directly to Central Station six times an hour; once an hour (44min past the hour) from 1am to 4.30am (10–13min; 27kr). Half these trains continue north to the town of Helsingør (45min; 63kr), calling en route at Nørreport (16min) and Øster-port (18min) stations. There's also a much slower city bus (#250S, 27kr; #96N night bus, 54kr) to Central Station and Rådhus-pladsen, which is only really convenient if you want to get off on the way. A taxi to the centre will cost about 180kr – there's a rank outside the arrivals hall.

There's a helpful **information desk** (daily 6am–midnight) in the sleek arrivals hall at Terminal 3 where you can pick up a copy of the English-language *Copenhagen This Week* and free maps of the city. They also run an efficient **hotel-booking service**

(daily 6am–11pm; 100kr per reservation) in conjunction with Wonderful Copenha-gen (see p.37) and generally offer some very good last-minute deals if you haven't booked accommodation already (see p.165). At the airport, there are also two late-opening **banks** (daily 6am–10pm), two 24hr ATMs, numerous car-rental agencies (see p.29) and a post office. The city's styl-ish *Hilton Hotel* is connected to the airport by a pedestrian walkway and is a beautiful place to kill some time if you arrive at the airport too early – conveniently, their lobby bar is equipped with arrival and departure screens.

If flying in with Ryanair, you'll arrive at **Malmö's** Sturup airport across the bridge in Sweden (see p.25). Transport into Copenhagen centre couldn't be easier with the *Flybuss 737* awaiting every Ryanair arrival and crossing over to Copenhagen Central Station 50min; 100kr). Alternatively, take the local airport bus *Flybuss* to Malmö Central Station 45min; 95SEK) and catch the train to Copenhagen from there (see p.154).

Copenhagen and Malmö

For centuries, the Swedish city of **Malmö** (in Danish, Malmø), 20km from Copenhagen across the Øresund, and the surrounding province of Skåne were part of a Danish empire with its capital in Copenhagen. With the Swedish capture of Skåne in the seventeenth century, however, Malmö was reduced from the second city of a major northern European power to a neglected outpost of a greater Sweden in which power rested firmly with distant Stockholm. The sense of rejection persists – Malmö's residents derisively call people from Stockholm *null åttas*, "zero-eights", after the telephone code for Stockholm.

In July 2000, Malmö's historical ties with the Danish capital were renewed with the opening of the **Øresunds Bridge** – Scandinavia's biggest-ever engineering project. The "bridge" (actually a road and rail link made up of a four-kilometre tunnel, a four-kilometre artificial island and an eight-kilometre cable bridge) has brought the two cities within a thirty-five-minute train ride of one another, effectively transforming Malmö into a satellite-cum-suburb of Copenhagen and placing the Danish capital at the heart of a new region, the so-called **Øresund**, which looks set to dominate the western Baltic for the foreseeable future.

Trains run roughly every twenty minutes from Copenhagen's Central Station to Malmö, via Copenhagen airport, with fast onward connections from Malmö to Stockholm, Gothenburg and Oslo. A single journey across the bridge by car costs 235kr.

By bus and train

All buses and trains to Copenhagen arrive at or near the **Central Station** (in Danish, Hovedbanegården or København H), the city's main transport hub, from where there are excellent connections to virtually every part of the city via bus or local train – but note, not the new metro (see p.26). The station is also home to an array of shops, a foreign-exchange bureau (daily 8am–9pm), a bicycle-rental service (see p.30), places to eat and, downstairs, left-luggage lockers (Mon–Sat 5.30am–1am, Sun 6am–1am; 30kr and 40kr for 24hr). The national train company, DSB, has a travel agency and information centre just inside the main entrance off Vesterbrogade (daily 6.30am–11pm; ☎70 13 14 15, ⊛www.dsb.dk).

Eurolines coaches (see p.23) from around Europe and buses from Malmö (Sturup) airport stop behind the station on Ingerslevgade, across from DGI-byen (see p.104).

Getting around

The best way to explore Copenhagen is either to walk or cycle: the inner city is compact, much of the central area pedestrianized, and there's a comprehensive network of excellent bike paths – you'll often find it just as quick to walk or cycle as to wait for a bus. For travelling further afield, there's an integrated network of buses, metros, S-Tog and local trains.

Tickets

All city transport operates on an integrated **zonal system** extending far beyond the suburbs and encompassing S-Tog trains, the metro system, regional trains and buses. There are an astounding 95 zones (pick up a free leaflet from any S-Tog station); you may find it easiest at first simply to state your destination and you'll be sold the appropriate ticket. The city centre and immediate area, as you'd expect, are in zones 1 and 2. **Fares** are based on a combination of zones and time: the cheapest ticket (*billet*) costs 18kr and is valid for one hour's travel within any two zones, with unlimited transfers between buses and trains. Another option is the **klippekort** ticket, a discount card containing ten stamps, which you cancel individually according to the length of your journey and the value of the *klippekort*. The cheapest *klippekort* costs 115kr, with each stamp being valid for an hour's travel within any two zones; each stamp in a 155kr *klippekort* is valid for one hour within any three zones – good value if you plan to travel outside the city centre – and is also valid to and from the airport. Unlimited transfers are allowed within the time period of the ticket, and two or more people can use the same *klippekort* simultaneously, provided you clip the required number of stamps per person. There's also an excellent-value **24-hour ticket** (105kr), which is valid on all transport in zones as far away as Helsingør and Roskilde, as well as night buses. Finally, a new option is the **Flexicard – 7 days**, which gives unlimited travel for seven days to whoever is carrying the cards, meaning that it can be shared as long as the people sharing aren't travelling at the same time. It costs 190kr for travel in two zones and 220kr for three. *Billets* can be bought on board buses or at train stations, while *klippekort*, 24-hour

tickets and Flexicard – 7 days are only available at bus or train stations and HT Kortsalg kiosks; *klippekort* should be stamped when boarding the bus or via machines on train-station platforms. Except on buses, it's rare to be asked to show your ticket, but if you don't have one you face an instant fine of 500kr. Route maps can be picked up free at stations, and most free maps of the city include bus lines and a diagram of the S-Tog and metro network.

By train

The **S-Tog** train service (⊛www.s-tog.dk; see colour map at the back of the book) is a metropolitan network laid out in a huge "U" shape and covering Copenhagen and the surrounding areas. Ten of its twelve lines stop at Central Station (in Danish, Hovedbanegården or København H), while the two remaining lines run a circular route around the centre. Each line has a letter, from A to M (some letters are not used), and is also colour-coded on route maps. Lines running similar routes, but stopping at fewer stations, have a + symbol after the letter (eg H+) so check carefully or you could whizz straight past your destination. Services run about every ten to fifteen minutes between 5am and 12.30am, and stations are marked by red hexagonal signs with a yellow "S" inside them.

Costing double its original budget, the state-of-the-art underground **metro system** (⊛www.m.dk) opened its first section in 2002 and a second a year later. Fast and efficient (departures every couple of minutes),

Useful bus routes

#5A Assistens Kirkegård, Nørrebrogade (near Skt Hans Torv and Blågårdsgade), Nørreport Station, Nørre Voldgade, Rådhuspladsen, Central Station.

#6A Sortedams Dosseringen (the lakes), Statens Museum for Kunst (Royal Museum of Fine Arts), Nørreport Station, Gammel Torv-Nytorv, Rådhusstræde, Vester Voldgade, Rådhuspladsen, Vesterport Station, Roskildevej, Frederiksberg Slot and the City Zoo.

#26 Valby Langgade, Carlsberg Brewery, Pile Allé, Frederiksberg Allé, Vesterbrogade, Central Station, Rådhuspladsen, Vester Voldgade, Kongens Nytorv, Dronnings Tværgade, Øster Voldgade, Østerport Station, Indiakaj, Langeliniekaj and the Little Mermaid.

#66 Åboulevard, Vesterport Station, Tivoli and Central Station, Christians Brygge on Slotsholmen, City Hostel, Christianshavns Torv, Christiania, Operaen.

Car parking

A **pay-and-display system** operates Monday to Friday 8am to 10pm and Saturday 8am to 5pm on the centre's streets (the area inside the lakes), with rates varying depending on which colour-coded zone you're in. Stretching out from the centre, the zones are red (25kr/hr), green (15kr) and blue (9kr). Each pay-and-display meter has a map on it detailing the extent of each zone. Outside the centre, there's two hours' free parking (Mon–Fri 8am–7pm), but you have to use a **P-disc** (rental cars come with them). You set the time you park on the hands of the clock, returning before your allotted time (indicated by signs) is up. Outside this period, there are no restrictions. "STOPFORBUD" means no stopping, whilst "PARKERING FORBUDT" means no parking unless a time limit is displayed, in which case you must use a P-disc. It's usually not too difficult to find a street parking space, but note that your car will be towed away if you overstay or park where you shouldn't. Downtown **car parks** are thin on the ground: there's a handy one at Israel Plads by Nørreport Station, one at Vesterbrogade 23 near Tivoli and the Central Station, and another attached to the Q8 station near Vesterport Station at Nyropsgade 42 (20kr/hr, 200kr/day).

it circumvents the Central Station in a "U" shape, connecting the island of Amager with west Copenhagen via two new stations conveniently located at Christianshavn and Kongens Nytorv. The metro's two lines – M1 and M2 – cross the S-Tog and regional trains at Nørreport, Flintholm and Vanløse. A final section of the metro is due to open in 2007, linking the city with Copenhagen airport. Metro stations are marked by a large red underlined "M" painted onto aluminium pillars.

Finally, a regional train network run by the **Danish State Railway** (DSB) connects the city to Helsingør and Roskilde, calling at Østerport and Nørreport stations and some suburban destinations on the way; remember that the S-Tog, metros and the regional trains depart from different platforms at Nørreport station.

By bus

The city's **bus** network (🌐 www.hur.dk) is much more comprehensive than the S-Tog system and can be a more convenient way to get around once you get the hang of finding the stops – marked by yellow placards on signposts – and as long as you avoid the rush hour (7–9am & 5–6pm). The excellent free city map produced by the Wonderful Copenhagen office (see p.37) includes a list of all bus routes in the centre. The city's bus terminal is a slick black building adjacent to the Rådhus, on the big open Rådhuspladsen, a block from both Central Station and

Tivoli; you can pick up bus-route maps here, and get general information about the metropolitan transport system. Other useful buses leave from Central Station's Vesterbro side entrance, the Tivoli side entrance, and the bridge at the end of the tracks. Buses with an "S" suffix only make limited stops, offering a faster service – check they make the stop you require before you get on. Buses with an "A" suffix indicate that the bus runs frequently. All buses have a small electronic board above the driver's seat displaying both the zone you're currently in and the time – so there's no excuse for not having a valid ticket. There's a skeletal **night-bus** service (running once or twice an hour), though fares are double daytime rates. Night-bus numbers always end with "N"; stops are well marked by yellow signs on major routes into and out of the city.

Harbour buses

Another option for getting around are the city-run yellow **harbour buses**, which sail along the harbour between Nordre Toldbod (near the Little Mermaid) and the Royal Library, stopping five times on the way (twice on the Christianshavn side). Services leave daily every twenty minutes from about 6.30am to 7pm (unless the harbour area is frozen) and cost 36kr (*klippekort* – see p.26 – can also be used). Tickets are valid for one hour and are transferable to the rest of the transport network; bikes cost an extra 17kr.

Compared to the canal tours (see p.28), this is a cheap way to experience Copenhagen from the waterfront.

By car

Given the excellent public transport system, the size of the city and the comparatively high price of petrol and parking, renting a car isn't really economical unless you're in a group. **Car rental** is expensive, though it's worth checking the cut-price deals offered by some airlines. You'll need an international driving licence and must be aged at least 20 to take to the roads, though many firms won't rent vehicles to anyone under 25. Costs start at around 3000kr a week for a small hatchback with unlimited mileage. Rent-a-Wreck (see p.29) offers the best deal for limited mileage (100km/day) at 2100kr

for a week – the cars aren't really wrecks, they're just not new.

Danes drive on the right, and there's a speed limit of 50kph in towns, 80kph in open country and 110kph on motorways. As in Sweden and Finland, headlights need to be used at all times. There are random breath tests for suspected drunken drivers, and the penalties are severe.

The national motoring organization, Forenede Danske Motorejere, operates a 24-hour breakdown service (☎45 88 00 25) for AA members; if you're not an AA member, Dansk Autohjælp (☎70 10 80 90) and Falck (☎70 10 20 30) can be summoned from call boxes by the road. A standard call-out fee will be charged – starting at 586kr per hour during weekdays and 1172kr per hour at the weekend.

Guided tours

If you've limited time or simply want someone else to do the hard work, then a **guided tour** might be a good option. There's a wide variety of tours available, suiting most needs, so it's mainly down to how you would like to get around (bus, boat, bicycle, kayak or by foot) and which sights you would like to take in.

City Safari Dansk Arkitektur Center, Gl. Dok, Strandgade 27B, Christianshavn ☎33 23 94 90, ⓦwww.citysafari.dk. Guided bike tours starting from in front of the old warehouse that's home to the Dansk Arkitektur Center (see p.68) on Strandgade, and visiting various well-known and not so well-known city attractions. "Historical Copenhagen" tours depart daily in summer (1.30pm; 250kr including bike hire; 3hr) and during the rest of the year according to demand – book in advance at all times. "Copenhagen by Night" evening tours depart daily in the summer (8pm; 250kr including bike hire; 3hr) and take in Istedgade's red-light district as well as the city's many beautifully illuminated squares and buildings, and include a night-time drink in one of the city's trendy cafés. There's a 30kr reduction if you bring your own bike.

Copenhagen Adventure Tours ☎40 50 40 06, ⓦwww.kajakole.dk. Original and challenging tours using well-designed, safe and easy-to-handle kayaks. Based at Christianshavns Kanal, Strandgade 49 in front of *Restaurant Kanalen*, these trips give a unique view of the city on their standard ninety-minute tours (May–Sept; 165kr), taking in the central city canals and Christianshavn; longer trips include the Little Mermaid and Holmen. The price includes a free drink in a canalside floating bar.

Copenhagen Sightseeing Tours ☎32 66 00 00, ⓦwww.sightseeing.dk. Eight different bus tours (with multilingual headphone commentary) departing from Rådhuspladsen in front of the Lure Players statue. Tours include a "City and Harbour" tour, by bus and boat (daily mid-April to mid-May daily 11.30am; mid-May to Sept 9.30am, 11.30am & 1.30pm; rest of the year Sat 10.15am, 11.15am & 12.15pm; 175kr; 2hr 30min); the "City Tour", which passes all the major sights (daily: mid-April to mid-May 11.30am; mid-May to Sept 9.30am, 11.30am & 1.30pm; 130kr; 1hr 30min); the "Open Top Tour", which runs a hop-on hop-off system and has a choice of three different routes, or all three combined (daily April–Sept every half hour between 9.30am and 5pm; from 120kr to 220kr); the "Grand Tour", which includes the Royal palaces and the parliament (daily 11am & Sat at 1.30pm; 195kr;

Car-rental agencies

Alamo US ☎ 1-800/462-5266, Ⓦ www.alamo.com.
Auto Europe US and Canada ☎ 1-888/223-5555,
Ⓦ www.autoeurope.com.
Avis UK ☎ 0870/606 0100, Ireland ☎ 021/428
1111, US ☎ 1-800/230-4898, Canada
☎ 1-800/272-5871, Australia ☎ 13 63 33 or
02/9353 9000, New Zealand ☎ 09/526 2847 or
0800/655 111, Ⓦ www.avis.com. Denmark
☎ 70 24 77 07 or 32 51 22 99 (airport).
Budget UK ☎ 087/156 5656, Ireland ☎ 09/0662
7711, US ☎ 1-800/527-0700, Canada
☎ 1-800/268-8900, Australia ☎ 1300/362 848, New
Zealand ☎ 0800/283 438, Ⓦ www.budget.com.
Denmark ☎ 33 55 05 00 or 32 52 39 00 (airport).
Europcar/Interrent UK ☎ 0870/607 5000, Ireland
☎ 01/614 2888, US and Canada ☎ 1-877/940 6900,
Australia ☎ 1300/131 390, Ⓦ www.europcar.com.
Denmark ☎ 33 55 99 00 or 32 50 30 90 (airport).

Europe by Car US ☎ 1-800/223-1516, Ⓦ www
.europebycar.com.
Hertz UK ☎ 020/7026 0077, Ireland
☎ 01/870 5777, US ☎ 1-800/654-3131, Canada
☎ 1-800/263-0600, Australia ☎ 08/9921 4052,
New Zealand ☎ 0800/654 321, Ⓦ www.hertz.com.
Denmark ☎ 33 17 90 20 or ☎ 32 50 93 00 (airport).
Holiday Autos UK ☎ 0871/222 3200, Ireland
☎ 01/872 9366, Australia ☎ 1300/554 432, New
Zealand ☎ 0800/144 040, Ⓦ www.holidayautos
.co.uk.
National UK ☎ 0870/400 4581, US ☎ 1-800/CAR-
RENT, Australia ☎ 02/13 10 45, New Zealand
☎ 03/366 5574, Ⓦ www.nationalcar.com. Denmark
☎ 39 63 23 75.
Rent-a-Wreck Denmark ☎ 70 25 26 70, Ⓦ www
.rent-a-wreck.dk.
SIXT Ireland ☎ 1850/206 088, Ⓦ www
.irishcarrentals.ie. Denmark Englandsvej 40 ☎ 32
48 11 00, Ⓦ www.sixt.dk.

2hr 30min). Other tours cover the rest of Zealand, taking in places such as Helsingør
and Roskilde. There's a ten percent discount if you book online.

DFDS Canal Tours ☎ 32 96 30 00, Ⓦ www.canaltours.dk. One of two companies
with guided tours around the canals and harbour. Two one-hour options (daily:
April–Oct departing every 30min between 10am and 5pm; Nov & Dec departing
every hour between 10am and 3pm) start from Nyhavn or Gammel Strand and take
in various city sights, including the Little Mermaid, Amalienborg Palace and the
Operaen; however, at 60kr, you'll get more for your money with Netto-Bådene (see
below). DFDS also run three hop-on hop-off **waterbus** routes (daily mid-May to
Aug leaving every hour between 10am and 5pm), one going east to the Trekroner
fort/island, one going west to the new Fisketorvet shopping complex, and one going
around the canals of Christianshavn; all three stop several times on the way. A two-
day unlimited-use ticket, which includes the open-top bus tours (see Copenhagen
Sightseeing Tours above) costs 220kr, a one-day ticket 50kr, and a single trip 30kr.
Bring a raincoat and warm clothing if the weather is bad, as the boats are quite
exposed.

Netto-Bådene ☎ 32 54 41 02, Ⓦ www.havnerundfart.dk. Offering a combination
of the two DFDS tours listed above, Netto-Bådene's one-hour trip for only 30kr is
a lot better value. Tours start at Holmens Kirke across from Børsen, pass Nyhavn,
Holmen, Nyholm, Amalienborg Palace and the Little Mermaid on the way, and
end up circumnavigating Slotsholmen before finishing back at Holmens Kirke.
Tours depart daily from April to mid-October between 10am and 5pm (July & Aug
10am–7pm) two to five times an hour.

Walking Tours A number of English-language guided tours are available from
various points throughout the city. Most unusual is the "Watchman's Round" starting
at dusk (daily mid-July to mid-Sept 9pm; rest of the year Fri & Sat 7pm; 50kr)
from Gråbrødre Torv in front of *Peder Oxe* restaurant. The tour takes roughly 1hr
15min and follows an "eighteenth-century watchman" on his round, while he tells
tales (in English) of the old city. Check Ⓦ www.nattevaegterne.dk.dk for more info.
Otherwise, the, Wonderful Copenhagen office on Berstorffsgade (see p.37) has a list
of tours taking in most of the city-centre highlights and lasting up to two hours.

Suncars UK ☎0870/500 5566, Ireland ☎1850/201 416, ⓦwww.suncars.com.

Taxis

Taxis are plentiful, but with a flat starting fare of 19kr, plus 11kr per kilometre travelled (14kr after 4pm and at weekends), they're only worthwhile if several people are sharing. There's a handy taxi rank outside Central Station, or phone Taxamotor (☎38 10 10 10 for a cab, ☎35 39 35 35 for a minibus). Alternatively, just hail one in the street – if it's showing a green "*Fri*" sign on top, it's available. A fun new addition to the scene are rickshaw-styled **cycle taxis**, which operate from April till October. Carrying a maximum of two people, they operate a flat starting fare of 35kr if you flag them down on the street, with an additional 3kr per minute until you reach your destination. Alternatively, contact Cykeltaxi (☎70 26 00 55, ⓦwww .cykeltaxi.com) or Copenhagen Rickshaw (☎35 43 01 22, ⓦwww.rickshaw.dk).

By bike

If the weather's good, the best way to see Copenhagen is to do as the locals do – up to 166,000 every day – and ride a **bicycle**. Cycling is also excellent for exploring the immediate countryside, as bikes can be taken for two hours on S-Togs for 10kr through any number of zones; you can also buy a special bicycle *klippekort*, valid for ten journeys and costing 95kr. The superb, city-wide cycle lanes make cycling

very safe, though remember that lights are a legal requirement at night (you'll be stopped and fined if the police catch you without them) and helmets are recommended at all times.

There are a number of outlets for **renting bikes** in central Copenhagen: Københavns Cyklebørs, Gothersgade 157, Indre By (Mon–Fri 8.30am–5.30pm, Sat 10am–1.30pm; ☎33 14 07 17, ⓦwww.cykelboersen.dk; 60kr/day, 270kr/week, 200kr deposit); Københavns Cykelcenter, Reventlowsgade 11, along the side of Central Station (Mon–Fri 8am–5.30pm, Sat 9am–1pm; ☎33 33 86 13, ⓦwww.copenhagen-bikes.dk; 75kr/ day, 340kr/week, 500kr deposit); Østerport Cykler, Oslo Plads 9, next to Østerport Station (Mon–Fri 8am–6pm, Sat 9am–1pm; ☎33 33 85 13, ⓦwww.oesterport-cykler.dk; 75kr/day, 340kr/week, 500kr deposit). Also bear in mind the summer-only free **City Bike scheme** (ⓦwww.bycyklen.dk), when two thousand free bikes (easily recognized by the advertisements painted onto their solid wheels) are scattered about the city at S-Tog stations and other busy locations; a refundable 20kr deposit unlocks one. The rules are simple: leave the bike in a rack when you've finished with it (you get your coin back automatically as you re-lock the bike), or just leave it out on a pavement, in which case someone else will happily return it and pocket the coin. Don't secure one with your own lock and don't take one outside the city limits (the old rampart lakes mark the border) or you risk a fine.

The media

Newspapers and magazines

Overseas newspapers are sold at the Magasin du Nord department store (see p.220), Illums Bolighus department store (see p.220), the stall on the eastern

side of Rådhuspladsen, and some newsagents along Strøget. Also check any of the newsagents in Central Station, which stock a large range of foreign newspapers and magazines. Most UK and US weekday titles cost 25–40kr and are available the day after publication.

If you can read Danish, your choices among the main daily **newspapers** (each costing 15–22kr) are *Politiken*, a reasonably impartial broadsheet with strong arts features; the conservative/centrist *Berlingske Tidende*; *Kristeligt Dagblad*, a Christian paper; *Jyllands-Posten*, a well-respected Jutland-based right-wing paper; and *Information*, left-wing and intellectual. The weekly *Weekendavisen*, published on Thursdays, has excellent background features. The best sports coverage can be found in the two tabloids: *BT*, which has a conservative bias, and *Ekstra Bladet*. You'll find excellent **entertainment listings** in *Politiken*, and every Thursday *Information* has a section devoted to listings, too. The free Danish **music** magazine, the monthly *Gaffa*, lists most of the bigger shows. You can find them in cafés, record shops and the like.

There's an **English-language newspaper**, *Copenhagen Post* (🌐 www.copenhagenpost .dk), which covers domestic issues and has an in-depth listings section; it comes out every Friday and costs 15kr.

Radio

There's a very short *News In English* programme weekdays at 10.30am, 5.05pm and 10pm on Radio Denmark International (1062MHz). The BBC World Service can be picked up on short wave 6195KHz, 9410KHz and 12,095KHz; you may also be able to pick up BBC Radio 4 on long wave 198Mhz.

BBC 🌐 www.bbc.co.uk/worldservice
Radio Canada 🌐 www.rcinet.ca
Voice of America 🌐 www.voa.gov

Television

After a slow start, **Danish television** has expanded rapidly. Fifteen years ago there was only one national station; today, there are four national and four cable channels. The four nationals are the non-commercial DR1 and DR2, and the commercial TV2 and TV2 Zulu – though, apart from the advertising, you'll probably struggle to spot the difference between them. The cable channels, some of which are shared with Sweden and Norway, are all commercial and prolific in American sitcoms and soaps (usually with Danish subtitles). If you're staying in a hotel, or a youth hostel with a TV room, you may also have the option of German and Swedish channels – plus a dozen cable and satellite stations.

Culture and etiquette

There is no single word in the Danish language for "**please**". So when a Dane doesn't say "please" when speaking to you in English, it's not because they're rude – the word just doesn't come naturally. Danes are also renowned for being direct and to the point, which can sometimes be interpreted as impolite – if they want something they say "Give me…" – but they're also extremely jovial and easy-going, seldom taking themselves too seriously.

Service is included on all restaurant, hotel and taxi bills, so unless you feel you've been given an exceptionally good service, tipping is not necessary.

Travel essentials

Costs

There's no getting away from the fact that Copenhagen is an **expensive** city, although you can cut costs substantially if you spend wisely.

If you come for just a few days, stay in youth hostels or on campsites and don't eat out, it's possible to survive on £25/US$45 a day. Otherwise, staying in cheap hotels and moving around the city visiting museums, eating in a restaurant each day, as well as buying a few snacks and going for a drink in the evening, you can expect to spend a minimum of £40–50/US$70–90 per day.

Crime and personal safety

Copenhagen is one of the most peaceful cities in Europe. Most public places are well lit and secure, the majority of people genuinely friendly and helpful, and street crime and hassle relatively rare.

It would be foolish, however, to assume that problems don't exist. Like any capital city, Copenhagen has its fair share of **petty crime**, fuelled by a growing number of drug addicts and alcoholics after easy money. Keep an eye on your cash and passport and you should have little reason to visit the **police**. If you do, you'll find them courteous, concerned and, most importantly, usually able to speak English. If you have something stolen, make sure you get a **police report** – essential if you are to make an insurance claim. Should you need them, **foreign embassies** in Copenhagen (see box on p.32) are are usually pretty helpful.

As for **offences** you might commit, **nude sunbathing** is universally accepted in all the major resorts (elsewhere, there'll be nobody around to care). Being **drunk** on the streets can get you arrested, and **drinking and driving** is treated especially rigorously. **Drug** offences, too, meet with the same strict attitude that prevails throughout the rest of Europe.

Travellers with disabilities

In many ways, Copenhagen is a model of awareness for travellers with disabilities: wheelchair access, other facilities and help are generally available at hotels, hostels, museums and public places.

There are **organized tours and holidays** specifically for people with disabilities – the contacts listed below will be able to put you in touch with specialists for trips to Copenhagen. The Danish Tourist Board (see p.37 for addresses and website) publishes the comprehensive 100-page *Access in Denmark – a Travel Guide for the Disabled*, which covers everything from airports to zoos. Also check Ⓦwww.visitcopenhagen .dk for specific information about disabled access to hotels, museums and public transport under the Practical Information tab.

People with a pre-existing medical condition are sometimes excluded from travel **insurance policies**, so read the small print carefully. To make your journey simpler, ask your travel agent to notify airlines or bus companies, who can cope better if they are expecting you. A **medical certificate** of your fitness to travel, provided by your doctor, is also extremely useful; some airlines or insurance companies may insist on it. Make sure that you have extra supplies of drugs – carried with you if you fly – and a prescription including the generic name in case of emergency. Carry spares of any clothing or equipment that might be hard to find; if there's an association representing people with your disability, contact them early in the planning process.

Dial ☏112 for police, fire or ambulance.
There are police stations at Halmtorvet 20 (☏33 25 14 48) and Store Kongensgade 100 (☏33 93 14 48), as well as Central Station.

Embassies and consulates in Copenhagen

Australian Embassy Dampfærgevej 26, 2nd floor ☏70 26 36 76, ⓦwww
.denmark-embassy.gov.au.
Canadian Embassy Kristen Bernikows Gade 1 ☏33 48 32 00, ⓦwww.canada.dk.
German Embassy Stockholmsgade 57 ☏35 45 99 00, ⓦwww.kopenhagen.diplo.de.
Irish Embassy Østbanegade 21 ☏35 42 32 33.
New Zealand Consulate Store Standstræde 21, 2nd floor ☏33 37 77 00, ⓦwww
.nzconsulate.dk.
Norwegian Embassy Amaliegade 39 ☏33 14 01 24, ⓦwww.norsk.dk.
South African Embassy Gammel Vartov Vej 8 ☏39 18 01 55, ⓦwww.southafrica.dk.
Swedish Embassy Skt Annæ Plads 15A ☏33 36 03 70, ⓦwww
.sverigesambassade.dk.
UK Embassy Kastelsvej 36–40 ☏35 44 52 00, ⓦwww.britishembassy.dk.
US Embassy Dag Hammerskjölds Allé 24 ☏33 41 71 00, ⓦwww.usembassy.dk.

Electricity

The Danish electricity supply runs at 220–240V, 50Hz AC; sockets generally require a two-pin plug. Visitors from the UK will need an adaptor; visitors from outside the EU may need a transformer.

Entry requirements

European Union, US, Canadian, Australian and New Zealand citizens need only a valid **passport** to enter Denmark for up to three months. South African citizens must obtain **visas** from the embassy in Pretoria (see details below) before travelling. Visas cost about R260, depending on the exchange rate, are valid for a maximum of ninety days and require proof of travel and health insurance. All other nationals should consult the relevant embassy about visa requirements.

For **longer stays**, EU nationals can apply for a residence permit while in the country, which, if it's granted, may be valid for up to five years. Non-EU nationals can only apply for residence permits before leaving home, and must be able to prove they can support themselves without working.

In spite of the lack of restrictions, **checks** are frequently made on travellers at the major points of entry. If you're young and are carrying a rucksack, be prepared to prove that you have enough money to support yourself during your stay. You may also be asked how long you intend to stay and why.

Danish embassies and consulates

The addresses given are for the main embassy or consulate in that country. To find out if there is a consulate in a major city nearer to your home, contact the main embassy or check their website.

Australia Consulates in Sydney: Gold Fields House, 21st floor, 1 Alfred St, Circular Quay, Sydney, NSW 2000, ☏061/29247 2224, ⓦwww.gksydney .um.dk; and Victoria: Ground Floor, 492 St Kilda Rd, Melbourne 3004, VIC ☏061/39866 1242.
Canada Embassy in Ottawa: 47 Clarence St, Pretoria Suite 450, Ottawa, Ontario K1N 9K1 ☏613/562-1811, ⓦwww.ambottawa.um.dk.
Ireland Embassy in Dublin: 121-122 St Stephen's Green, Dublin 2 ☏01/475 6404, ⓦwww .ambdublin.um.dk.
New Zealand Consulate in Wellington: Level 7, Forsyth Barr House, 45 Johnston St, Wellington 6001 ☏04/471 0520, ⓦwww.nishconsulatesnz .org.nz.
South Africa Embassy in Pretoria: Parioli Office Park, Block B2, Ground Floor, 1166 Park St, Pretoria ☏012/430 9340, ⓦwww.ambpretoria.um.dk.
UK Embassy in London: 55 Sloane St, London SW1X 9SR ☏020/7333 0200, ⓦwww.amblondon .um.dk.
US Embassy in Washington: 3200 Whitehaven St NW, Washington DC 20008 ☏202/234-4300, ⓦwww.denmarkemb.org.

Health

Most visitors to Copenhagen will, of course, enjoy a trouble-free trip, but should you require medical attention, then you can rest assured that health care in Denmark is superb. There are **emergency departments** at Amager Hospital, Italiensvej 1, Amager (℡32 34 32 34); Bispebjerg Hospital, Bispebjerg Bakke 23 (℡35 31 35 31) and Frederiksberg Hospital, Nordre Fasanvej 57, Frederiksberg (℡38 16 38 16). They provide free treatment for EU and Scandinavian nationals, though citizens of other countries are unlikely to have to pay. For **medical emergencies**, call ℡122.

If you need a **doctor**, call ℡33 15 46 00 (Mon–Fri 8am–4pm) and you'll be given the name of one in your area; outside these hours, call ℡70 13 00 41. Doctors' fees start at 400kr, to be paid in cash. If you're an EU citizen and you have a European Health Insurance Card (EHIC) – available from post offices in your home country – you can claim back doctors' fees and charges for medicine from the local health department. You'll need to produce the relevant receipts and card.

For **dental emergencies**, contact Tandlægevagten, Oslo Plads 14 ℡35 38 02 51 (Mon–Fri 8am–9.30pm, Sat & Sun 10am–noon), but be prepared to pay at least 200kr on the spot.

Copenhagen's two main 24-hour **pharmacies** are Steno Apotek, Vesterbrogade 6C in front of Central Station (℡33 14 82 66) and Sønderbro Apotek, Amagerbrogade 158, Amager (℡32 58 01 40).

Insurance

Most people will want to take out some kind of comprehensive **travel insurance** for their trip. A typical policy usually provides cover for the loss of baggage, tickets and – up to a certain limit – cash or cheques, as well as cancellation or curtailment of your journey.

Before paying for a new policy, however, it's worth checking whether you are already covered. Some all-risks home insurance policies may cover your possessions when overseas, and many private medical schemes include cover when abroad. In Canada, provincial health plans usually provide partial cover for medical mishaps overseas, while holders of official student/teacher/youth cards in Canada and the US are entitled to meagre accident coverage and hospital in-patient benefits. Students will often find that their student health coverage extends during the vacations and for one term beyond the date of last enrolment.

Internet

Internet access is available **free of charge** at Use It, Rådhusstræde 13, and at the city's libraries (not the Royal Library). **Internet cafés** are pervasive; the Sidewalk Express Internet café chain is rapidly spreading its sphere of influence, with branches all over the city, including the Central Station (19kr/hr, tickets are transferable between branches), while other cafés include the huge Boomtown, Axeltorv 1–3 (daily 24hr; ⓦwww.boomtown .net); B1, Bragesgade 1, Nørrebro (Mon–Thurs & Sun 11am–1am, Fri & Sat 11am–4am; ⓦwww.b1.dk); games shop Faraos Cigarer, Skindergade 27 (Mon–Sat 10am–midnight, Sun noon–midnight; ⓦwww.faraos.dk); and Nethulen, Istedgade 114, Vesterbro (Mon–Fri 9.30am–11pm, Sat–Sun 4–11pm; ℡33 24 04 07). Prices generally range from 15 to 25kr per hour. Alternatively, hotels, hostels and some sleep-ins will offer Internet access.

Rough Guides travel insurance

Rough Guides has teamed up with Columbus Direct to offer you **travel insurance** that can be tailored to suit your needs. Products include a low-cost **backpacker** option for long stays; a **short break** option for city getaways; a typical **holiday package** option; and others. There are also annual **multi-trip** policies for those who travel regularly. Different sports and activities (trekking, skiing, etc) can usually be covered if required.

See our website (ⓦwww.roughguidesinsurance.com) for eligibility and purchasing options. Alternatively, UK residents should call ℡0870/033 9988; US citizens should call ℡1-800/749-4922; Australians should call ℡1300/669 999. All other nationalities should call ℡+44 870/890 2843.

Laundry

All bigger hotels generally provide a **laundry** service – but at a cost. It's generally cheaper to go to one of the many laundry outlets spread across the city. Central places include: Istedgades Møntvask, Istedgade 45; Quickvask, Rosenørns Allé 37; Møntvask, Fælledvej 23; and Vasketeria, Dronningensgade 42. An average load costs about 30kr. Alternatively, head for the new Laundromat Café, Elmegade 15 where you can have a bite to eat while your laundry gets done for 32kr per load (see p.189).

Left luggage

The DSB Garderobe office downstairs in Central Station **stores luggage** for 30kr per item per day and has lockers for 30 and 40kr per day. There are also lockers free for one-day storage at Use It, Rådhusstræde 13. Copenhagen Airport's left-luggage facility is in the walkway between Terminal 2 and Terminal 3, and charges 30kr per day (max 1 month). There are also small and large lockers for 20kr and 50kr per day respectively (max 3 days).

Lost property

The police department's **lost-property** office is at Slotsherrensvej 113, Vanløse ☎38 74 88 22. For items lost on a bus, contact the bus information office on ☎36 13 14 15; lost on a train or S-Tog, the central train information office on ☎70 13 14 15; lost on the metro, call ☎70 15 16 15; lost on a plane, contact the airline or Copenhagen Airport ☎32 47 47 25.

Mail

Like most other public bodies in the country, the Danish **post office** runs an exceedingly tight ship – within Denmark, anything you post is almost certain to arrive within two days. You can buy stamps from most newsagents and from post offices. The main post office is at Købmagergade 1 (Mon–Fri 10am–5pm, Sat 10am–2pm) and there's a late-opening one inside the Central Station (Mon–Fri 8am–9pm, Sat & Sun 10am–4pm). Mail under 50g costs 7kr to other parts of Europe, and 8kr to the rest of the world. Poste restante is available at any post office,

and many hotels, youth hostels and campsites will hold mail ahead of your arrival.

Maps

The **maps** in this book should be adequate for most purposes, but drivers, cyclists and hikers will require something more detailed. The tourist office gives out reasonable city maps, but anything better you'll have to buy.

The best **city** maps are produced by Kraks either in booklet form at various scales, or as a folding map at 1:15,000. Country maps of **Denmark** are produced by Kümmerley & Frey (1:300,000), Ravenstein (1:500,000), and Baedeker (1:400,000). The **provinces** of Denmark are covered by the 1:200,000 Kort og Matrikelstyren series. The Danish Youth Hostel Association also produces a very informative country map (including all hostels, campsites, ferry links and cycle routes), which you can order free of charge from ⓦ www.danhostel.dk.

Money

The Danish currency is the **krone** (plural kroner), made up of 100 øre, and comes in notes of 1000kr, 500kr, 200kr, 100kr and 50kr, and coins of 20kr, 10kr, 5kr, 2kr, 1kr, 50øre and 25øre. At the time of writing, the exchange rate was approximately 10.7kr to the pound, 7.4kr to the euro and 5.7kr to the US dollar. For the latest rates, go to ⓦ www .xe.com.

Banks are plentiful, and the easiest place to change traveller's cheques and foreign cash; there's a uniform commission of 30kr per transaction, so change as much as is feasible in one go. Banking hours are Monday to Wednesday and Friday 10am to 4pm, Thursday 10am to 6pm. The airport and Central Station have late-opening exchange facilities, which charge a similar amount of commission.

Forex exchange bureaux charge only 20kr to exchange cash and 10kr to exchange traveller's cheques but are much rarer; there's one at Central Station (daily 8am–9pm), one at Nørre Voldgade 90, near Nørreport Station (Mon–Fri 9am–7pm, Sat 10am–4pm), and one at Gothersgade 8, near Kongens Nytorv (Mon–Fri 9am–7pm, Sat 10am–4pm).

Alternatively, the red Kontanten high-street cash machines (**ATMs**) give cash advances

Public holidays

New Year's Day; Maundy Thursday; Good Friday; Easter Sunday; Easter Monday; Common Prayer Day (fourth Friday after Easter); Ascension Day (fifth Thursday after Easter); Whit Sunday and Whit Monday (seven weeks after Easter); Constitution Day (June 5); Christmas (December 24–26).

on credit cards and, if you've a Link, Cirrus or Maestro symbol on your ATM card, will allow you to withdraw funds from your own account in local currency (check with your home bank), which can work out cheaper than changing cash or traveller's cheques.

Opening hours and public holidays

Shop **opening hours** are Monday to Thursday 10am to 5.30pm, Friday 10am to 6pm or 7pm and Saturday 9am to 1pm or 2pm; shops are closed on Sundays. Supermarkets stay open a bit later. On the first Saturday of the month, shops stay open until 5pm.

Most shops and businesses are closed on **public holidays** (see box above), and transport services are reduced.

Phones

Public telephones come in two forms. Coin-operated ones are white and require a minimum of 3kr for a local call (the machines irritatingly swallow one of the coins if the number is engaged), and 5kr to go international. Cards for the blue cardphones come in denominations of 30kr, 50kr and 100kr and work out a little cheaper – they're sold in newsagents and post offices. Most hotel rooms have a phone, but it's much cheaper to make calls from the public phone at reception. Youth hostels and campsites

generally have public phones; if not, the warden will probably let you use the house one for a payphone fee.

You should be able to use your **mobile phone** in Denmark if it's been connected via the GSM system common to the rest of Europe, Australia, New Zealand and South Africa. This means that the vast majority of mobile phones from these countries will work here; though, if you haven't used your mobile abroad before, you should check with your phone company as some mobiles are barred from international use. The North American mobile network is not compatible with the GSM system, so you'll need a tri-band phone that will be able to switch from one band to the other. If you plan to make a lot of mobile calls while in Denmark, you could also invest in a Danish SIM card for use in your phone; these are available in all mobile phone shops. For 99kr, you'll get a Danish number plus about forty minutes of domestic calling time. The most commonly used network is TDC (the national landline network), but coverage with Orange, Telia and others is just as good. Top-up cards can be bought in supermarkets, kiosks and phone shops.

Calling Denmark from abroad, the **international code** is ☎45; codes for international calls from Denmark are given below. To make a **collect international call**, dial

Calling home from abroad

Note that the initial zero is omitted from the area code when dialling the UK, Ireland, Australia and New Zealand from abroad.

US and Canada international access code + 1 + area code.
Australia international access code + 61 + city code.
New Zealand international access code + 64 + city code.
UK international access code + 44 + city code.
Ireland international access code + 353 + city code.
South Africa international access code + 27 + city code.

☎80 30 40 00 for the operator and ask to be connected to the operator in your own country, who will then put through the collect call – full instructions for this "Country Direct" system are displayed in phone booths (in English), and you can dial ☎80 60 40 50 for free assistance. Be warned that **directory enquiries** (international ☎113, domestic ☎118) are expensive – the initial charge of 8kr per minute climbs ridiculously high whilst the operator puzzles out your request. Almost all operators speak English. To save money try a phone book (there should be one in all public phone booths), the national phone company's website (🌐www.tdc.dk), or the online (Danish-language) yellow pages (🌐www.degulesider.dk).

Time

Denmark is one hour ahead of GMT, six hours ahead of US Eastern Standard Time, and nine ahead of US Pacific Standard Time.

Taxes

A sales tax, MOMS, of 25 percent is added to almost everything you buy – but it's always included in the price. Non-EU citizens can claim a refund at the airport, provided you fill out a Global Refund Cheque at the point of purchase.

Tourist information

Before you leave home, it's worth contacting Danish **tourist boards** for free maps, timetables, accommodation listings and brochures – though don't go mad, since much of what you'll need can easily be obtained once you arrive. There's also a wealth of information available online; we've included a selection of general sites below.

Once you're in the country, Wonderful Copenhagen's Copenhagen Right Now **tourist office** (May–June Mon–Sat 9am–6pm; July–Aug Mon–Sat 9am–8pm, Sun 10am–6pm; Sept–April Mon–Fri 9am–4pm, Sat 9am–2pm; telephone enquiries Mon–Fri 10am–4pm ☎70 22 24 42; 🌐www.visitcopenhagen.dk), across the road from the Central Station at Vesterbrogade 4A, offers maps, general information, and accommodation reservations for hotels and hostels

(booking fee 100kr). The office also distributes the free *Copenhagen This Week*, an up-to-date monthly news and listings magazine. Far better for youth and budget-oriented help, though, is the **Use It** information centre (mid-June to mid-Sept daily 9am–7pm, mid-Sept to mid-June Mon–Wed 11am–4pm, Thurs 11am–6pm, Fri 11am–2pm; ☎33 73 06 20, 🌐www.useit.dk), centrally placed in the Huset complex at Rådhusstræde 13. A wide range of help for travellers is available, including poste restante and free email services, accommodation (staff fall over themselves to help find you a room in the busy summer period) and entertainment information, luggage-storage facilities and an extremely useful free magazine called *Playtime*.

If you plan to visit a lot of museums, either in Copenhagen or in nearby towns such as Helsingør and Roskilde, you might want to buy a **Copenhagen Card**, which comes in versions valid for either 24 hours (199kr) or 72 hours (429kr). The card covers transport on the entire metropolitan system (which includes the towns mentioned above) and gives entry to most museums in the area. Obviously their worth will depend on your itinerary, but you can certainly save money if well used – especially since it also gets you twenty to fifty percent discounts on some car hire, ferry rides, theatre tickets and on certain museums. The cards are available from tourist offices, hotels and travel agents in the metropolitan region, and at train stations.

Danish tourist board offices abroad

Australia Level 4, 81 York Street, Sydney, NSW 2000 ☎02/9262 5832, 🌐www.scandinavia .com.au.

Canada Box 115, Station N, Toronto, ON M8V 3S4 ☎416/823-9620.

Ireland No tourist board office, but the embassy (see p.33) handles tourist information.

New Zealand No tourist board office but the embassy (see p.33) supplies tourist information.

South Africa No tourist board office, but the embassy (see p.33) handles tourist information.

UK 55 Sloane St, London SW1X 9SY ☎020/7259 5959, 🌐www.visitdenmark.com.

US Scandinavian Tourist Board, 655 3rd Ave, 18th floor, New York, NY 10017 ☎212/885-9700, 🌐visitdenmark.com.

Tourist offices and government sites

Australian Department of Foreign Affairs
ⓦ www.dfat.gov.au, ⓦ www.smartraveller.gov.au.
British Foreign & Commonwealth Office
ⓦ www.fco.gov.uk.

Canadian Department of Foreign Affairs
ⓦ www.dfait-maeci.gc.ca.
Irish Department of Foreign Affairs ⓦ www
.foreignaffairs.gov.ie.
New Zealand Ministry of Foreign Affairs
ⓦ www.mft.govt.nz.
US State Department ⓦ www.travel.state.gov.

The City

The City

Slotsholmen

T he small island of **SLOTSHOLMEN** is the historical and geographical
heart of Copenhagen. It was here, in 1167, that Bishop Absalon founded
the castle, or *slot*, that became the nucleus of the future city, and it's
been the seat of Danish rule ever since. Set imperiously apart from the
bustling commercialism of Indre By, Slotsholmen is packed with historic buildings housing government and royal offices and a quirky collection of **museums** – even if you're choosy, it will take the best part of a day to explore.

The island is dominated by the massive Christiansborg complex, an absorbing, if sometimes confusing, collection of the surviving portions of the various
palaces and castles that have occupied the site since Absalon put it on the map.
At the heart of the complex, the austere grey bulk of **Christiansborg Slot**,
built early last century, is home to the Danish parliament and the dazzling
Kongelige Repræsentationslokaler. Behind it lies the elegant courtyard known
as the **Ridebane**, all that remains of the original Baroque palace built by Christian VI in the early eighteenth century and still home to the Royal Stables and
Royal Riding School, as well as a couple of minor, specialized museums.

On the northern side of the complex are the delightful **Christiansborg
Slotskirke** of 1826, and **Thorvaldsens Museum**, a charming collection of the
work of the nineteenth-century Danish sculptor, while several older buildings to
the south date from the time when Slotsholmen was at the heart of Christian
IV's drive for naval expansion – the most impressive is now home to the **Tøjhusmuseet** with its world-class collection of guns and cannons. Just beyond, a tranquil
garden leads to the more refined collections of the **Det Kongelige Bibliotek** and
its sleek modern extension, the **Den Sorte Diamant**, as well as the newest – and
arguably best – of the area's bevy of museums, the **Dansk Jødisk Museum**.

Opening hours for the various Slotsholmen sights vary considerably, with
many closed on Monday and some only open afternoons, so plan carefully if
time is limited. The best day to visit is Sunday when everything, with the exception of Det Kongelige Bibliotek is open. Buses #1A, #2A, #15, #26 and #29
stop on Christiansborgs Slotsplads for sights on the northern side of the island;
#47 and #66 from Central Station skirt along the southern harbour side of the
island, passing the Sorte Diamant.

Christiansborg Slot

The history of Christiansborg (see the box on p.43 for a full account) is insepa-
rably linked to that of Copenhagen. Since the late twelfth century, there has
been a castle of some sort on the site: the current **Christiansborg Slot** (⊛www
.ses.dk/christiansborg), a hefty granite-faced neo-Baroque building topped
by an enormous green copper spire, was constructed between 1907 and 1928

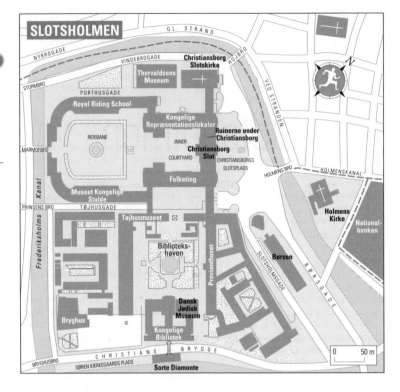

using the remains of the previous palace destroyed by fire in 1884. Its illustrious occupants include the Folketing (Danish Parliament), Supreme Court, prime minister's office and the Royal Reception Rooms.

The **main entrance** is on the square of **Christiansborgs Slotsplads** – long-time favourite spot for demonstrations against king or parliament – adorned with Bissen's pompous equestrian statue of Frederik VII. For a more attractive approach to the palace, head along Frederiksholms Kanal and across the eighteenth-century **Marmorbro** (Marble Bridge), the original entry point for Christian VI's castle, which leads you into the Ridebane and gives a fine view of the palace complex.

Folketing

Folketing (ⓦwww.folketinget.dk), home to the Danish Parliament, is located in Christiansborg Slot's south wing – facing the palace, walk left around the outside of the building from Christiansborg Slotsplads to reach the entrance. You can visit the main parliamentary chamber, the **Folketingssal**, and watch from the public galleries at any time during the surprisingly informal parliamentary sittings (usually from 1pm on Tues & Wed, and from 10am Thurs & Fri; no sessions June–Sept) and see Danish democracy at work, but you'll get a much better impression of it all by taking one of the free guided tours in English (July to mid-Aug Mon–Fri & Sun 2pm; Oct–May Sun 2pm). Well-informed guides lead you up the magnificent staircase to the seemingly endless **Vandrehal** (Hall

Christiansborg through the ages

In 1167, **Bishop Absalon** of Roskilde was granted the small village of Havn (on the site of modern Indre By) by his foster brother, King Valdemar the Great. Absalon set about constructing a castle to protect herring traders in the village from Wendish pirates, and the castle's strategic placement subsequently ensured Danish domination of Øresund and a large part of the Baltic, until in 1369 a strong Hanseatic fleet finally succeeded in occupying the town and set about methodically dismantling the castle to ensure that it would never be rebuilt.

A new castle, **Københavns Slot**, constructed by the church to replace Absalon's castle, was completed in 1417, and promptly confiscated by the Danish king, Erik of Pomerania, who made it the seat of Danish rule and residence of the royal family. Over the years, the *Slot* was extended and modernized innumerable times – Christian IV completely refurbished it, adding a spire to the infamous Blue Tower (see p.45). Over the years, foreign visitors and dignitaries became increasingly amused by the *Slot*'s mishmash of architectural styles, until, to avoid further ridicule, the newly crowned Christian VI decided in 1730 to have the castle demolished and a much grander palace, inspired by the Rococo palaces of France's Louis XIV, erected in its place. Architects from all over Europe were called in to furnish **Christiansborg**, as it became known, with some of the finest art and decoration of the period. Christian VI died long before the palace was completed in 1766, and only 28 years later, in 1794, it burnt down in all its splendour – the Ridebane with its two low, Baroque wings (which now house the Royal Stables, the Royal Riding School and the small Theatre Museum) are all that remain.

The building of a **second Christiansborg** was delayed by the country's dire position following the war with England and the bombardment of Copenhagen in 1807. The palace square and its ruins were used as emergency housing for homeless Copenhageners, and when construction finally began, the walls of the ruins were incorporated into the new palace to save money. By 1828, a new Romanesque-style palace had arisen, but its lifetime was short: in 1884 it, too, burnt to the ground. The chapel – the present Christiansborg Slotskirke – is all that remains from this second Christiansborg.

Today's Christiansborg Slot, the **third Christiansborg**, took 21 years to complete, since the three parties it was to house – the royal family, the parliament and the supreme court – couldn't agree on a suitable style. In the end, the royal family decided to stay at Amalienborg (see p.83), leaving the building, for the most part, to the other two pillars of Danish society parliament and Supreme Court.

of Wandering), where the original Danish constitution from 1849 is exhibited in a silver chest, along with other important historical documents. They'll also explain who sits where – briefly, the 179 members sit grouped in their political parties, with the Cabinet occupying the front seats on the right side of the chamber; on the left side are special galleries reserved for the royal family and representatives of the Supreme Court, who attend the opening debate of the Folketing on the first Tuesday in October.

De Kongelige Repræsentationslokaler

The royal presence at Christiansborg is today limited, for the most part, to **De Kongelige Repræsentationslokaler** (Royal Reception Rooms; guided tour only, English: May & Sept daily, 1pm & 3pm; June–Aug daily 1pm; Oct–April Tues–Sun 3pm; 60kr), located in the palace's north wing – go through the main entrance into the Inner Courtyard and they're on your right, marked by the red sentry box. The rooms are used mainly as a place for the royal family to wow important visitors, though given the Danish royals' easy-going attitude, the formality and opulence of these meticulously kept chambers can come as a surprise. The entertaining tours keep things lively with a sprinkling of royal anecdotes and gossip as you amble through the succession of sumptuous, chandelier-decked rooms. Particularly noteworthy are the **Throne Room**, whose marble walls, covered in richly decorated silk from Lyon, make it a suitably grand spot for greeting guests, and the Alexander Hall, encircled by Bertel Thorvaldsen's magnificent frieze depicting Alexander the Great's arrival into Babylon.

The real highlight, though, is the **Great Hall**, adorned with Bjørn Nørgaard's wonderfully vibrant **tapestries** (a fiftieth birthday gift to the queen from the Danish business community), woven in the famous Gobelin workshops in Paris and depicting the history of Denmark in a refreshingly modern and colourful way that somehow fits perfectly in the otherwise classical room. The rather unflattering portrayal of the queen with long arms, huge hands and high forehead was skilfully explained away by Nørgaard as symbolic of her intelligence and ability to embrace the people; similarly, Prince Frederik's pink flush represents his being next in line to the royal "red" throne. The guides usually whizz through the first few, ending up with the tapestry charting the twentieth century – an engrossing collage of events and personalities with cameo appearances by The Beatles, Bob Dylan and Hitler among others.

The Danish monarchy

The Danish monarchy is one of the oldest in the world, but the royal line of the current monarchy, the **House of Glücksborg**, only dates back to 1853 and the reign of Christian IX, who was nicknamed the "Father-in-law of Europe" as a result of having married off his female progeny to various European royals (including Alexandra, who married Edward VII of England). Denmark's rulers were always men, until Denmark's first and current queen, **Margrethe II** (1940–), came to the throne in 1972. The head of the current royal family is highly educated and independent, with her own interests and work (as a stage designer and translator). Together with her French husband, the **Prince Consort, Henrik II**, she has done much to make the monarchy more approachable and human, although one aspect of her relaxed public demeanour – her chain-smoking – has been criticized in some quarters. Her husband, never as popular a figure, also recently came under public scrutiny for his penchant for dog meat, a habit from his childhood in Vietnam, and one that he maintains – despite being such an avowed dog-lover that he has published a book of poems eulogising his pet dachshunds. The heir to the throne, **Crown Prince Frederik**, is currently riding a wave of popularity; the seemingly eternal bachelor, once a regular face in the trendy bar scene around Skt Hans Torv, married his Tasmanian wife, Crown Princess Mary, in 2005, and they now have a son, Christian. His younger brother, **Prince Joachim**, divorced from his Hong Kong-born wife, Princess Alexandra, in 2003 – they have two young sons, Prince Nikolai and Prince Felix.

Like their British counterparts, the Danish monarchy has been pretty much stripped of any real power, but is for the most part respected by ordinary Danes – a proudly patriotic lot, on the whole, who see their royal family as a living manifestation of the country's history and tradition. You'll encounter little cynicism towards them and their burden to the taxpayer, not least because they have reduced the pomp to a minimum. Not that they live the simple life – in addition to the largely ceremonial splendour of De Kongelige Repræsentationslokaler (see p.43), they have several palaces, including their principal home, **Amalienborg** (see p.83); a summer residence at Fredensborg (see p.140); and, for visits to Jutland, the Marselisborg and Gråsten palaces.

Ruinerne under Christiansborg

In 1907, during the digging of the extraordinarily deep foundations necessary for Christiansborg's soaring new spire, the foundations from previous castles – **Absalon's castle** and **Københavns Slot** (see box on p.43) – were discovered. Prior to this, nobody had known what Absalon's castle had looked like – or, indeed, whether it was just a myth – so massive effort went into the excavation. The inconspicuous entrance to the **ruins** (Ruinerne under Christiansborg; May–Sept daily 9.30am–3.30pm; Oct–April Tues, Thurs, Sat & Sun 9.30am–3.30pm; 35kr) is via a staircase on the right as you pass through the *slot*'s main entrance. From here you head down into two massive subterranean rooms, connected by archways, which follow the circumference of Absalon's castle. Diagrams and explanations in English help decipher the stone and brick jumble of ring walls, foundations, drains and wells, indicating which bits belong to which castle, and though it's still fairly easy to lose the plot, it's all surprisingly absorbing, the mood enhanced by the subdued lighting and eerie silence. There's also the odd juicy historical footnote to keep things interesting: the second room contains the foundations of the **Blue Tower**, the notorious prison of Københavns Slot where Princess Leonora Christina, daughter of Christian IV, was held captive from 1663 to 1685 by her father's successor, Frederik III, officially for treason, unofficially on the orders of the queen, who was jealous of her beauty.

You'll find more detailed background information and exhibits (as well as a useful short film) relating to the succession of castles – and the fires that have ravaged them – in the new **exhibition** adjacent to the ruins, including astonishingly intricate pieces of carved granite and sandstone discovered during excavations – it's thought they formed part of Absalon's chapel and were dumped here by the Hanseatic fleet while the castle was being dismantled in 1369.

Ridebane

Walk through Christiansborg Slot's main entrance and the Inner Courtyard to reach the **Ridebane** (Royal Riding Ground) whose buildings, sole survivors from the original Baroque Christiansborg that burnt down in 1794, still largely serve their original function as home and training ground for the royal horses. The courtyard, overlooked by an equestrian statue of Christian IX and flanked by two long, low wings that curve around to meet at the Marmorbro, is a pleasant and peaceful spot and offers a fine view of the palace as a whole. If you're lucky, you may see the queen's horses being exercised here in the morning; alternatively, look in at the magnificent Royal Riding School, housed in the north wing of the courtyard and open most days until 4pm. This exquisite, light-filled indoor riding arena, flanked by delicate arches and a balcony running into a royal box at the far end, is considered Denmark's most important piece of eighteenth-century architecture and gives a clear indication of how highly equestrian skills were valued.

Museet Kongelige Stalde og Kareter

In the south wing of the Ridebane is all that remains of the **Museet Kongelige Stalde og Kareter** (Royal Stables & Coaches Museum; May–Sept Fri–Sun 2–4pm; Oct–April Sat & Sun 2–4pm; 20kr), which once occupied both wings and housed the royal family's retinue of two hundred horses (there are now just twenty). Even if you're not interested in horses, the stables are worth seeing for their unexpectedly lavish interiors, with pillars, vaulted ceilings, and walls and cribs of Tuscan marble – apparently, not even the king's own chambers were this extravagantly decorated. To the right, as you enter, the **Harness Room** contains a motley collection of old riding uniforms, harnesses and horse portraits – which shouldn't keep you long. Further on, through the stables, the **Coach Museum** displays the royal family's collection of coaches and carriages (some of them still in use), ranging from Dowager Queen Juliane Marie's state coach from 1778 – the collection's oldest and most elaborately decorated carriage – to Frederik IX's black Bentley T, left here since his death in 1972.

Teatermuseet I Hofteatret

Incongruously situated above the Royal Stables, the **Teatermuseet I Hofteatret** (Theatre Museum in the Court Theatre; Tues & Thurs 11am–3pm, Wed 11am–5pm, Sat & Sun 1–4pm; 30kr; ⑩ www.teatermuseet.dk) occupies the charming former Court Theatre of 1767. When Christian VII came to the throne in 1766, he immediately set French architect Nicolas-Henri Jardin the task of turning an old tack room into a small Italian-style theatre (the first Christiansborg lacked a theatre, thanks to the pietistic Christian VI, who prohibited theatre performances throughout Denmark). It remained in use until the fire authorities closed it down in 1881, fearful of a repeat of the disastrous theatre fire that occurred earlier that year in Vienna.

The building reopened as the Theatre Museum in 1922; each of its rooms explores a particular theme of Danish theatrical history – opera, pantomime, ballet and drama – from the seventeenth century to the present day with the aid of photographs, prints, paintings, video and assorted memorabilia. The exhibitions aren't particularly captivating and there are few labels in English, but the auditorium itself is an unexpected gem, its deep, sloping stage, plush velvet upholstery, elegant royal boxes and beautifully decorated oriental ceiling (painted for a royal masquerade in 1857) evoking an atmosphere of theatrical excitement, best experienced during one of the plays and concerts occasionally held here – for more information, consult the tourist office (see p.37) or see ⑩ www.kulturnaut.dk.

Around Christiansborgs Slotsplads

Back on Christiansborgs Slotsplads, the graceful, white-domed building tacked on the northwest end of the palace is **Christiansborg Slotskirke** (Palace Chapel; Sun noon–4pm and daily noon–4pm during Easter, July and third week of Oct; free; ⑩ www.ses.dk/christiansborg), all that remains of the second Christiansborg, which burnt down in 1884. Consecrated in 1826, the chapel – designed by C.F. Hansen, one of the most important Danish Golden-Age architects – is a beautiful example of the simple Neoclassical architecture typical of the period. Ironically, having escaped the fire of 1884, the chapel went up in flames in 1992 when a flare from a passing boat landed on its roof during Copenhagen's Lent carnival – the dome collapsed and the inside was seriously damaged. The lavish custard-and-cream-coloured marble stucco interior has since been returned to its original state, with Thorvaldsen's magnificent angel frieze encircling the dome and Bissen's four angel reliefs seeming to float from the walls beneath. Originally the parish church of the royal family, it was demoted in 1926 and now only hosts the occasional christening and lying in state. Services are no longer held here (with the exception of the annual opening of parliament) and the chapel is mainly used by the Royal Danish Music Conservatory for organ lessons. Concerts are sometimes held here (check with the tourist office; see p.37).

Thorvaldsens Museum

Tucked behind Christiansborg Slotskirke, **Thorvaldsens Museum** (Tues–Sun 10am–5pm; July & Aug guided tours in English Sun 3pm; 20kr, free on Wed; ⊕www.thorvaldsensmuseum.dk) is a refreshing antidote to the power and pomp of Slotsholmen's historical heavyweights. The Neoclassical building, with its striking ochre facade and eye-catching frieze, was purpose-built in 1839 to house the enormous collection of works and personal possessions (and the body) of Denmark's only sculptor of note – **Bertel Thorvaldsen** (see box on p.48). Though the name is unlikely to ring any bells, in his time Thorvaldsen enjoyed international renown as sculptor to Europe's elite, and while none of the pieces is famous in its own right, it makes for an pleasant wander amid the roll call of famous and infamous gods and mortals – Byron, Christian IV, Napoleon and Hercules among others – set off beautifully by the richly coloured walls, mosaic floors and finely painted ceilings. The excellent, free audioguides help bring it all to life with useful background on classical mythology and artistic interpretation.

On the **ground floor**, the hall to the left of the entrance is stuffed with the plaster models of some of his most important commissions – hulking homages to the likes of Pope Pius VII and Maximilian I – but the numerous small rooms surrounding the inner courtyard where the sculptor is buried are far more rewarding, housing a succession of more delicate works that reflect his love for classical antiquity. Highlights include the enchanting *Cupid and Psyche* (room 2), *Jason with the Golden Fleece* (room 5) – bristling with masculinity and new-found power – and *Mars and Cupid* (room 7), depicting the eternal tussle of love and war. Further along, in the **Christ Hall**, are the huge, grubby casts (left uncleaned for fear of erasing the sculptor's original marks) of the statues of Christ and the Apostles that cut such a dash in Vor Frue Kirke (see p.53). Look out, too, for the debonair and self-congratulatory sculpture of the man himself in room 20.

The **first floor** displays Thorvaldsen's considerable, but unexceptional, collection of **antiquities** – ancient Egyptian artefacts, greek coins and pottery and

△ Thorvaldsens Museum

Bertel Thorvaldsen

Born into a poor family, **Bertel Thorvaldsen** (1770–1844) had negligible schooling but plenty of talent, and at the age of 11 drew his way into the Danish Academy of Fine Arts. However, with Neoclassicism in full swing, **Rome** beckoned, and when he got the chance to visit the city in 1797, he found his spiritual home, staying on for forty years. Of his early days in Rome, he said, "Every day I hurried to the Vatican and devoured as much as I could of the works of Antiquity". Inspired by the wealth of classical tradition around him, he began to perfect his own trademark heroic, classical sculptures – well-proportioned, graceful figures with contemplative, absorbed expressions. Before long he was fulfilling prestigious commissions for Europe's most powerful players – chief among them the Alexander frieze for the Palazzo del Quirinale to commemorate Napoleon's entry into Rome, and Pope Pius VII's tomb for the basilica in St Peter's. But Thorvaldsen never forgot his native city and played his part in the cultural and artistic rejuvenation of a Copenhagen half destroyed by fires and British bombs, with several important commissions, including the Christ and Apostles for Vor Frue Kirke and the frieze in Christiansborg Slotskirke. He eventually **returned to Denmark** in 1838 to a hero's welcome, and died six years later, leaving his sculptures and private collections to the nation. Thorvaldsen was something of a wit, too. Asked by the Swedish artist J.T. Sergel how he managed to make such beautiful figures, he held up the scraper with which he was working and replied, "With this".

Etruscan gold jewellery – as well as some of his furniture and paintings, including numerous self-portraits. If you're still up for more, the **lower ground floor** has the inevitable film on his life and art, as well as several rough cuts of the finished models upstairs, and a display on how a sculpture is made. After you exit, walk around the building to see the magnificent painted frieze by Jørgen Sonne, which shows hat-doffing citizens lining up to welcome the sculptor home after his many years in Rome.

Børsen, Holmens Kirke and Nationalbanken

At the eastern end of Christiansborgs Slotsplads, the flamboyant red-brick building with the distinctive gabled green copper roof and fanciful spire formed out of four entwined dragons' tails is the seventeenth-century **Børsen** (Stock Exchange) – centrepiece of Christian IV's plan to make Copenhagen the centre of trade in the Baltic region. The building served as a stock exchange before money traders and bankers began moving in during the eighteenth century. It's now owned by the Chamber of Commerce and is not open to the public.

Just across the canal, **Holmens Kirke** (Mon–Sat 9am–noon; summer till 2pm; @www.holmenskirke.dk) also caught the eye of the ambitious king. Originally built as an anchor forge for the naval dockyard in 1562, it was converted it into a church for naval personnel from Bremerholmen (the naval yard) and Slotsholmen in 1619, and it has changed little since. The long chapel by the canal (go through the door to the left of the altar), added in the early eighteenth century, is dedicated to Denmark's seafaring heroes, several of whom are buried here. The church's other claim to fame is that the present queen, Margrethe II, was married here in 1967.

Just east of the church, occupying the entire block between waterfront Havnegade and Holmenskanal, is the subdued, black presence of **Nationalbanken** (National Bank), the final project of Denmark's revered architect and designer, Arne Jacobsen (see **Danish design** colour section), who died before it could be completed. Ever mindful of the bigger picture, Jacobsen designed the part of the bank nearest to Holmens Kirke on one level so as not to compete with the church and Børsen.

South of Christiansborg

The buildings in the area **south of Christiansborg** are mostly much older than those of Christiansborg and are connected to the expansionist Christian IV (1577–1648) and the period when Slotsholmen was home to the Danish Royal Navy. With military domination of the Baltic in mind and relations with Sweden permanently on a war footing, Christian IV transformed the area south of the then Københavns Slot into a dock and supply depot capable of feeding his ever-expanding naval fleet – hence the predominance of large, functional red-brick constructions capped by massive tiled roofs. However, modern architecture does get a look-in with the impressive **Den Sorte Diamant**, occupying a peaceful waterfront location and the perfect spot for a coffee or lunch break, while the area is also home to the **Tøjhusmuseet** and the excellent new Libeskind-designed **Dansk Jødisk Museum**.

Tøjhusmuseet

Walking from Christiansborgs Slotsplads past the main entrance to the Folketing and along Tøjhusgade you come to the exhaustive **Tøjhusmuseet** (Royal Danish Arsenal Museum; Tues–Sun noon–4pm; 40kr; free Wed; ⓦwww.thm .dk), appropriately housed in the old Tøjhus (Arms House). Completed in 1604, this huge armoury was created to supply Christian IV's navy with cannons, guns, ammunition and gunpowder. Ships docked at the adjacent naval basin (now the Bibliotekshaven see below), to be loaded with arms from the Tøjhus, and clothes, food and drink from the **Provianthuset** (Victuallers' Building), on the eastern side of the basin. Eighty years later, the royal naval base moved to Nyholm on Christianshavn (see p.74) and the Tøjhus and Provianthuset fell into disuse (the latter now houses parliamentary offices and isn't open to the public).

As you'd expect, the collections are unlikely to excite unless you're into displays of military hardware, and it doesn't help that most of the signs are in Danish only, but the sheer scope of the paraphernalia on display is undeniably impressive – it's reputedly the world's finest collection of eighteenth- and nineteenth-century armaments. On the ground floor, cannons (some dating back to the fifteenth century), tanks and artillery line both sides of the enormous **Cannon Hall** – at 156m the longest arched room in Europe, and a handsome sight in itself with its succession of whitewashed arches and expanse of cobbled floor. On the first floor, the even longer **Armoury Hall** displays endless rows of swords and firearms in chronological order starting with a prototype gun from around 1400, with just the odd suit of armour for relief – look out for Christian IV's breastplate and guns halfway along. Needless to say, the glorification of weaponry can get overwhelming, though the friendly guides do their best to humanize the experience with insights into the exhibits.

Det Kongelige Bibliotek and Den Sorte Diamant

The basin in which ships used to dock while being provisioned at the Tøjhus and Provianthuset was filled in during the 1860s and is now the **Bibliotekshaven** (Royal Library Garden; entrance on Tøjhusgade) – a peaceful spot for a picnic, with shady lawns, a fountain and fishpond, and assorted statues, including one of a lovesick Søren Kierkegaard looking over to where his fiancée, Regine Olsen, used to live. At the far end of the garden stands **Det Kongelige Bibliotek** (Royal Library), a romantic, Venetian-inspired building with large, curved windows and slim pillars, built in 1906 to house the extensive collections begun by Frederik III over two and a half centuries earlier. You can't actually get in here – walk around the right side of the building to the stunning black-granite and glass extension known as **Den Sorte Diamant** (Black Diamond; building Mon–Sat 8am–7pm, free; library & exhibitions Mon–Fri 10am–7pm, Sat 10am–5pm, 30kr; ⊛www.kb.dk; to arrange guided tours in English contact ☏33 47 48 80 or ⊛booking@kb.dk). Connected to the original library by a glass walkway above the road, the Diamond tilts elegantly on its glass base to the edge of the harbour, dominating the waterfront and dwarfing all around it. Inside, the glass-walled foyer with harbour views and soaring, light-filled atrium create an exciting public space that includes a concert hall, bookshop (with a decent English paperbacks section), café, and the expensive *Søren K* restaurant (the only restaurant on Slotsholmen). The lower ground floor is given over to varied temporary exhibitions (30kr) drawing on the library's collections of books, prints and music, as well as changing selections from the archives of the **National Museum of Photography**, which also has its home here. The information desk can tell you what's on and will give you a free floorplan. You'll get a better impression of the building as a whole by heading up the travelator onto the glass walkway, with its ceiling mural by Danish expressionist painter Per Kirkeby. You're free to wander across to the old library, but the reading rooms and collections, which include manuscripts by Hans Christian Andersen, Karen Blixen and Søren Kierkegaard, are for members only.

Dansk Jødisk Museum

Designed by Daniel Libeskind, architect of the Jewish Museum in Berlin and the impending Ground Zero memorial, the new **Dansk Jødisk Museum** (Danish Jewish Museum; June–Aug Tues–Sun 10am–5pm; Sept–May Tues–Fri 1–4pm, Sat & Sun noon–5pm; 40kr) recounts the largely peaceful coexistence of Jews and Danes in Denmark for over four centuries. The concept of *Mitzvah*, or "good deed", runs through the museum, Libeskind taking as his inspiration one of the few Jewish success stories of World War II – the escape from imminent deportation to concentration camps of 7000 Jews, helped across the Øresund to safety in neutral Sweden by the Danish Resistance, the Danish people and reputedly several German officers who turned a blind eye (see box on p.51). It's a fitting and, at times, moving memorial to this proud period in Denmark's history and the tolerance of the Danes themselves, moving deftly from the events of 1943 to broader themes such as the history of Jewish immigration to Denmark, what it means to be Jewish, and the concept of "homeland", all amply illuminated by personal histories and possessions, and a beautiful array of paraphernalia used in Jewish rituals – prayer shawls, Torah bells and shields, and an exquisitely illustrated eighteenth-century copy of the *Haggadah* (the story of the Exodus from Egypt). The displays are perfectly set off by the striking architecture: a series of sloping corridors – all jutting angles and rods of light – whose layout corresponds to the interlaced Hebrew letters of the word "*Mitzvah*". The brick, vaulted ceiling is the only visible reminder that the museum is housed in Christian IV's old royal boathouse (it was absorbed into the library building in 1906), a fitting location as it was Christian who first invited wealthy merchant Jews to settle in Denmark in 1616, enticing them with the privilege of a tax-free status for 25 years.

Flight to Sweden

Exploiting the Nazis' desire for collaboration, the Danish government had, for the first few years of **occupation**, managed to keep their Jewish population safe from persecution, refusing to enforce the special laws applied to Jews in other occupied countries, such as the wearing of the Star of David. This **protected status** couldn't last forever, though, and in September 1943, the issue of the Danish Jews was brought to the attention of Hitler himself by Werner Best, the ambitious head of the German Legation in Denmark. The Führer's subsequent order that **Endlösung** (the "Final Solution") should now be extended to Danish Jews disgruntled many prominent Nazis, who were mindful of disrupting the so-far peaceful occupation and beginnings of collaboration. Their reservations were ignored, and desperate to avoid the impending confrontation with the Danish government and political fallout for his ally and boss, **C.F. Duckwitz**, a high-ranking official at the German Legation, embarked on a frantic and secret round of meetings (probably sanctioned by a now-anxious Best) with Swedish ministers, who proposed to Berlin that Sweden give safe haven to all Danish Jews. Again, their suggestions fell on deaf ears, and Best was told to proceed – the date was set for October 2 that year. Having exhausted all diplomatic routes and with just four days to go, Duckwitz leaked the information to the Danish authorities – a message that was quickly disseminated via the congregation at the Copenhagen synagogue to every Jew in Denmark. By the time the Gestapo began knocking on doors, most Jews had already fled their homes and were either escaping across the Ønesund Sound or lying low in hiding places up and down the coast.

The **Danish population** played a crucial role in helping their Jewish compatriots to escape – offering them shelter, raising funds, volunteering their boats as the Danish Resistance found their traditional escape routes swamped under the volume of refugees. In small fishing towns along the Zealand coast, inhabitants improvised **escape routes**; 1800 Jews fled from Gilleleje alone, the town's fishermen ferrying the waiting escapees out night after night to a larger vessel on its return journey from delivering potatoes. All but a few hundred of Denmark's 7500 Jews made it safely across to Sweden – some were discovered by the Gestapo (including 80 who had been hiding in the attic of Gilleleje church), others were too old or sick to flee. Those captured were sent to a concentration camp in Czechoslovakia, where, as a final, happy endnote to this remarkable story, most survived the war. An insight into Denmark's position in World War II can be had at the Frihedsmuseeet (see p.85).

Bryghus

While you're in the vicinity it's worth having a quick look at the historic **Bryghus** (Brewery), another Christian IV construction, which looms over the northern side of Søren Kierkegaards Plads. A classic building of its time, this monumental red-brick hulk, with a massive roof, had the important task of housing the king's brewery and providing rations to the thirsty sailors, as well as defending what was then the most outlying point of Slotsholmen. Beer was brewed here until 1767, when the building partially burnt down, since when it has served as a storage facility for the navy and later for the Tøjhursmuseet. It's now in private hands and not open to the public.

Indre By

Compared to the monumental edifices of Christiansborg across the Slotsholmen canal, the district of **INDRE BY** presents Copenhagen on a more human scale. The heart of both medieval and modern cities, Indre By (Inner City) is where it all began – the site of the small and marshy fishing village of Havn, whose fortunes were transformed by the arrival of Bishop Absalon in 1167 (see box on p.43). Whilst Absalon and his successors raised their castles on the island of Slotsholmen, the settlement of Havn prospered through tax and trade, acquiring the name of København (Merchant's Harbour) and becoming capital of Denmark in 1445. Within its fortifications – which endure as a ring of parks, lakes and green areas – Copenhagen grew rapidly. Although it was subsequently ravaged by a series of major fires, and bombarded by first the Swedish and then the British, the medieval town's tangle of tiny streets, squares and ancient churches survived and is still very much in evidence, forming a sharp contrast to the relatively modern areas outside the old fortifications, where permanent settlement only started after 1851.

Indre By is very much the public face of Copenhagen; the hub of the city's day-to-day activity and its main shopping district, it's a maze of lively, attractive streets and squares perfectly suited to idle ambling (or serious shopping) amongst crowds of locals, tourists and street entertainers. It's all the more enjoyable for the fact that its two main thoroughfares are pedestrianized and wide enough to accommodate the inevitable hordes of shoppers. The first is **Strøget**, the colloquial name (it's not on any street signs) given to the series of connecting streets (Frederiksberggade, Nygade, Vimmelskaftet, Amagertorv and Østergade) that run across Indre By from Rådhuspladsen in the west to Kongens Nytorv in the east. The other main street, **Købmagergade**, leaves Strøget at Højbro Plads, heading north towards Nørreport Station via Kultorvet. You won't find much beyond mainstream chain stores, department stores and big-name designers on either, but a dip into the side streets reveals an enticing array of second-hand, antique and small Danish shops, as well as many popular and unusual bars, cafés and restaurants.

Indre By also has its fair share of historic buildings, churches and museums. Foremost among these is Christian IV's wonderfully quirky **Rundetårn**, which offers a chance to escape the crowds for a fantastic view over the city, while, close by, the eclectic collections of the **Musikhistorisk Museum**, **Arbejdermuseet**, **Post & Tele Museum** and **Museum Erotica** make for enlightening diversions from shopping. At some point or another most visitors make it to **Nyhavn** – a bevy of colourful restaurants and bars in a picture-postcard canalside setting, east of Kongens Nytorv, that draws tourists by the boatload.

Indre By is served by two metro stations: Nørreport (also an S-Tog stop) on its northwestern side, at the top of Købmagergade, and Kongens Nytorv on the eastern side. Given the narrow, largely pedestrianized streets, bus access is limited to the encircling main roads; several buses stop at Nørreport Station (the best starting point for the shops and museums on Købmagergade), including the #5A, #6A and #14, all of which continue round to the southern border of Indre By, particularly useful for the shops and restaurants of the Latin Quarter. Bus #350S runs along the northern side of Indre By – good for the smaller, trendier and more eclectic shops around Store Regnegade and Grønegade – while for the sights on Kongens Nytorv and Nyhavn, there's the metro or numerous buses (#1A, #15, #19, #26 and #350S).

Along Frederiksberggade to the Latin Quarter

Heading east from Rådhuspladsen, **Frederiksberggade**, five minutes from Central Station, is the first – and tackiest – of the series of streets that make up **Strøget**. The fast-food joints, souvenir shops and touristy pubs aren't the best introduction to the area, but you soon reach Kattesundet on the left, which leads to the altogether trendier area centred on **Larsbjørnstræde**, one of the liveliest streets in the city. Despite being nicknamed *Pisserenden*, "the urinal" (in its dilapidated former days it was a favourite spot for people to relieve themselves), the street has shed its smelly past and now overflows with trendy new and used clothes shops, independent music stores, second-hand bookshops and chic cafés; it also has a buzzing nightlife including much of the city's lively gay scene. The quieter streets crossing Larsbjørnstræde – **Studiestræde** and **Skt Peders Stræde** – are also worth exploring whether you want to kit yourself out in vintage denim or leather bondage gear. Shopping done, it's a few minutes' walk to the more rarefied atmosphere of the Latin Quarter, home of the city's university and several old churches.

The Latin Quarter

At the eastern end of Skt Peders Stræde is Copenhagen's **University**, the oldest in Scandinavia, founded in 1475 to train Catholic priests. The university sits at the heart of the so-called **Latin Quarter** – a reference to the fact that Latin was once the *lingua franca* here. It's a far cry from its lively Parisian namesake, however – this quiet bit of Indre By is now largely deprived of its intellectual buzz, as most of the university departments have moved out of the city centre. The impressive neo-Gothic main building dating from 1836 is now used mainly for administration – statues of the university's most distinguished graduates, including Nobel Prize-winner Niels Bohr, who discovered the structure of the atom, line the building's side. Rather more of an academic aura pervades **Fiolstræde**, on the other side of the main building, a lovely pedestrianized street hosting a fine array of antiquarian and new bookshops (see p.220 for more details).

Immediately south of the university, on the peaceful, cobbled Frue Plads, **Vor Frue Kirke** (Our Lady's Church; daily 8am–5pm) is surprisingly modest, given its status as Copenhagen's cathedral. Built on the site of a twelfth-century church, the dusky pink Neoclassical edifice dates only from 1829, when it was erected to a design by the ubiquitous C.F. Hansen, town planner and architect, amidst the devastation caused by the British bombardment of 1807. Hansen's simple designs were a distinctive feature of Copenhagen's Golden Age. Inside, the weighty figure of Christ behind the altar merits a look, as do the solemn

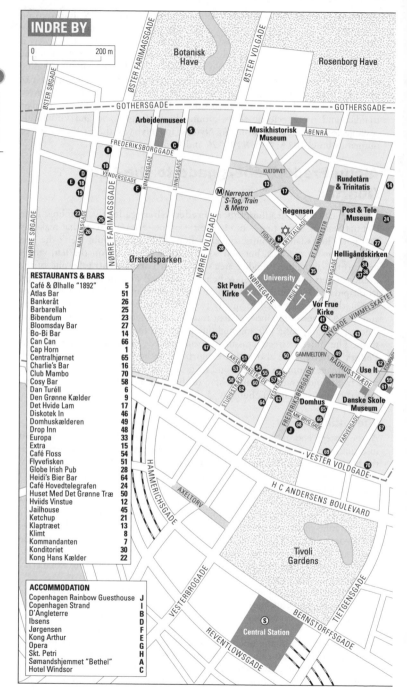

INDRE BY

0   200 m

Botanisk Have

Rosenborg Have

GOTHERSGADE — — — — — — — GOTHERSGADE

Arbejdermuseet **5**

Musikhistorisk Museum

ÅBENRÅ

FREDERIKSBORGGADE

C

10

D

E **18**

19

23

25

26

VENDERSGADE

F

RIMMERSGADE

LINNÉSGADE

KULTORVET

13

17

Rundetårn & Trinitatis

14

ØSTER SØGADE

NØRRE SØGADE

NANSENSGADE

NØRRE FARIMAGSGADE

Ørstedsparken

M Nørreport S-Tog, Train & Metro

Regensen

Post & Tele Museum **24**

27

NØRRE VOLDGADE

HAUSER PL

KRYSTALGADE

St. KANNIKESTR

H

28

31

35

University

34
36
37

Helligåndskirken

Skt Petri Kirke

NØRREGADE

FRUE PL.

SKINDERGADE

Vor Frue Kirke

VIMMELSKAFTET

NYGADE

44

45

46

41
42

43

47

LARSBJØRNSSTR.

51

53

54
55
66

50

GAMMELTORV

49

RÅDHUSSTRÆDE

Use It **52**

58

STUDIESTRÆDE

62

60

57

56

64

VESTERGADE

NYTORV

59
61

63

FREDERIKSBERGGADE

Domhus **65**

66

Danske Skole Museum

FREDERIK BRYG GADE

68

J

TEGLGÅRDSTR.

67

FARVERGADE

VESTER VOLDGADE

69

70

H C ANDERSENS BOULEVARD

HAMMERICHSGADE

AXELTORV

Tivoli Gardens

VESTERBROGADE

BERNSTORFFSGADE

TIETGENSGADE

REVENTLOWSGADE

S Central Station

RESTAURANTS & BARS

Café & Ølhalle "1892"	5
Atlas Bar	51
Bankeråt	26
Barbarellah	25
Bibendum	23
Bloomsday Bar	27
Bo-Bi Bar	14
Can Can	66
Cap Horn	1
Centralhjørnet	65
Charlie's Bar	16
Club Mambo	70
Cosy Bar	58
Dan Turéll	6
Den Grønne Kælder	9
Det Hvide Lam	17
Diskotek In	46
Domhuskælderen	49
Drop Inn	48
Europa	33
Extra	15
Café Floss	54
Flyvefisken	51
Globe Irish Pub	28
Heidi's Bier Bar	64
Café Hovedtelegrafen	24
Huset Med Det Grønne Træ	50
Hviids Vinstue	12
Jailhouse	45
Ketchup	21
Klaptræet	13
Klimt	8
Kommandanten	7
Konditoriet	30
Kong Hans Kælder	22

ACCOMMODATION

Copenhagen Rainbow Guesthouse	J
Copenhagen Strand	I
D'Angleterre	B
Ibsens	D
Jørgensen	F
Kong Arthur	E
Opera	G
Skt. Petri	H
Sømandshjemmet "Bethel"	A
Hotel Windsor	C

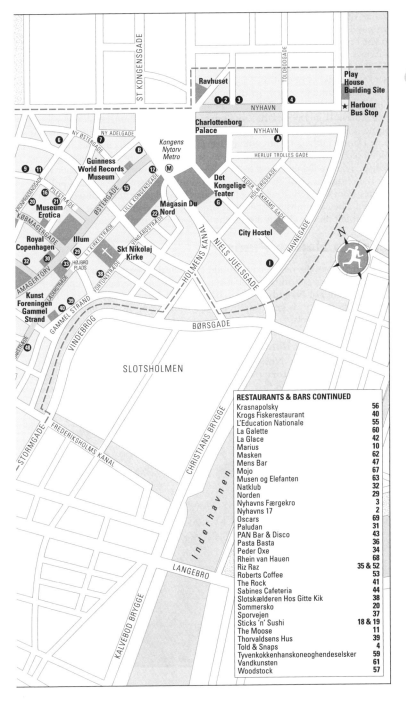

RESTAURANTS & BARS CONTINUED

Krasnapolsky	56
Krogs Fiskerestaurant	40
L'Education Nationale	55
La Galette	60
La Glace	42
Marius	10
Masken	62
Mens Bar	47
Mojo	67
Musen og Elefanten	63
Natklub	32
Norden	29
Nyhavns Færgekro	3
Nyhavns 17	2
Oscars	69
Paludan	31
PAN Bar & Disco	43
Pasta Basta	36
Peder Oxe	34
Rhein van Hauen	68
Riz Raz	35 & 52
Roberts Coffee	53
The Rock	41
Sabines Cafeteria	44
Slotskælderen Hos Gitte Kik	38
Sommersko	20
Sporvejen	37
Sticks 'n' Sushi	18 & 19
The Moose	11
Thorvaldsens Hus	39
Told & Snaps	4
Tyvenkokkenhanskoneoghendeselsker	59
Vandkunsten	61
Woodstock	57

statues of the apostles – some crafted by Bertel Thorvaldsen (see p.48), others by his pupils – that line the nave. Copenhagen Royal Chapel boys' choir is based at Vor Frue; check the cathedral website for details of concerts.

Across from the university on the other side of Nørregade, **Skt Petri Kirke** (St Peter's Church; May–Nov Tues–Fri 11am–3pm, Sat noon–3pm; ⓦwww .sankt-petri.dk) is one of the city's best-preserved medieval buildings. Built as a Roman Catholic church in the mid-fifteenth century, it became the king's cannon and bell foundry following the Reformation in 1536, until its donation by Frederik II in 1585 to the city's substantial German Lutheran congregation. Some sermons are still held in German (Sun 11am), although the church is now Danish Lutheran. The central nave and choir of the present building are its oldest sections, although the church's most interesting feature is the atmospheric Italian-style sepulchral chapel from 1683 (25kr); its numerous tombs and crypts are the resting place of many prominent Danish members of court and political figures from the period of absolute monarchy, including the architect Nikolai Eigtved. The cannonballs suspended from the chapel ceiling are just some of the 150 that fell on the church during the 1807 British bombardment.

East to Højbro Plads

Back on Strøget, the next section, heading northeast as far as the bustling square of Højbro Plads (a natural point for a coffee or lunch break), comprises the hectic stretches of **Nygade**, **Vimmelskaftet** and **Amagertorv**, though there's ample opportunity to get away from the main throng by heading down the numerous side streets.

Gammeltorv and Nytorv

At the junction with Nørregade, Strøget is flanked by the busy squares of **Gammeltorv** and **Nytorv** ("old" and "new" squares), two large ancient spaces that mark the site of the first marketplace in Havn when it was still a fishing

△ Kompagnistræde, Indre By

village – a tradition kept alive today by a few fruit-and-veg stalls and the odd stall selling jewellery and bric-a-brac. The wide, gently sloping expanse and presence of the city's C.F. Hansen-designed **Domhus** (Law Courts), with its suitably forbidding row of Neoclassical columns, lend a faintly Roman whiff to Nytorv, and it's a refreshingly open spot to sit with a drink and watch the stream of shoppers passing along Strøget.

Gammeltorv's most striking feature is the **Caritas Fountain**, by Statius Otto, dating from 1608. Ten years older than the similarly risqué – but much more famous – Manneken Pis in Brussels, the fountain's water flows from Caritas's breasts and from the little boy at her feet taking a leak (the three holes were sealed with lead during the puritanical nineteenth century). The fountain supposedly symbolizes Christian IV's compassion for his people: the well on top of which it stands was Copenhagen's first external water supply, linked by lead piping to a source 6km north of the city.

A short detour south from Nytorv down Rådhusstræde brings you to lively **Kompagnistræde**, one of Europe's best hunting grounds for antiques. The range of outlets here, both up- and down-market, yields all sorts of treasures if you look hard enough, from Persian carpets and oak furniture to silver candlestick holders, ancient plates, delicate crystal glassware and collectable children's toys. On the way, at Rådhusstræde 6, you'll pass the **Danske Skolemuseum** (Mon–Fri 10am–4pm, Sun noon–4pm; 30kr; ⊛www.skolemuseum.dk), only really worth a visit if you happen to be interested in educational history – even then, the reconstructed classroom from 1900, old school uniforms and assorted, outmoded teaching aids do little to enlighten, though plans are afoot to expand the exhibitions.

Gråbrødretorv

Continuing east down Nygade, then left just before reaching Helligåndskirken down cobbled Valkendorfsgade and through Kringlegangen – a pedestrian passageway that goes straight through no. 17 – will bring you to **Gråbrødretorv**, a charming, enclosed square with more than its fair share of good cafés and restaurants. The square dates back to 1238 when Franciscan monks started the city's first monastery here – the name Gråbrødretorv (Grey Brothers' Square) is a reference to their grey habits. The monks left Copenhagen shortly before the Reformation, and today the square is a gathering place for locals in the know, who come in good weather to dine well or just sit by the fountain and enjoy a cold *høker* beer. Concerts and buskers provide entertainment during the summer.

Helligåndskirken and Amagertorv

Returning to Strøget brings you to **Helligåndskirken** (Church of the Holy Ghost; Mon–Fri noon–4pm), founded in 1296 as part of a Catholic monastery of the same name, and one of the oldest churches in the city. The monastery was dissolved during the Reformation, but the building survived as a Lutheran parish church until being completely gutted by the Great Fire of 1728; it has been largely rebuilt since. Entrance is through a beautifully carved sandstone portal, dating back to 1620, which was originally intended for the old stock exchange (Børsen) on Slotsholmen; inside, look out for an impressive altarpiece donated by Christian VI depicting the ascension of Christ. Also dating from 1296, **Helligåndshuset** (entered from the church close, left of the main church entrance), the west wing of the original monastery, survived the fire and is today the only completely preserved medieval building in Copenhagen. It's now used for book fairs, art shows and other exhibitions, and is worth a look for the formidable vaulted ceiling and slender granite columns.

From Helligåndskirken, you're on the broader, lighter Amagertorv section of Strøget, accentuated by the beautiful mosaics of **Bjørn Nørgaard** (famous for the Queen's Tapestries; see p.44) that in 1994 replaced the street's old cobbled stones.

On the north side of Amagertorv, the four torchbearers of classic Danish design are banded together under the name of **Royal Copenhagen** (ⓦwww .royalshopping.com): Georg Jensen's Silverware Shop, Royal Copenhagen Porcelain and Antiques, Holmegaard Glass and the furniture and household design Mecca of Illums Bolighus (see "Shopping" p.220 for more details). Danish design at its best, if most traditional, it's all classy, beautifully crafted and expensive stuff – the queen is a customer – and makes for an aspirational browse. Georg Jensen became famous in the early twentieth century for his Art Nouveau silverware ranging from jewellery to cutlery, and there's a small museum in the shop dedicated to him and his designs, including some beautiful examples of his early work. Next door, the Royal Copenhagen Porcelain and Antiques shop is housed in one of Copenhagen's oldest buildings (dating from 1616); the exquisite porcelain comes from the most famous Danish factories, and you can also watch the signature blue designs being painted by an in-house artist. Upstairs, **Konditoriet** (see p.180) offers some of the best – and most expensive – pastries in Copenhagen. If you want to see how Royal Copenhagen porcelain is made, there's a small visitors' centre at the former factory site at Frederiksberg (see p.109), with a discount shop, too.

Højbro Plads and around

Højbro Plads, at the busy junction of Amagertorv and Købmagergade, was created to make space for the city fire brigade's trucks after the devastating fire of 1795 – the streets here were too narrow for the trucks to get through, resulting in the fire spreading uncontrollably in the tightly packed area. Today, it's lined with banks and other relatively dull buildings, though the two perennially popular cafés *Europa* (see p.179) and *Norden* (see p.181), and an abundance of street entertainers and buskers, guarantee a lively atmosphere, and in summer there's usually a small jazz band playing. The eye-catching **Storkespringvandet** (Stork Fountain, though the birds which adorn it are actually herons) has repeatedly been a focal point of Danish anti-establishment culture, most memorably during the Flower Power era, when hippies sat around it singing protest songs, though today it's more likely to be surrounded by rollerbladers, dazed shoppers and a few local drunks.

The southern end of **Højbro Plads** is dominated by an equestrian statue of the founder of Copenhagen, Bishop Absalon, positioned on the spot where he is presumed to have first sighted Slotsholmen, site of his future castle. The statue, by Wilhelm Bissen, dating from 1901, was criticized for its aggressive portrayal of Absalon – perched on a rearing charger, he looks more like a warrior than a man of the church – though the plinth, by Martin Nyrop, was much praised; some critics even suggested that horse and rider be removed, leaving the plinth alone to stand as a more worthy memorial to the bishop. At the bridge, Højbro, peer down into the canal on the left to see the enchanting underwater sculpture of *The Merman and his Seven Sons*.

Around Gammel Strand

To the right of Absalon's statue on Højbro Plads is the delightful canalside stretch of **Gammel Strand** (Old Beach), where you'll encounter another, more earthy statue, *The Fisher Woman*, commemorating the tough ladies who used to line up along the beachfront here, selling the fish their husbands had caught. Keeping tradition alive, there's usually a fish stall here in summer trading all manner of seafood to tourists hanging around for the next DFDS boat (see p.29 for more details). From Gammel Strand, there's a fine view across the canal to Slotsholmen, with the brightly coloured Thorvaldsens Museum standing out next to Christiansborg and Christiansborg Slotskirke, best appreciated during spring and summer from the outside tables of the row of cafés and restaurants here, including the popular *Thorvaldsens Hus* (see p.182) and, a few doors further along, Denmark's oldest and most famous (read expensive) fish restaurant, *Krogs* (see p.180).

Squeezed in between the cafés and restaurants, at no. 48, is a fine building housing the city's oldest art gallery **Kunstforeningen Gammel Strand** (Tues, & Thurs–Sun 11am–5pm, Wed 11am–8pm; 50kr; ⊛www.kunstforeningen.dk), where, over three floors with striking views of the city, you can catch temporary exhibitions of modern and contemporary art. The **Photographic Centre** (25kr; ⊛www.photography.dk) to the right of the main entrance has temporary exhibitions of the work of renowned local and international photographers.

In summer, there's also a good **flea market** here (Sat 8am–4pm) – a chance to pick up, among other things, a piece of Royal Copenhagen Porcelain at a price approaching affordable.

North along Købmagergade

From Højbro Plads you can either continue east along the Østergade section of Strøget to Kongens Nytorv – a route described on p.63 – or head north up Indre By's other main shopping street, **Købmagergade**, which winds its way past a few museums and the unmissable Rundetårn to Kultorvet, where it changes its name to Frederiksborggade.

Købmagergade now rivals Strøget for mainstream shops and chain stores, though for something different, you need only dive off into the smaller streets to the right – in particular the hyper-trendy knot of lanes centred on **Kronprin-sensgade**, Store Regnegade, Ny Østergade and Grønegade, where a number of independent Danish fashion designers have outlets (see "Shopping", p.216, for more details). On the corner of Købmagergade and Strøget, **Illums Bolighus** department store (see also p.220) is Copenhagen's classiest, with the usual range of designer fashions and merchandise, as well as several cafés and a supermarket.

Museum Erotica

At Købmagergade 24, red banners and a red-carpeted, peepshow-style entrance announce the **Museum Erotica** (May–Sept daily 10am–11pm, Oct–April Mon–Thurs & Sun 11am–8pm, Fri & Sat 10am–10pm; 89kr; catalogue 20kr; ⊛www.museumerotica.dk), part shrine to all things erotic, part historical romp through sexual history. It's entertaining enough, and despite sporadic attempts at historical and social context, never takes itself too seriously, often succumbing completely to the titillatory nature of its subject matter with an overdose of in-your-face photos and hilariously tacky tableaux. It kicks off with a few rooms devoted to the origins of erotic art – ancient Greek vases depicting the symbolic value of the phallus and Indian miniature paintings of the *Kama Sutra*, among other things – before moving on to more loosely themed exhibits on the likes of erotic nineteenth-century photography, lurid tales of royal exploits, and the history of prostitution in Copenhagen. The section on the more modern era focuses on the legalization of pornography with wall-to-wall *Playboy* pin-ups, a whole room devoted to Marilyn Monroe as sex symbol, and another on the sex lives of famous people from Charlie Chaplin to Karl Marx, who apparently liked telling dirty jokes. From here on, though, the erotic is pretty much replaced by the explicit with a selection of the museum founder Ole Ege's 1970s pornographic films shown in a small cinema providing a hard-core finale.

Post & Tele Museum

Altogether more prosaic exhibits can be found nearby at Købmagergade 37, in the **Post & Tele Museum** (Tues & Thurs–Sat 10am–5pm, Wed 10am–8pm, Sun noon–4pm; 40kr, free on Wed; @www.ptt-museum.dk), which charts the history of communication in Denmark from Christian IV's 1624 decree establishing the Danish Royal Post Office to modern-day mobile phones. On the whole, it does a good job of bringing its rather dry subject matter to life with a well-displayed collection of old telephones, radio equipment, mock-ups of old post offices, philatelic displays and historical artefacts such as Denmark's first mail coach, its egg-shaped mail drum designed to minimize air resistance, allow water to run off, and prevent the coachman from taking along passengers. Sadly, things aren't helped by the fact that the labels are all in Danish, though you can pick up a free, if rather confusingly organized, English translation from the desk on the second floor. A less taxing highlight is the museum's pleasant, rooftop café *Hovedtelegrafen* (see p.179), which offers delicious food and a fine view.

Rundetårn

Købmagergade's historic landmark, and one of the city's most intriguing sights, the 42-metre-high **Rundetårn** (Round Tower; June–Aug Mon–Sat

Christian IV: The architect king

The layout of present-day Copenhagen is largely thanks to **Christian IV**, despite the fact that he ruled more than three hundred years ago (1588–1648), and was broke for most of his reign. Not only did he extend the city northwards, to include Rosenborg and Frederiksstad, but he also fortified its defences, building Kastellet to the north, creating a ring of moats and ramparts (today's Tivoli Ørstedsparken, Botanisk Have and Østre Anlæg) to the west, and reclaiming the Christianshavn area, in the east, from the sea – a series of sweeping changes that earned him the moniker "the Architect King"..

The list of his architectural achievements is long. Shortly after taking over the country's reins (his father Frederik II died when Christian was 10) he instigated the construction of a naval yard and supply depot, a brewery – for the navy – and an arsenal (today's **Tøjhusmuseet**; see p.49) next to his castle on Slotsholmen, **Københavns Slot**. Of these, only Københavns Slot is gone; apparently, Christian made such a mess of its refurbishment that future kings were too embarrassed to have visitors here and decided to tear the whole thing down and start afresh, replacing it with the grander Christiansborg Slot. Christian returned to form with **Rosenborg Slot** (p.78), which he gradually built up from a mere summer-chalet to the romantic Dutch-Renaissance palace that rises over Kongens Have today.

Of his more unusual feats, the **Trinitatis** complex (p.61) is arguably his greatest – a combined church, university library and astronomical observatory, whose church tower, **Rundetårn** (see above), with its spiral cobbled ramp leading all the way up to the still-functioning observatory, is one of the best places from which to view the city's skyline (and may well have been built for that reason). Looking southwest from here you can see another of Christian's quirky mementos, the **Caritas Fountain** (p.57) on Gammeltorv, linked to the city's first external water supply, a gift from the Architect King to his people.

10am–8pm, Sun noon–8pm; Sept–May Mon–Sat 10am–5pm, Sun noon–5pm; 25kr; ⍟www.rundetaarn.dk) stands two-thirds of the way up the street – an enduring testament to a king's vision It was built by Christian IV as part of the **Trinitatis** complex, which combined three important facilities for seventeenth-century scholars and students: an astronomical observatory, a church and a university library. The tower functioned both as observatory lookout and as the Trinitatis church tower – and perhaps also as a vantage point from which Copenhagen's citizens could admire Christian's additions to the city. It's still a functioning **observatory** – making it the oldest in Europe – and the public can view the winter night sky through the astronomical telescope (mid-Oct to mid–March Tues & Wed 7–10pm). Inside the tower a wide, cobbled ramp spirals its way to the top for a wonderful view of the hive of medieval streets below and the city beyond. Legend has it that Peter the Great sped to the top on horseback in 1715, pursued by the tsarina in a six-horse carriage – a smoother technique than descending on skateboard, a short-lived fad in more recent times. Left unused for many years, the **library** in the church attic has been restored and turned into a gallery featuring changing artistic, cultural and historical exhibitions; entered from halfway up the Rundetårn ramp, it's a convenient spot for a break. It's also worth peeping into the **church** itself (Mon–Sat 9.30am–4.30pm); rebuilt in Baroque style following the Great Fire of 1728, it is still affiliated to the university's student congregation.

North to Kultorvet

A quick detour left down Krystalgade, takes you past **Regensen** on the left-hand corner, a crooked, old student hostel originally founded by Frederik II in 1628 for students without means, a function it still fulfils today. Many of Denmark's most prominent philosophers lectured here, and over the years Regensen became the hub of the city's intellectual life. Further down Krystal-gade, on the right-hand side, is Copenhagen's **synagogue**, a classical-style basilica dating from 1833. It's the main synagogue for Denmark's Jewish community, but is only open during services.

The short stretch from Rundetårn to Kultorvet is unremarkable, as is **Kultorvet** itself, though it buzzes with life during the summer months when its numerous restaurants, cafés and music venues offer entertainment to satisfy most tastes and ages. Close to Nørreport Station, it's also an easy place to stagger home from after a lively night out.

Musikhistorisk Museum

Just north of Kultorvet, at Åbenrå 30, the thoroughly entertaining **Musikh-istorisk Museum** (Musical History Museum; May–Sept Mon–Wed & Fri–Sun 1–3.30pm; Oct–April Mon, Wed, Sat & Sun 1–3.30pm; free; ⍟www.musikhistoriskmuseum.dk), set in three lovely eighteenth-century houses, has an impressive quantity of musical instruments and sound-producing devices spanning the globe and the last thousand years. Naturally, the bulk comes from Denmark, and there are some subtle insights into the social fabric of the nation to be gleaned from the yellowing photos of country dances and other get-togethers hung alongside the instruments. There are recordings of most of the instruments to listen to (helpful with some of the odder ones, where it's a mystery even which end the sound comes out) and two rooms where children can play with sounds. Jazz and classical concerts are occasionally held in the small concert hall – check details with the museum on ☎33 11 27 26.

Around Nørreport

Less musical sounds are provided by the cars hurtling along Nørre Voldgade, north of Kultorvet, which marks the position of the former ramparts and the end of the pedestrianized streets of the old city. The site of the Nørreport city gate is now occupied by **Nørreport Station**, Copenhagen's busiest train station. No construction was allowed in the area outside the old ramparts until 1851, which is why most developments in the area north of Nørre Voldgade up to the lakes are relatively new.

Israels Plads and Ørstedsparken

Shortly after the old city gates were demolished, Copenhagen's vegetable and flower market moved from Christianshavn to what is now **Israels Plads**, just northwest of Nørreport Station. It didn't take long, however, before the surrounding area was completely built up and, as further expansion became impossible, the market moved again, this time to Valby. The fruit, vegetable and flower retailers stayed behind, however, and are still much in evidence today, trying to out-shout and out-sell one another. There's a **flea market** on the playground behind the vegetable market on Saturdays, where you may find some good deals if you're lucky, though rumour has it that many of the stands are owned by mainstream city shops.

Just west of Israels Plads, the pretty **Ørstedsparken**, one of the city's most popular gay cruising grounds, is named after the famous Danish physicist, H.C. Ørsted, who discovered electromagnetism. It's one of the few areas where the layout of the old ramparts has been preserved – the lakes here (part of the old defence system) follow the shape of the former battlements – and there are also a number of statues scattered on and around the hillocks, sponsored by brewing magnate Carl Jacobsen. In the summer, you can get refreshments at the park café in the centre and watch the world pass you by.

Arbejdermuseet

On the far side of Nørre Voldgade, halfway down Rømersgade at no. 22, is the **Arbejdermuseet** (Workers' Museum; daily 10am–4pm, Nov–June closed Mon; 50kr; ⓦwww.arbejdermuseet.dk), housed in the former Workers' Hall (still used for occasional union meetings) and an engrossing guide to working-class life in Copenhagen from the 1870s onwards.

It's best to begin on the third floor with useful background on the history of the **labour movement** in Denmark and around the world – look out for the original copy of the 1899 "September Accord" that started the ball rolling in Denmark by giving workers the right to organize into unions. The rest of the permanent exhibition relies heavily on reconstructed scenes chronicling the workers' living and working conditions, starting on the second floor with an apartment that housed generations of a working-class family from 1885 to 1990, and continuing on the more engaging first floor with a Copenhagen street of the 1950s, complete with shop windows hawking the consumer durables of the day and the Fifties-style museum coffee-shop where you can buy a cup of an old-fashioned coffee and chicory blend. Further on, a drab house interior, complete with suitably wretched-looking mannequins, evokes the life of a working-class Nørrebro family during the **1930s depression**; the apartment of the **1950s** with family photos, newspapers and TVs showing newsreels of the time is a far brighter affair, its occupants clearly benefiting from the influx of Marshall Plan American funding to a battered postwar Europe.

The ground floor and basement are given over to the shop and temporary exhibitions on topics ranging from Nelson Mandela to the Paris Commune. Look out for one of the museum's most recent acquisitions, a copy of the Saint Petersburg statue of **Lenin** demoted to a small, dark, closed-off museum back yard. Sculpted in 1985 for one of the few communist unions in Denmark, the Danish Seaman's Union, it was donated to the museum following the fall of communism. Only moved here in 1998, it created a massive stir: critics demanded that, if the statue was to be displayed at all, then Lenin should be depicted as an executioner and mass murderer; the museum insisted it be exhibited for his visit to Copenhagen – and this building – during the Socialist World Congress in 1910, seven years prior to the October Revolution, and for his efforts to promote international socialism throughout the world. The museum won the ideological tug-of-war, but the debate (read class struggle) continues.

In the street-front section of the basement, the cosy **restaurant** *Café & Ølhalle* (see p.178 for full review) has been restored to its 1892 state and serves traditional Danish food (lunchtime only) – it's a lovely spot for lunch and the only listed restaurant in the city.

East to Nyhavn

Back at Højbro Plads, head east off the square along the alley named Lille Kirkestræde and then left to reach the grandiose **Skt Nikolaj Kirke**. Although one of the oldest churches in Copenhagen, and mother church of the Danish Reformation in 1536, it hasn't been used for ecclesiastical purposes since 1795, when the city's second great fire destroyed everything except the tower (which, ironically enough, was subsequently used to house the municipal fire brigade). The massive red-brick church wasn't rebuilt until early in the twentieth century, and now, as the **Kunsthallen Nikolaj** (daily noon–5pm; 20kr, Wed free), houses stimulating exhibitions of contemporary art: the main body provides a grand venue for multimedia art shows; the tower is mostly used for audio and video installations.

Heading east along the final section of Strøget – here called **Østergade**, and undoubtedly the most exclusive section of the entire thoroughfare – you'll pass the likes of Versace, Hermes and Chanel and, on the left, the quaint alleyway and courtyard of **Pistolstræde**, home to a handful of super-cool Danish design shops. Also along this stretch, at no. 16, is the **Guinness World Records Museum** (mid-June to Aug daily 9.30am–10.30pm; Sept to mid-June Mon–Thurs & Sun 10am–6pm, Fri & Sat 10am–8pm; 83kr, 122kr for joint ticket with the Exploratorium, 232kr including Ripley's Believe It Or Not and Hans Christian Andersen's Wonderful World (see p.91); ⑳www .topattractions.dk) – much as you'd expect, with family-oriented exhibits on the world's tallest, smallest and fastest. Out to the back, and along the same theme, the **Mystical Exploratorium** (same hours; 60kr, 122kr for joint ticket with the World Records Museum, 232kr including Ripley's Believe It Or Not and Hans Christian Andersen's Wonderful World; ⑳www.topattractions.dk) offers a chance to explore odd natural phenomena, such as how weather works and how it can be manipulated (at least on a small scale).

Kongens Nytorv

For most Copenhageners, Strøget ends, rather than begins, at **Kongens Nytorv**. This is where the shopping spree finishes and the search for a place to sit down and rest your feet starts. In summer, weary shopaholics head for the outdoor seats of the square's high-ceilinged, glass-fronted cafés; in winter, for the cosy dens selling *gløgg* and *æbleskiver* (warm, mulled wine with nuts, raisins and spices, served with round dough balls).

At the centre of Kongens Nytorv is an equestrian statue of Christian V, who completed the square by ordering the owners of land bordering it to erect houses of a certain regal standard or sell up, which is why the square is entirely surrounded by pompous-looking buildings from the seventeenth century, such as the swish *Hôtel d'Angleterre*. In more recent times, it has become the tradition for newly graduated high-school students to celebrate by dancing around the king's statue in a ring – watch out for cheery, white-clad youngsters in late spring. In winter, the square is transformed into a free open-air ice-skating rink; a stall nearby rents out skates. On the right, as you leave Strøget, is the **Magasin du Nord** – after Illums Bolighus, the city's most exclusive department store, with a large English-language magazine section in the basement.

The southern end of the square is dominated by the grand late-nineteenth-century **Det Kongelige Teater** (Royal Theatre; guided tours every Sun at 11am; 75kr; book in advance Mon–Sat noon–6pm on ☏33 69 69 69; ⊛www .kgl-teater.dk). Hans Christian Andersen supposedly tried his luck here as a ballet dancer while attempting to court the prima ballerina. True to his reputation, he failed miserably but wrote yet another fairy tale with a rosy ending. Until recently, the theatre was one of the few in the world where ballet, opera and drama were performed under one roof. However, conditions became too cramped, and in 2005 the grand, new Operæn (see p.73) opened on Holmen. With a flash play house (see p.88) expected to open in 2008 around the corner from Nyhavn, only ballet will be performed on the old regal stage in future years. An extension to the theatre was also added in 1931, **Stærekassen**, in Danish Art Deco style, its plain surfaces and clean decoration in sharp contrast to the Italianate "old stage", as the main building is now called. The front of the main entrance is adorned with statues depicting poet Adam Oehlenschläger and playwright Ludvig Holberg, both prominent in eighteenth-century Danish cultural life. For details of performances at Det Kongelige Teater, see p.207 and p.209.

Next door to the theatre is **Charlottenborg Palace** (daily 10am–5pm, Wed until 7pm; ⊛www.charlottenborg-art.dk), built by an illegitimate son of Frederik III in 1677 and now the oldest building on the square. It was handed over to the Royal Academy of Fine Arts in 1754, since when many prominent artists, including Thorvaldsen (see p.48), have lived here. It's still home to the Royal Academy, and though there are no specific public displays, it's worth dropping in just to glimpse the palace's elegant interior. The spacious, light rooms of the **exhibition hall** (30kr) at the back, in a separate building from 1883, provide a perfect setting for eclectic Danish and international exhibitions of contemporary art, architecture and decorative art.

Nyhavn

Nyhavn (New Harbour) – created in 1671 as a canal leading from the city's main port to Kongens Nytorv – is mostly known for its sunny northern side, with its long row of bars, cafés, taverns and restaurants set in brightly coloured and picturesque gabled houses, some dating back as far as 1681. During the past twenty years, this canalside promenade has become one of the trendiest places in the city to live and be seen, a complete turnaround from its seedy past as a disreputable sailors' haunt. In summer, it's packed with locals and tourists eating, drinking or whiling away some time before the next DFDS boat to the Little Mermaid and Christianshavn (see p.29 for details).

On the corner of Nyhavn and Bredgade, the **Ravhuset** (Amber Museum; daily: mid-May to mid-Sept 10am–7.30pm; mid-Sept to mid-May 10am–5.30pm; 25kr; ⓦwww.houseofamber.com) is located on the first floor of the Amber House, a historic building from the 1670s now devoted to producing and selling amber artefacts. The small museum takes you through the economic and geological history of amber, while rows of display cases equipped with magnifying glasses show specimens of the many odd creatures found trapped in the resin from the enormous pine forests of northern Europe twenty to fifty million years ago. There's also an in-house craftsman showing how amber is worked, plus the world's largest piece of Baltic amber, a massive lump weighing 8.8kg.

Christianshavn

Facing Indre By and Slotsholmen across the waters of Inderhavnen, and linked to them by Knippelsbro, is the charming island of CHRISTIANSHAVN. Nicknamed "Little Amsterdam" on account of its pretty canals, cobbled streets, and old Dutch-style houses with brightly painted facades, it's a laid-back area with a cosy, neighbourhood feel and a pleasant spot to hang out with a *høker* beer while watching the boats meander up and down the canals.

Until the seventeenth century, however, Christianshavn didn't even exist. The area was under water, creating a breach in Copenhagen's defences that left the city vulnerable to attack from the sea, until **Christian IV** reclaimed an arc of land in the early 1600s and built a ring of defensive fortifications on it. An autonomous borough was created to house Dutch merchants, with a Dutch architect, Johan Semp, employed to plan the new district. The Dutch merchants never arrived and the island was instead distributed between rich Danish merchants and aristocrats, who moved into the elegant dwellings along the waterfront and Wilders Kanal, and the workers, who were assigned the dark and dingy areas in between. For much of the next three hundred years Christianshavn prospered from the trade created by the huge naval base on the adjacent islands of **Holmen**, and from the late 1800s to mid-1900s, with the large commercial shipbuilding yards of Burmeister & Wain. Today, many of its waterfront warehouses and fine naval buildings have been transformed into offices, cultural centres, educational institutions and expensive housing developments, while the Operæn, the new opera house, has placed the island firmly at the forefront of the city's cultural scene.

Christianshavn's ordered grid of streets, pretty canals and moatside paths – along with its well-placed cafes and restaurants – make it perfectly suited to idle exploration. The sights are, for the most part, low-key, but you won't want to miss **Vor Frelsers Kirke**, with its magnificent spire; the attention-grabbing **Operæn**; or the "free city" of **Christiania**, whose alternative, independently run community has long been one of Copenhagen's major tourist attractions, albeit one now deprived of its famous street of hash stalls. **Christianhavns Torv**, halfway along the busy main thoroughfare of **Torvegade**, is the district's hub and a natural starting point – the metro station is here, as are stops for all buses crossing Christianshavn. Buses can get you to within five minutes' walk of most of the sights: #2A from Central Station and #19 and #350S from Kongens Nytorv stop on Torvegade, from where it's all pretty walkable, or you can pick up #66, which runs from Torvegade along Prinsessegade (past the main entrance to Christiania) and on to Holmen and the Operæn. Alternatively, it's a nice trip on the harbour bus #901 or #902, which drops you at the Operæn.

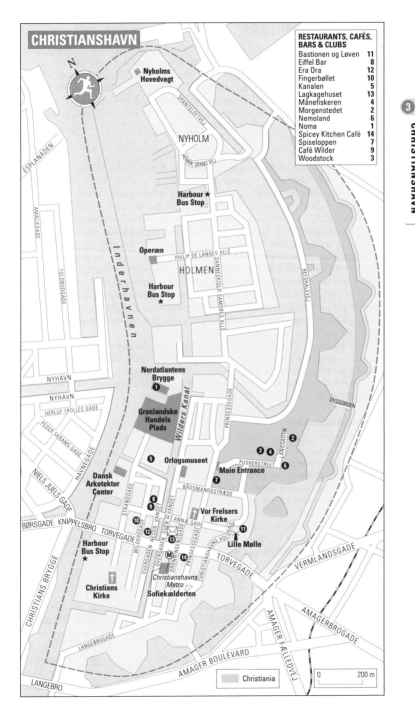

CHRISTIANSHAVN

RESTAURANTS, CAFÉS, BARS & CLUBS

Bastionen og Løven	11
Eiffel Bar	8
Era Ora	12
Fingerbøllet	10
Kanalen	5
Lagkagehuset	13
Månefiskeren	4
Morgenstedet	2
Nemoland	6
Noma	1
Spicey Kitchen Café	14
Spiseloppen	7
Café Wilder	9
Woodstock	3

Nyholms Hovedvagt

NYHOLM

SPANTELOFTVEJ

HENRIK SPANS VEJ

Harbour Bus Stop ★

Operæn

PHILIP DE LANGES ALLÉ

HOLMEN

DANNESKIOLD SAMSØES ALLÉ

Harbour Bus Stop ★

REFSHALEVEJ

Inderhavnen

ESPLANADEN

AMALIEGADE

TOLDBODGADE

DYSSEBROEN

NYHAVN

NYHAVN

HERLUF TROLLES GADE

PEDER SKRAMS GADE

HAVNEGADE

NIELS JUELS GADE

Nordatlantens Brygge ❶

Grønlandske Handels Plads

Wilders Kanal

PRINSESSEGADE

LANGGADEN

❷

❸ ❹

❺ Orlogsmuseet

Main Entrance

PUSHERSTREET

❻

❼

Dansk Arketektur Center

❽
❾

BÅDSMANDSSTRÆDE

STRANDGADE

SKT ANNÆ GADE

Vor Frelsers Kirke ℹ

NEDER VANDET

❿

⓬ ⓭

OVERGADEN OVEN VANDET

PRINSESSEGADE

CHRISTIANSHAVNS VOLDGADE

Bastionen og Løven ⓫

Lille Mølle

BØRSGADE KNIPPELSBRO TORVEGADE

OVERGADEN

DRONNINGENSGADE

⓮

TORVEGADE

VERMLANDSGADE

Harbour Bus Stop ★

CHRISTIANS BRYGGE

Christians Kirke ℹ

Sofiekælderten

Ⓜ Christianshavns Metro

AMAGERBROGADE

AMAGER FÆLLEDVEJ

AMAGER BOULEVARD

LANGEBROGADE

LANGEBRO

LANGE

Christiania

0   200 m

Along Strandgade

From the small, undistinguished (except for the Lagkagehuset bakery; see p.221) square of Christianshavns Torv, cross the Wilders Kanal and walk up Torvegade until you come to **Strandgade**, whose eastern side is home to some of the island's oldest houses. As interesting as its few rather specialized sights is the chance to head off the street's western side to explore Christianshavn's peaceful and much-renovated harbour front, whose gigantic converted warehouses offer a glimpse of the island's trading past.

Christians Kirke

At the southern end of Strandgade, **Christians Kirke** (daily: March–Oct 8am–6pm; Nov–Feb 8am–5pm) is squeezed between apartment blocks on one side and the waterfront headquarters of the Danish bank Nordea – four magnificent rectangles of glass and copper – on the other. Completed in 1759 to a design by Nicolai Eigtved, the court architect responsible for Amalienborg (see p.83), the Rococo church was built for the city's German Lutheran community. The exterior is unremarkable – Eigtved saved his creative flourish for the theatrical interior designed in line with the Lutheran principle of the importance of the sermon: the central and prominent pulpit allowed the preacher to connect more freely with the congregation while the three-storey arched gallery offered everyone the same visual and auditory experience. The church's unusual design has given it excellent acoustics: rock and classical concerts, theatre and ballet are occasionally performed here – you can get a calendar of events from the tourist office (see p.37) and the church itself.

Before leaving, it's worth taking a quick look into the **crypt** (entrance around the left side of the church), lined with numerous small chapels, while if you turn left on exiting the church gates and walk through the bank complex, you'll reach the harbour front for a fine view across the Inderhavnen to Den Sorte Diamant (see p.50).

Dansk Arkitektur Center

Heading north along Strandgade across Torvegade, you pass the massive dirty-yellow-brick eyesore of the Danish Foreign Ministry before reaching **Dansk Arkitektur Center** (Danish Architecture Centre; daily 10am–5pm; free; ⓦwww.dac.dk) on the waterfront at Gammel Dok. The temporary exhibitions (labels in Danish only) verge on incomprehensible but the building itself – a beautiful renovation of what is one of the oldest warehouses in Christianshavn – is worth a peek inside. The bookshop stocks Denmark's largest selection of titles on architecture and design (most of them in English), and the café (11am–4pm), with its lovely view over the harbour, is a pleasant spot to break for coffee. In the same building, the **National Workshop for Arts and Crafts** (closed to the public) rents out studios to struggling artists.

Nordatlantens Brygge

Pushing on a bit further along Strandgade and crossing over onto another small island, you reach the wide, windswept expanse of **Grønlandske Handels Plads** (Greenlandic Trading Square). Ships from Denmark's old colonies in the North Atlantic – Greenland, Iceland and the Faroe Islands – used to dock here, and the cargoes of dried fish, whale oil and skins were stored or treated in the enormous warehouses before being sold off to the rest of Europe. The warehouses were turned into offices in the early 1980s – the Danish Red Cross and Danish Polar Centre are among the new inhabitants – and the whiff of fish is long gone, but the square still flies the flag for North Atlantic relations in the new **Nordatlantens Brygge** (North Atlantic House; ⓦwww.bryggen.dk; daily 10am–5pm except Tues). Housed in the magnificent warehouse that dominates the square, its aim is to promote artistic, commercial and cultural links between the North Atlantic countries, and to present contemporary North Atlantic art and culture, though it's a bit hit and miss as to whether you'll find anything of interest in the temporary exhibitions (40kr). It's also home to the diplomatic representations of the three countries – always useful to know if you need a visa for Greenland – and the Michelin-starred, Nordic-inspired restaurant *Noma* (see p.183). The **shop and craft centre**, **Tranhuset** (Mon–Fri 10am–5.30pm, Sat 11–3pm), located out the back in the former factory where whales were boiled for lamp oil, is a showcase for the more practical arts and crafts of the region, though the seal-fur gloves, bags and hats, racks of mink coats and fish-skin lampshades might prove a bit too much for some.

Wilders Kanal and Orlogsmuseet

Lapping the eastern side of Grønlandske Handels Plads and running north-south down the centre of the island, the delightful **Wilders Kanal** – Christianshavn at its most Dutch – bristles and tinkles with the bobbing masts and halyards of its many sailing boats, especially thick around the small marina at its northwestern end. The lively cobbled streets of Overgaden Oven Vandet and Overgaden Neden Vandet flank its length, and though they harbour no compelling tourist sights, a stroll along the banks taking in the grand and colourful old buildings, cafés and locals pottering about on their boats is one of the island's highlights.

The nautical theme continues on the corner of Bådsmandsstræde (Boatswain's Alley) and Overgaden Oven Vandet in the cheery yellow Naval Hospital of 1780, now home to the **Orlogsmuseet** (Royal Danish Naval Museum; Tues–Sun noon–4pm; 40kr, free on Wed ⓦwww.orlogsmuseet.dk). Devoted to the illustrious history of the Danish Navy, the museum's pride and joy is its collection of four hundred intricate **ship models** – some dating back to the sixteenth century. Ships' equipment, uniforms, weapons, nautical instruments, maritime art and minutely detailed models of the many sea battles the Danish Navy has fought (they even include cotton-wool smoke clouds from the cannons) make up the rest of the collection. You can also go aboard the *Spækhuggeren* (Killer Whale) submarine – radio broadcasts help you to relive the

△ Crusing on the Wilders Kanal

moment it narrowly escaped the Germans during World War II – or clamber up onto the bridge of a torpedo boat. There's an eating area downstairs where you can tuck into your packed lunch in the company of a selection of cannons, and a **children's museum** where kids can scramble around on bits of ships.

Vor Frelsers Kirke and Lille Mølle

Just south of the Orlogsmuseet, soaring skywards through the trees on Skt Annæ Gade, is the unmistakable copper-and-gold spire of Christianshavn's famous landmark, **Vor Frelsers Kirke** (April–Aug Mon–Sat 11am–4.30pm, opens noon on Sun; Sept–March Mon–Sat 11am–3.30pm, opens noon on Sun; spire closed Nov–March and on wet and windy days; ✆www.vorfrelserskirke.dk). Completed in 1696 in Dutch Baroque style, it was the first church to be built following the 1660 declaration of absolute monarchy, and Christian V took the opportunity to ram the point home with a generous sprinkling of his initials and symbols.

The lavish **spire**, with its helter-skelter exterior staircase and large golden globe carrying a three-metre Jesus waving a flag, was added to the otherwise plain exterior in the mid-eighteenth century, instantly becoming one of the city skyline's most recognizable features – it's said to have been used as a target by Nelson during the 1807 bombardment, though fortunately he only managed to hit a leg. Rumour also had it that the spire's architect, Laurids de Thurah, threw himself off the top when he discovered that the stairs wound to the right instead of the left, as the king had requested, though this has since been proved untrue – de Thurah died penniless seven years after the spire's completion. To ascend the spire (20kr) you'll have to climb a total of 400 steps, 150 of them outside, slanted and slippery (especially after rain), and gradually becoming smaller and smaller. The reward for reaching the top, however, is a great **view** of Copenhagen and beyond.

Inside, the Baroque extravagance reaches its peak in the showy **altar**, depicting a gilded sun (representing God) breaking through black clouds to shine on frolicking cherubs and archangels. To the left of the altar, the white marble font surrounded by menacing marble toddlers was intended as a fertility charm for the childless wife of Frederik IV. The two stucco elephants appearing to hold up the gigantic **organ** were included due to their association with the king – the animal became the symbol of the nation's highest order, the Order of the Elephant, started by Christian V and still in existence today. If you want

Walking the bastions

One of the unsung highlights of a visit to Christianshavn is a walk along the picturesque moat on the eastern side of the island. **Lille Mølle** (see p.71) makes a good starting point, from where you can head north through **Christiania** (see p.71), either along the top of the bastions themselves for fine views over the moat and Free City, or along the narrow path that winds its way along the water's edge through Christiania and continues by way of a minor road up to **Nyholm** (see p.74). The latter is a pretty walk, negotiating the rambling track through Christiania's waterside homes with just the wind in the reeds and the cries of waterfowl to break the silence. Alternatively, you can head **south** from Lille Mølle, crossing over Torvegade and following the line of the moat until you reach Langebro, from where you can cross back into the city proper. This stretch is noisier and more built up, and is also a popular jogging path, but it offers a scenic route back into town if you have time (45min walk).

to hear the magnificent organ, there are services every Sunday at noon from May to September.

Continue to the end of Skt Annæ Gade and head up onto the ramparts to **Lille Mølle** (guided tours in Danish only June–Sept Sat & Sun at 1pm, 2pm & 3pm; 50kr; tickets from *Bastionen og Løven* (see p.182) on same day; for English tours call ☏33 47 38 38), the only surviving example of the many windmills that formerly stood on the Christianshavn ramparts. Built in 1783 to a Dutch design, the windmill ground wheat for the ever-increasing numbers of Copenhageners until being converted into a private home at the beginning of the twentieth century. In 1973 it was given to the National Museum by its flamboyant owners, and today it bears witness to their lavish lifestyle, with many odd rooms furnished in a mixture of styles from quaintly Germanic to romantic British. Next door, in the miller's old domicile, is *Bastionen og Løven*, a fine restaurant with outdoor seating on the edge of the ramparts.

Christiania

Stretching for almost a kilometre along either side of the moat north of Lille Mølle, the remarkable "Free City" of **Christiania** (⊛www.christiania.org) is living proof of Copenhagen's liberal social traditions. Ever since a group of young and homeless people colonized the complex of disused military barracks in the spring of 1971, the area has excited controversy, sympathy and admiration in equal amounts. Declared a "Free City" by its residents later that year – with the aim of operating autonomously from Copenhagen proper and pursuing more egalitarian and environmentally friendly lifestyles – it inevitably became best known outside Denmark for its open selling of hash on "Pusherstreet", while its continued existence on some of Copenhagen's finest real estate has fuelled one of the longest-running debates in Danish society.

Initially categorized and tolerated by those in power as a "social experiment" (a term dismissed by Christianites themselves), Christiania has had a roller-coaster ride at the hands of successive governments, who either largely left the community alone or tried to bring it under the city's municipal machinery. Time after time Christiania has mobilized itself, mustering popular, political and legal support to repel any attempts to curtail its freedoms, no doubt helped by the fact that, when push came to shove, politicians proved too wary of potential electoral damage at the hands of the Free City's broader public support. Not that Christiania is a hippie paradise – an inevitable by-product of its idealism and freedoms is that it has, at times, been a refuge for petty criminals and undesirable characters. But the problems have been overplayed by its critics, and though there have been sporadic raids and police crackdowns on drugs – the latest in 2004 – the authorities have mostly proved tolerant of the open trade in hash (use and possession of which is still illegal in Denmark), in the knowledge that Christiania has enforced, as far as possible, its own ban on hard drugs imposed in the late 1970s following problems caused by an influx of heroin.

However, Christiania's **future** hangs in the balance under the current right-wing government, which has been strident in its disapproval of the rebel in its midst. In 2004, faced with imminent police action, Christiania made a pre-emptive strike by removing the biggest stick the government had to beat it with: the hash booths on Pusherstreet. The street may now be a far less enticing place for many, and it remains to be seen whether Christiania will continue to pull in one million visitors a year now that its infamous attraction is gone, but the "Free City" bought itself extra time to fight the longer-term threat to its future: proposed new property laws that would enforce private ownership of homes and render Christiana's policy of collective use – no one owns their own home – illegal, so opening the door for property developers. The Free City has to mobilize itself yet again in the face of what it sees as inevitable gentrification into a "cappuccino quarter" but, for the time being at least, its one thousand inhabitants continue to make an economic, social and environmental success of their long-running "experiment" (see p.72).

Walking around Christiania

Christiania has a few entrances but for ease of orientation it's best to head for the **main entrance** on Prinsessegade (the others are on the corner of Prinsessegade and Bådsmandsstræde and at Bådsmandsstræde 43), which leads you straight into the heart of the Free City, close to its "**tourist office**" – the small shack on the right 50m or so in. Here, you can pick up the excellent *Christiania Guide* (5kr), which gives the lowdown on the area's turbulent history and includes a map locating all the places of interest; you can also buy a T-shirt or car sticker to help the cause. Don't be intimidated by the idea of wandering around by yourself: naturally, the area has a grungy, offbeat feel and you'll still get more than the odd whiff of dope but the atmosphere is welcoming and relaxed (cars aren't allowed). Moreover, Christianites are used to the constant influx of the curious and sympathetic, although residents ask tourists, reasonably enough, not to enter their gardens or photograph them without asking first. It's worth joining one of the **guided tours** (July & Aug daily 3pm; Sept–June Sat & Sun 3pm; 1hr 30min; 30kr; booking advisable in summer ☎32 57 96 70) that leave from the main entrance. Conducted by residents, they're a good introduction to the nooks, crannies and workings of this rather complex community.

Covering almost 85 acres, Christiania spreads out in a loose network of unpaved paths and small green open spaces on both sides of Christian IV's old moat between Christianshavn and Amager (a bridge, Dyssebroen, connects the two sides), many of its ramshackle homes hugging the reedy water's edge in a picture of rural charm. As you'd expect given its military past, its buildings are a peculiar mix of huge old barracks and warehouses – livened up with a generous splattering of vivid murals and now housing community projects including workshops, art centres and crèches – and small, colourful homes cluttered with flowerpots and all manner of decoration. There's also a good smattering of cafés and shops selling locally made goods.

The best place to start your wanderings is in the large converted warehouse to the right of the main entrance – the **Loppe building** – whose music venue *Loppen* (see "Live Music", p.201) and highly-rated restaurant *Spiseloppen* (see "Eating", p.183) have ensured its fame beyond the Free City's walls. It also houses **Gallopperiet**, Christiania's art gallery and information centre (Tues–Sun noon–5pm), and the *Info* café and craft shop. Continuing straight ahead you soon come to the city's hub, where you'll find most of its bars, cafés and nightlife as well as the closest Christiania gets to a commercial centre – **Carl Madsen Plads** – a small square lined with stalls selling snacks, cheap clothing, CDs, jewellery, incense and the like. The square marks the start of the once infamous **Pusherstreet**, now only really noteworthy for the Sunshine Bakery (a good spot to pick up a picnic lunch), and the large building on the left, **Operæn** – a musical venue (see "Live Music", p.201), community centre, children's theatre and jazz club. Push on instead to the small square on the right, crowded in summer with the chilled-out clientele of *Nemoland* (see "Drinking", p.196), Christiania's most popular bar. Pusherstreet ends at the huge ex-military riding hall, **Den Grønne Hal** (Green Hall), a one-stop new and second-hand shop for Christianites, piled high with everything from building materials to

Anarchy rules

A colony of hippies it may be, but given its low budget – 18 million krone per year raised through residential rents, business revenue and metered utilities – Christiania is a pretty well-organized community. From this **common purse** it has to pay municipal taxes, electricity and water bills, rubbish-collection fees and for the maintenance and running of all of its buildings and services, such as the post office, youth clubs and playgrounds. Christianites aren't all sitting around smoking pot either: eighty percent of the community are in **work**, half with "straight" jobs in the city, the rest employed within Christiania itself.

Adhering to anarchist principles of a social system based on voluntary cooperation not government, there's no hierarchy of rule, and community-related decisions are reached by **consensus** not votes, with a representative of each of the fourteen area committees regularly attending the **Common Meeting**, which makes Christiania-wide decisions, sets the annual budget, negotiates with outside authorities and, when necessary, acts as a kind of court, settling private disagreements that can't be resolved at the Area Meetings. Increasingly severe building restrictions imposed by the city council have meant that planning permission to build a new home is rarely, if ever, granted, so property only becomes available as people leave or die; should you be taken with the idea of living in the Free City, you'll have to wait for an advertisement in Christiania's weekly gazette, *Ugespejlet*, and put your case to an interview panel.

fuel to clothes. From here, head left along **Langgaden** (Long Street), a quiet, mostly residential street that runs parallel to the moat and from where narrow paths lead up on to the bastions. The path leading up from the Buddhist Stupa at the entrance to the residential quarter known as Mælkebøtten will take you down to the water's edge at the Dyssebroen, from where you can either cross the bridge to an even quieter, greener area of the Free City, or continue your ramble in either direction along the waterside path (very muddy in winter) for a look at some more of Christiania's alternative dwellings.

Holmen

Continuing north from Christiania along Prinsessegade brings you to the area of **Holmen** – five reclaimed islands, formerly home to the old naval station founded by Frederik III. The base of the Danish fleet from the middle of the seventeenth century, it was a small town in its own right, with all manner of factories and workshops attending to the navy, and its own schools, churches, courts and hospitals catering to the huge workforces stationed there. Most of the base was moved elsewhere in the early 1990s and the area, as home to several prestigious **art schools**, is now busy producing Denmark's next generation of architects, movie directors, musicians and actors. There's nothing in particular to do here, but the atmospheric, old listed buildings (the navy employed only the best architects) and laid-back campus-feel make it an enjoyable area to wander around and it's worth getting up close to Holmen's famous landmark, the new **Operæn**.

Operæn

Occupying a prime waterfront spot at the northern end of Philip de Langes Allé, Copenhagen's state-of-the-art **Operæn** opened in 2005 – funded by Denmark's richest man, the 91-year-old shipping magnate Maersk Mc Kinney

Møller. The work of the country's leading architect, Henning Larsen, the opera house is an undeniably bold and original, if not immediately appealing, building, completely dominated by the immense slab of the 158-metre-long **"floating" roof**, which extends 32m beyond the orb-like foyer and stepped entrance plaza out to the water's edge like a giant diving board. A generous gift and significant boost to the city's cultural life it may be, but the project hasn't escaped criticism: the press sniped at Møller's insistence on total control over what was a public project, while the building's critics have likened the glass and metal facade of the foyer to the grille of a 1955 Pontiac, called the auditorium's gold-leaf ceiling vulgar and questioned the location, suggesting that the building reduces the dome of the royal palace of Amalienborg across the harbour to a bit-part player in the city's skyline. However, it's a hit with the public, with many performances selling out way in advance, and the acoustics are world class. The building is at its most striking by night, but at any time, it's worth popping into the wonderful light-filled **foyer** (daily 10am–9pm, closes to non-ticket holders 4hr before performances) to admire the three stunning multi-faceted glass globes suspended from the ceiling and the sumptuously rich maplewood shell that encases the auditorium as though it were a giant musical instrument. Should you want to see more, you'll have to get tickets for a **performance** (see p.207) or join a **guided tour** (Sat & Sun 9.30am & 4.30pm; 100kr).

Nyholm

If you've come this far, it's worth pressing on a bit further north to the island of **Nyholm** (daily 8am–sunset), with its naval station and a few gems of naval architecture. Head up Henrik Spans Vej for 200m or so till you get to Nyholms Hovedvagt; the former main gate dates from 1745 and is one of Holmen's oldest buildings, with a slightly out-of-proportion tower capped by a huge crown – the Danish flag is still raised and lowered here by the navy every sunrise and sunset. Next door is the Elephanten Dock, constructed on an old ship that was deliberately sunk to establish the foundations of the dock. There's a line of old cannons nearby, and you can walk along the top of the fortifications overlooking Inderhavnen – on a sunny day, the view from here over to mainland Copenhagen and the spires and domes of Frederikstad is incomparable.

Rosenborg, Frederikstad and Kastellet

There's quite a contrast between the narrow, tangled streets of Indre By and the open parks and boulevards of the more modern areas on the northeastern side of the city centre. This part of Copenhagen owes its character to two royal builders, Christian IV – creator of the fanciful palace of **Rosenborg Slot** and the more functional fortress of **Kastellet** to the north – and Frederik V, whose name is preserved in the district he created, **Frederikstad**, a sumptuous royal quarter boasting proud aristocratic monuments such as the Marmorkirken and the palaces of Amalienborg. Some of the city's main **art museums** are also found here: the huge Statens Museum for Kunst and the Hirschsprungske Samling, both El Dorados for art lovers, and the Kunstindustrimuseet, a must-see if you're interested in Danish design.

Public transport connections for these areas are as follows: for Rosenborg, the Botanisk Have and Statens Museum for Kunst, either buses #6A, #26, #150S #350S or Nørreport and Østerport station. The Hirschsprungske Samling is reached via buses #14 and #40. Buses #1A, #15, #19 and #29 go to Amalienborg, Kastellet and the Little Mermaid (it's a ten-minute walk from the bus stop to the Mermaid).

Rosenborg

Immediately north of Gothersgade, the medieval streets of Indre By give way to regal boulevards surrounding the fairy-tale palace of **ROSENBORG Slot**, once protected to the west by the old city ramparts, which have since been converted into open parks and now house the glorious cornucopia of Copenhagen's **Botanisk Have** and Østre Anlæg. Scattered around the parklands are some good museums, including the **Geologisk Museum**, the **Den Frie Udstilling** exhibition hall, and the impressive artworks of the **Statens Museum for Kunst** and the **Hirschsprungske Samling**. The primarily residential area immediately south and east of Rosenborg Slot is worth seeking out for the **Davids Samling**, with its fine Islamic collection (currently closed

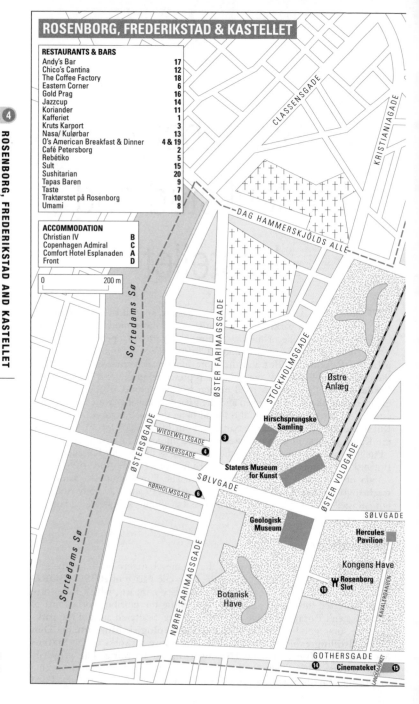

ROSENBORG, FREDERIKSTAD & KASTELLET

RESTAURANTS & BARS

Andy's Bar	17
Chico's Cantina	12
The Coffee Factory	18
Eastern Corner	6
Gold Prag	16
Jazzcup	14
Koriander	11
Kafferiet	1
Kruts Karport	3
Nasa/ Kulørbar	13
O's American Breakfast & Dinner	4 & 19
Café Petersborg	2
Rebétiko	5
Sult	15
Sushitarian	20
Tapas Baren	9
Taste	7
Traktørstet på Rosenborg	10
Umami	8

ACCOMMODATION

Christian IV	B
Copenhagen Admiral	C
Comfort Hotel Esplanaden	A
Front	D

0   200 m

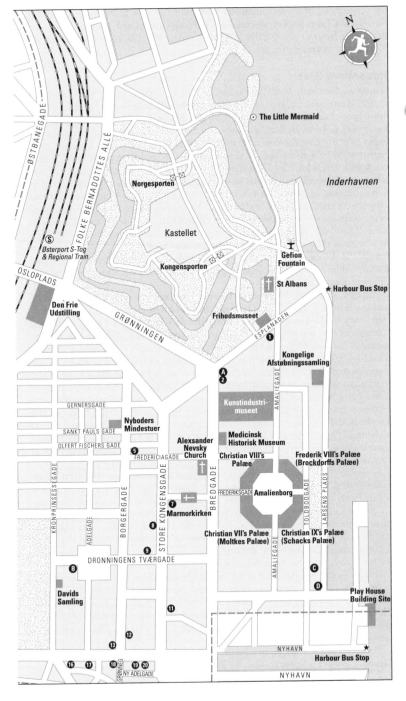

⊙ The Little Mermaid

Inderhavnen

Nørgesporten

Kastellet

Ⓢ Østerport S-Tog
& Regional Train

Kongensporten

Gefion
Fountain

✠ St Albans

★ Harbour Bus Stop

OSLOPLADS

Den Frie
Udstilling

GRØNNINGEN

Frihedsmuseet

ESPLANADEN

❶

Ⓐ
❷

Kongelige
Afstøbningssamling

AMALIEGADE

GERNERSGADE

Kunstindustri-
museet

Nyboders
Mindestuer

SANKT PAULS GADE

OLFERT FISCHERS GADE

Medicinsk
Historisk Museum

❺

Alexsander
Nevsky
Church

Christian VIII's
Palæe

Frederik VIII's Palæe
(Brockdorffs Palæe)

FREDERICIAGADE

KRONPRINSESSEGADE

FREDERIKSGADE

Amalienborg

BREDGADE

STORE KONGENSGADE

ADELGADE

BORGERGADE

❼ ✠
Marmorkirken

TOLDBODGADE

LARSENS PLADS

❽

Christian VII's Palæe
(Moltkes Palæe)

Christian IX's Palæe
(Schacks Palæe)

❾

AMALIEGADE

DRONNINGENS TVÆRGADE

Ⓑ

Ⓒ

Davids
Samling

Ⓓ

Play House
Building Site

❶❶

❶❷

❶❸

NYHAVN

★
Harbour Bus Stop

❶❻ ❶❼ ❶❽ ❶❾ ❷⓪

GRØNNEG

NY ADELGADE

NYHAVN

for renovation), the rows of quaint old sailor cottages at **Nyboder**, and, for film buffs, **Cinemateket**, devoted to all things film related. It should be noted that, apart from museum cafés and hotel restaurants, places to eat are thin on the ground in this entire area.

Rosenborg Slot

Rising enchantingly from the carefully manicured lawns of Kongens Have, the Dutch-Renaissance palace of **Rosenborg Slot** (May & Sept–Oct daily 10am–4pm; June–Aug daily 10am–5pm; Nov–April Tues–Sun 11am–2pm; 65kr, 80kr for a joint ticket with Amalienborg valid for 2 days; @www.rosenborg-slot.dk) looks like a setting for one of Hans Christian Andersen's more romantic tales. Surrounded by a moat and decorated with spires and towers, the playful, red-brick palace was built by Christian IV in 1606 as a summer residence, and was where he drew his final breath more than forty years later. Over the centuries it has become a storehouse for various royal collections, which now include artworks, a small armoury and assorted curiosities, along with well-preserved living quarters and the crown jewels. A central part of Rose Tremain's historical novel *Music and Silence* (see p.257) takes place at Rosenborg during the reign of Christian IV, and provides good background reading if you want an insight into life at the castle in the days when it was lived in. Today's museum (opened to the public in 1833) is chronologically organized, each room devoted to a different monarch.

The first section of the **ground floor** of the castle is devoted to Christian IV and is a relatively dark affair – oak-panelled rooms, royal busts and grand paintings of sea battles abound. Further along, the dark panelling in Frederik III's and Christian V's rooms gives way to stuccoed nymphs and marble, and the atmosphere is lightened by some bizarre oddities glorifying the absolute monarchs. The highlight is a seventeenth-century armchair with hidden tentacles in the armrests that would grab the wrists of anyone unlucky enough to sit in it. The victim would then be doused in water before being released to the sound of a small trumpet. Look out, too, for the golden elephant chair in room 6 with elephant trunks as legs, used by the king when handing out Orders of the Elephant, the absolute monarchy's finest military order. There's also a piece of alchemical "gold" (item 612) – the lead it was made from is kept beside it – and there's also a small armoury featuring crossbows, ornate rapiers and dozens of flintlock pistols.

Access to the two upper floors is via a spiral stone staircase. The **first floor** is dedicated to seven more rulers – Frederik IV to Frederik VII – and is a labyrinth of rooms stuffed with largely uninspiring pieces of furniture or artwork. The one highlight is the **Mirror Cabinet** – all four walls are covered in mirrors – designed to indulge the kings' erotic fantasies: the floor mirrors allowed him to peer up his partner's dress, before whisking her off to a connecting bedroom. The **second floor** is dominated by the **Long Hall**, its walls covered with enormous tapestries from 1690 showing Christian V's victories in the Scanian War of 1675–79. It's also home to one of the biggest collections of silver furniture in the world (from the 1700s) and three large silver lions that used to guard the king's throne. Left of the Long Hall is the Flora Danica porcelain room with almost two thousand pieces of delicate royal porcelain (each decorated with different hand-painted plants or flowers; see p.109) from the 1790s.

Back outside, a small flight of stairs leads down to the **basement** where the **Green Cabinet** is home to a sumptuous collection of regalia and jewellery – an elaborate embroidered saddle takes centre stage. A further flight of stairs leads down through massive steel doors into the **Treasury**, where you're immediately confronted by Christian III's magnificent Sword of State, dating from 1551, beyond which are hundreds of incredibly detailed gold items and the fabulous silver Oldenborg Horn, allegedly dating from 989 AD. In the bottom section of the basement are two cases containing the present queen's **crown jewels** and those of earlier monarchs, encrusted with jewels and precious stones. The largest piece, the Crown of the Absolute Monarchs, weighs in at over 2kg and includes a sapphire weighing over an ounce.

Kongens Have

Central Copenhagen's oldest and prettiest park, **Kongens Have** (Royal Gardens; daily 6am–sunset; free) – known also as Rosenborg Slotshave – was established in 1606 by Christian IV to provide Rosenborg Slot with a place in which the royal family could grow vegetables and flowers. The gardens still preserve much of their original layout, with a grid of wide lanes and narrower pathways. From the palace, it's a short stroll down to the park's southern entrance on Gothersgade, where two large plinths, topped with gold domes, neatly frame Kavalergangen (Squire's Lane), originally used as a jousting run. Walk down here to the **Hercules Pavilion** – there's a small café here during the summer and, next door, a novel children's play area complete with large wooden dragons for clambering on. Look out, too, for the statue of a solemn-looking Hans Christian Andersen a couple of hundred metres east of here, towards Kronprinsessegade. During summer months, the garden is often host to live music and theatre performances, and jugglers from around the world gather here to share tricks of the trade. The puppet theatre (June–Aug Tues–Sun 2pm & 3pm; free) along the outer wall of Kronprinsessegade is worth checking out and especially popular with kids.

Davids Samling

Housed in an eighteenth-century house on Kronprinsessegade, east of Kongens Have, the **Davids Samling** Islamic collection (Tues & Thurs–Sun 1–4pm, Wed 10am–4pm; free; ⓦwww.davidmus.dk) is an Aladdin's cave of Persian, Arabian and Indian antiques dating back to the sixth century (it also houses a less noteworthy collection of antique European furniture and porcelain). The well laid-out collection includes everything from delicate embroidered silks to savage-looking daggers, and there's also an extensive assortment of miniatures and illuminated manuscripts and Korans, dating back to the thirteenth century, from all over the Islamic world. The museum is closed for refurbishment until June 2008.

Cinemateket

Opposite the Kongens Have on Gothersgade, **Cinemateket** (Film House; Tues–Fri 9.30am–10pm, Sat & Sun noon–10pm; free; ⓦwww.cinemateket.dk) is a state-of-the-art complex dedicated to all things connected to the big screen. Occupying a restructured office block, the curious interior contains a large black sarcophagus-like edifice, which encloses two of Cinemateket's screens (see p.210). Other parts of the building are sometimes used as a gallery – expect to see cutting-edge, if not always interesting, Danish art. There's also a book- and video shop, and a trendy café-restaurant (see p.210), but the main attraction is **Videotek** (Tues–Fri 2–10pm, Sat & Sun noon–10pm) with over 3000 films to choose from (a full catalogue is available at ⓦwww.katalog.dfi.dk) and free viewing facilities in the basement.

Botanisk Have

Established on their present site in 1874, the **Botanisk Have** (Botanical Gardens; May–Sept daily 8.30am–6pm; Oct–Apirl Tues–Sun 8.30am–4pm; free; ⊛www.botanic-garden.ku.dk) occupy the levelled bastions of the old city fortifications – the zigzagging nature of the lakes inside reveals their original function as a protective moat. The gardens boast a small coniferous forest, rock gardens, and waterfalls populated by herons, ducks and freshwater terrapins, while three greenhouses hold wonderful collections of citrus fruits, succulents and cacti. The largest is the circular **Palmehus** (daily 10am–3pm), where massive palms hang lazily in the steamy atmosphere over ponds festooned with water lilies – a walkway runs around the top of the interior if you want to get up among the treetops. There are also collections of some economically and medicinally important plants from the tropics, including spices, cacao, coffee and coconut. Next to the Palmehus, the enthralling **Kaktushus** (Wed, Sat & Sun 1–2pm; free) contains around a thousand species of cacti and succulents. Next door, the **Orkidehuset** (Wed, Sat & Sun 2–3pm; free) houses over six hundred types of orchids, whose fragrant smells permeate the air. Light refreshment is available at *Café Paradisfugl* next to the Palmehus.

Geologisk Museum

At the northeastern corner of Botanisk Have, by the junction of Sølvgade and Øster Voldgade, the interesting **Geologisk Museum** (Geological Museum; Tues–Sun 1–4pm; 25kr, free Wed; ⊛www.geological-museum.dk) is housed in a grand old university building. It has exhibits depicting how geological forces shaped the Earth's landscape and life, a vast collection of minerals and, most interestingly, a startling collection of **meteorites** from a major fall thousands of years ago in Cape York, Greenland – some have been cut into enormous slices, creating strange, mirror-like effects. The collection's two biggest meteorites, "Savik" and "Agpalilik", are displayed outside – Savik, the smaller of the two, has pitted sides, the result of generations of Inuits hammering away at it to procure iron for knives and harpoons. Also look out for the world's largest mussel (found in Greenland), a fossilized bivalve 178cm long and 83 million years old. If you're into crystals and polished stones, check out the museum shop on the ground floor.

Statens Museum for Kunst

Situated in the southeastern corner of Østre Anlæg park is the **Statens Museum for Kunst** (Royal Museum of Fine Arts; Tues & Thurs–Sun 10am–5pm, Wed 10am–8pm; free; 70kr for special exhibitions; ⊛www.smk.dk), a huge affair with a wide-ranging exhibit housed in two contrasting wings: the older Dahlerup Building, containing classical works ranging from Tintoretto through to the Danish Golden Age, and the bright and airy new wing, devoted to contemporary works and a stimulating children's museum. Doing the entire museum in one go can be somewhat overwhelming and you may be better off focusing on only a few selected sections. Alternatively, break up your visit with a pit stop at the museum's excellent café.

Ascending the main stairs from the entrance hall of the **Dahlerup Building** leads to an enormous collection of works from all over Europe from the beginning of the fourteenth century to the end of the nineteenth, including rooms devoted variously to the almost photographic images of the Dutch and Flemish masters, Italian religious paintings (including a number by Tintoretto) and a smattering of lesser-known Brueghels, Rembrandts and Van Dycks.

Danish design

The Danes' love affair with design has been going on for a century, its guiding principle – the successful merging of form and function – seen in the capital today in everything from chairs to Bang & Olufsen electronics to the new metro system. Core to the Danish attitude to design is the relationship between the user and the product – the ultimate aim to produce an object that fulfils its function, yet, at the same time, is aesthetically appealing.

Interiors and furniture

Danish designers have always been driven by a democratic, social ideal that good design is the right of all, as essential in the home as in public arenas – after all, it's a country where the climate means a lot of time is spent indoors. Pioneers of the 1920s such as **Poul Henningsen** and **Kaare Klint** got the ball rolling with their classic designs; the former depressed by the dreary lighting in most homes set about designing lamps that transformed rooms with their effective, subtle distribution of light, the latter took classics of furniture design and reworked them for modern needs. But it wasn't until the 1940s and 1950s that Danish design became an international phenomenon with the work of creative visionaries such as **Hans J. Wegner**, who took chair design to new heights with such classics as the Round Chair (1949), interiors and furniture designer, **Finn Juhl**, who furnished parts of the UN building in New York, the prolific **Arne Jacobsen** and **Børge Mogensen**, who went so far as to calculate the average dimensions of household objects and find out how many of each the average person owned in a quest to design perfect storage systems. Danish design became synonymous with outstanding craftsmanship, innovative style, pared-down simplicity and from there on purity of line – a combination that has driven design principles ever since. The torch was carried from thereon by the likes of **Vernor Panton**, with his more futuristic moulded plastic chairs in bright, bold colours, and **Poul Kjærholm**, whose steel-framed chairs have also become timeless classics.

Arne Jacobsen

For many, it's the Copenhagen-born architect/designer, Arne Jacobsen (1902–71), who symbolizes Danish design at its best and whose legacy is the most enduring. Still revered,

copied, exhibited and coveted, classic "AJ" designs pervade the city – in its shops, cafés, restaurants and hotels, and the skyline itself. Espousing the modernist idea of **Gesamtkunstwerk** or "total work of art", he turned his hand to everything from furniture to cutlery to coffee pots to buildings, a vision at its most ideologically complete in the swish **Radisson SAS Royal Hotel** (see p.169), for which he designed everything from the door handles to the high-rise building itself. However, it's probably for his iconic **chairs**, the "Number 7", the "Ant", the "Swan" and the "Egg" – the latter two designed specifically for the *SAS Royal Hotel* and famous for their natural, curvy shapes intended to suggest the presence of the human form even in its absence – that he is most remembered. "The Ant", his model for a simple, armless chair and named after its insect-like waist, was created from a single piece of moulded wood, the prototype for the stackable plastic chair designed by Verner Panton.

Danish design in Copenhagen

Radisson SAS Royal Hotel Arne Jacobsen's signature creation – pop into the sleek lobby for a taste of AJ style and a brief rest in the sumptuous Swan and Egg chairs. See p.169.

Dansk Arkitektur Center Temporary exhibitions and an excellent selection of books on design and architecture. See p.68.

Dansk Design Center The country's showcase for cutting-edge design exhibitions, along with a small selection of timeless classics and a great shop. See p.94.

Kunstindustrimuseet The new exhibition on twentieth-century design gives you the lowdown on such heavyweights as Kaare Klint, Poul Henningsen and Arne Jacobsen. See p.84.

Illum Bolighus and Paustian These two flagship stores for Scandinavian design are a real treat – everything from lighting to coat hooks to iconic chairs. For more on shopping for design, see p.218.

Twentieth-century Danish design icons

The successful combination of a highly stylized aesthetic with basic utilitarian demands has seen many Danish products become design icons. Most of the selected list below can be seen at the Dansk Design Center (see p.94); if you'd like to take your very own piece of Danish design history home with you, upmarket secondhand furniture/design shops (see p.218) are often a fruitful hunting ground, or you can pick up a modern incarnation from stores such as Illums Bolighus and Paustian (see p.219).

Stacking Chair (Verner Panton, 1959). Panton's simple "S" form chair in bright colours was the first single-piece, injection-moulded plastic chair paving the way for mass production of great design.

Monkey (Kay Bojesen, 1951). A silversmith by training, Bojesen nevertheless became more famous for his charming, beautifully crafted wooden toys with moveable limbs, which are still popular with kids today.

PK22 Easy Chair (Poul Kjærholm, 1956). His armless, steel-framed, wicker or rattan chair became an instant success for its simple lines and relaxed style.

Number 7 Chair (Arne Jacobsen, 1955). With its sensuous, cinched waist, almost triangular backrest and spindly steel legs, this is the most reproduced chair in the world, having sold over five million copies.

PH Lamp (Poul Henningsen, 1925). The first of the lamps that were to revolutionize lighting in Danish homes, its multiple small reflector shades broke up the light and diffused it evenly, removing glare.

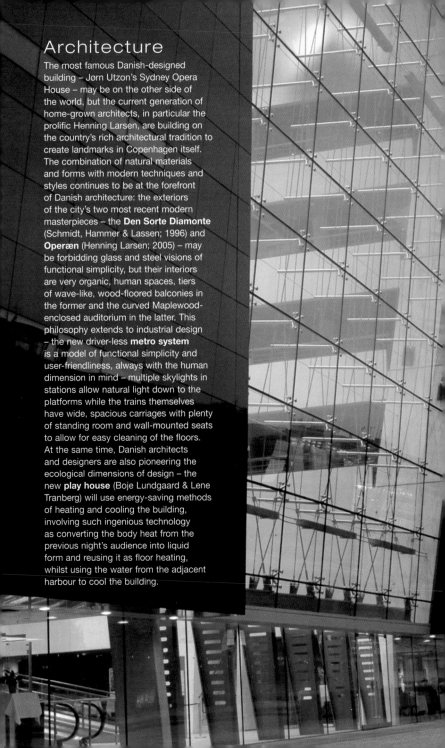

Architecture

The most famous Danish-designed building – Jørn Utzon's Sydney Opera House – may be on the other side of the world, but the current generation of home-grown architects, in particular the prolific Henning Larsen, are building on the country's rich architectural tradition to create landmarks in Copenhagen itself. The combination of natural materials and forms with modern techniques and styles continues to be at the forefront of Danish architecture: the exteriors of the city's two most recent modern masterpieces – the **Den Sorte Diamonte** (Schmidt, Hammer & Lassen; 1996) and **Operæn** (Henning Larsen; 2005) – may be forbidding glass and steel visions of functional simplicity, but their interiors are very organic, human spaces, tiers of wave-like, wood-floored balconies in the former and the curved Maplewood-enclosed auditorium in the latter. This philosophy extends to industrial design – the new driver-less **metro system** is a model of functional simplicity and user-friendliness, always with the human dimension in mind – multiple skylights in stations allow natural light down to the platforms while the trains themselves have wide, spacious carriages with plenty of standing room and wall-mounted seats to allow for easy cleaning of the floors. At the same time, Danish architects and designers are also pioneering the ecological dimensions of design – the new **play house** (Boje Lundgaard & Lene Tranberg) will use energy-saving methods of heating and cooling the building, involving such ingenious technology as converting the body heat from the previous night's audience into liquid form and reusing it as floor heating, whilst using the water from the adjacent harbour to cool the building.

The **new wing**, accessible via the ground floor or by two footbridges from the Dahlerup Building, is an impressive architectural pile spread over five floors. Its light and spacious design makes an excellent home for an extensive, if rather lightweight, collection of contemporary art – you may feel it's the building rather than the paintings that grabs your attention. There's also an excellent **children's museum** on the ground floor, with stimulating temporary exhibits drawn from the permanent collection, thoughtfully hung at a lower, child-friendly height, and paper and paint with which kids can create their own works of art.

The main body of the collection, on the second and third floors of the new wing, highlights most major movements of the twentieth century. The **second floor** has a large sample of Danish and international work – the colourful post-surrealist abstractions of the CoBrA movement (made up of mid-twentieth-century artists from *CO*penhagen, *BR*ussels and *A*msterdam – hence the name) are particularly well represented. Elsewhere, look for the enormous, quirky photographic self-portrait by Gilbert and George and, in an adjacent room, Dane Øyvid Nygaard's impressive sculpture *The Light Conductor*, reminiscent of the Silver Surfer, the Marvel comic-book character. The rest of the second floor holds a largely uninspiring cache of works by contemporary German artists and a small collection of Danish and US sculpture.

The **third floor** features an important collection of modernist works, including a small selection of the Danish artist Asger Jorn's dramatic canvases, examples of works from twentieth-century movements such as Surrealism and Expressionism, and pieces by Picasso and Matisse – look out for the latter's *The Green Line*, in which a severe-looking Madame Matisse is unceremoniously bisected into contrasting halves by a noticeable green line.

Hirschsprungske Samling

Crossing Østre Anlæg from the Statens Museum for Kunst brings you to the back of the Greek-inspired Neoclassical pavilion that houses the **Hirschsprungske Samling** (Hirschsprung Collection; Mon & Wed–Sun 11am–4pm; 35kr, Wed free; ⊕www.hirschsprung.dk), by far the finest collection of nineteenth-century Danish art in the city. The collection was donated to the Danish state in 1902 by second-generation German-Jewish immigrant and tobacco magnate Heinrich Hirschsprung – there's a large portrait of him smoking a cigar in the entrance hall.

Following the collection clockwise takes you through all the major periods of nineteenth-century Danish art. The **Golden Age** (roughly 1810–40) is initially reflected through a collection of Eckersbergs – one of Denmark's first professional artists, whose work was rooted firmly in romantic and idealistic traditions (*Woman Before a Mirror* is typical, with a poetic picture of a flesh-and-blood Venus de Milo) – and his students, such as Christen Købke and William Bendz.

In **room 13** are the remarkable historical paintings of Kristian Zahrtmann, a late nineteenth-century artist known for his colourful portrayals of eighteenth-century royal scandals, such as the ill-starred liaison between Princess Caroline Mathilde, the English wife of the particularly mad Christian VII, and Prime Minister Count Struensee (Caroline Mathilde was sent into exile in Germany; Struensee was beheaded for treason). **Room 15** contains one of the collection's most popular paintings, Harold Slott-Møller's *Spring*, a simple but engaging image of a young girl, her hair garlanded with yellow flowers. The haunting symbolism of the almost pre-Raphaelite paintings of Ejnar Nielsen and Vilhelm Hammershøi takes centre stage in **room 19** – Nielsen's *The Blind*

Girl is particularly melancholy. **Room 20** contains a large collection of works by painters from Skagen – a town on the northernmost tip of the country renowned for its bewitching light – some of whom Hirschsprung personally supported. P.S. Krøyer's depictions of the beaches around Skagen give a real feel for the qualities of its strange light.

Den Frie Udstilling

A rather strange-looking wooden building directly opposite Østerport station, at the northeastern tip of Østre Anlæg, **Den Frie Udstilling** (The Free Exhibition; daily 10am–5pm; 30kr; ⊕www.denfrie.dk) is the place to check out Denmark's budding young artists – note, though, that it's "free" as in free space rather than free entry. The exhibition hall was built in 1898 by an artists' collective looking for a place to exhibit and sell their work, and the same collective still runs the hall today. Many of the big names of Danish art, such as Asger Jorn and Christian Lemmerz, have shown work here at various times, but the exhibitions, as you might expect, can vary dramatically in quality. The building itself is virtually unchanged since 1898, with creaky, old wooden floors, and natural light spilling in through the glass roof – a great exhibition space, though unfortunately the greenhouse effect created by the roof makes it too hot to be used in high summer.

Nyboder

Heading back down Kronprinsessegade towards the city centre, any left turn before you reach Sølvgade and Kongens Have will take you into the striking cobbled streets and ochre terraces of the Nyboder district, built by Christian IV in the seventeenth century to provide free housing for his sailors, and supposedly the world's first terraced houses. It's a pleasant enough place to wander about, even if it does all look a little bit too perfect to be true – in fact, all but one of the rows of buildings here are nineteenth-century reconstructions. The solitary original row that does survive, dating from the 1630s, runs along Sankt Pauls Gade and now houses the small and reasonably interesting **Nyboders Mindestuer** museum (Wed 11am–2pm, Sun 11am–4pm; 10kr), containing a collection of furniture and domestic objects reflecting life at Nyboder in the 1880s.

Frederikstad

Bordered by the Inderhavnen harbourfront to the east and cut in two by the broad sweep of Bredgade, the **FREDERIKSTAD** district was commissioned by Frederik V and designed by Danish architect Nicolai Eigtved, as a royal quarter fit for a noble elite. Containing the residence of Danish royalty, **Amalienborg**, and the grandest place of worship in the city, **Marmorkirken**, Frederikstad raised Copenhagen to new levels of urban elegance.

Marmorkirken

Easy to spot at the end of Frederiksgade, topped by a large green dome modelled on – and intended to rival – St Peter's in Rome, the grandiose **Marmorkirken** (Marble Church, officially called Frederikskirken; Mon–Thurs 10am–5pm, Fri–Sun noon–5pm; ⊕www.marmorkirken.dk) was commissioned by Frederik V to be a splendid centre of worship befitting his new royal quarter. Originally designed by Eigtved, Frederik V himself laid the church's first stone in a grand ceremony in 1749. After Eigtved's death in 1754, however, the scheme ran into difficulties, and in 1770 the exorbitant cost of the Norwegian marble being used in the church's construction forced Count Struensee to abandon the project. The building was then left in disarray for a century, while various plans were mooted as to what to do with it – one proposed turning it into a gasworks – until N.F.S. Grundtvig (see p.123) finally had it completed using cheaper Danish marble (there's a portrait of him in the church, unmissable with flowing white beard and bald head, and a statue of him outside). The church was consecrated in 1894, 145 years after the foundation stone was laid.

The **interior** is grandly proportioned, if a bit drab – if you look at the walls, you can see the materials change from expensive Norwegian to cheaper Danish marble about a quarter of the way up. The best reason to visit, however, is to climb the steep, twisting steps, all 260 of them, to the top of the **bell tower** (mid-June to Aug daily 1 & 3pm; Sept to mid-June Sat & Sun 1 & 3pm; 25kr; they are very precise about these times). A guide will take you through the passages and staircases that lead to the summit, where the grand vista of Copenhagen is laid before you. The ascent involves entering the space between the inner and outer domes before climbing through a trap door and out into the elements. On a clear day, you can see out to Malmö, Helsingør and across the city to Roskilde – look for the arrows on the bell tower. No matter what the weather is like, though, you can't miss Operæn, the new opera house, across the water, the harbourfront location a heated topic of discussion (see p.74). For music closer to home, the Marmorkirken stages concerts, normally on Wednesdays at 4.30pm and usually free – pick up a full programme at the church or check ⊛www.marmorkirken.dk/koncert.html.

Next door to Marmorkirken are the gilded onion domes of the **Alexsander Nevsky Church** (Tues–Thurs 11.30am–1.30pm), Denmark's only functioning Russian Orthodox Church with three shiny golden onion-shaped cupolas. Inside, look for the "weeping" icon behind the pavilion selling postcards, *Jerusalem Mother of Christ*, which from time to time – last on March 10, 1996, according to the caretaker – allegedly sheds miraculous tears.

Amalienborg

Across from Marmorkirken, along Frederiksgade, you cross Bredgade to reach Amalienborg Slotsplads, a square surrounded by the four palaces of **Amalienborg**, the centrepiece of Frederikstad and the home of the Danish royal family since 1794 when their former residence, Christiansborg, burnt down. Originally site of Queen Sophie Amalie's (wife of Frederik III) summer residence, which, in 1689, had also burnt down, killing almost two hundred party-goers in the process, the square was left vacant for more than sixty years until the newly crowned Frederik V decided to build a Louis XV-inspired model town (styled on Paris's Place de la Concorde) in the area. Designed by Eigtved, the four almost identical palaces (completed in 1760) are functional rather than sumptuous, and the whole ensemble is striking for its accessibility and openness rather than its grandeur – you're free to wander around the Slotsplads, though you'll be challenged by the bearskin-hatted **Livgarden** (Life Guards) if you get too close to the palaces. Hang around long enough and you may even catch a glimpse of Denmark's first family.

The first palace to the left of Frederiksgade – Christian VIII's Palæe – is home to the **Danske Kongers Kronologiske Samling** (Royal Danish Collection; May–Oct daily 10am–4pm; Nov–April Tues–Sun 11am–4pm; 50kr, joint ticket with Rosenborg Slot 80kr; ⊛www.amalienborgmuseet.dk), which includes a part of the royal family's living quarters that have been turned into what

④

is basically a shrine to the monarchy. Queen Margrethe has had a sizeable input into designing the museum, as well as putting together the cover of the collection's catalogue – decide for yourself whether she got the job on merit. The museum itself is a mishmash of family mementos, stuffed animals, garish military pictures and carefully preserved living quarters shielded from the hoi polloi behind glass screens. The rooms of previous kings (the present queen is the first female monarch in recent times) do reveal something of their character – some are stuffed full of assorted regalia and military tackle; others are more homely affairs, with family portraits, pipes and slippers. There are also dull collections of jewellery and an absorbing Europe-wide royal family tree revealing the generations of inbreeding that have gone into producing the monarchs of today.

Diagonally across the Slotsplads, past the enormous **equestrian statue** of Frederik V – which reputedly cost more than the four palaces combined, thanks to sculptor Jacques Saly, who, invited to Copenhagen to create the work, spent thirty years in the city living it up at the court's expense – is the queen's current residence in Christian IX's (her father's) Palæe, or Schacks Palæe; for obvious reasons this is off limits to the public. Left of here, when facing the statue, Christian VII's Palæe (also known as Moltke's Palæe) is the royal guesthouse and occasionally houses exhibitions related to royal Copenhagen. To the right, Frederik VIII's Palæe (also called Brockdorff's Palæe) is today home to the crown prince and his young family. It is currently undergoing extensive refurbishment, scheduled to be finished in 2009, presumably to make the building fit for a future king.

Every day at noon, the Livgarden perform a **changing of the guard**, during which they march back to their barracks beside Rosenborg Slot. A marching band is added to the procession if the queen or any other member of the royal family is in residence.

Medicinsk-Historisk Museum

Returning towards Marmorkirken, a right turn down Bredgade brings you to the grisly **Medicinsk–Historisk Museum** (Medical History Museum; guided tours only: in English July & Aug Wed–Fri & Sun 1pm; rest of the year only in Danish Wed–Fri 11am & 1pm, Sun 1pm; 30kr; ⊛www.mhm.ku.dk), situated in a wing of what was originally the Danish Academy of Surgery, designed by Peter Meyn in 1787, and thus one of the few classical buildings in this area not designed by Eigtved. The museum's macabre account of Denmark's medical history features aborted foetuses, syphilis treatments, amputated feet, eyeballs and a dissected head, along with the original dissection auditorium around which the gore-splattered pioneers of Danish surgery learnt their trade. A couple of early and late eighteenth-century dental surgeries, complete with hand-drills and sinks using recycled and often bloody water, finish off the exhibition. The guides are well-informed medical students and the tour takes roughly 1hr 30min.

Kunstindustrimuseet

Continuing north along Bredgade, the **Kunstindustrimuseet** (Danish Museum of Decorative Art; permanent exhibition June–Aug Tues–Sun noon–4pm; Sept–May Tues & Thurs–Sun noon–4pm, Wed noon–6pm; temporary exhibits and post-1900 collection June–Aug Tues–Fri 10am–4pm, Sat & Sun noon–4pm; Sept–May Tues & Thurs–Fri 10am–4pm, Wed 10am–6pm, Sat & Sun noon–4pm; 40kr; ⊛www.kunstindustrimuseet.dk) is housed in the former Royal Frederiks Hospital, a Rococo building from 1757. The museum traces the development of European – and particularly Danish – design, as well as examining the influence of Eastern styles on Western design through a notable collection of Oriental furniture, ceramics and other exhibits. Most of the museum is used for displaying items from the permanent collection, which covers the period from the Middle Ages to 1900. One wing (on the right as you enter) is kept for later pieces, and for temporary exhibits focusing on Danish design. Note that these two parts of the collection have slightly different opening hours (see opposite).

Oriental exhibits include a collection of early Japanese porcelains and sword-hilt *tsuba*s decorations, along with some Chinese Ming vases, all displaying styles from which Europeans were to derive later designs. Early examples of styles borrowed from the East are shown through decorative work on Baroque furniture, while a section devoted to British design displays copies of Chinese lacquerware, Chippendale furniture and a toiletry set given to the unfortunate Princess Caroline Mathilde (see p.81). The Study Collection upstairs focuses on the development of European porcelain from its beginnings in the early eighteenth century, with pieces such as the first glazed European porcelain from Meissen, Germany, up until the late nineteenth century, with emphasis on Danish porcelain production in the district of Amager (Royal Copenhagen still make porcelain today in Frederiksberg, and it's possible to purchase exact copies of eighteenth-century pieces from their shop; see p.109). On a slightly more offbeat note are the ceramic pieces produced by Gauguin – who was married to a Dane – including a unique ceramic self-portrait.

The last part of the collection is dedicated to Danish designers of the twentieth century, focusing on the avant-garde, and featuring the simplistic Kaare Klint and intricate Poul Henningsen lamps, and chairs of Wegner and Arne Jakobsen, plus other more abstract pieces.

To the right by the main entrance, the museum's excellent café serves good-value Mediterranean-style food, and in the summer, there's outdoor service in a pleasant courtyard shared with the popular open-air Grønnegårds theatre.

Kastellet and around

At the far end of Bredgade, the straight streets of Eigtved's Frederikstad are replaced by the green open spaces of Churchillparken and **KASTELLET**. There's a distinct military feel to this part of the city, with both the **Frihedsmuseet**, detailing Denmark's struggles against the Nazis during World War II, and Kastellet, Europe's oldest working fort, situated here. Nearby is that enduring symbol of the city, the **Little Mermaid**.

Frihedsmuseet

Situated within Churchillparken – a small park named after the British wartime leader – the **Frihedsmuseet** (Resistance Museum; May–Sept Tues–Sat 10am–4pm, Sun 10am–5pm; Oct–April Tues–Sat 10am–3pm, Sun 10am–4pm; free; ⓦwww.natmus.dk) offers a comprehensive account of Denmark's role in World War II, using video displays (with English dubbed versions), personal accounts, and exhibits such as resistance broadsheets, home-made weapons and printing presses.

The museum also grasps the thorny issue of the Danish government's **collusion** with German rule. Denmark, uniquely amongst the countries invaded by the Nazis, was afforded a kind of independence. The price of this was a large degree of collaboration: the Danish government was convinced that a

Europe-wide Nazi victory was inevitable, and displays show the signed agreements between the two countries, while uniforms of the Danish Freikorps – volunteers who joined the German army – bear witness to the degree to which some Danes aligned themselves with the invaders.

Initially slow to offer armed resistance, the first Danish acts of sabotage were carried out in 1942 by a group of teenage boys from Århus called the **Churchill Gang** (photographs and filmed interviews with them are on display). These acts of sabotage gave impetus to other groups, largely made up of illegal Danish communists, and the period of collusion ended with a number of uprisings in 1943, which led to the Germans imposing martial law, imprisoning hundreds and engaging in acts of terror against the Danish population. There are some dramatic photographs (and mundane police reports) of these first acts of sabotage, along with home-made printing devices, machine guns and bombs.

Another act that infuriated the Nazis was the mass evacuation of Denmark's **Jewish population** – all but a tiny percentage were saved from the death camps by the Danish government's refusal to collaborate on this issue and the efforts of ordinary Danes, who helped Jews escape to neutral Sweden. Personal accounts, video interviews and original maps showing the escape routes attest to the courage shown during this episode of the war (see also box on p.51).

One of the most moving parts of the exhibition is just in front of the large stained-glass windows in a section called **"The Dead"**, showing the original wooden posts to which arrested resistance fighters were tied and shot, along with last letters to loved ones from those sentenced to death.

Gefion Fountain

Just past the museum is the incongruous British St Alban's Church, beside which is the dramatic **Gefion Fountain**. The fountain is based on the story of the goddess Gefion who, according to legend, was promised as much land as she could plough in a single night. She promptly turned her four sons into oxen and ploughed out a chunk of Sweden (creating Lake Vänern), then picked it up and tossed it into the sea – where it became the Danish island of Zealand.

△ Gefion Fountain

Created in 1908 by Anders Bundgaard, the fountain is one of the largest public monuments in Copenhagen, depicting an enormous bronze Gefion with her four oxen pulling a plough, water coming out as mist from their nostrils and cascading down from behind the plough in a series of steps from which huge snakes coil out of the bubbling water.

Kastellet

Just past Churchillparken are the unmistakable ramparts and moats of **Kastellet** (The Citadel; daily 6am–10pm; free). Conceived by Christian IV as the key element in the city's defences, the fortress has been occupied by troops since 1660, making it the oldest still-functioning military base in Europe, and it remains the only part of the city's ancient defence system still in use. The star-shaped fortress is formed by five grass-covered bastions surrounded by a series of moats; it can be entered via one of two gates – Kongensporten, near Churchillparken to the south, and Norgesporten, at the opposite end near the Little Mermaid – which are linked by a thoroughfare flanked by barracks and storehouses. Due to its secure nature, Kastellet was also used as a prison – the windows in the west wall of the Kastellet church were bricked up so that those attending services did not have to look at the detainees in the prison building in front, although small holes were cut through, allowing prisoners to hear the words of the Lord. Count Struensee was held here after he was caught having an affair with Princess Caroline Mathilde (see p.81).

  Kastellet's principal attraction has for generations been the chance it offers for a leisurely stroll around its bastions and ramparts. In the late 1990s, extensive restoration works were initiated by the city council (funded by Maersk McKinney Møller, sponsor of the new opera house) and the entire area now stands pretty much as it did in the nineteenth century, with the curious addition of sheep to maintain the grass on the slanted slopes of the inner ramparts. Remember that in part this is still a working military complex – these days mainly with administrative duties – and some areas are off limits to the public: keep an eye out for the *Adgang Forbudt* ("No Entry") signs. Kastellet's church sometimes holds free classical concerts on Sundays.

The Little Mermaid

A stone's throw from Kastellet (take Norgesporten gate) on the stretch of coastline called Langelinie, and poised on a pile of carefully positioned rocks by the harbour's edge, is Copenhagen's most famous symbol, the statue of the **Little Mermaid** (Den Lille Havfrue). Created in 1913 by Edvard Eriksen, this rather plain bronze figure has become the city's de facto emblem despite its modest dimensions, and continues to hold a powerful sway over the imagination of Danes and visitors alike, conjuring up a period when Copenhagen was the fairy-tale capital of the world. Tour buses and tour boats arrive here in a steady stream throughout the summer with hordes eager to photograph themselves with the mermaid whilst trying to avoid the less scenic industrial harbour in the background.

  Inspired by the 1837 Hans Christian Andersen story of the same name, the statue was commissioned by Carlsberg brewery boss and art lover Carl Jacobsen after he had seen a performance of a ballet based on the *Little Mermaid* story at the Royal Theatre. The prima ballerina in that production, Ellen Price, was to have been the model for the statue, but her reluctance to pose nude for Eriksen forced him to use his wife as a model for the mermaid's body – only the face is Price's. Jacobsen originally wanted the mermaid to have the traditional fish's tail, but Eriksen noted that in Andersen's story the mermaid exchanges her golden hair and beautiful voice for legs – hence the final statue, with the outline of a mermaid's tail between two human limbs.

Continuing north on **Langelinie** towards Nordhavnen and Østerbro (see p.115) will take you along one of Copenhagen's most popular Sunday destinations. On a sunny day, this stretch of coast – with its numerous hot-dog stands and ice-cream booths – is crowded with a happy mix of rollerbladers, joggers, dog walkers and old-age pensioners all enjoying the wonderful view of the Trekroner Bastion and the Swedish coast beyond.

Larsens Plads

South of Langelinie and the Gefion Fountain, the pedestrian stretch of Larsens Plads runs along the Frederikstad waterfront back to Nyhavn, its length lined with robust red-brick warehouses stemming from Copenhagen's maritime trading days but now housing converted flats – some of Copenhagen's most sought after residential property. Roughly halfway along lies the huge **Den Kongelige Afstøbningssamling**, and further towards Nyhavn, is the stylistic Amaliehaven park, where the new play house is being built next to an old granary now housing Hotel *Copenhagen Admiral* Toldbodgade (see p.167).

Kongelige Afstøbningssamling

Housed in a West Indian warehouse, **Den Kongelige Afstøbningssamling** (Royal Cast Collection; Wed 2–8pm, Sun 2–5pm; free; ⓦwww.smk.dk) is an enormous assortment of plaster casts of statues and reliefs from temples, churches and public places throughout the world. The collection was begun in the mid-eighteenth century by the Royal Academy of Art for students to use when practising their drawing skills. Following a period of grandeur during the Golden Age in the nineteenth century, when the casts were on prominent display, the collection spent decades hidden away in this warehouse while paintings took the museum's centre stage as the more worthy art form. In the late twentieth century, following restoration on the by-now dilapidated casts, the warehouse opened to the public. It now houses more than 2600 pieces – casts of the world's oldest, largest and most important statues and reliefs, dating back four thousand years – and is undeniably astounding. Root around for a while and you'll see Louvre's magnificent *Venus of Milo* (no.434), and casts of all of Michelangelo's works including *Maria and the Dead Jesus* (no.115), the original statue made in one single piece of marble in meticulous detail, Jesus' arm almost lifelike with protruding veins. Donatello's complete works are also here, the most famous of which is *Erasmo da Narni* (no.1170), a horse-and-rider statue that, not surprisingly, took six years to complete.

5

Rådhuspladsen and around

S andwiched between Indre By to the east and Vesterbro to the west, the area around the buzzing town hall square, Rådhuspladsen, is Copenhagen at its most frivolous, touristy and sometimes downright tacky, bursting with virtually every kind of populist amusement you could imagine: if you want to ride one of the world's oldest rollercoasters, pose next to a wax model of Hans Christian Andersen or catch the latest IMAX movie, look no further. Top of the bill are the **pleasure gardens of Tivoli**, the country's top tourist attraction and synonymous with Copenhagen at its most innocently pleasurable. Tagging along for the ride are plenty of other mass-appeal family amusements of varying quality including the mannequin celebrities of **Louis Tussauds**, the **Tycho Brahe Planetarium** and the entertainment complexes lining the otherwise drab **Axeltorv**.

That said, the area is far more than an enormous fairground. Just south of the Rådhuspladsen lurk a few of the city's cultural heavyweights: the **Ny Carlsberg Glyptotek** with its soothing collections of sculptures and paintings; the unmissable **Nationalmuseet**, home to many of Denmark's historic treasures; and the **Dansk Design Center**, slick temple to urban cool. Finally, at some point you're likely to pass through **Central Station** itself, built in 1911 and resembling a red-brick neo-Gothic cathedral. Inside, you'll have to look up past the humdrum rows of shops on the concourse to the high ceiling and wooden beams to get a sense of its former splendour.

All the sights in this chapter are a five- to ten-minute walk from Central Station (served by buses #2A, #5A, #10, #15, #26 and #250S, among others) or Rådhuspladsen bus terminal (buses #2A, #5A, #8, #14, #16 and #250S). Buses #2A, #6A, #29 and #250S will get you a little closer to the Nationalmuseet, Ny Carlsberg Glyptotek and the Dansk Design Center. For the Tycho Brahe Planetarium, Vesterport is the nearest station; alternatively, buses #14 and #15 run along Gammel Kongevej.

Rådhuspladsen

Flanked by two busy roads, the oblong, pedestrianized expanse of **RÅDHUSP-LADSEN** (City Hall Square) is central Copenhagen's principal square, though you're more likely to come across it by accident than design, en route to Tivoli or the shops of Indre By. The striking Rådhus (City Hall) aside, it's not the

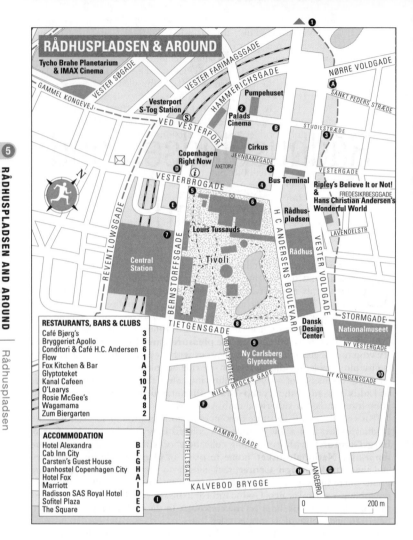

RÅDHUSPLADSEN & AROUND

Tycho Brahe Planetarium
& IMAX Cinema

Vesterport
S-Tog Station

Copenhagen
Right Now

Pumpehuset

Palads
Cinema

Cirkus

Bus Terminal

Ripley's Believe It or Not!
&
Hans Christian Andersen's
Wonderful World

Rådhus-
pladsen

Rådhus

Louis Tussauds

Central
Station

Tivoli

Dansk
Design
Center

Nationalmuseet

Ny Carlsberg
Glyptotek

RESTAURANTS, BARS & CLUBS

Café Bjørg's	3
Bryggeriet Apollo	5
Conditori & Café H.C. Andersen	6
Flow	1
Fox Kitchen & Bar	A
Glyptoteket	9
Kanal Cafeen	10
O'Learys	7
Rosie McGee's	4
Wagamama	8
Zum Biergarten	2

ACCOMMODATION

Hotel Alexandra	B
Cab Inn City	F
Carsten's Guest House	G
Danhostel Copenhagen City	H
Hotel Fox	A
Marriott	I
Radisson SAS Royal Hotel	D
Sofitel Plaza	E
The Square	C

0   200 m

most scenic of Copenhagen's squares – part transport hub (the city's main bus terminal is at one end), part tourist trap, with its fair share of fast-food joints and family amusements – but it's always lively with a café, *pølser* stands and assorted street vendors. Once a lowly hay market, it was elevated to its present status after 1851 when the old city ramparts were demolished and it was decided to build a new city hall here, on what was then the largest available central space. The resulting Rådhus is an impressive building worth a little exploration; look out for the statue of Hans Christian Andersen on its southern side, his head turned towards the screams emanating from Tivoli's rollercoasters.

There's little else of interest on the square itself, though a few overpriced family attractions vie for attention on either side. To the south, at HC Andersens Blvd 22, is **Louis Tussauds** (daily 10am–11pm; last admission one hour before closing; 80kr; ⓦwww.tussaud.dk), the Danish version of London's Madame Tussauds. It's the usual roll call of waxwork Hollywood stars, pop icons and historical figures, with a few famous Danes, including the royal family, thrown in for good measure and a pretty section dedicated to fairy tales and Hans Christian Andersen. On the northern side of Rådhuspladsen, at no. 57, is a **Ripley's Believe It Or Not!** (mid-June to Aug daily 9.30am–10.30pm; Sept to mid-June Mon–Thurs & Sun 10am–6pm, Fri & Sat 10am–8pm; last entry one hour before closing; 83kr, 141kr combined ticket with Hans Christian Andersen's Wonderful World; ⓦwww.topattractions.dk) – the American chain of tacky temples to the bizarre and freakish, based on the 1930s travels and cartoons of Robert L. Ripley. Adults will squirm at the unreconstructed mish-mash of bearded-lady-style exhibits and "ethnic" curios such as the Ecuadorian shrunken head (revolving on a stick for complete viewing), but it's a hit with the kids. The new **Hans Christian Andersen's Wonderful World** exhibition (same hours; 83kr or combined ticket with Ripley's for 141kr), in the same building, is a light-hearted jaunt through his life history and works, again aimed squarely at the kids, with mock-ups of his childhood home, study and so on and animated tableaux of his ever-popular fairy tales (astonishingly, only the Bible has been translated into more languages). For a more serious treatment of his life and literary contribution, you'll have to head off to the museums in his birthplace of Odense (see p.149).

Rådhus

Occupying as much space as the square itself, the monumental red-brick **Rådhus** (Mon–Fri 10am–4pm, free; guided tours Mon–Fri 3pm, Sat 10am & 11am, 30kr; ⓦwww.copenhagencity.dk), topped with an impressive bell tower, was designed by Martin Nyrop and completed in 1905. The gold figure above the main entrance is Bishop Absalon (see p.43), founder of the city. You're free to wander around during working hours, though given the building's massive size and the ease with which you can get lost, it's worth joining a guided tour. Beyond the impressive entrance, the spacious and elegant main hall has retained most of its original features, such as the Italianate wall decorations – Nyrop was heavily influenced by Tuscan architecture – and the sculpted oak banisters heading up from the ground floor. Upstairs, the reception hall and balcony overlooking the square are used for civic celebrations. The guided tours take you behind locked doors to a series of impressive wood-panelled rooms, including the Meeting Hall (where the 55 city council members meet every second Thursday) and the Banqueting Hall, lined with the coats of arms of Denmark's merchant towns.

At 106m, the city-hall **tower** (guided tours June–Sept Mon–Fri 10am, noon & 2pm, Sat noon; Oct–May Mon–Sat noon; 20kr) is Denmark's highest. It's about three hundred steps up to the balcony, and a further fifty through a narrow passageway to the spire, passing the bells used as Danish Radio's hourly chime, but you'll be rewarded with a view of the city and northeast down the length of Strøget all the way to Kongens Nytorv.

In a side room close to the entrance, what looks like a mass of inscrutable dials is in fact the astronomical timepiece of **Jens Olsen's World Clock** (Mon–Fri 8.30am–4.30pm, Sat 10am–1pm; 10kr). Set going in 1955, the clock features a 570,000-year calendar plotting eclipses of the moon and sun, solar time, local time and various planetary orbits – all with incredible accuracy. It's fascinating to watch, too, as hundreds of ticking dials track the movements of the planets.

In the summer, the building's enclosed courtyard **garden** (daily 10am–4pm) is a peaceful spot to take a break; it's open to the public but largely used by city-hall workers on their lunch break.

Tivoli

Across HC Andersens Boulevard from the Rådhus, with its main entrance at Vesterbrogade 3, is Denmark's most popular tourist attraction. Ninety percent of all foreign visitors to the city flood through the gates of **Tivoli** (ⓦwww .tivoli.dk) each summer, and though there are few rides here to compete with the white-knuckle thrills of modern theme parks, its popularity shows no signs of fading, while to the Danes it's nothing short of a national treasure. The opening of Tivoli for the new season in April is one of Copenhagen's major annual celebrations, and anyone who is anyone will have booked tables at one of the garden's posh restaurants.

Opened in 1843, Tivoli was the brainchild of architect/publisher/entertainment guru George Carstensen, who was inspired by the pleasure gardens of Europe, in particular London's Vauxhall Gardens. Though the number of rides has grown over the years from two to around twenty-five, it has stayed faithful to its creator's ideal – the delightful landscaped gardens, fairground stalls, plentiful restaurants, bandstands, theatres and concert halls as much a part of the experience as the rides. All in all, it's an expensive day out, with prices for food around twenty percent higher than the outside world and those for alcoholic drinks a white-knuckle ride in themselves, but a few hours spent wandering among the revellers of all ages indulging in the mass consumption of ice cream, with the squeals from the rides echoing round the park, is an experience well worth having, while on a fine summer's night, with the twinkling illuminations and **fireworks** exploding overhead (every Wed & Sat at 11.45pm), it's almost magical.

As one of the few still-functioning nineteenth-century pleasure gardens, Tivoli has its historical aspect, too, with a number of playful and well-maintained period buildings, notably the Chinese-style, open-air **Pantomime Theatre**.

Built in 1874, this now hosts the world's only regular performances of classical pantomime, a delicate art form, somewhere between ballet and mime – plus an element of farce – derived from Italian *commedia dell'arte*. Look out, too, for the fairy-tale *Nimb* restaurant, a slightly dilapidated white wood-and-plaster confection built in Moorish style, and the Chinese pagoda by the boating lake. Some of the fairground **rides** are also pretty old: don't miss the rickety wooden Mountain Roller Coaster, dating from 1914 – each train has its own brakeman – and the tiny Ferris wheel nearby, looking like a decorated museum piece. If this all sounds just too tame, head for the more recent rides – the Golden Tower and the Monsoon, that will have you plunging vertically from a height of 60m and narrowly

△ The Demon, Tivoli

Tivoli practicalities

The Tivoli **summer season** runs from mid-April to the third week of September. **Opening hours** are: Mon, Tues, Wed, Thurs & Sun 11am–11pm, Fri 11am–12.30am, Sat 11am–midnight (from mid-June to mid-Aug: Mon, Tues, Weds, Thurs & Sun closes at midnight, Fri & Sat at 12.30am), with most rides opening at 11.30am, though be warned that some don't open till 2pm. Entrance **tickets** cost 75kr for adults, 35kr for children (ages 3–11); on top of that you'll be paying 15–60kr (depending on thrill factor) per ride, so if you're planning on riding several, it's worth investing in a **multi-ride ticket** (200kr for adults, 150kr for children). The **Christmas season** begins the fourth week of November (check the website – see p.92 – for the exact date), ending on December 23. If you want to **leave and re-enter Tivoli** – to get a more reasonably priced lunch outside or stagger your visit throughout the day to make the most of the variety of entertainment on offer – get your hand stamped on exit. **Eating** in Tivoli, though expensive, is all part of the day out, with the whole range of eating options on offer – see the Tivoli box in "Eating" (p.186) for listings.

escaping a drenching respectively; the Star Flyer, at 80m the world's tallest carousel; and the Demon, a stomach-churning three-loop roller coaster.

Music, some of it free with the admission price, plays a large part in Tivoli; check the posters around the park for details of that day's events. The renowned and recently revamped **Concert Hall** (ticket only; see p.202), which now also features a stunning saltwater aquarium in its basement, features big-name stars – from Anne-Sophie Mutter to Beck – as well as classical concerts. There are also several smaller venues – the Sex Pistols once played in one of them – and bandstands playing jazz and blues, while the open-air stage "Plænen", given over most of the time to displays of acrobatics and dance, hosts Danish rock bands (and the occasional international rock and pop act) free every Friday at 10pm (see p.202).

Tivoli is also open during Danish half-term in October for a **Halloween** themed extravaganza, and the weeks around **Christmas**, when the festive spirit is cranked up with even more spectacular lighting displays, a "Christmas Market", Christmas theatre performances, on ice-skating rink by the Chinese pagoda, and all sorts of Christmas nibbles and warming *glögg* – while the braziers and torches help keep the worst of the chill at bay. Note, though, that at this time of year you may not find all of the rides working; around twenty percent are closed during the winter.

Axeltorv

Directly opposite the main entrance to Tivoli is the bland **Axeltorv**, complete with tacky faux-classical statues and bordered on one side by the empty, run-down Scala centre (set to become a hotel in the near future), and on the other by bowling alleys, games arcades and the Axelborg entertainment centre. The eye is drawn to the end of the square and the seventeen-screen **Palads Cinema** – a garish white, pink and orange pile resembling a huge Battenburg cake. Built in 1917 to replace the old central station, Palads acquired its distinctive decor in 1987, when artist Poul Gernes was brought in to redesign the exterior: the decoration survived the predictable storm of criticism and is now a Copenhagen landmark.

The most interesting building on Axeltorv is **Cirkus**, a circular, domed, pseudo-Roman auditorium with seating for two thousand people. Built in

1905, it was used as a proper circus until the 1960s, since when it has hosted everything from boxing matches to a talk by the Dalai Lama – it's now the venue of a huge restaurant with nightly cabaret, stage shows and dancing. The splendid auditorium has fantastic acoustics and, despite its size, is surprisingly intimate; the striking painted frescoes of circus scenes that run round the interior frieze are originals from 1905.

Just to the west, on the corner of Vesterbrogade and Hammerichsgade, the *Radisson SAS Royal* hotel (see p.169), Denmark's first skyscraper, brought a taste of American glamour and hotel chic to the city when it was built in the 1960s. The architect, Arne Jacobsen (see the *Danish design* colour section) designed everything from the furniture to the door handles and cutlery; it's worth popping into the lobby for a look at his work, still highly popular today.

Tycho Brahe Planetarium

At Gammel Kongevej 10, a five-minute walk west from Axeltorv and pleasantly situated at the southeastern corner of Skt Jørgens Sø (the southernmost of the lakes that enclose central Copenhagen), is the **Tycho Brahe Planetarium** (Mon–Fri 9.30am–9pm, Sat & Sun 10.30am–9pm; 25kr exhibition only, 95kr including IMAX film; ⊛www.tycho.dk). Named after the famous sixteenth-century Danish astronomer who discovered the constellation Cassiopeia, this distinctive cylindrical, sand-coloured brick affair is home to a rather pedestrian exhibition on the stars, planets and space travel, with the obligatory lump of moon rock. The only real reason to come here is the **IMAX cinema**, which shows hourly films (you'll need to hire headphones with English translations; 15kr), though they're more likely to be about ancient Egypt, deep-sea exploration or dolphins than anything astronomical.

Dansk Design Center

A few minutes' walk southeast of Tivoli and the Rådhus, at HC Andersens Blvd 27, is the Henning Larsen-designed, glass-fronted **Danish Design Centre** (Mon–Fri 10am–5pm, Wed open till 9pm & free from 5pm, Sat & Sun 11am–4pm; 40kr; ⊛www.ddc.dk), research facility and showcase for the country's outstanding design industry (see the *Danish design* colour section). It's largely given over to temporary exhibitions – anything from design concepts to displays of award-winning furniture; the tiny permanent exhibition in the basement won't keep you more than the minute or so it takes to peruse the small selection of design icons such as Wonderbras, Zippo lighters, jeans, computers and coffee pots. The café is a pleasant spot for a coffee or light lunch, but it's the **shop** that makes it worth the effort, with an excellent range of books on design and architecture, plus drawers full of dinky designer gadgets – a chance to acquire the latest bottle opener, key ring or cutlery. For more on *Danish design* see the colour section.

Ny Carlsberg Glyptotek

A little further on, at Dantes Plads 7, is the recently revamped **Ny Carlsberg Glyptotek** (Tues–Sun 10am–4pm; 40kr, Wed & Sun free; ⊛www.glyptoteket .dk), Copenhagen's finest art gallery, opened in 1897 by the philanthropic Carlsberg brewing magnate Carl Jacobsen (see p.106) as a venue for ordinary people to see the collection of classical and modern art that he had generously donated to the state. Its focal point is the delightful glass-domed **Vinter Have**

(Winter Garden), filled with soaring palm trees, a fountain and statues – Jacobsen correctly guessed that the heat and tropical plantlife here would lure visitors who wouldn't be interested by the works of art alone, and even on a freezing winter's day a wander through this lush atrium and the extensive collections of Etruscan, Greek, Roman, Egyptian, French and Danish artworks can prove both a physically and mentally warming experience. Furthermore, the Vinter Have's highly rated **café** (see p.185) makes a perfect spot for a morning coffee and pastry or lunch.

The building itself is in three sections centred on the Vinter Have. The entrance is through the long, low and rather self-important facade of the **Dahlerup building**, completed in 1897 and largely given over to French and Danish sculpture and Danish painting. From here you pass through into the **Kampmann building** (there's a good view of the exterior from outside at the back, where a tiered pyramid looks dramatically down over Rodin's *The Thinker*), added to the original Glyptotek in 1906 to house the antiquities collection. Off to the left is the stunning modern **French Wing**, housing the wonderful collection of French painting. At a push, it's possible to see the entire works in a few hours; if time is limited, the excellent Rodins, the Ancient Rome and Etruscan collections, and the Impressionist and Post-Impressionist paintings in the French Wing shouldn't be missed. Be sure to grab a **floor plan** as the layout of the three buildings can be a little confusing.

French and Danish sculpture and Danish Golden Age painting

The entrance hall leads you into the oldest section of the gallery, the Dahlerup building, where, spread over two floors, you'll find the collections of French sculpture and Danish sculpture and painting. The **French sculpture** collection is dominated by a particularly fine haul of **Rodins** – the largest outside France. Many of the exhibits were created for his "Gates of Hell" doors commissioned for a new museum of decorative art in Paris and inspired by the Inferno from Dante's *Divine Comedy* – damned souls undergoing various torments and agonies for their sins or indulging in passionate clinches sure to send them straight to hell, including a version of *The Kiss*. Other parts of this section include a dramatic collection of white marbles: you'll find Marqueste's theatrical *Perseus slaying Medusa* set amidst a raft of huge, full-bodied women and muscular men by various other artists, and a series of ornate busts by Carpeaux.

The **Danish sculpture and painting** is, unsurprisingly, rather less stimulating, though it does provide a good reflection of Golden Age painting with some idealized landscapes by C.W. Eckersberg, some more realistic paintings depicting the travails of Danish peasants by Marstrand, and a few decorative frescoes by Herman Freund, a close colleague of Bertel Thorvaldsen (see p.48), whose sensual relief *The Three Graces* is on display.

Antiquities collection

Beyond the enticing Vinter Have, in the Kampmann building, the antiquities collection has received the full modernization treatment: now called The **Mediterranean Horizon**, it's a worthy attempt to go beyond merely labelling the treasures from Ancient Greece, Rome, Egypt, Etruria and the Near East by setting the context within which the works were created. With this in mind, the first few rooms, "The Ancient Mediterranean", provide the geographical, cultural and artistic background to the various periods and cultures, in the process exploring the links between them and using selected pieces from the collections to highlight artistic concepts and themes of the time. This all sets the scene perfectly for a better appreciation of the antiquities collections themselves. Look out, in particular, for the **Greek and Roman** portrait sculpture and statues; an amusing mix of the greats – the portrait of Caligula, which still retains some of its original paint, and large Alexander the Great are particularly striking – and some surprisingly warts-and-all private portraits of rich commoners. There's a small but excellent collection of **Egyptian** artefacts – statuary, stelae, tomb models, reliefs and the obligatory handful of mummies – but it's the large and diverse haul of **Etruscan** works that really stands out. This distinct civilization from central Italy, whose origins date back to around 700 BC, was eventually incorporated into the Roman world around the first century BC but Etruscan culture heavily influenced that of the Romans and therefore persisted. The exhibition explores the development of Etruscan culture, religion and society through its impressive array of artefacts – the votive offerings, sculptures, figurines, funerary items, and jewellery providing ample evidence of the Etruscans' mastery of gold, bronze, terracotta and stone, while their characteristic sarcophagi topped with the reclining, contented-looking statues of their owners offer some insight into the reverence they had for their dead and the ancestor cults that grew up as a result.

French Wing

The last section of the Glyptotek is the self-contained, Henning Larsen-designed **French Wing** (rooms 56–66; access from the Vinter Have), opened in 1996 to house the museum's excellent collection of nineteenth-and twentieth-century French painting from David to Gauguin. The result – the exterior in particular – is an architectural triumph: a huge white vault in the most minimalist of contemporary architectural styles, which blends extraordinarily well into its classical context. Linked to the other two buildings by arches and walkways, the wing's glimmering white surface creates a real sense of light and space, particularly when sunlight spills in through the glass roof.

On the lower ground floor (rooms 56–60), precursors of the Impressionists and artists from the Barbizon school are well represented with works by Corot, Delacroix, Courbet and Manet, including a version of the latter's well-known *Execution of Emperor Maximilian* and *The Absinthe Drinker*, its dark tones and subject matter a contemporary comment on those brushed aside during the modernization of society. The ground floor is given over to the **Impressionists** (rooms 61 & 62), with some exquisite Monets – notably *The Lemon Grove*, a wonderful play of colour and technique – a few lesser-known Renoirs and a complete set of charming Degas bronze figurines. The exhibition continues upstairs with the **Post Impressionists** (rooms 63–66), including works by Toulouse-Lautrec, Pissarro, Bonnard and Van Gogh – look out for his luscious *Pink Roses*, a wonderful example of his ability to bring nature to life on the canvas. Gauguin is particularly well represented with over thirty paintings. Be sure to see *Tahitian Girl*, a painting that really emphasizes his unique style of bright primary colours, flat shapes and heavy contours that resulted from his search for a more organic, primitive source for his art.

Nationalmuseet

To the east of Rådhuspladsen, on Ny Vestergade, is the excellent – and now free – **Nationalmuseet** (National Museum; Tues–Sun 10am–5pm; ⓦwww .natmus.dk), housed partly in an elegant eighteenth-century royal palace and home to the country's finest collection of Danish artefacts from the Ice Age to the present day, though be warned that the Prehistoric Denmark galleries, featuring the Viking collections, are undergoing extensive **renovations** and will be closed to the public until 2008 (with the exception of the Rune Room, see p.98). There's still plenty to see, though: Danish history from 1050 AD onwards is unaffected and there's a fantastic ethnographic collection including one of the largest displays of Inuit artefacts in the world, as well as a modest exhibit of Egyptian and classical antiquities, plus the Royal Coin Collection. All of the displays are amply labelled in English. Attached to the main collection is a **children's museum**, where kids can clamber in a Viking ship, fire toy cross-bows from model castles and try out various costumes.

The museum's collections of Danish history and culture are spread over three floors on the right as you enter; the ethnographic collections, temporary exhibits and children's museum are all on the left; classical antiquities are on their own on the top floor. Free floor plans are available from the information desk in the entrance hall. While you could do it all in one day (stopping for lunch in the café), it's worth breaking your visit up into more manageable chunks to get the most out of the collections.

Prehistoric Denmark and the Viking Age

Already the undisputed highlight of the museum, when it reopens in May 2008, with its swanky new galleries, the **Prehistoric Denmark and the Viking Age** collection promises to be an even more dazzling display of the country's 14,000 years of prehistory. The remarkable number of intact finds on display here is due to the country's peat bogs, which acted as a preservative on anything buried in them, often precious objects deliberately thrown in to curry favour with the marsh gods. The earliest moments of Danish civilization are represented with various skulls (many bearing evidence of gruesome deaths), carefully crafted flint tools, stunning amber pieces and necklaces, and a full-sized skeleton of an *auroch* – a very large (and now extinct) indigenous buffalo – replete with Stone Age hunting wounds. In the excellent Bronze Age section, a good sense of the lives of the early settlers is gained by the collection of 3500-year-old oak coffins, which contain domestic items along with the grisly, desiccated remains of their human occupants – the best preserved belongs to the **Egtved Girl**, whose clothes, comb, bracelets and blonde hair have all survived eerily intact. Other Bronze Age highlights include the beautifully crafted **Trundholm Sun Chariot** (1400 BC) – an enchanting model made by sun-worshippers that depicts a magical horse-drawn chariot pulling a gold-leaf sun disc across the heavens – and a fine array of *lurs*, sacred horn-like musical instruments used in ritual ceremonies.

Further on, the Iron Age collection's horde of gold artefacts is resplendent, though the superlative **Golden Horns** outshine all others with their delicate decoration of figures and animals. They're considered the most important finds from Danish antiquity, though the ones you see here aren't the original fifth-century AD versions (they were stolen from Christiansborg Slot in 1802 by a goldsmith who melted them down into jewellery and belt buckles) but reconstructions commissioned by Frederik VII.

The **Viking collection** makes for a superlative finish to the period. The idea that the Vikings were a distinct culture and people has been challenged in recent years – even some of the artefacts most closely associated with them, such as the characteristic horned helmets (examples of which are on display), predate them by centuries. Whatever the truth, the period from the birth of Christ to the triumph of Christianity in Scandinavia in about 1100 AD saw the establishment of a sophisticated seafaring culture in the region, with extensive trade routes, military prowess, and colonies in France, Britain and Ireland. Many of the everyday tools and artefacts from this period, including clothes and weapons, are on display, and there are also ample examples of shimmering filigree silver jewellery, coins and ingots, many of them from private stashes buried by the wealthy in times of unrest.

Also in this part of the museum is the **Rune Room** (still open to visitors) – take the corridor leading to the right from the entrance cloakroom – with its enthralling section on the ancient Germanic alphabet, used, especially in Scandinavia, from the third century AD to the end of the Middle Ages. There are a number of original, boulder-sized rune stones from Jutland and Lolland – erected by the wealthy in memory of the dead – and a small exhibit that translates the symbols.

The Middle Ages to the present day

Upstairs on the first floor, the story continues with an extensive collection of religious and royal paraphernalia, weapons, furniture and household objects spanning the Middle Ages and the Renaissance. The collection is particularly strong on the relics of **Danish Christianity** – stern-looking late-Viking crucifixes give way to more naturalistic representations, while the Latin alphabet arrives to replace the Germanic runes. There are rooms full of the intricate crafts used to glorify Christ (and the Church), with elaborate **gold altars**, wonderful ceremonial robes and grails. Look out, too, for the practical fifteenth-century **portable altar** (room 104) – *the* must-have travel accessory for the wealthy – in the form of a hinged box that opened up to reveal a diptych of biblical scenes intricately carved in ivory. Other highlights include a fantastic collection of jewel-encrusted rings, made to be worn outside the gloves of the wearer, and an armoury of alarming implements. The displays of royal regalia aren't really in the same league, and many of the more interesting pieces are in Rosenborg Slot (see p.78), but a cabinet in room 114 contains a trio of gold treasures: a tankard given to Christian IV as a christening present; his incredibly ornate display dagger; and Frederik II's ring with the name of his wife, Sofie, touchingly engraved on the inside. After this wonderful array of historical artefacts the collection jumps to the nineteenth century with a disappointing run of portraits of Danish worthies and a series of elaborate seventeenth-century Rococo interiors – the preserved section of the royal palace that served as the home of various crown princes and was left untouched by the museum when it took over the palace in the late 1800s.

If you've not yet had enough, head up to the second floor where the exhaustive "**Stories of Denmark**" picks up the account from 1660 to the present day with an enormous array of objects ranging from royal garments to pop posters to plastic bowls spotlighting key historical and cultural events in the country's history. Weaving together big themes such as "Denmark at War", "The State and the Church" and "Absolute Monarchy", with popular movements including the advent of trade unions, women's rights and current issues such as immigration, it's a somewhat overambitious attempt to combine the history of the state with the story of its people, and is best skimmed through lest the sheer sweep of history and level of detail leave you rather more dazed than informed.

The ethnographic, classical antiquities and numismatic collections

The bulk of the rest of the museum is taken up by the huge and exceptionally diverse **ethnographic collection**, "Peoples of the Earth". Beautifully displayed in manageable, well-labelled sections, it's a captivating journey through non-European art and culture with Africa, China, India and Japan particularly well represented. Exhibits range from a feathered Peruvian mummy to African jewellery to Native American totem poles to exquisite tea paraphernalia from China. Given the extent of the collections, it's wise to focus on particular areas of geographical interest, though the section on **Inuit culture**, spread over the first and second floors and featuring exhibits from Northern Canada, Alaska and Greenland, shouldn't be missed – on the first floor, look out for the wonderful example of Inuit reliance on lucky charms and protective amulets to ward off evil spirits and enemies in the small coat dating to 1923 and belonging to Tertaq (the Amulet Boy), at six years old the most powerful person in his tribe. It has no less than eighty protective amulets affixed to it, including a grisly array of dead animals, skins and unidentifiable desiccated items, and was acquired in Canada by the Inuit/Danish arctic explorer **Knud Rasmussen** on his fifth Thule expedition. There are more details of Rasmussen's various expeditions, aimed at documenting the culture of the Inuit tribes, upstairs where the collection continues with case after case of whalebone carvings, harpoons, sealskin kayaks, furry boots and clothing, and spooky-looking sealskin whaling costumes – the beautiful multicoloured beading and lacework on the festive costumes provides welcome evidence of a lighter side to Inuit life.

Should you have the energy left to climb all the way to the top of the museum, you'll be rewarded with a refreshingly small selection of **Egyptian** and **classical antiquities**, featuring a few mummies and, more impressively, a good collection of glazed decorative pottery from the city states of Greece, while coin and medal enthusiasts might want to feast their eyes on the museum's **numismatic collections** spanning Ancient Greece and Rome, the history of Danish coinage and plentiful exhibits from around the world.

Vesterbro and Frederiksberg

T he two districts immediately west of the city centre, Vesterbro and Frederiksberg, couldn't be more different. **Vesterbro** has always been determinedly working class, and also has the city's highest multicultural mix, yet despite encroaching gentrification, it's still Copenhagen's red-light district and one of the most colourful areas of the city, with the broadest selection of affordable ethnic restaurants and shops. In stark contrast to Vesterbro's vibrant and vivid street life, **Frederiksberg**'s wealthy residents tend to stay behind the doors of their grand villas, and the district's spacious and leafy roads are relatively lifeless. Conservative to the core, Frederiksberg is renowned for its low taxes and expensive housing. Situated on the land leading up to Frederiksberg Slot, the monarch's former summer residence, the area was originally used to grow crops and keep livestock for the royal household, and was ruled directly by the king. Even now it retains a regal aura, and is still administered by its own council, independent of the city.

Both areas have their share of tourist pulls, though they're fairly spread out and will involve a couple of short bus hops. Vesterbro's main daytime attractions are limited to the famous **Carlsberg Brewery Visitor Centre**, on the western edge of the district, and the exhaustive but informative **Københavns Bymuseum**. It's at night, however, that the area really comes into its own with its wealth of good, cheap restaurants, trendy bars, clubs and music venues. Most visitors who make it out to Frederiksberg are there either for **Copenhagen Zoo**, a tour of the **Royal Copenhagen Porcelain Visitor Centre**, or the area's real highlight, the sprawling green oasis of **Frederiksberg Have**. Weather permitting, it's well worth forgoing Frederiksberg's undistinguished eating options in favour of a picnic in the park. With more time to spare, you might want to take in one or two of the area's clutch of small, rather offbeat museums.

Central Station is the closest station to Vesterbro, although to reach the sights on the area's western edges and those in Frederiksberg you'll probably want to save your legs and take a bus. Bus #6A heads all the way up Vesterbrogade for Københavns Bymuseum and Copenhagen Zoo. Bus #26 heads up Vesterbrogade, branching off along Frederiksberg Allé to the main gates of Frederiksberg Have, before turning left along Pile Allé past the Bakkehus Museet and Carlsberg Brewery. Buses #14 and #15 run along Gammel Kongevej for the northern edge of Frederiksberg Have and the Porcelain Visitor Centre; and on to the zoo. Istedgade is served by bus #10 as far as Enghave Plads.

Vesterbro

After the old city ramparts fell in 1851 and construction on areas outside the former defences took off on a massive scale, **VESTERBRO** was quickly bought up by entrepreneurs, who crammed in as many housing blocks with minuscule flats as possible. Overcrowded and mismanaged for decades, it was not until the mid-1960s that the area's deplorable state was recognized by the city council. Eventually, in the 1980s, and wise from their experiences at Nørrebro a few years earlier – when local residents had clashed with police after historic buildings were torn down to make way for concrete housing blocks – it was decided to renovate rather than rebuild, and a long-term project to renew derelict areas of the city by the year 2010 was initiated. Large sections of Vesterbro have to date been restored – flashy streetside cafés have popped up on the corners of Halmtorvet, the preserve, just a few years ago, of drug dealers and prostitutes – though sadly the rapid gentrification that's followed has meant that many of Vesterbro's original inhabitants, and much of the area's immigrant community, have had to leave, unable to afford the hiked-up rents.

Vesterbro is crossed by the roughly parallel streets of **Vesterbrogade**, **Istedgade** and **Sønder Boulevard**, running from Central Station at the eastern end of the district to the Carlsberg Brewery in the west. Vesterbrogade, the northernmost of the three, is the district's main artery and one of the city's principal shopping streets. More affordable than Strøget, it sells everything from clothes to designer kitchenware, and also has some good restaurants and nightlife.

The area around Istedgade by Central Station is the only part of the city where you might feel a little vulnerable at night – this is home to what's left of the city's red-light district, and drunks, drug dealers and junkies still hang around amidst the porn shops, dodgy clubs and tattoo parlours. Paradoxically, a high police presence probably makes this one of the safest areas in the city. Crossing Istedgade here, but decidedly less seedy in themselves, are the city's two so-called "hotel streets" – **Colbjørnsensgade** and **Helgolandsgade**. In a desperate attempt to avoid the district becoming a working-class stronghold, the city council decreed that all houses in these two streets were to have a minimum of four rooms. Their attempt had an unexpected outcome: shortly after they were built, many of the buildings were converted into the hotels that are still here today. It's worth pressing on further along Istedgade for a more representative taste of Vesterbro life; beyond Gasværksvej, the street starts to clean up its act and the porn shops give way to a more workaday mix of cafés, clothes shops, Turkish, Chinese and Thai grocers, and *halal* butchers.

Halmtorvet and around

Nowhere is the cleanup and rejuvenation of the Vesterbro area more obvious to the casual visitor than in the area around **Halmtorvet**, at the southern end of Helgolandsgade. This initial stretch of Sønder Boulevard has been scrubbed clean and covered in a currently rather lifeless expanse of cream-coloured paving dotted with saplings and strategically placed benches. A trio of bland, bistro-style cafés lines one side, while the other is taken up by the beautifully restored **Øksnehallen**, the hall of a former cattle market of 1901. This small area was once home to many of the city's slaughterhouses and meat markets; the slaughterhouses have moved, but the low-rise blue and white buildings to the west still house wholesale butchers and fish suppliers. The Øksnehallen (Mon–Sun 11am–6pm; ⊛www.dgi-byen.dk/oeksnehallen) is now used for temporary exhibitions (admission varies), usually concentrating on contemporary culture,

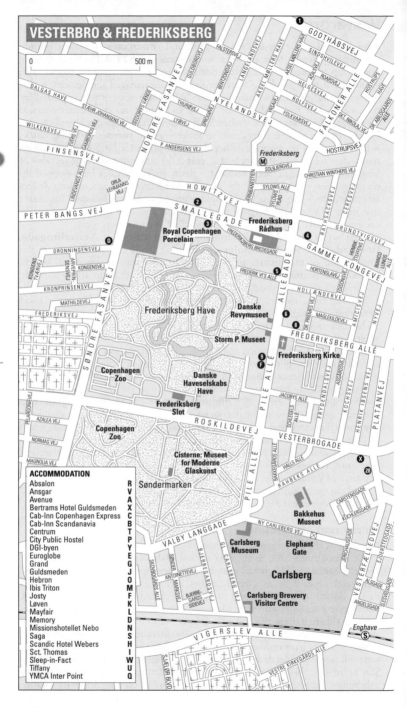

VESTERBRO & FREDERIKSBERG

0 ——————— 500 m

GODTHÅBSVEJ
FALSTERSVEJ
GULDBORGVEJ
BENZONSVEJ
LANGELANDSVEJ
AKSEL MØLLERS HAVE
AKSEL MØLLERS HAVE
SINDSHVILEVEJ
ADM. GJEDDES HAVE
ROARSVEJ
HELGESVEJ
HOSTRUPS HAVE
SKT. NIKOLAJ VEJ
DR. ABILDGAARDS ALLE
FALKONER ALLE

DALGAS HAVE
STÆHR JOHANSENS VEJ
SEEDORFS VÆRFT
THURØVEJ
SPRGGØ
LYØVEJ
NORDRE FASANVEJ
NYELANDSVEJ
PRØVEJ
FOLKVARSVEJ
ROLFSVEJ

WILKENSVEJ
EVERS VEJ
GAMBORGS VEJ

FINSENSVEJ
LINDEVANGS ALLE
ORLA LEHMANNS VEJ
P. ANDERSENS VEJ

Frederiksberg
(M)
SOLBJERGVEJ
JERNBANESTIEN
CHRISTIAN WINTHERS VEJ
HOSTRUPSVEJ

PETER BANGS VEJ
HOWITZVEJ ❷
SYLOWS ALLE
SYLOWS PLADS
RATHSACKSVEJ
CERESVEJ

SMALLEGADE
DRONNINGENSVEJ ❸
Royal Copenhagen Porcelain
FREDERIKSBERG BREDEGADE
Frederiksberg Rådhus
GRUNDTVIGSVEJ ❹
GAMMEL KONGEVEJ
HENRIK STEFFENS VEJ
BIANCO LUNDS ALLE

KONGENS TVÆRVEJ
ARVEPRINS SENSVEJ
KONGENSVEJ
KRONPRINSENSVEJ

FREDERIK VI'S ALLE ❺
HORTENSIAVEJ
HOLLÆNDERVEJ
EDISONSVEJ
AMICISVEJ
NYVEJ

MATHILDEVEJ
FREDERIKSVEJ

Frederiksberg Have
Danske Revymuseet ❻
DR. PRIEMES VEJ
MAGLEKILDEVEJ
Storm P. Museet ❽

FREDERIKSBERG ALLE
ASGÅRDSVEJ
ASSARSVEJ
KOCHSVEJ
HENRIK IBSENS VEJ
PLATANVEJ

❾ **Frederiksberg Kirke**
FREDERIKSBERG KIRKE
F

PELARGONIEVEJ
AZALEA VEJ

Copenhagen Zoo
Danske Haveselskabs Have

NORMAS VEJ
MAGNOLIA VEJ

Frederiksberg Slot

Copenhagen Zoo

ROSKILDEVEJ

JACOBYS ALLE
PILE ALLE
SCHLEGELS ALLE
FRYDENDALSVEJ

VESTERBROGADE

Cisterne: Museet for Moderne Glaskunst
Søndermarken
BAKKEGÅRDS ALLE
HALLS ALLE
RAHBEKS ALLE
X
28

CARSTENSGADE
KÜCHLERSGADE

ACCOMMODATION	
Absalon	R
Ansgar	V
Avenue	A
Bertrams Hotel Guldsmeden	X
Cab-Inn Copenhagen Express	C
Cab-Inn Scandanavia	B
Centrum	T
City Public Hostel	P
DGI-byen	Y
Euroglobe	E
Grand	G
Guldsmeden	J
Hebron	O
Ibis Triton	M
Josty	F
Løven	K
Mayfair	L
Memory	D
Missionshotellet Nebo	N
Saga	S
Scandic Hotel Webers	H
Sct. Thomas	I
Sleep-in-Fact	W
Tiffany	U
YMCA Inter Point	Q

Bakkehus Museet

VALBY LANGGADE
NY CARLSBERG VEJ

SKOVBOGÅRDS ALLE
SØNDR. ALLE
ANTOINETTEVEJ
BJERREGÅRDSVEJ
BJERRE-GÅRDS SIDEVEJ
GL. CARLSBERG VEJ

Carlsberg Museum
Elephant Gate

Carlsberg

Carlsberg Brewery Visitor Centre

JERICHAUSGADE
VESTERFÆLLEDVEJ
EJDERSTEDGADE
ALSGADE
SLESVIGSGADE
ANGELSGADE

VIGERSLEV ALLE
Enghave
(S)

VESTRE KIRKEGÅRDS ALLE
SLÆLØR BLVD

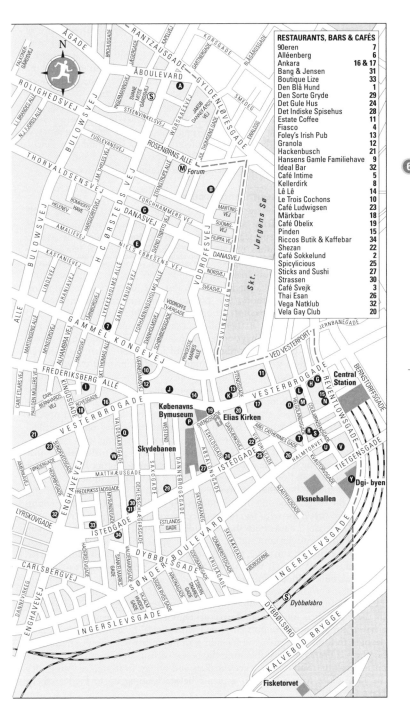

RESTAURANTS, BARS & CAFÉS	
90eren	7
Alléenberg	6
Ankara	16 & 17
Bang & Jensen	31
Boutique Lize	33
Den Blå Hund	1
Den Sorte Gryde	29
Det Gule Hus	24
Det Indiske Spisehus	28
Estate Coffee	11
Fiasco	4
Foley's Irish Pub	13
Granola	12
Hackenbusch	21
Hansens Gamle Familiehave	9
Ideal Bar	32
Café Intime	5
Kellerdirk	8
Lê Lê	14
Le Trois Cochons	10
Café Ludwigsen	23
Märkbar	18
Café Obelix	19
Pinden	15
Riccos Butik & Kaffebar	34
Shezan	22
Café Sokkelund	2
Spicylicious	25
Sticks and Sushi	27
Strassen	30
Café Svejk	3
Thai Esan	26
Vega Natklub	32
Vela Gay Club	20

design, photography, art and fashion, but it's worth popping in irrespective of what's on to admire the light and spacious interior, which preserves most of its original features, including the arched, wood-beamed ceiling typical of market places from the period. Looking west up Sønder Boulevard, you can't miss the bold **trompe l'oeil mural** painted on the side of a building, one of the finest examples of many such modern murals dotted around Vesterbro.

Nestling behind the Øksnehallen and signalled by a distinctive concrete climbing tower on the corner of Tietgensgade, the **DGI-byen** centre (Mon–Thurs 6.30am–midnight, Fri 6.30am–7pm, Sat & Sun 9am–5pm; @www .dgi-byen.dk) offers superb sports and conference facilities, including the fantastic Vandkulturhuset (Swim Centre; see p.228), a top-of-the-range restaurant, and a pricey hotel designed in classic Scandinavian minimalist style (see p.170).

Københavns Bymuseum and around

Fifteen minutes' walk northwest of DGI-byen on Vesterbrogade is the small, triangular **Vesterbros Torv**. Popular in the summer with its outdoor bars and cafés, the square's main feature is the **Elias Kirken**, designed by Martin Nyrop, creator of the Rådhus, in 1908, and exhibiting the same Italian-inspired architecture. A bit further along Vesterbrogade, at no. 59, the **Københavns Bymuseum** (City Museum; daily 10am–4pm; 20kr, free on Fri, closed Tues; @www.bymuseum.dk) is a slightly confusing but interesting introduction to the capital's chaotic history. The fifteenth- and sixteenth-century city is brought to life through reconstructions of ramshackle house exteriors and tradesmen's signs. Looking at these, the subsequent impact of Christian IV's expansive building programmes (see box on p.60) becomes resoundingly apparent, and there's a large room recording the form and cohesion that this monarch and amateur architect gave the city, including a few of his own drawings. The rest of the city's thousand-year history is told by an array of paintings, photos, miniature models of the town, and items from daily life in various periods. Try to catch the free half-hour slide show (in English at 11.15am, 12.45 & 2.15pm), which presents a good, clear introduction to the city's history. Head upstairs for the small room devoted to **Søren Kierkegaard** (see box, opposite), filled with bits and bobs – caricatures of the man himself, furniture from his home, paintings of his girlfriend Regine Olsen, jewellery, books and manuscripts – that form an intriguing footnote to the life of this nineteenth-century Danish writer and philosopher, and one of the most interesting parts of the museum.

The collection is housed in a distinguished building of 1787 that was formerly home to the Royal Shooting Brotherhood; their suitably sumptuous Banqueting Hall on the first floor with its riot of stuccowork angels dates to a renovation of 1896. Outside, it backs onto the brotherhood's old firing range, Skydebanen, now a children's playground and unremarkable apart from its curious back wall, **Skydebanemuren**, a massive, twelve-metre-high red-brick wall adorned with the brotherhood's logo. It was erected in 1887, allegedly to protect passers-by from stray bullets, though rumours suggest that its real purpose was to protect the snobbish brotherhood from the distracting sight of Vesterbro poverty.

Continuing west for a couple of minutes along Vesterbrogade brings you to the right turn into **Værnedamsvej**. Dubbed "Little Paris", this street is a haven for the food connoisseur, lined with speciality shops, many of them devoted to food and drink, and including an impressive selection of traditional butchers, a French bakery (boasting the best croissants in Scandinavia), an ice-cream parlour, fishmongers, cheesemakers and ethnic fruit-and-veg shops. It's the ideal place to put together a picnic before heading up to Frederiksberg Have (see p.107).

The name of **Søren Kierkegaard** is inextricably linked with Copenhagen, yet his championing of individual will over social conventions and his rejection of materialism did little to endear him to his fellow Danes. Born in 1813, Kierkegaard believed himself set on an "evil destiny" – partly the fault of his father, who is best remembered for having cursed God on a Jutland heath. Weighed down by his father's endless lectures on the suffering of Christ and the inevitable misery of the world, the young Kierkegaard developed a morbid, depressive and, at the age of 25, deeply religious, personality. This combination of periodic depressions and religious devotion led him in 1841 to end his engagement to the love of his life, Regine Olsen, for fear of drawing her into his melancholy and himself away from God. The resulting emotional trauma saw him flee to Berlin where he turned feverishly to writing, with the publication in 1843 of his first book *Either/Or* – a philosophical examination of the conflicting emotions of his doomed love affair – and a concerted writing spell that lasted ten years. Few people understood *Either/Or* with its discussion of the two worlds – the "aesthetic" (man's love of the bodily, sensory, material world and all its sins) and the "ethical" (man's relationship with the spiritual and eternal) – and the individual's resulting "dread" or angst at trying to reconcile the two. Kierkegaard, however, came to revel in the enigma he had created, becoming a "walking mystery in the streets of Copenhagen" (he lived in a house on Nytorv). He was a prolific author, sometimes publishing two books on the same day, and often writing under pseudonyms. His greatest philosophical works, *Either/Or, The Concept of Dread* and *Fear and Trembling*, were written by 1846 and are often claimed to have laid the foundations of **existentialism**. Kierkegaard died in 1855, emotionally exhausted by his various quarrels with rival philosophers, writers and the Church itself; it was to be another sixty years before his work gained international recognition.

Carlsberg Brewery Visitor Centre

It's a twenty-minute walk west from Værnedamsvej along Vesterbrogade, then left along Pile Allé, to the **Carlsberg Brewery Visitor Centre** at Gamle Carlsberg Vej 11 (Tues–Sun 10am–4pm; 40kr; ⊛www.visitcarlsberg.dk). Carlsberg sadly no longer offers tours of the brewery itself, whose low hum and pungent whiffs pervade the air, having replaced them with this decidedly less inspiring multimedia centre. The exhibition, in an old brewhouse dating to 1906, kicks off with the world's largest collection of beer bottles from around

△ Carlsberg Brewery

the globe, before a detailed tour takes you through the history of beer-brewing in Denmark from the Bronze Age – Egtved Girl (see p.97) had a small pot at her feet containing the first known Danish beer – and the role of beer in Danish social history with juicy tales including Christian IV's legendary benders. It then moves on to the story of the founder, brewer Jacobsen, and Carlsberg itself, complete with models of old workers' quarters, tableaux demonstrating the brewing process, and old brewing machinery, all accompanied by a plethora of videos, photos and diagrams. It's not nearly as exciting as a noisy brewery in full action, though Carlsberg have at least retained the tradition of handing out beer in the bar at the end of your visit, overlooking the new fully operational Jacobsen Microbrewery – always the busiest part of the centre.

While you're in the vicinity, have a look at the wonderful **Elephant Gate** behind the visitor centre on Ny Carlsberg Vej: four elephants carved in granite supporting the building that spans the road. Just before the gate, on the right in brewery founder Jacobsen's old house, is the decidedly less popular **Carlsberg Museum** (Mon–Fri 10am–3pm; free), not surprising given its alarmingly scientific panels detailing the complicated chemical equations involved in the brewing process and research into how to get the perfect head of foam. The assortment of old advertising campaigns makes for lighter entertainment, and there's a section on various countries' per capita Carlsberg consumption – Germany has the highest.

Frederiksberg

"A city within the city" is how the residents **FREDERIKSBERG** like to describe their independent district. Positioned between the districts of Vesterbro and Nørrebro, it covers a large area – almost twice the size of Indre By – and, with its own industry, shopping streets, city hall, and now also a much-needed metro station, tries to be completely self-contained. Away from the main roads you'll find street after street of the district's distinctively grand **villas**, quite unlike the apartment blocks characteristic of residential areas in other parts of the city. The first

Carlsberg: The pursuit of the perfect pint

Danes have been knocking back **Carlsberg beer** since the mid-nineteenth century when J.C. Jacobsen, a young Copenhagen brewer, established a brewery on a hill at Valby calling it Carlsberg (Carl's hill) after his son. Using Bavarian-style brewing techniques it was a runaway success, prompting young Carl to set up his own brewery "New Carlsberg" in 1871. Ahead of his time, J.C. set great store by scientific research as the basis for improving production, setting up a research laboratory in 1875 and expressing his overall aims for the company in a mission statement entitled "The Golden Words" that went so far as to make profit a secondary consideration to the quest for the perfect pint. As the two breweries prospered and the money flowed in, both father and son sought to use their wealth for the greater good: J.C. through the Carlsberg Foundation that funded and supported Danish scientific research; Carl, with his more artistic leanings, through the **New Carlsberg Foundation**, among whose achievements was the establishment in 1897 of the sculpture and art museum, the Ny Carlsberg Glyptotek (see p.94), which the foundation still runs today. This munificence wasn't just a glorified PR exercise, since the Carlsbergs extended their social principles to their workforce; in a time when there was no social security, Carlsberg employees received medical aid and pensions, as well as additional perks such as annual balls and picnics and, of course, a daily beer ration. Carlsberg merged with the other Danish beer giant Tuborg in 1970, becoming Carlsberg A/S, whose brands are drunk all over the world but with only seven percent of its sales in Denmark.

one was erected in 1846, and between them they represent the work of some of Denmark's most distinguished architects, from Functionalists to Neoclassicists.

Frederiksberg Allé and Runddel

Just beyond Københavns Bymuseum (see p.104), **Frederiksberg Allé** branches off Vesterbrogade to the right. Sloping gently and lined with rows of trees, this long, wide boulevard was originally built by Frederik IV as a private road to his summer residence, Frederiksberg Slot, and even today along its grand length you'll find an impressive array of old apartment buildings and a number of theatres. At **Frederiksberg Runddel** (Circus) the road joins Pile Allé and Allégade and becomes the main entrance to Frederiksberg Have. Look out on the left for the **Frederiksberg Kirke** – a delightful, ivy-clad, 1734 octagonal church built by Dutch farmers coerced here by Christian II to grow vegetables and care for the royal livestock.

As well as being transformed into an open-air ice-skating rink in winter, the *runddel* is home to two eclectic collections. First up, immediately on the left, is the entertaining **Storm P. Museet** (May–Oct Tues–Sun 10am–4pm; Nov–April Wed, Sat & Sun 10am–4pm; 30kr; ⊛www.stormp-museet.dk), packed with the satirical cartoons that made "Storm P" (Robert Storm Petersen) one of the most popular by-lines in Danish newspapers during the 1920s, as well as his enormous collection of pipes, and other personal effects. Even if the humour is not to your taste, you'll leave the museum with an insight into what the Danes, at least in the early part of the last century, found amusing. A video in English gives some background on the man's work.

A short walk along Allégade, at no. 5 is the **Danske Revymuseet** (Danish Revue Museum; Tues–Sun 11am–4pm; 35kr; ⊛www.revymuseet.dk). With hardly any English labelling, you'll have to be a bit of a devotee of revue theatre to get much out of the collection of pictures, theatrical props, costumes, posters, programmes and other artefacts associated with the entertainers who used to amuse – and ridicule – rich city folks on their weekend outings to the Frederiksberg countryside.

Pile Allé and Allégade

From Frederiksberg Runddel, you can either head straight into Frederiksberg Have (see overleaf) or strike off to the south or north depending on your time and tastes. **Pile Allé**, the road heading south of Frederiksberg Runddel, is famous for the many small, ornate gardens that line its western side, collectively known as **Danske Haveselskabs Have** (10am–sunset; free) and base of the Danish Horticultural Society; the entrance is through the white gate on the left hand side of the *runddel*. The formally laid out gardens are stuffed with a mishmash of amazing plant environments, the odd peacock strutting about to complete the picture, and make a pretty setting for the jazz concerts hosted here during summer. Further along Pile Allé, amidst a few so-called "family gardens" – popular restaurants formerly catering for palace staff, these days renowned for their sublime traditional Danish lunches accompanied by the obligatory snaps (see "Eating", p.187, for recommendations) – is the **maze**, shaped in the form of a Tuborg beer label. There are great views of Frederiksberg Slot from hereabouts.

The road heading north from the *runddel* is **Allégade**, the original main street of the now vanished village of Ny Amager, which housed Dutch immigrant farmers in the seventeenth century. It leads to Gammel Kongevej – Christian IV's main road to Frederiksberg Slot, replaced by Frederiksberg Allé a hundred years later – and Frederiksberg Rådhus, on the corner of Smallegade. One of the city's biggest and most colourful flea markets takes place in the car park behind the Rådhus on Saturdays from May to October. From the Rådhus it's just a fifteen-minute walk up Smallegade to the Royal Copenhagen Porcelain Visitor Centre (see opposite), though you might prefer to take the more scenic route through the park.

Frederiksberg Have and Frederiksberg Slot

From the main entrance on Frederiksberg Runddel, the expansive English-style gardens of **Frederiksberg Have** (daily 6am–sunset; free) stretch north toward Smallegade and south towards Frederiksberg Slot amidst a network of pathways, lakes and canals that criss-cross the beautiful lime-tree groves. Throughout the eighteenth century, the city's top nobs came here to mess about in boats, though nowadays you'll have to settle for one of the tours in the large, manned rowing boats that depart regularly from in front of Frederiksberg Slot. The grassy slopes, ponds and fountains attract hordes of picnicking locals in summer, especially when the park becomes a regular venue for live music and theatre. Romantic follies, temples and grottoes abound; look out for the colourful **Chinese Folly** (June–Aug Sun 2–4pm) on one of the park's picturesque islands – it was built in 1799 and used for Frederik VI's tea parties – and the Neoclassical **Temple of Apis**, west of the palace near the zoo, dating from 1804 – and despite the twentieth-century graffiti, a real architectural gem.

At their southern end, the gardens take on a distinctly more ordered, French-inspired look as they slope up to the pale yellow **Frederiksberg Slot**; the castle and its immediate environs are all that remain of the original Baroque style of the park, the rest having been transformed, according to the latest fashions, into English romantic style in the late 1700s. The *slot* (guided tours Jan–May & Aug–Nov on the last Sat of the month at 11am & 1pm; 25kr) was built by Frederik IV in the early eighteenth century on top of Valby Bakke hill, from where it would originally have commanded an uninterrupted view of the city ramparts and the Swedish coastline. Extended many times since, it acquired its present shape under Christian VI in 1735, and was the royal family's summer residence until the mid-1800s, when it was taken over by the Danish Officers' Academy. It's worth joining a guided tour to see the evocative interior, with its imposing stucco work and ceiling paintings, along with the secret passageway leading down to an enormous marble bathtub (supposedly a secret meeting place of Princess Caroline Mathilde and her lover Count Struensee) and the black-and-white chequered kitchen, where she used to make pancakes. Have a look, too, at the exquisitely fashioned Baroque decorations in the adjacent palace chapel.

To the south of the *slot*, across Roskildevej, **Søndermarken** is a further sprawling expanse of greenery, equal in size to Frederiksberg Have, though much less rigorously landscaped. It's another of the city's regular summer venues for concerts. The strange glass pyramid structure unceremoniously plonked on the left of the lawn is the opening to the rather atmospheric if bizarre **Cisternerne: Museet for Moderne Glaskunst** (Cisternerne: Museum of Modern Glass Art; Feb–Nov Thurs & Fri 2–6pm, Sat & Sun 11am–5pm; 40kr; ⓦwww.cisternerne.dk) – an underground exhibition of stained-glass works set in the damp environs of the former water cisterns.

Copenhagen Zoo

Bordering the southwest corner of Frederiksberg Have, next to Frederiskberg Slot, is **Copenhagen Zoo** (March Mon–Fri 9am–4pm, Sat & Sun 9am–5pm; April, May & Sept Mon–Fri 9am–5pm, Sat & Sun 9am–6pm; beginning to mid-June & mid to end-Aug daily 9am–6pm; end of June to mid-Aug daily 9am–10pm; Oct daily 9am–5pm; Nov–Feb daily 9am–4pm; 100kr; ⓦwww.zoo.dk), one of the oldest and largest in Europe, with over 2500 animals. The zoo tries to keep its animals in enclosures that reproduce their natural environments as closely as possible – their reputable breeding results testify to their success. That said, it's still rather depressing watching the huge bears and big cats pacing around their compounds, though the African savannah area in the section south of Roskildevej is a more uplifting, open-plan affair with giraffes, impala and okapi looking a little more at home. The zoo's latest star attractions are two Tasmanian Devils, a gift from the Australian government to Crown Prince Frederik and his Tasmanian born wife Mary, though the classy elephant enclosure, being designed by Norman Foster and due to open in 2008, should be another highlight. The zoo also has a special **children's section** where kids can touch domestic animals such as goats, sheep, cows and horses (see p.235).

Bakkehus Museet

Southeast of Frederiksberg Have, just north of the Carlsberg Visitor Centre, at Rahbeks Allé 28, the **Bakkehus Museet** (Bakkehus Museum; Wed, Thurs, Sat & Sun 11am–3pm; 10kr; ⊛www.bakkehusmuseet.dk) is located in what is claimed to be the oldest house in Frederiksberg, dating from the seventeenth century. The museum provides a charming insight into the literary milieu of Denmark's Golden Age; the Rahbæk family – Knud Lyhne Rahbæk, critic, writer and manager of the Royal Theatre and his wife Kamma – lived here from 1802 to 1830, hosting a popular salon for Danish literary personalities such as Hans Christian Andersen and Adam Oehlenschläger (author of the Danish national anthem), who were frequent guests. The peaceful museum preserves the house more or less as the Rahbæks left it, with period furniture, various portraits, personal effects and publications dating to the time. Look out for Rahbæk's study, with his diary open on the desk and, in Kamma's delightfully cosy corner room, papier-mâché replicas of the cakes served at the famous salon. Unfortunately, there's no labelling in English, but the very helpful curator is always willing to answer any questions you might have. The recently restored kitchen leads through to a succession of rooms given over to almost two hundred tiny portraits of the Danish high and mighty who flocked to Paris from the 1790s onwards to have their profiles immortalized by French portrait artist Gilles Louis Chrétien. In a continuation of the literary traditions of the house, the upstairs apartment is let to a struggling poet of the moment, who gets to live here rent-free for four years.

Royal Copenhagen Porcelain Visitor Centre

The only real attraction on the northern side of the park is the **Royal Copenhagen Porcelain Visitor Centre** at Søndre Fasanvej 5 (Mon–Fri 9am–4pm; 40kr; ⊛www.royalcopenhagen.com), founded by Dowager Queen Juliane Marie in 1775. Two unique types of porcelain design have made the factory world famous: "Flora Danica", a multi-coloured wildflower pattern – no two pieces are the same – and "Musselmalet", with blue decorations based on Meissen models. The factory has since moved to its current site in Glostrup, but the visitor centre that has taken its place features two surprisingly interesting short films that tell the history of the world-famous porcelain and, more importantly, detail the painfully delicate process of making both Flora Danica and Musselmalet, showing the way the porcelain is shaped, fired, hand painted, re-fired and repainted (sometimes with gold). There are also three factory workers at the ready who, thanks to their skilful techniques and years of practice – make porcelain painting look easy; until you have a go yourself, that is, which they're more than happy to let you. If you're inspired to take home a piece of this pricey porcelain, check out the attached **factory shop** (Mon–Fri 9am–5.30pm, Sat 9am–2pm) where it's sold at reduced prices, though many will still find 1000kr for a cup and saucer beyond the bounds of reason.

Nørrebro and
Østerbro

To the north and east of the city centre are the districts of **Nørrebro** and **Østerbro** (North Bridge and East Bridge), built up in the mid-nineteenth century after the devastation of the British bombardments in 1801 and 1807, when the city's old defences – by now deemed pretty useless – were abolished and the land outside the old ramparts opened up to house the ever-increasing population. Their similar age apart, the two districts have deeply contrasting histories: Nørrebro's is one of deprivation and social struggle followed by more recent immigration, gentrification and today's almost Parisian feel; Østerbro's is one of traditional wealth and privilege – hence the rather smug feel of the district today, though its leafy ambience makes it a pleasant enough place.

Nørrebro is served by buses #5A and #350S, which head up Nørrebrogade, from Nørreport station, past the Assistents Kirkegård. Bus #3A crosses Nørrebrogade at Elmegade and continues east past Sankt Hans Torv and the Politihistorisk Museum to Østerbro via Rigshospitalet and Nordre Frihavnsvej, ending at Nordhavn station. Østerbro's two other stations – Østerport, to the south, and Svanemøllen, to the north – are used by both the regional and S-Tog trains; the line runs roughly parallel with the coast and with Østerbrogade to the west. Buses #1A and #14 ply Østerbrogade past Fælledparken, Parken Stadium and the Experimentarium. The western side of Fælledparken, and the Zoologisk Museum, is reached by bus #150S.

Nørrebro

Working-class **NØRREBRO** is synonymous with Copenhagen at its most rebellious. As the city expanded beyond the old ramparts, huge slum tenements began to spring up to house Copenhagen's newly industrialized working class, and by the end of the nineteenth century, Nørrebro had established itself as one of the country's most politicized areas – local residents were later instrumental in forming both the Danish trade union movement and the Social Democratic Party, Denmark's biggest political party.

Nørrebro's resilience was expressed in more dangerous circumstances when local residents led the fight against the Nazis during World War II – you can see pictures of them on the barricades at the Frihedsmuseet (see p.85). The immediate postwar period was rather quiet, but by the 1960s Nørrebro

The Danes are well known for their political and social tolerance, but in the 1980s the activities of a radical squatting movement, the **BZ** (a shortening of the Danish word *beseat*, meaning "to occupy"), led to massive and violent street confrontations with the authorities. Based mainly in Nørrebro – then a very run-down area – the BZ's initial aim, apart from alleviating a chronic housing shortage, was to establish an autonomous youth centre outside the control of the city council. After gaining wide-spread public support, they were given Ungdomshuset (literally "The Youth House"). Even so, increasing confrontation followed, particularly during the eviction of a large squat in Ryesgade in 1985, when thousands of police – the country's biggest ever peacetime deployment – faced down a large group of squatters armed with petrol bombs and sticks.

The **violence** reached a peak in 1993 when, following Denmark's decision to sign the Maastricht Treaty, the police lost control of an anti-EU protest organized by the BZ on Nørrebrogade. In the ensuing chaos, several officers fired into the crowd and eleven demonstrators were shot – some in the back – in the worst incident of civil violence in Denmark's history. Fortunately, nobody was killed.

Today, BZ lacks the popular support it once had, and Nørrebro now faces new problems, such as the perceived exclusion of immigrants from Danish society. In November 1999, after a number of incidents, a large-scale riot developed along the Blågårdsgade following the threatened expulsion from Denmark of a second-genera-tion Turkish immigrant, during which local youths hurled petrol bombs at the police from hastily erected barricades.

Nowadays, you can be certain that if anything happens in the political arena that invokes a mass public response (the last was Denmark's decision to send troops and equipment to the 2003 war in Iraq), Dronnin Louises Bro – connecting Nørrebro with Indre By – is first port of call for the demonstrators.

residents were again challenging authority, first in anti-Vietnam War protests, later in protesting about local issues such as housing and public parks. By the 1980s, this had transformed into one of Europe's most radical squatting move-ments, the BZ (see box above).

In the 1980s, an influx of immigrants started to arrive in Nørrebro, bringing some much-needed cultural diversity to the city, while large numbers of Danish yuppies have also moved in, taking advantage of low property prices. Their joint arrival has been accompanied by a wonderful mix of markets, ethnic food stores and restaurants, and a vast selection of sometimes pretentiously groovy cafés, bars and clubs.

Skt Hans Torv and Politihistorisk Museum

At the heart of Nørrebro is the small Skt Hans Torv, formerly working class, now transformed into a hub of gentrified Parisian-style cafés and bars. The trendy home of Copenhagen's young and gifted – or at least rich – this was a favourite hangout of Denmark's "dynamic" thirty-something crown prince, Frederik before he got married and started a family.

Just down Fælledvej from Skt Hans Torv is Nørrebro's only – and curiously appro-priate – museum, the **Politihistorisk Museum** (Police History Museum; Tues, Thurs & Sun 11am–4pm; 25kr), a fascinating, if somewhat macabre, document of crime, detection and incarceration, housed in one of the city's first purpose-built police stations – the infamous Station 6. On the ground floor, the exhibits initially focus on the gruesome methods of social control employed in medieval times, as well as the uniforms and brutal cudgels of the city's early nightwatchmen. There

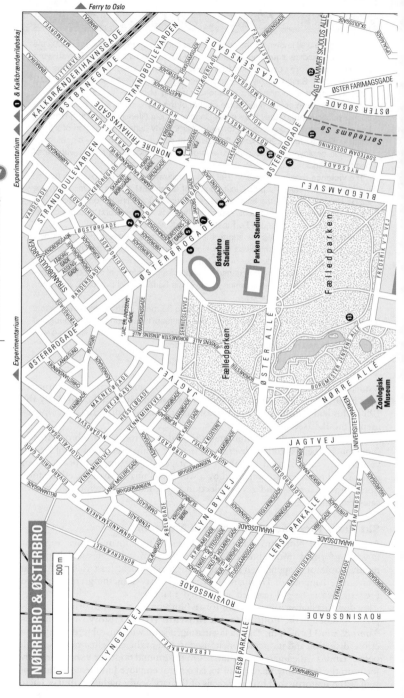

NØRREBRO & ØSTERBRO

500 m

Ferry to Oslo

Experimentarium

Experimentarium

Kalkbrænderiløbskaj

Østerbro
Stadium

Parken Stadium

Fælledparken

Fælledparken

Zoologisk
Museum

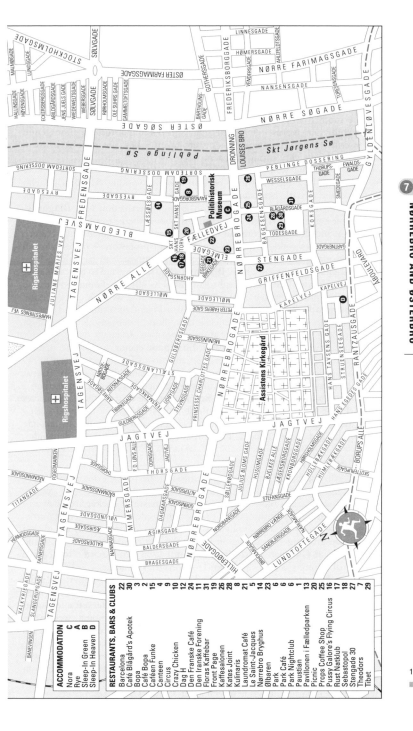

ACCOMMODATION

Nora	C
Rye	A
Sleep-In Green	B
Sleep-In Heaven	D

RESTAURANTS, BARS & CLUBS

Barcelona	22
Café Blågård's Apotek	30
Bopa	3
Café Bopa	2
Caféen Funke	15
Canteen	4
Circus	9
Crazy Chicken	10
Dag H	12
Den Franske Café	24
Den Iranske Forening	11
Floras Kaffebar	31
Front Page	19
Kaffesalonen	26
Nørrebro Bryghus	14
Ølbaren	28
Kates Joint	8
Kulinaris	21
Laundromat Café	5
Le Saint-Jacques	14
Nørrebro Bryghus	23
Park	6
Park Café	6
Park Nightclub	6
Pavillonen i Fælledparken	1
Picnic	13
Props Coffee Shop	20
Paustian	25
Pussy Galore's Flying Circus	16
Rust Natklub	17
Sebastopol	18
Stengade 30	27
Theodors	7
Tibet	29

are grim, old holding cells (in which you can temporarily lock yourself up), and a pair of impressive antique Nimbus police motorbikes, amongst dozens of other exhibits.

The stairwell contains an array of copies of famous artwork, while the second floor is dedicated almost solely to crime and criminals. One room delves into the history of the various facets of the city's once-illegal sex industry – there's a large collection of porn discreetly held in drawers under the display cases – while another concentrates on forgery and smuggling, and a third on murder. Each exhibit here is cross-referenced to drawers holding disturbing photographs of the crime scene from which they were taken – best not to look in them unless you have a very strong stomach.

Back outside, the well-preserved streets around Skt Hans Torv still capture the flavour of how life must have been in this old working-class district, with narrow streets of dark, brick tenements. Heading south from the Politihistorisk Museum down Fælledvej brings you to the large intersection with **Blågårds-gade**, a pleasant, pedestrianized street that is now at the heart of Copenhagen's immigrant and alternative communities, where south Asian and Middle Eastern immigrants rub shoulders with ex-squatters and protestors – there's also an intriguing multicultural blend of inexpensive restaurants and bars along here, and a pleasant tree-fringed square, **Blågårds Plads**, converted to an ice-skating rink during winter (see p.226), and surrounded by alfresco dining spots in the summer. Two other streets, both parallel to Fælledvej, are worth looking out for. **Ravnsborggade** to the southeast has an unusual blend of second-hand – some call it antique – furniture and knick-knack shops, interspersed with Danish designer-clothes shops; a definite Saturday-morning shopping destination for the young and trendy. To the northwest, **Elmegade** stands out with its mass of small, quirky deli-bars, where you can get all sorts of food from eastern European to Japanese sushi as well as plain old organic sandwiches, and, of course, coffee of every type imaginable. If you want a view while you lunch, then a bench in the sun by the **Sortedams Sø** rampart lake further to the east makes an ideal spot. The semicircle of man-made rampart lakes is a favoured outing destination, especially for Sunday-morning strolls, and the numerous lakeside cafés are packed as they struggle to satisfy the never-ending brunch demands.

Assistens Kirkegård

Head northwest from Elmegade, either through the backstreets or up Nørre-brogade, and you'll eventually arrive at the unmistakable, graffiti-covered yellow walls of Copenhagen's most famous cemetery, **Assistens Kirkegård** (dawn to dusk; free). Originally positioned in open countryside outside the city's north-ern gate, the cemetery was founded in 1760 – in an area previously designated for tobacco growing – as a place in which the city's poorer inhabitants could enjoy a decent Christian burial. It wasn't until 1785 that it started to become the eternal resting place of choice for Copenhagen's wealthier gentlefolk.

The Kapelvej entrance, where you'll find an information office with maps, is the best place to start. Close to here (and well signposted) are the cemetery's two most internationally famous graves, those of **Hans Christian Andersen** and **Søren Kierkegaard**, but don't expect anything grand: both graves, though well main-tained, are pretty nondescript. Rather more imposing is the owl-topped tomb of the Bohr family, where Nobel Prize-winning Danish physicist Niels Bohr is interred. Also keep an eye out for the grave of Martin Andersen Nexø, the famous Danish communist and author of *Pelle the Conqueror* (subsequently turned into an Oscar-winning film), and for the "Jazz Corner", where the American musician Ben Webster is buried alongside several lesser-known Danish jazz players.

Assistens' open green spaces offer a welcome respite from the confined streets of Nørrebro, and during the summer many locals can be seen picnicking and sunning themselves (more or less covered) amongst the gravestones – if you want to join them, avoid the garden of remembrance, where the ashes of the departed are scattered over inviting grassy lawns.

Østerbro

Stretching from the fringes of Fælledparken in the west through to the commercial docks, warehouses and wealthy residences along the Øresund coast to the east, the salubrious suburb of **ØSTERBRO** stands in marked contrast to the narrow streets and tenements of Nørrebro. Originally a watering hole full of taverns en route to the hunting grounds of Dyrehaven and the amusements at Bakken (see p.119), Østerbro is nowadays predominantly home to Copenhagen's moneyed classes, who luxuriate in the expensive houses along its coastal fringes. Nearer to the city centre, the district's broad avenues are home to ornate apartment blocks and most of the city's embassies, including that of the US, focal point of many a demonstration. More affordable apartment blocks are tucked away in the residential backstreets connecting main thoroughfare Østerbrogade with Strandboulevarden. This is also where many of the area's quainter cafés are found. Behind Strandboulevarden, across the railway tracks, the Nordhavn harbour area has undergone rapid changes in recent years, from industrial harbour to gentrified office zone with a few exclusive restaurants and lifestyle shops. The ferry to Oslo also departs here – after it was moved from Kvæsthusbroen in the centre to make room for the impending play house – from a funky, glass-covered DFDS terminal that looks almost science-fiction-like at dawn and dusk. Further along the harbourfront, Denmark's most internationally known architect, Jørn Utzon – famous for the Sydney Opera House – has designed a number of buildings, including the Paustian building now housing a fashionable furniture and indoor design boutique and an exclusive restaurant.

Fælledparken and Parken Stadium

At the western edge of Østerbro lie the wide-open spaces and tree-lined avenues of **Fælledparken** (Community Park), an enormously popular swathe of greenery. Originally pastureland for Copenhagen's livestock, and then shooting range for the Danish military, it finally reached its present incarnation in 1906 as a recreational space for the city's workers. The large area is constantly under development with new playgrounds opening or different tree species being planted. It's also long been home to Copenhagen's supposedly best skateboarding rink, and every weekend during summer young – and not so young – semi-serious football enthusiasts meet up on the park lawns to kick a ball about. The latest addition is the Scent Garden – in the southeastern corner near the main entrance at Trianglen, the square where Østerbrogade, Nordre Frihavnsgade and Blegdamsvej meet – developed specifically for visually impaired visitors, and the park also hosts workers' fairs, free live concerts and carnivals (see "Festivals and events", p.230).

On the eastern fringe of Fælledparken is the huge, 41,000 all-seater **Parken Stadium** (ⓦwww.parken.dk). There has been a football stadium on this site for almost a hundred years – five of Copenhagen's football clubs played here at one time – and it's now the home of the Danish national team and FC Copenhagen (usually known as FCK), while big-name acts such as Bruce Springsteen, U2 and Robbie Williams also perform here from time to time. In July, there are one-hour tours of the stadium (Tues & Thurs 11am & 1pm;

△ Fælledparken

40kr) in English and Danish, where you're regaled with anecdotes, shown around the grounds, and told about all the technicalities involved in building and maintaining a stadium this large. Notice especially the massive sliding roof, apparently one of a kind. Next door is the much smaller **Østerbro Stadium**, home to athletics meetings and football team B93 – look out for the splendid entrance on Østerbrogade, topped with bronze figurines engaging in miscellaneous sporting activities. Further details about football matches at Parken and Østerbro are given on p.225.

Zoologisk Museum

The area immediately to the west of Fælledparken is occupied by Copenhagen's main hospital, Rigshospitalet, and by various departments of the university, amongst which is the **Zoologisk Museum** (Zoological Museum; Tues–Sun 11am–5pm; 50kr; ⓦwww.zmuc.dk), in the modern building at Universitetsparken 15 on the fifth floor – look out for the magnificent metallic cockroach on the roof of the entrance made by Kim Olesen. Walk inside, past the stuffed polar bear, and catch the lift up to the museum. First founded in 1622 (and thus the oldest museum in Denmark and one of the oldest in Europe), the collection is curently being restored and expanded.

The present collection is made up mainly of an impressive array of **stuffed animals**, starting with Danish wildlife and moving on through the fauna of rainforests, savannahs, ice floes and deserts: the close-up views of long-deceased exotic animals such as armadillos, anteaters and various apes are educational, if a bit creepy. Particularly impressive are the stuffed elephant seals and walruses, which are immense – as are the skeletons of sperm and Greenland whales. Also look out for the display covering the post ice-age period, with life-size woolly mammoths and ice effects. The museum also has a very popular **children's section** (see p.237).

Experimentarium

Designed to make the sciences more accessible to the masses, **Experimentarium**, sited in the old Tuborg brewery bottling hall on the northeastern edge of Østerbro (Mon & Wed–Fri 9.30am–5pm, Tues 9.30am–9pm, Sat & Sun 11am–5pm; 120kr; ⓦwww.experimentarium.dk), makes for an educational and entertaining few hours, particularly if you've got children (if not, try to visit during a weekday afternoon, as the place tends to get overrun with kids in the mornings). Every six months or so a section of the exhibition changes – check out what's currently happening on their website.

Not strictly a museum, Experimentarium describes itself as a "science centre" where everybody can get a hands-on experience of the physics, biology and chemistry that shape our lives. Most of the exhibits – such as the Emotion Tester, which judges your reaction to pictures of fluffy kittens, naked men/women and sweaty feet – are great fun. There are also lectures giving simple explanations of scientific topics illustrated by down-to-earth experiments using things like bubbles and prisms. Further scientific demonstrations are conducted throughout the museum by guides (called "pilots"), who introduce you to processes ranging from cheese-making to dissection – you can even have a go at cutting up a cow's heart or lung yourself, if the urge takes you.

8

The suburbs

openhagen's suburbs are relatively characterless, though there are a few attractions dotted about here and there, along with a number of surprisingly good beaches and refreshing tracts of open park and woodland within easy reach of the city centre. To the north are the determinedly populist attractions of the **Danmarks Akvarium** and the brash **Bakken** amusement park, along with the cultured **Ordrupgaard** art museum, the idyllic **Frilandsmuseet** and the curious **Grundtvigs Kirke**, commemorating one of the nation's most celebrated priests and scholars. South of the city you'll find the controversial **Arken** museum of modern art, as well as the large island of **Amager**, with its pleasing mixture of beaches, parkland and nature reserve. All the places listed here are fairly easily reached by public transport from central Copenhagen.

Charlottenlund and Danmarks Akvarium

North of the centre, a twenty-minute S-Tog ride on line C or a forty-minute #14 bus ride past some of the country's most expensive real estate brings you to the notoriously snooty suburb of **Charlottenlund**. From the train station – walk up the station concourse and turn right – it's a ten-minute walk through woods to the immaculate lawns and tree-lined avenues of **Charlottenlund Palace** and its gardens – an excellent spot for a picnic. The bus drops you off on Kystvejen in front of the Akvarium, meaning you'll miss the Charlottenlund Palace grounds if you arrive this way. Built for, and named after, Christian VI's sister Charlotte Amalie in 1731, the palace continued to house numerous royals until 1936, when it was donated to the fish research unit of the Danish Ministry of Agriculture. You can't go into the palace itself, but the gorgeous, leafy gardens (free) are open 24 hours a day.

The white building, a short walk beyond the palace towards the sea, holds the **Danmarks Akvarium** (Danish Aquarium; Feb–April & Sept–Oct 10am–5pm; May–Aug 10am–6pm; Nov–Jan 10am–4pm; 85kr; @www .danmarks-akvarium.dk), home to over three hundred species of fish, plus crocodiles, turtles, frogs and a tank of mudskippers – remarkable creatures, half-fish, half-reptile, which hop between land and water (the bigger ones sometimes hop straight out of their tank into the crocodile pool below, never to return). The tropical collection is an exotic and enticing blend of colourful creatures and rare corals, along with some sharks and a vicious-looking shoal of piranhas, which you can watch being fed at 2pm on Wednesday, Saturday and Sunday. Look out, too, for the coelacanth preserved in alcohol – a mysterious, prehistoric-looking fish thought to have been extinct for sixty million years until a live specimen was netted in the Indian Ocean in 1938; further examples have continued to turn up occasionally off the coast of southern and eastern Africa. In a designated children's area (weekends and holidays 11am–4pm) to the right behind reception, there are three touch pools where you're allowed to handle native marine animals such as hermit crabs, plaice, shrimp and sea anemones. Marine biology students are on hand to answer questions about the animals' habitats and ecology.

Continuing towards the sea from the aquarium past the popular *Jorden Rundt Café* (see p.191), you arrive at a stretch of lawn leading to a small sandy **beach**. On hot days, you can hardly move here for exposed flesh, and even in winter some hardy souls like to take a dip in the Sound. On the left of the beach there's a small private bathing pier (Søbadet; June–Aug 9am–7pm; 20kr) with showers, toilets and a café. Note that an enclosed section of Søbadet is divided into male and female nudist bathing areas. To the right of Søbadet are the remains of **Charlottenlund Fort**, Copenhagen's most northerly fortification from 1888, closed down in 1932, and now, with its few abandoned cannons and magnificent views over the city and out to sea, part of the excellent *Charlottenlund Fort* campsite (see p.174).

Klampenborg and Bakken

If you continue northwards on bus #14 or take the C-line S-Tog to its last stop, you reach the wealthy suburb of **Klampenborg**. Turning right out of the station brings you to the attractive and very popular **Bellevue Beach** – nudists to the left when facing the sea – the preferred spot for Copenhagen's poseurs, where beautiful young things lounge around on the sand pretending to read French existential novels.

Turn left out of the station and walk for ten minutes through Dyrehaven woods (see below) to reach the **Bakken** amusement park (July to mid-Aug daily noon–midnight; March–June & mid-Aug to mid-Sept Mon–Fri 2pm–midnight, Sat 1pm–midnight, Sun noon–midnight; pass for all 34 rides 199kr; ⓦwww.bakken.dk). Compared to the supposedly genteel Tivoli, Bakken is a strictly blue-collar affair, with dozens of brash beer halls, cheap restaurants and fairground rides whose colourful trashiness provides a welcome contrast to the staid atmosphere of many of Copenhagen's other attractions. It also boasts about being the oldest surviving amusement park in the world – a claim the park's antiquated wooden roller coaster would seem to bear out. The third weekend of March, when Bakken opens for the new season, is a big annual event, with Copenhageners congregating en masse to sample the latest attractions, and a mass rally of city bikers turning up to mark the occasion.

Almost entirely surrounding Bakken is the enormous **Dyrehaven** (Deer Park), a former royal hunting ground that is still home to large numbers of deer and whose ancient oak and beech woods (up to 300 years old) are a wonderful spot for walking, picnicking and relaxing. In the middle of the park, and at its highest point, is a unique Rococo hunting lodge, Eremitagen (closed to the public), built in 1736 by Christian VI. Designed by Laurids de Thurah – also known for his contributions to Frederiksberg Slot (see p.108) and the first Christiansborg (see p.43) – this is considered his masterpiece and worth taking a few minutes to appreciate. Today, it's still occasionally used by the royals to impress foreign dignitaries. Strolling back towards Klampenborg along Christianholmsvej, a left turn at the *Peter Lieps Hus* restaurant (see p.192) gives superb views over the Øresund. If you head in the opposite direction from the restaurant, following the edge of Dyrehaven west on Klampenborgvej, or alternatively taking bus #388 towards Lyngby, you reach the art museum at

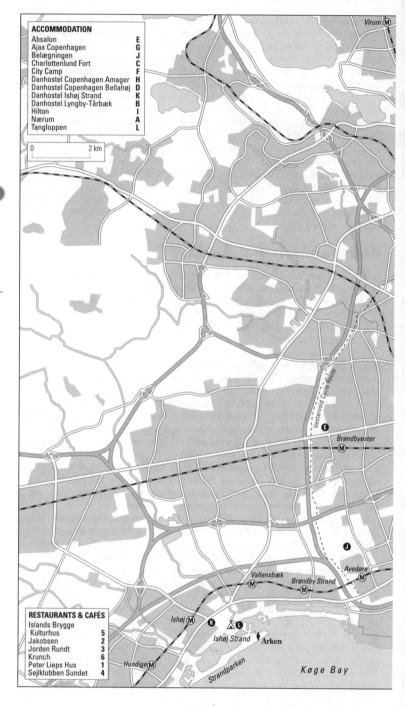

ACCOMMODATION
Absalon   E
Ajax Copenhagen   G
Belægningen   J
Charlottenlund Fort   C
City Camp   F
Danhostel Copenhagen Amager   H
Danhostel Copenhagen Bellahøj   D
Danhostel Ishøj Strand   K
Danhostel Lyngby-Tårbæk   B
Hilton   I
Nærum   A
Tangloppen   L

0   2 km

RESTAURANTS & CAFÉS
Islands Brygge
 Kulturhus   5
Jakobsen   2
Jorden Rundt   3
Krunch   6
Peter Lieps Hus   1
Sejlklubben Sundet 4

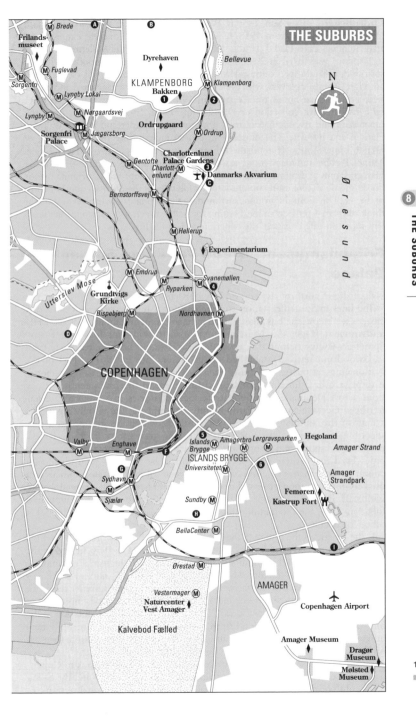

THE SUBURBS

N

Frilands-
museet

Ⓜ Brede   Ⓐ

Ⓑ

Dyrehaven

Bellevue

KLAMPENBORG
Bakken ❶   Ⓜ *Klampenborg*
                        ❷

Ordrupgaard   Ⓜ *Ordrup*

Charlottenlund
Palace Gardens
Gentofte   ❸ Danmarks Akvarium
Ⓜ *Charlott-* Ⓒ
   enlund

Ⓜ *Fuglevad*
Sorgenfri
Ⓜ *Lyngby Lokal*
Lyngby Ⓜ Ⓜ *Nørgaardsvej*
Sorgenfri
Palace   Ⓜ *Jægersborg*

Ⓜ *Bernstorffsvej*

Ⓜ *Hellerup*

◆ *Experimentarium*

Ⓜ *Emdrup*   *Svanemøllen*
            Ⓜ *Ryparken* ❹
Grundtvigs
Kirke
Bispebjerg

Utterslev Mose

Ⓓ   *Nordhavnen* Ⓜ

COPENHAGEN

Valby   *Enghave*
Ⓜ   Ⓜ   Ⓕ Islands ❺
                   Brygge Ⓜ Amagerbro *Lergravsparken*
Ⓖ   ISLANDS BRYGGE Ⓜ   Ⓜ Hegoland
                   Universitetet Ⓜ   ◆
Ⓜ *Sydhavn*   ❻   *Amager Strand*
Ⓜ *Sjælør*   Amager
                   Sundby Ⓜ   Strandpark
                                        Femøren ◆
            Ⓗ   Kastrup Fort ⚔
         BellaCenter Ⓜ

Ⓘ
Ørestad Ⓜ

                                AMAGER
Vestermager Ⓜ
Naturcenter ◆   ✈
Vest Amager   Copenhagen Airport

Kalvebod Fælled

                   Amager Museum ◆
                              Dragør
                              Museum ◆
                        Mølsted ◆
                        Museum

Øresund

❽

THE SUBURBS

Ordrupgaard (Tues–Sun 1–5pm, Wed until 8pm; 65kr; ⊛www.ordrupgaard .dk), a manor house from 1918. A modern, bunker-like concrete extension by Iraqi architect Zaha Hadid (famous for the Mind Zone at the Millennium Dome in London) was added in 2005, which, although blending in smoothly with the surrounding landscape, contrasts sharply with the stately home – it created a stir amongst Danish art lovers, who preferred Ordrupgaard as it was: rural and digni-fied. The original house was donated in 1951 to the Danish State – together with its extensive collection of Danish and French Impressionist art from the nineteenth and twentieth century – by insurance magnet and banker Wilhelm Hansen and his wife. The outstanding display includes the finest collection of French Impressionist art in northern Europe, comprising pieces by Manet, Degas, Monet, Renoir and many more, as well as changing exhibits from the period. The Hansen family's furniture has, to a large extent, been kept in the original manor house, giving an interesting insight into the lifestyles of the Danish country gentry of the day. The beautiful grounds surrounding the buildings – whatever you might think of them – provide an ideal setting for such a fine museum, while the excel-lent museum café enhances the experience even further.

Frilandsmuseet, Brede Værk and Sorgenfri Palace

Half an hour north of the city on bus #184 from Nørreport, or by B or B+ S-Tog lines to Sorgenfri station and then a fifteen-minute walk past Sorgenfri Palace (see below, the bus takes you straight to the main entrance), is the **Fril-andsmuseet** (Open-Air Museum; mid-April to mid-Sept Tues–Sun 10am–5pm; free; ⊛www.natmus.dk), a wonderful mixture of heritage park, city farm and woodland retreat. Established on its present site in 1901 as part of the Nationalmuseet (it had previously been in Kongens Have next to Rosenborg), it displays over a hundred buildings dating back to the seventeenth century from across Denmark, including its former territories in southern Sweden, northern Germany and the Faroe Islands. The office at the entrance provides a map of the lopsided cottages and farmsteads, which are grouped together according to region, and furnished according to various trades – bakers, potters, blacksmiths and so on – offering a vivid picture of how rural commu-nities lived in northern Europe in times past. The museum is involved in a countrywide initiative to conserve Danish breeds of domesticated animals that used to populate the farms, and it also runs a number of well-planned events, with staff in period costume engaging in arts and crafts such as weaving and folk dancing – the programme varies from week to week, so ask at the ticket office for details.

At the far end of the museum, the **Brede Værk** (Industrial Works of Brede) is a large textile mill and factory that operated here from 1831 to 1956, fuelled by the Mølleåen river. Around the mill and factory parts of the industrial community have been preserved – factory workers' cottages, a children's nursery and vege-table allotments. Next to the factory, the mill owner's grand summer residence (tours only; June–Aug Sun noon and 1.30pm; 50kr) gives a good impression of the wealth made by the industry, and "The Cradle of Industry" exhibition in the mill's main factory building (mid April to mid-Sept Tues–Sun 10am–5pm; free) provides a vivid description of the impact of the industrial revolution, focusing on the contrast between the rich mill owners and their workers.

Brede train station is by the entrance to Brede Værk, and to get back to Copen-hagen you can either catch a private train to Jægersborg where B and B+ S-Tog trains continue on to the city centre, or you can make an interesting diversion past the Frilandsmuseet again and south through the park to the splendid **Sorgenfri Palace**, one-time home of Frederik V (now home to Count Christian of Rosenborg and closed to the public). Cross Kongevejen in front of the palace to take S-Tog B or B+ back from Sorgenfri station.

Grundtvigs Kirke and Utterslev Mose

Five kilometres north of the city centre, and fifteen minutes by bus #6A, #66 or #69, is the magnificent yellow-brick **Grundtvigs Kirke** (Mon–Sat 9am–4pm, Thurs until 6pm, Sun noon–4pm winter until 1pm), overlooking the city from the top of Bispebjerg hill. It was designed in 1913 by Peder Vilhelm Jensen-Klint – father to Kaare Klint who is famous for designing the Klint lamp – as a monument to the Danish theologian and pedagogue N.F.S. Grundtvig (see box below). Resembling a kind of enormous church organ, with parallel yellow-brick buttresses running upwards, the church dwarfs the neighbouring housing that was built using similar motifs. Inside, the cavernous, unadorned space and large, high windows provide a suitably reverential atmosphere, with wonderful acoustics and beautiful natural lighting.

About one kilometre west of the church – head along På Berget and then Mosesvinget – is the large lake and park of **Utterslev Mose**, an excellent place for biking, walking, sunbathing and picnics. The park stretches about 3km west to the old outer defences at Husum, where you reach a cycle path that circumnavigates the city, running almost solely through green areas. Maps of the cycle route are available at ⓦwww.dcf.dk.

Arken and Strandparken

Situated 20km southwest of the city centre on a beautiful windswept beach near the working-class suburb of Ishøj is the controversial **Arken** museum of

---

N.F.S. Grundtvig and the Folkehøjskole

Although less well known internationally than his contemporaries Søren Kierkegaard and Hans Christian Andersen, **N.F.S. Grundtvig** left the most indelible mark on Danish history and culture. As a man given to manic bouts of frenzied activity – he is still the most prolific Danish author ever – Grundtvig forged a career as a priest and scholar, developing the grand humanist vision that would go on to shape almost every aspect of Danish cultural and social life. To many, his lasting legacy was the establishment of the uniquely Danish **Folkehøjskole** (People's High School) system, residential colleges for adults offering courses in arts, crafts and, more recently, computers and the media. In these schools, Grundtvig's philosophy of equality, democracy, participation and the pursuit of knowledge was put into practice. The first school opened in 1844, and they soon spread throughout the country and abroad – there are now schools as far afield as the US, India and Nigeria.

One of the main principles of the Folkehøjskole is to provide an education that eschews the usual authoritarian teacher–pupil relationship in favour of shared experience and knowledge. Schools also avoid competitiveness (there are no exams) and vocational training – the aim is to produce rounded human beings rather than good little workers. If you're interested in attending one, contact the International People's College in Helsingør (Montebello Allé 1, 3000 Helsingør ⓣ49 21 33 61, ⓦwww.ipc .dk), one of the few places in Denmark where courses are taught in English. They run a variety of courses varying in length from eight to twenty-two weeks; expect to pay about 1725kr per week – less for the longer courses – including board and lodging.

modern art (Tues & Thurs–Sun 10am–5pm, Wed 10am–9pm; 40kr; ⓦwww. arken.dk). The obscure location – take S-Tog line A, A+, E or EX to Ishøj, and then bus #128 or a 25-minute walk – seems almost wilfully perverse for a museum that aspires to be an internationally recognized showcase for the contemporary arts, but it's worth the trouble of getting there, and you'll also find a fantastic beach right on the museum's doorstep.

It was originally intended to build Arken (The Ark) actually in the sea, though environmental concerns prevented this, and it was finally placed on the seafront instead. The building resembles a beached sailing ship – a striking sight when seen from across the dunes, with its large, white, angled expanses and steel wings. The interior, formed by an intersecting hall and a narrower corridor, is slightly bewildering, and the unusual character of the building and its location can tend to overwhelm the exhibits themselves. The museum is used for temporary exhibitions devoted to modern art and a constantly expanding permanent collection centered on Nordic art post 1990, among them the massive Asger Jorn abstracts by the ticket desk. Check out the steel-and-marble toilets in the basement – a work of art in themselves. On the first floor, there's an excellent restaurant with great views over the bay.

While in the area, take the time to explore a recently developed bit of beachfront – **Strandparken** – running for roughly 7km between the two harbours of Brøndby and Hundige. The ecology of this fabulous man-made stretch of predominantly reclaimed coastline ranges from windblown salt meadow and heather-covered dunes – recently inhabited by large colonies of grey and Canada geese in the winter and tufted duck, merganser, coot and swans in spring and autumn – to artificial islands and fine sandy beaches ideal for summer frolicking. This is also the site of the stunningly located *Tangloppen* campsite (see p.175) halfway along the beach and a few hundred metres from Arken. At the park's eastern end, just behind Brøndby harbour, the Vestervold-kanal runs out into the sea. The canal is all that remains of the city's outer rampart ring from 1888 and continues inland in a semicircle for 14km all the way to Utterslev Mose (see p.123). A cycle path running alongside it provides a great incentive to experience this historic landscape – today a protected conservation area – by pedal power.

Amager

Just southeast of the city centre, and connected to it by a series of lifting bridges, is the large island of **Amager** (pronounced "Ama"). Although within walking distance of the city, the area feels quite separate, and the locals – the so-called "Ama'rkaner" (a play on the word "American") – have a reputation for being rougher and tougher than their "mainland" counterparts. Since the mid-1990s, however, transport developments have linked Amager more closely with the city, and the atmosphere of the island is gradually beginning to change. In particular, the **Øresunds Bridge** (see p.25), connecting Copenhagen – via Kastrup and Copenhagen Airport on Amager – to Malmö in Sweden, has had a dramatic effect, and connecting trains and a new metro network – final stages due for completion in 2007 – mean that a large chunk of Amager is now (or will shortly become) accessible by fast public transport.

Islands Brygge

Crossing Langebro from HC Andersens Boulevard and Rådhuspladsen (bus #5A, #12, #33, #40 or #250S) brings you to the harbour strip of **Islands Brygge**, just south of Christianshavn. Named after the first passenger ferries from Iceland that docked here in the early twentieth century, Islands Brygge was, until the mid-1980s, a working industrial harbour, and off limits to the public; in recent years, though, it has had a complete facelift, and is now one of the most popular places to hang out during hot summer days. Just next to the bridge, the Islands Brygge Harbour Pool (see p.227) attracts crowds during summer and is where **Havneparken** starts – a grassy strip following the coastline for approximately 400m and a pleasant spot to laze in the sun. The first building within Havneparken – moving southwards – is Islands Brygges Kulturhus (see p.203), the local cultural centre hosting bands and entertainment all year round. From the terrace of the centre's laid-back waterfront café/restaurant (see p.191) you can look out across the new developments on Kalvebod Brygge on the opposite bank of Inderhavnen. Continuing south along the promenade lining the harbour's edge, the upside-down hull of an old wooden ferry balancing on two poles provides cover for Havneparken's small stage, and is the park's landmark.

South of Havneparken, still on the waterfront, are some of Copenhagen's most prestigious new residential buildings. Two of these, the Wennberg Silo and the Gemini Residence, right next to each other, are considered architectural masterpieces in the way they have incorporated the former industrial silos of the sites into the buildings, maintaining a rough and powerful industrial look with glass and concrete.

Amager Strandpark

Along the eastern coastline, the newly developed **beach** area known as Amager Strandpark (Ⓦwww.amager-strand.dk) is another of the island's big attractions (Lerparken metro station or bus #12). Over the past three years, this area has undergone some dramatic changes. Previously a quiet, unpretentious beach, Amager Strandpark now encompasses a two-kilometre-long artificial island of beautiful, soft sandy beaches, heaving with people during summer and on a par in popularity with the beaches to the north of the city (see p.119). Facing Sweden across the Øresund and with the Øresunds Bridge to the south, the island's bunker-like, concrete structures housing free toilets and showers also give excellent views. Between the island and Amager "mainland" a shallow laguna has been created, ideal for kids to paddle in, and offering kayaking and other watersports. At the northern end, where Øresundsvej meets Amager Strandvej, an old public bathing pier still remains – Helgoland Søbadeanstalt – where 12kr buys you access to changing rooms, showers and a kiosk. The pier is divided into three sections: a communal section, where swimwear is obligatory, and a male and female section where nudist bathing is the norm.

About 1.5km south along the beaches you reach **Kastrup Fort**, a remnant of the city's fortification from 1886 that never came into use. In the 1930s, the area was handed over to the city as a community park, but during World War II the occupying German army moved in and incarcerated German deserters here – the bullet holes in the concrete walls bear witness to the many executions that took place. Today, the fort is open to the public, though not much of its past is evident, apart from the casemate and some old cannons. There's a good kids' playground, however, and, during summer months, a restaurant (see p.192), plus fantastic views of the Swedish coast, while the botanically inclined will be impressed by the number of rare red horse chestnut trees growing here. Just a few metres south of the fort is a section of the coast called **Femøren** (named after the five-øre coin), where during summer weekends music lovers are drawn in their thousands to inexpensive open-air rock concerts – check the notice board at Use It (see p.371) or Amager Strandpark's website for what's on.

Ørestad

Another new development is the **Ørestad** area, south of the motorway on the way to the airport (Ørestad station). What was, just a couple of years ago, ploughed fields is today northern Europe's biggest shopping mall, the rather ironically named Fields (see p.220), built in anticipation of the seventy thousand or so residents that will soon be calling this area home, and – due to open in 2007 – an exciting **national television centre** (Universitetet metro station). Inspired by a Middle Eastern *kasbah*, the multimedia centre will be divided into four segments, connected by streets and squares, one of which will be an extraordinary sounding 26,000 square-metre amphitheatre-style concert hall, covered in a light-penetrating screen that will be used to show images from within.

Kalvebod Fælled

Amager's other big draw, the enormous **Kalvebod Fælled** nature reserve on the island's western side, is remarkable for its proximity to the city – no other European capital has a reserve of this size so close to its centre. Reclaimed from the sea during World War II in an effort to create work for unemployed Danes who might otherwise have been deported to Germany, it's now home to an amazing number of predatory birds, including kestrels, blue hawks and buzzards. Up until recently, the reserve was a military firing range, and as large areas are still being cleared for potentially explosive debris, it's strongly recommended that you stick to the marked paths.

The **Naturcenter Vestamager**, at the fringe of the reserve, offers free bike rental (call ☎35 52 04 03 to book in advance – a good idea during school holidays) and free camping for two nights in designated campsites. Reaching the centre has become a lot easier with the recent opening of the Vestamager metro station ten minutes' walk away (follow the signboards).

△ Dragør harbour

Dragør

East of Kalvebod Fælled, in the southeastern corner of Amager, lies the atmospheric cobblestoned fishing village of **Dragør** (bus #30 from Råhuspladsen, #350S from Nørreport station), which, until the opening of the Øresunds Bridge a few years ago (see box p.25), was the departure point for ferries to Sweden. It now mainly survives on tourism and the high incomes of its city-commuting inhabitants – properties in Dragør do not come cheap. Apart from meandering around the quaint streets you could check out the, couple of good local history museums in Dragør. The first of these is the summer-only **Dragør Museum** (May–Sept Tues–Sun noon–4pm; 20kr), by Dragør harbour, devoted to the maritime history of the village, from the thirteenth-century herring trade to the arrival of the Dutch in the early sixteenth century. There's also a large display of model ships, navigation instruments, and curios collected by sailors during their travels to distant parts of the world. Docked outside is the *Elisabeth K571* fishing boat, which was used to transport Danish Jews across to Sweden during the World War II (see p. 51); a display inside the museum gives a full account of the event. Also on the harbour is the museum-run warehouse café *Pakhuset* (daily 10am–4pm), which hosts gigs every Saturday during summer and specializes in smoked-herring sandwiches using herring from the traditional smoke house just around the corner. In the centre of the old village on Dr Dichs Plads, **Mølsteds Museum** (May–Aug Sat & Sun noon–4pm; free) displays paintings by local celebrity Christian Mølsted (1862–1930), known for his atmospheric and colourful depictions of the land- and seascapes around Dragør.

Another museum, the **Amager Museum** (May–Sept Tues–Sun noon–4pm; Oct–April Sun noon–4pm; 30kr), at Store Magleby village on the road leading back to Copenhagen (buses #30 or #350S), is housed in two of Amager's old four-winged farmhouses. In the early sixteenth century, Christian II invited a group of farmers from Holland – at the time, a more agriculturally advanced nation than Denmark – to settle here to produce food for the royal household. Twenty-four families arrived, and they and their descendants stayed for three centuries, continuing to live in the Store Magleby and Dragør area and leaving only for their weekly trips to the Amagertorv market in Indre By. Amongst their many achievements they were responsible for introducing the carrot to Denmark. The museum comprises two working farms, complete with livestock and vegetable patches, their interiors kept as they would have been at the time. Museum staff demonstrate how the Dutch grew their crops and kept their animals, as well as explaining the distinctive dress and cultural traditions they introduced to Denmark.

If you manage to time your visit with the last weekend of July, you may want to consider staying for the annual **Dragør Music Festival** (@www .dragoermusikfest.dk), featuring mostly Danish bands (folk as well as rock). It's a good opportunity to experience a real village festival, with lots of great food and a jovial atmosphere. Be warned, however, that you probably won't get much sleep.

9

Out of the city

The area around Copenhagen is steeped in history, with a plethora of castles, museums and sites of natural beauty offering a huge range of opportunities for day-trips or longer stays, and all easily accessible on fast public transport links from Copenhagen's Central Station. Heading **north** up the coast, you can stop off at the **Karen Blixen Museum** or the excellent collection of modern art at **Louisiana**, before continuing on to **Helsingør**, with its magnificent castle of Hamlet fame, from where it's then just a short side-trip to a string of fantastic beaches along the north coast. Nearby, inland, is the grand **Frederiksborg Slot** in the town of Hillerød, while, to the west of the city, is the unmissable ancient Danish capital of **Roskilde**, with its fascinating Viking ship museum. On the coast to the south of Copenhagen, the historic town of **Køge** has a charming medieval centre and long, sandy beaches; to its west lies another former Danish capital, **Ringsted,** rich in medieval ecclesiastical history – a fact attested to by the royal tombs within the town's massive twelfth-century church. Further west, at **Trelleborg**, stand the preserved remains of an excavated Viking fortress. Continuing on across Storebælt via the architecturally stunning tunnel-bridge connecting Zealand and the island of Funen, you come to **Odense**, Denmark's third city and famous as Hans Christian Andersen's birthplace, with two museums devoted to him. The city also offers a number of worthwhile art galleries and museums, as well as excellent restaurants and nightlife.

You needn't confine yourself to Denmark on your day-trips either: the southern Swedish medieval town of **Malmö** is within easy reach across the Øresunds Bridge; once Denmark's most important city after Copenhagen, this historic regional capital has the museum-packed Malmöhus castle as its main attraction, and a pleasant, strollable centre bustling with Copenhageners looking for bargains.

North Zealand and Roskilde

The **coast north of Copenhagen**, as far as Helsingør, rejoices under the tag of the "Danish Riviera", a label that neatly describes its line of tiny one-time fishing hamlets, now inhabited almost exclusively by the wealthy. It's best seen on the hour-long bus journey (#388) north to Helsingør from Klampenborg, itself the last stop on line C or F+ of the S-Tog system. There's also a frequent fifty-minute train service between Copenhagen and Helsingør; it's quicker than the bus, but you won't see much unless you break the journey, since views are obscured by trees almost the entire way. Heading inland from the north coast takes you past Hillerød, home of the stunning Frederiksborg Slot and Museum of National History, precariously positioned across three small islands on an artificial lake. Transport to Hillerød from Helsingør and the north coast is limited to slow regional trains, one line heading south from Gilleleje and one southwest from Helsingør.

West of Copenhagen, the city of **Roskilde** is an easy train ride from the capital. Strategically positioned on the banks of Roskilde Fjord, the former capital's attractions come from both its Viking and royal connections and make a rewarding day-trip.

Karen Blixen Museum

A visit to the **Karen Blixen Museum** (May–Sept Tues–Sun 10am–5pm, Oct–April Wed–Fri 1–4pm, Sat & Sun 11am–4pm; 40kr; ⓦwww .karen-blixen.dk), at Rungsted Strandvej 111, is easily combined with a trip further up the coast to Louisiana and Helsingør. The museum is housed in the family home of the writer who, while long a household name in Denmark for her short stories (often written under the pen name of Isak Dinesen) and outspoken opinions, enjoyed a resurgence of international popularity during the mid-1980s when the film *Out of Africa* – based on her 1937 autobiographical account of running a coffee plantation in Kenya and her love affair with the dashing English hunter Denys Finch-Hatton – won seven Oscars. Often nominated for the Nobel Prize for Literature, she never won it; Ernest Hemingway, on winning the award in 1954, said it should have gone to her.

Blixen lived in the house after her return from Africa in 1931 until her death in 1962, and much of it is maintained as it was during her final years – even if you've never read any of her work, it's hard not to be impressed by the accounts of her spirit, strength and passion, which shine through the museum. Upstairs, a small exhibition describes her eventful life – her father committed suicide and she married the twin brother of the man she loved, among other things – amply illustrated with glamorous photos of her with various celebrities, while exhibits include a collection of first editions and the tiny typewriter she used in Africa. The **living quarters** (timed admission) feature a short film of her life and work, a gallery showing a collection of her paintings and drawings (she was an accomplished artist but dropped out of art school in her late teens) and several rooms with furniture, personal effects and photographs, including several of Denys Finch-Hatton, left as they were when she died. The light-filled study at the end is where she wrote most of her books, surrounded by mementoes of her time in Kenya and with lovely views out to sea. You might find the museum's grounds as interesting as the museum itself. It's backed by delightful woodlands, established as a **bird sanctuary** by Blixen, and is also her final resting place – a simple **grave** beneath a huge beech tree. The ticket office can provide a map of the grounds and you can follow the path back on to Rungstedvej, from where it's just five minutes' walk back to the station.

The closest station is Rungsted Kyst, on the *regionaltog* line, from where it's a fifteen-minute walk to the house – turn left out of the station, right onto Rungstedvej, then right at the harbour, from where the house is signposted – or a short ride on bus #388. Bus #388 also makes the longer ten-kilometre journey from Klampenborg S-Tog station.

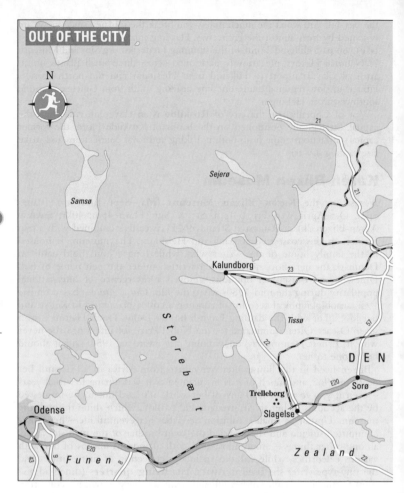

Louisiana

In Humlebæk, a sizeable coastal village three train stops before Helsingør, you'll find **Louisiana** (daily 10am–5pm, Wed until 10pm; 72kr; ⓦwww .louisiana.dk), one of Europe's most intriguing modern-art museums. With its compelling mixture of unusual architecture and outstanding modern art in a memorable natural setting – right on the Øresund coast – it's worth at least half a day's exploration, though be prepared for huge crowds on summer weekends. Most of the displays are permanent, although the museum also hosts excellent temporary exhibitions, plus regular concerts of chamber music and solo recitals, often featuring internationally renowned performers (see their website for more details). The gallery's layout and frequent rearrangement to accommodate the temporary exhibitions can make for some confusion, but the **collection** – divided between the museum buildings

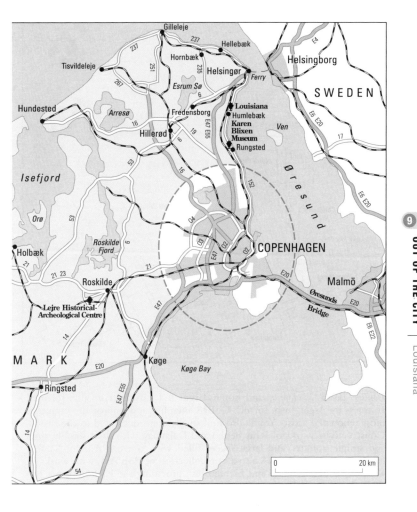

and the sculpture garden outside – reflects most of the important art movements of the twentieth century.

The entrance is through a nineteenth-century villa (built by a man whose three wives were all called Louise, hence the museum's name), beyond which stretches a twisting array of glass corridors, laid out in a roughly circular shape and offering stunning views out over the gardens and sculptures. Start walking clockwise around the gallery, through a section usually given over to temporary exhibits, to reach a light-filled, purpose-built gallery that sets off perfectly the visual impact of **Giacometti**'s gaunt bronze figures – many of his original sketches are here, too. Corridors connect from here with a collection of work by artists of the **CoBrA** movement (named after the cities of Copenhagen, Brussels and Amsterdam), a left-wing collective of artists characterized by their distinctive and colourful abstracts. Here you'll find Henry Heerup's odd wood sculptures, including the bizarre

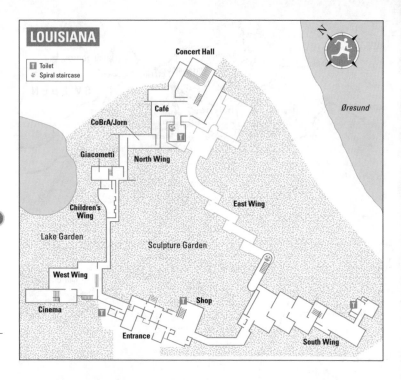

Ironing Board Madonna, and some large and characteristically tortured abstracts by Asger Jorn, former CoBrA member and one of the country's most renowned artists. You'll also find small rooms dedicated to the bright, Constructivist works of Rodchenko and Delaunay, with their straight lines and simple colours, and large spaces filled with German Anselm Kiefer's energetic canvases. There's also a fine collection of **Pop Art**, with works by Warhol, Robert Ryman and Lichtenstein providing the backdrop to Claes Oldenburg's models of oversized cigarette butts and a lunchbox, and Jim Dine's stark *White Bathroom*.

The grounds **outside** are dotted with small copses and carefully tended lawns overlooking an old harbour, scattered amongst which is a fantastic array of world-class sculpture, most of it specifically designed for this site. Here you'll find the strange, flat, abstract sculptures of Alexander Calder rubbing shoulders with Max Ernst's surreal creations, and Henry Moore's dramatic *Bronze Woman* perched on a small hill, with the Øresund and distant Sweden providing a stunning backdrop. Louisiana also has an imaginative **children's wing** where kids can paint and hear stories (see "Kids Copenhagen", p.236). Outside, an adventure playground, designed by renowned Italian nature-artist Alfio Bonnano, features enormous birds' nests and playful houses made of boats.

The gallery is situated at the northern edge of the village, on Gammel Strandvej 13, it's a short signposted walk from the train station or bus #388 stops right outside.

Helsingør

Some 45km north of Copenhagen and just 45 minutes on the *regionaltog* from Copenhagen, **HELSINGØR** is strategically positioned on the four-kilometre strip of water linking the North Sea and the Baltic, facing the Swedish town of Helsingborg on the opposite coast. The town's wealth was founded on the Sound Toll of 1429, which was levied on passing ships right up until the nineteenth century, when shipbuilding restored some of Helsingør's fortunes after the toll was abolished. Today, it's the ferries crossing to and from Sweden that account for most of the town's livelihood, with boatloads of Swedes taking advantage of the easily accessible (and relatively cheap) booze, though the local economy is also significantly bolstered by the many visitors who come each year to see the mighty Kronborg Slot.

Kronborg Slot

Tactically placed on a sandy curl of land extending seawards into the Øresund, the **Kronborg Slot** (April & Oct Tues–Sun 11am–4pm, May–Sept daily 10.30am–5pm, Nov–March Tues–Sun 11am–3pm; 60kr, joint ticket with Handels og Søfartsmuseet 75kr; ⓦwww.kronborg.dk), a fifteen-minute walk from the train station, dominates Helsingør. Famous principally as the setting – under the name of Elsinore Castle – for Shakespeare's *Hamlet*, it's still uncertain whether the playwright actually ever visited Helsingør (see box p.134), but the association endures in Kronborg's thriving trade in *Hamlet* souvenirs and the annual staging of the play in the castle grounds (see p.208 for details)

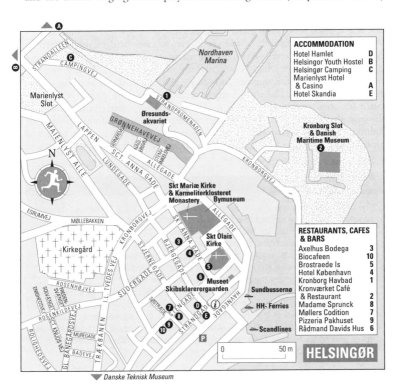

ACCOMMODATION

Hotel Hamlet	D
Helsingør Youth Hostel	B
Helsingør Camping	C
Marienlyst Hotel & Casino	A
Hotel Skandia	E

RESTAURANTS, CAFES & BARS

Axelhus Bodega	3
Biocafeen	10
Brostraede Is	5
Hotel København	4
Kronborg Havbad	1
Kronværket Café & Restaurant	2
Madame Sprunck	8
Møllers Codition	7
Pizzeria Pakhuset	9
Rådman Davids Hus	6

0   50 m

HELSINGØR

Danske Teknisk Museum

– a tradition started in 1816. In 2000, the castle was awarded UNESCO World Heritage Site status and a ten-year project was initiated to restore the building to the height of its glory; be prepared for a little disruption in some rooms due to ongoing restoration work. **Guided tours** of the royal chambers take place in English daily at 2pm, and well-informed attendants also hover in every room ready to answer questions.

Originally constructed in the fifteenth century by **Erik of Pomerania**, the fortress of Krogen was for hundreds of years the key to control of the Øresund (Helsingborg on the other side of the strait was also under Danish rule), enabling the Danish monarchs to extract a toll from every ship that passed through it. During the sixteenth century, **Frederik II** rebuilt (and renamed) the castle as a splendid Renaissance palace with sumptuous interiors, commissioning Dutch architect Antonius Van Opbergen, who took his ideas from the Dutch Renaissance buildings of Antwerp. Upon completion in 1585 it stood in all its grandeur as the largest castle in northern Europe and its international reputation soon caught Shakespeare's ear. However, in 1629, during the reign of Frederik's son, **Christian IV**, the castle was largely destroyed by a massive fire – only the royal chapel survived – and the cost of rebuilding it would have bankrupted the struggling Danish state had Christian IV not doubled the Sound Toll. Christian's castle had lavish Baroque interiors – liberally sprinkled with his distinctive monogram – though he opted to rebuild the exterior to the same Renaissance style. His enjoyment of the castle (supposedly his favourite) was short-lived; only twenty years after the fire, the hapless fortress was bombarded and overrun by the Swedes, who carted off most of its treasures. Over the next three centuries, the castle was largely given over to military use, being deemed too uncomfortable for the royals – in 1924, the military moved out and a major restoration programme began.

Even now, as you enter the castle via a series of gates, bridges, moats, earthen ramparts and brick defences, you get a sense of its former power, with antique cannons pointing menacingly out across the narrow sound. Crossing over the final bridge, you go through the forbidding Dark Gate, to the small forecourt and castle courtyard. The main keep is rather ornate, with plenty of Renaissance features, two spindly towers roofed with green copper jutting out into the usually blustery sky, and another tower providing a fully functioning lighthouse. The **interior** isn't as grand as you might expect: white walls and wood floors long ago replaced the more lavish gilt-leather wall cladding and

Kronborg and Hamlet

The origins of the story of a tragic Danish prince stretch back far beyond Shakespearean times. The earliest mention of a character called **Amled** can be found in a story, derived from Icelandic and Celtic sagas, written around 1200 by one of Bishop Absalon's scribes, a certain Saxo Grammaticus. An Elizabethan version of the Hamlet story, thought to have been written by **Thomas Kyd**, had already appeared on the London stage twenty years before Shakespeare's *Hamlet* was produced in 1602. Quite how the semi-mythical Danish prince and the very real Danish castle became connected isn't entirely clear, though it's probable that Elizabethan England got wind of Kronborg from sailors who had passed through the Øresund, returning with stories of the mist-shrouded fortress that subsequently metamorphosed into Shakespeare's Elsinore. Another vague theory has it that Shakespeare spent part of his so-called lost years, between 1585 and 1592, in Kronborg rather than in Spain as was previously believed.

black-and-white floor tiles, and the furniture, though beautiful, is rather sparse. That said, the rooms are still impressive: the second floor houses the **private apartments**, with the King's Chamber and Queen's Chamber adorned with magnificent fireplaces and fine, circular ceiling paintings. On the third floor, the **ballroom**, at 62m, is the longest hall in northern Europe and a stunning space, though sadly lacking most of its original features. The paintings hanging along its length are from a series commissioned by Christian IV for Rosenborg Slot (see p.78); fourteen splendid tapestries woven in 1590 and part of a series depicting Danish kings once decorated the ballroom during festivities, seven of them are now on display in the **Little Hall**. In the **Corner Room** – part of the guest suite of James VI of Scotland (later James I of England) and his wife, who was Christian IV's sister – you can see the original flooring that was once laid throughout the castle. From here on, it's a lighter, brighter affair in the series of panelled and stuccoed eighteenth-century chambers of Frederik V.

Be sure to see the beautiful **Chapel**, directly across the courtyard from the ticket office: the only part of the castle to survive the fire of 1629, its elaborate and colourful carving, at its zenith in the royal pew opposite the pulpit, gives an idea of the richness of the castle's original Renaissance interiors. An altogether gloomier atmosphere pervades the dark, labyrinthine **casemates** (cellars; guided tours daily noon & 1.30pm) where the body of Holger Danske, a mythical hero from the legends of Charlemagne, is said to lie, ready to wake again when Denmark needs him – although the Viking-style statue depicting the legend detracts somewhat from the cellars' authentic aura of decay. The castle also houses the **Handels og Søfartsmuseet** (Danish Maritime Museum; same hours as the castle; 40kr; joint ticket with Kronborg Slot 75kr; ⓦwww .maritime-museum.dk), a well-displayed jaunt through the history of Danish seafaring up to the modern day domination by the Maersk shipping dynasty, featuring what is reputedly the world's oldest ship's biscuit, ship figureheads of busty Viking maidens, and the usual nautical trinkets and paintings. There are interesting sections on the Sound Toll, the Danish East India Company and the valuable work of the ice-breaking ship *SS Storebjørn* from 1922, whose lovely wood-panelled officers' saloon, complete with table laid for dinner, is a sight to behold. The **coastal batteries**, worth a stroll for some gusty fresh air and views over the Sound, are open from sunrise to sunset.

The town

Helsingør itself is a lively town with a well-preserved **medieval quarter**. At its heart is the bustling pedestrianized main street, **Stengade**, linked by a number of narrow alleyways lined with rickety half-timbered houses, to **Axeltorv**, the town's small market square (markets on Wed, Fri & Sat mornings) and a good spot to linger over a beer. Near the corner of Stengade and Skt Anna Gade is the town's cathedral, the red-brick, copper-spired **Skt Olai's Kirke** (daily: May–Aug 10am–4pm; Sept–April 10am–2pm), extensively remodelled and expanded over the centuries from its humble origins as a Romanesque church founded in 1200. Inside, the white walls set off the run of dark portraits of past rectors, en route to the fussily ornate white and gold altar. Look out, too, for the font, to the left of the entrance, its balusters given by wealthy citizens and engraved with their children's names. Just beyond is the fifteenth-century **Skt Mariæ Kirke** (Mon–Sat 9am–noon, Thurs also 4–6pm) with its pretty red-brick cloister, and the adjacent **Karmeliterklosteret** (guided tour only, summer Mon–Fri at 2pm; 20kr), the best preserved medieval monastery in Scandinavia. Erik of Pomerania gave the site to Carmelite monks in 1430; following the Reformation, in 1541, the monastery was turned into a hospital for the old and poor, during which time it prided itself on its brain opera-tions. The unnerving tools of this profession are still on show next door, at Skt Anna Gade 36, in the **Bymuseum** (Town Museum; daily noon–4pm; 20kr), an otherwise rather dry trawl (no English labelling) through Helsingør's history. You'll get a better sense of what the town was all about at the **Museet Skibsklarerergaarden** (Shipping Agent's House; Mon–Fri noon–4pm, Sat 10am–1pm), on Strandgade 91, a gorgeous eighteenth-century building once occupied by agents responsible for collecting the Sound Toll. The rooms have been reconstructed much as they were during the last days of the toll (it was abolished in 1857) and there's also a shop done out in period style – now selling a motley selection of treats and trinkets – complete with a blackboard chalked up with the names of ships once present in the Sound and the captains who skippered them.

There's not much else to keep you in town; those with kids might want to make the ten-minute walk north of the centre to the harbour at Strandprom-enaden 5, where the **Øresundsakvariet** (Øresund Aquarium; daily: June–Aug 10am–5pm; Sept–May Mon–Fri 10am–4pm, Sat & Sun 10am–5pm; 50kr; ⊛www.oresundsakvariet.ku.dk) is home to a collection of local sea critters, some of which can be approached close up in the "touch basin". A further fifteen minutes' walk northwest out of town (continue to the end of Skt Anna Gade and follow the signs straight ahead), the stately Neoclassical pile of **Marienlyst Slot** (daily noon–4pm; 30kr) was built in the eighteenth century as a royal summer residence – ideally situated to make the most of the cooling sea breezes and stunning views. There's not much to see in the Louis XVI-style interior; the rooms are largely devoid of furniture with just the odd gilt mirror and chandelier to set the tone, but the collection of paintings, most of local seascapes and the brooding Kronborg over the centuries, are wonderfully atmospheric and include a few by Golden Age painter C.W. Eckersberg. You can walk up behind the palace into the hilly gardens (the ticket desk will give you a map) where you'll find a shady glade and a statue marking the supposed site of "Hamlet's Grave". In the other direction out of town, southwest along Kongevejen (bus #805 from the train station, towards Espergæde) is the **Danske Teknisk Museum**, Fabriksvej 25 (Danish Science and Technology Museum; Tues–Sun 10am–5pm; 65kr ⊛www.tekniskmuseum.dk), a huge hangar filled with all manner and vintage of planes, trams, fire engines, cars, steam locomo-tives and the like.

Practicalities

You can pick up a free map from the **tourist office** (third week of June to third week of Aug Mon–Thurs 9am–5pm, Fri 9am–6pm, Sat 10am–3pm; rest of year Mon–Fri 10am–4pm, Sat 10am–1pm; ☎49 21 13 33, ⊛www.visithelsingor .dk), across Strandgade from the train station at Havnepladsen 3. If you want to stay overnight in high season, it's wise to book ahead as it gets very busy and the town has surprisingly few **hotels**. The cheapest option is the *Skandia*, Bramstræde 1 (☎49 21 09 02, ⊛www.hotelskandia.dk; 750kr), which is decent and clean; some rooms have a shared bath. A bit more upmarket is *Hamlet*, Bramstræde 5 (☎49 21 05 91, ⊛www.hotelhamlet.dk; 995kr), a friendly and comfortable three-star with its own restaurant. If you can afford it, head for the resort-style *Marienlyst Hotel and Casino* (☎49 21 40 00, ⊛www.marienlyst .dk), Nordre Strandvej 2, which benefits from a lovely seafront location, and has restaurants, a beach park, spa and pool. You'll pay 1675kr for a standard double (extra 150kr for a sea view) but holiday rates (weekends and school holidays) reduce this by about thirty percent.

The **youth hostel**, *Helsingør Hostel* (☎49 21 16 40, ⊛www.helsingorhostel .dk; Feb–Nov; dorm beds 115kr per person), is literally on the beach – a twenty-minute walk to the north along the coastal road (Nordre Strandvej), or take bus #340 from the station and get off just after the sports stadium. The *Helsingør Camping* **campsite**, at Standalleen 1 (☎49 21 58 56, ⊛www .helsingorcamping.dk), is closer to town and also by a beach, between the main road Lappen (which begins where Skt Anna Gade ends) and the sea.

For **eating**, Stengade offers the full range of fast food, cafés and restaurants; for light lunches or snacks, *Møllers Konditori*, at no. 39, is a lovely old-fashioned bakery and café that's been here since 1855. For something more substantial, there's *Madame Sprunck* at no. 48, an characterful, old timbered building in a tiny courtyard; the cosy café serves up good pasta, burgers and salads, while upstairs is a more formal restaurant (evenings only, ☎49 26 48 49) with meat and fish mains from 192kr. Alternatively, *Pizzeria Pakhuset*, no.26 (☎49 21 10 50), offers excellent, cheap, authentic pizza and pasta. Skip dessert and head off to Brostræde where *Brostræde Is* sells immense home-made **ice creams**.

Away from the centre, *Kronværket Café & Restaurant*, in the castle approaches, is an excellent spot for coffee or lunch (try the sumptuous brunch for 99kr), and an atmospheric place for an evening meal with a three-course gourmet menu for 289kr (book ahead on ☎44 47 73 02). A similarly impressive loca-tion can be found at *Kronborg Havbad*, Strandpromenaden 6 (☎49 20 20 45) – a bright, modern restaurant specializing in fish, and boasting lovely views across the harbour,

Given the proximity of the capital, **nightlife** of note is a rare commodity, but for an evening drink, stroll the streets on either side of Stengade, where there are several decent bars, including *Biocafeen*, Stengade 26, with live music in the evenings, and *Axelhus Bodega*, at Sudergade 27, just off Axeltorv – a friendly, cheap local bar. *Hotel København*, at Skt Anna Gade 17, has a lively atmosphere, good music and a pool table; look for the window stuffed full of beer steins. You'll find a more genteel and relaxed ambience at the cosy, candlelit *Rådmand Davids Hus* on Strandgade 70. Rowdier boozing goes on at the top end of Axeltorv, popular with Swedes taking advantage of Denmark's more liberal licensing laws.

Onwards from Helsingør: the North Zealand coast

An overnight stay in Helsingør or a long day-trip from Copenhagen would allow you to see a little of the beautiful (and very popular in summer) North Zealand coast, which boasts some of the best beaches in Zealand and a clutch of attractive fishing towns. The glorious sandy swathes at **Hellebæk** and **Horn-bæk** (the best option for an overnight stay) are within easy reach of Helsingør, either by bike, local bus or a network of private trains, while the fishing town of **Gilleleje** – just forty minutes by train from Helsingør – is a lovely spot for a fish lunch or dinner.

Hellebæk and Hornbæk

A string of fine beaches can be found simply by following Nordre Strandvej from Helsingør towards the sleepy village of **HELLEBÆK**, some 5km north. At Hellebæk itself, part of the beach is a well-known, if unofficial, venue for nude bathing. Trains from Helsingør stop at Hellebæk and then continue for 7km to the moderately larger **HORNBÆK**, blessed with excellent beaches, sand dunes and fabulous views over the sea towards Kullen, the rocky prom-ontory jutting out from the Swedish coast. Harbour and beaches aside, there's not much to see in the town itself, but there's a lovely pine forest – **Hornbæk Plantage** – bordering the beaches to the east of town, its cool, shady paths a great place for a walk or bike ride. The excellent **tourist office** (mid–June to Aug Mon 1–7pm, Tues & Thurs 1–5pm, Wed & Fri 10am–5pm, Sat 10am–2pm; rest of the year same hours but closed Tues; ☎49 70 47 47, ⊛www.hornbaek. dk), in the library just off the main street, has maps of the forest with trails marked and can advise on cycle hire.

Hornbæk is an attractive, relaxed spot to **stay overnight**. The staff at the tourist office can find you private rooms from 420kr, as well as summer cottages (both for a 20kr booking fee). Or, from mid–June to mid–August, try the homely, farmhouse pension *Ewaldsgården*, (☎49 70 00 82, ⊛www.ewaldsgaarden .dk; 715kr) close to the train station at Johannes Ewalds Vej, and ten minutes' walk from the beach, which has single, double and family rooms. Alternatively, around the corner at Sauntevej 18, *Hotel Bretagne* (☎49 70 16 66, ⊛www .hotelbretagne.dk; 1395kr) has a superb location on Hornbæk's lake and offers charming rooms with a seaside feel (some with shared bathroom). Hornbæk's **campsite** (☎49 70 02 23, ⊛www.camping-hornbaek.dk) is beautifully situ-ated on the edge of Hornbæk Plantage, and is just ten minutes' walk from the beach. For **food**, nothing beats the pricey but delicious fresh fish and seafood from the fish shop *Fiskehuset* (Mon–Fri 9am–5.30pm, Sat & Sun 9am–2pm) on the harbour; there are a few tables outside, but their takeaway menu means you can eat delicious fresh fish anywhere along the beach. If you'd rather something more formal, head for *Restaurant Hansen's Café* (⊛www.hansenscafe.dk) on Havnevej 9, which has bags of olde-worlde charm, great Danish-French cook-ing and outside seating in summer.

Gilleleje

From Hornbæk, trains continue along the coast to **GILLELEJE**, another appealing fishing town that does a roaring tourist trade. The town's beaches aren't the best along the coast, but there's a pretty working **harbour** bristling with boats and lined with restaurants serving the local catch – *Gilleleje Havn Restaurant* does excellent traditional lunches; further along the harbour, *Adam-sen's Fisk*, next to the smokehouse and shop of the same name, is a small kiosk selling a variety of fish-filled rolls for 35kr.

While in Gilleleje, it's worth negotiating at least some of the footpath that runs along the top of the dunes, where, in 1835, **Søren Kierkegaard** took lengthy contemplative walks, later recalling: "I often stood there and reflected over my past life. The force of the sea and the struggle of the elements made me realize how unimportant I was." Ironically, so important has Kierkegaard become that a monument to him now stands on the path bearing his maxim: "Truth in life is to live for an idea." The tourist office has maps of the different routes he used to walk.

Hillerød and around

The inland town of **Hillerød** is forty minutes by S-Tog from Helsingør, and a similar distance from Copenhagen (last stop on S-Tog lines A and E). Hillerød itself is unremarkable but it basks in the glow of the glorious **Frederiksborg Slot**, a castle that, for sheer splendour and romance, comfortably pushes the more famous Kronborg into second place, lying decorously across three small islands within an artificial lake and set within magnificent Baroque gardens.

△ Frederiksborg Slot

Buses #701 and #702 run from the train station to the castle, or it's a twenty-minute walk, following the signs (*Slottet*) through the town centre.

Frederiksborg Slot (daily: April–Oct 10am–5pm; Nov–March 11am–3pm; 60kr; ⊛www.danishcastles.com) was originally the home of Frederik II and birthplace of his son Christian IV, who, at the turn of the seventeenth century, began rebuilding the castle in an unorthodox Dutch Renaissance style. It's the unusual aspects of the design – a prolific use of towers and spires, Gothic arches and flowery window ornamentation – that still stand out, despite the changes wrought by a serious fire in 1859 and subsequent restoration.

Since 1882, the interior has functioned as a **Museum of National History**, largely funded by the Carlsberg brewery magnate Carl Jacobsen, and intended to heighten the nation's sense of history and cultural development. It's a good idea to get an audioguide (20kr) to get the most out of the sixty-odd rooms charting Danish history since 1500. Many are surprisingly free of furniture and household objects, and attention is drawn to the ranks of portraits along the walls – a motley crew of flat-faced kings and thin consorts who between them ruled and misruled Denmark for centuries. A few rooms deserve special mention. **The Rose** (room 19; to the left of the ticket office) has been reconstructed to look as it did in the time of Christian IV, when it served as a dining room, its low vaulted ceiling and imitation gilt-leather creating a lavish yet intimate space. On the first floor, the **chapel**, where Denmark's monarchs were crowned between 1671 and 1840, is exquisite, its vaults, pillars and arches gilded and embellished, and the contrasting black marble of the gallery riddled with gold lettering. The shields, in tiered rows around the chapel, are those of the knights of the Order of the Elephant – an honour begun by the king in the late seventeenth century that continues to the present day (Churchill and Montgomery were recipients but it's now limited to Danish royalty and foreign heads of state). From the chapel, head through room 23 along the Privy Passage to Christian V's **Audience Chamber** (room 24) – the only living quarters from the seventeenth-century to have been preserved and a Baroque triumph of stucco and marble flourishes. The **Great Hall**, above the chapel, is a reconstruction, but this doesn't detract from its beauty. It's bare but for the staggering wall and ceiling decorations: tapestries, wall reliefs, portraits and a glistening black marble fireplace. In Christian IV's day the hall was a ballroom, and the polished floor still tempts you to some fancy footwork as you slide up and down its length.

It's worth setting aside some time for the **Modern Collection** on the third floor – effectively Denmark's national portrait gallery with paintings, busts and photos of more recent royals, politicians, scientists, writers and artists, including Karen Blixen, the explorer Knud Rasmussen, Niels Bohr, and a rather camp and gory self-portrait by Lars Von Trier (on the balcony section). Room 82 is devoted to the current royal family – look out for the portrait of Margrethe II by Andy Warhol.

Away from the often crowded interior, the **Baroque gardens**, on the far side of the lake, are astonishingly intricate in their landscaping, with a cascade of canals and fountains (summer only) and some excellent photogenic views of the castle from their stepped terraces. The quickest way to them is through the narrow **Mint Gate** to the left of the main castle building, which adjoins a roofed-in bridge leading to the King's Wing. From the castle you can take the **footpath** that skirts the lake into town – it's a pretty ten-minute walk to Torvet, Hillerød's main square. In summer, you can also do a thirty-minute trip on the lake aboard the *M/F Frederiksborg* **ferry**, which leaves every half-hour from outside the castle (mid-May to mid-Sept Mon–Sat 11am–5pm, Sun 1–5pm; 20kr).

Practicalities

The **tourist office** is at Møllestræde 9 (mid-June to Aug Mon–Fri 10am–6pm, Sat 10am–3pm; Sept to early June daily 10am–5pm ☎48 24 26 26, ⊛www. hillerodturist.dk), off the main shopping street Slotsgade. For good **food**, you needn't even leave the castle confines: ⅔ *Spisestedet Leonora* (daily 11am–4pm) set in one of the gatehouses, serves fantastic smørrebrød starting at 44kr a piece – one should suffice unless you're really hungry. In the town itself, *Encore Café & Brasserie* on Torvet, the pretty square overlooking the lake, has burgers, salads and sandwiches, as well as delicious cakes, or try *Engelhardt's Café*, in the shopping arcade, Slotsarkaderne, which does good-value sandwiches and light snacks.

There's really no reason to stay overnight unless you want to combine your trip with a visit to Fredensborg Slot (see below). **Accommodation** is limited: the tourist office can arrange **bed and breakfast** for around 150kr per person (25kr booking fee); the other budget option is the *Nordiske Lejerskole og Kursuscenter*, Lejerskolevej 4 (☎48 26 19 86, ⊛www.nordlejr.dk), which has inexpensive private rooms with shared bathrooms as well as dorms (120kr). There's also a **campsite**, 1km south of the centre by the agricultural show-ground at Blytækkervej 18 (☎48 26 48 54, ⊛www.hillerodcamping.dk; Easter to mid-Sept). With a bit more money, you could opt for the recently renovated three-star *Hotel Hillerød*, Milnersvej 41 (☎48 24 08 00, ⊛www.hotelhillerod.dk; 1110kr), south of Hillerød centre, off Roskildevej, and about 2km south of the castle, with bright and clean, if a little characterless, rooms.

Fredensborg Slot

While in Hillerød, it's worth making a detour to a current royal residence – the picturesque **Fredensborg Slot** (July daily 1–4.30pm; guided tours 40kr; joint ticket with the Reserved Garden 60kr) in the small town of Fredensborg (15min on the train towards Helsingør). Built by Frederik IV to commemorate the 1720 Peace Treaty with Sweden, the palace is only open in July, when the queen is away staying at her summer home, Marselisborg, in Århus. During this period there are also guided tours of the so-called **Reserved Garden** next to the palace where you'll find the queen's veggie patch and herb garden, and a grand orangery stuffed with citrus trees, olive trees and the like. The rest of the extensive **Baroque gardens** – grand, seemingly endless, tree-lined avenues radiating out from the palace down to the waters of the beautiful Esrum Sø – are open year round (daily dawn–dusk; free). In the gardens, be sure to see **Normandsalen**, seventy life-size sandstone statues of eighteenth-century Norwegian and Faroese peasant folk arranged in a grassy amphitheatre; the statues on display are replicas of the disintegrating originals carved in 1773 that were intended as an ethnographical record of the various folk costumes of the region. For **food**, head down to the lakeside *Skipperhuset* (May–Oct noon–6pm; book ahead on ☎48 48 17 17) for a beautifully presented traditional Danish lunch; alternatively, it's just a five-minute walk into town, where you'll find several bakeries and cafés.

Roskilde and around

The ancient town of **ROSKILDE**, less than half an hour away by train, was seat of the country's ecclesiastical and royal power from the eleventh to the fifteenth centuries. There's been a community here since prehistoric times, and the Roskilde Fjord later provided a route to the open sea that was used by the Vikings. But it was the arrival of Bishop Absalon in the twelfth century (see box on p.43) that made the place the base of the Danish church – and, as a consequence, the national capital for a while. Roskilde's importance waned after the Reformation, and it came to function mainly as a market for the neighbouring rural communities – much as it does today, as well as serving as dormitory territory for Copenhagen commuters. The ancient centre makes Roskilde one of Denmark's most appealing towns, though in high season, especially, it can be crammed with day-trippers seeking the dual blasts from the past supplied by its royal tombs and Viking boats; while the first week of each July sees a massive influx of visitors when it hosts the **Roskilde Festival** – one of Europe's biggest and most well-known open-air rock events (see p.231).

The Town

The major pointer to the town's former status is the fabulous **Domkirke** (April–Sept Mon–Sat 9am–4.45pm, Sun 12.30–4.45pm; Oct–March Tues–Sat 10am–3.45pm, Sun 12.30–3.45pm; 25kr), burial place of Danish royalty and one of Scandinavia's most important religious sites. The cathedral was originally founded by Bishop Absalon in 1170 on the site of a tenth-century church erected by Harald Bluetooth, and finished during the fourteenth century – although portions have been added right up to the twentieth century. The result is a mishmash of architectural styles, though one that hangs together with surprising neatness. Every square inch seems adorned by some curious mark or etching, but it's the claustrophobic collection of coffins containing the regal remains of twenty-one kings and eighteen queens in four large **royal chapels** that really catches the eye. The most richly endowed of these is that of Christian IV, a previously austere resting place jazzed up – in typical early nineteenth-century Romantic style – with bronze statues, wall-length frescoes and vast paintings of scenes from his reign. A striking contrast is provided by the simple red-brick chapel just outside the cathedral, where Frederik IX was laid to rest in 1972. Try to arrive at the Domkirke just before the hour to see and hear the animated medieval **clock** above the main entrance: a model of Skt Jørgen

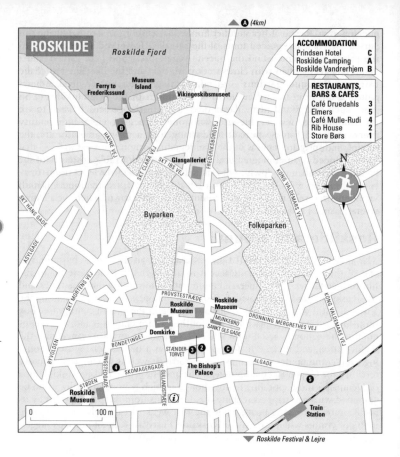

ROSKILDE

Roskilde Fjord

▲ Ⓐ (4km)

ACCOMMODATION
Prindsen Hotel   **C**
Roskilde Camping   **A**
Roskilde Vandrerhjem   **B**

RESTAURANTS, BARS & CAFÉS
Café Druedahls   **3**
Elmers   **5**
Café Mulle-Rudi   **4**
Rib House   **2**
Store Børs   **1**

Ferry to Frederikssund
Museum Island
Vikingeskibsmuseet

Glasgalleriet

Byparken

Folkeparken

N

PROVSTESTRÆDE
Roskilde Museum
Roskilde Museum
Domkirke
MUNKEBRO
SANKT OLS GADE
DRONNING MERGRETHES VEJ
STÆNDER-TORVET
The Bishop's Palace
ALGADE
SKOMAGERGADE
GULLANDSTRÆDE
Roskilde Museum
ⓘ
Train Station

0   100 m

▼ Roskilde Festival & Lejre

9 OUT OF THE CITY | Roskilde and around

gallops forward on his horse to wallop the dragon and the hour is marked by the creature's squeal of death. Upstairs in the Great Hall, a small **Cathedral Museum** (April to mid-June Mon–Fri 11am, 1pm & 2pm, Sat 10am, Sun 1pm & 2pm; mid-June to Sept Mon–Fri every 30min between 11.05am and 2.35pm, Sat every 30min between 9.05am and 11.35am, Sun every 30min between 1.05pm and 3.35pm; Oct–March Tues–Fri noon & 1pm, Sat noon, Sun 1pm & 2pm) provides an engrossing introduction to the Cathedral's colourful history. Ask one of the staff to open up the museum for you.

From one end of the cathedral, the **Arch of Absalon** (a roofed passageway only accessible to the Danish clergy), feeds into the yellow **Bishop's Palace**. The incumbent bishop nowadays confines himself to one wing, while the others have been turned into showplaces for (predominantly) Danish art. The main building houses the **Museet for Samtidskunst** (Museum of Contemporary Art; Tues–Fri 11am–5pm, Sat & Sun noon–4pm; 30kr), whose diverse temporary exhibitions often reflect current trends. The theme continues in the west wing, where the **Palæfløjen** gallery (Tues–Sun noon–4pm; free), run by the local arts society, extends outdoors, turning up a collection of striking sculpture beneath the fruit trees of the bishop's garden. The less compelling **Palace Collections** (mid-May to mid-Sept daily 11am–4pm; mid-Sept to mid-May Sat & Sun 2–4pm; 25kr) are made up of paintings, furniture and other artefacts belonging to the wealthiest Roskilde families of the eighteenth and nineteenth centuries.

The **Roskilde Museum**, close to the cathedral at Skt Ols Gade 18 (daily 11am–4pm; 25kr), is a little more enticing, with strong sections on medieval pottery and toys. Look out for the strange photos that satirist Gustav Wied (who lived in Roskilde for many years and whose rooms are reconstructed here) took of his family. The museum extends to Ringstedgade 6, a shop kitted out in early twentieth-century style, where locals dutifully turn up to buy traditional salted herring and sugar loaves.

More absorbing, and better known, is the excellent **Vikingeskibs Museet** (Viking Ship Museum; daily: May–Sept 9am–5pm, 60kr; Oct–April 10am–4pm, 45kr; @www.vikingeskibsmuseet.dk), set in the green surrounds of Strandengen on the banks of the Roskilde Fjord fifteen minutes' walk north of the centre. The museum is one of the country's finest, with five massive exemplars of grand Viking shipbuilding: a deep-sea trader, a merchant ship, a man-of-war, a ferry and a longship – all retrieved from the bottom of the fjord, where they had been sunk to block invading forces. Together, they give an impressive indication of the Vikings' nautical versatility, their skills in boat-building, and their far-ranging travels to places as various as Paris, Hamburg and North America. The material does a good job of portraying a balanced view of Viking history – they sailed abroad not only to rape and pillage, as much historiography would suggest, but also to find places where they could settle down and farm. Try to catch the film downstairs first (shown in English on request), which goes into fascinating detail about the project to restore the ships, helping to bring the main exhibits alive. In the manicured **grounds** outside the museum, boat-building and sail-making demonstrations take place throughout the year, while during the summer months, you can experience the seaworthiness of the reconstructed ships moored on the fjord – you'll be handed an oar when you board and be expected to pull your weight as a crew member (50min; 50kr).

Whilst in town, take a moment to inspect the **Glasgalleriet**, Vindeboder 1 (Mon–Fri 10am–5.30pm, Sat & Sun noon–4.30pm; free; @www.glasgalleriet .dk), a good little glasswork gallery in the old Roskilde Gasworks building between the harbour and Byparken, the city's central park. This quiet park, offering great vistas to the fjord, was once the stronghold of Viking power – a spot now marked by a hard-to-find plaque and a walking path to town.

Practicalities

Roskilde is only thirty minutes from Copenhagen by train, but if you're heading towards Odense (see p.147), it's convenient enough to **stay** here for the night. *Prindsen Hotel* at Algade 13 (T46 30 91 00, @www.hotelprindsen .dk; 950kr) is comfortable and central; alternatively, there's the well-designed **youth hostel**, *Roskilde Vandrerhjem*, located at the harbour next to the Viking Ship Museum at Vindeboder 7 (T46 35 21 84, @www.danhostel .dk/roskilde), which has dorms (150kr), double rooms (420kr), a communal kitchen and a view of the water. Finally, there's a **campsite**, *Roskilde Camping*, on the wooded edge of the fjord about 4km north of town – an appealing setting that means it gets very crowded at peak times (T46 75 79 96, @www .roskildecamping.dk; early April to mid-Sept); it's linked to the town centre by bus #603 towards Veddelev. For general information or to arrange a private room, call in at Roskilde's central **tourist office** at Gullandstræde 15 (April to late June Mon–Fri 9am–5pm, Sat 10am–1pm; late June to mid-Aug Mon–Fri

9am–6pm, Sat 10am–2pm; mid-Aug to March Mon–Thurs 9am–5pm, Fri 9am–4pm, Sat 10am–1pm; ☎46 31 65 65, ⊛www.visitroskilde.com).

Eating well isn't a problem in Roskilde, with plenty of options for all budgets – most of the restaurants, cafés and pubs are scattered through the maze of streets branching off the Domkirke, with a handful on Skomagergade and Algade, just to the south. Good options include *Café Druedahls*, Skomagergade 40, a modern café offering salads, sandwiches and a wide range of interestingly flavoured teas, and *Rib House*, Djalma Lunds Gaard 8, whose lunch menu of ribs, steaks and burgers is among the city's best deals. On the waterfront at Havnevej 43, and across the docks from the Viking Ship Museum, you'll find *Store Børs*, which does smørrebrød and salmon specials from 78kr. Alternatively, you can rustle up a picnic from the Irma supermarket at 21 Skomagergade, and head for the pleasant little park at the top of the stairs behind the harbour, from where there are good views of the town.

In the evenings, serious party animals head to Copenhagen, but a few spots in the town centre offer less frenetic **entertainment,** including *Elmers,* Heste-torvet 1, a student bar that stays open late, and *Café Mulle-Rudi*, Djalma Lunds Gaard 7, a lively disco.

Lejre Historical-Archeological Centre and Ledreborg Slot

Iron Age Denmark is kept alive and well at the **Lejre Historical-Archeological Centre**, 8km west of Roskilde, by volunteer families who admirably spend the summer living in a reconstructed Iron Age settlement, farming and carrying out domestic chores using implements – and wearing clothes – copied from those of the period. Modern-day visitors are welcome (May–June & early-Aug to mid-Sept Tues–Fri 10am–4pm, Sat & Sun 11am–5pm; July to mid-Aug daily 10am–5pm; 75kr; ⊛www.lejrecenter.dk), and can try their hand at grinding corn or paddling a dugout canoe. The serious academic purpose here is to gain an understanding of family life in Denmark 2500 years ago, but it's fun to visit as a day-trip. To get here, take a local train from Roskilde to the village of Lejre; from Lejre station, bus #233 covers the 4km to the entrance.

If you have time to spare on your way back, get off the bus a few stops before the train station at **Ledreborg Slot** (June & Sept Sun 11am–5pm; July–Aug daily 11am–5pm; 75kr; ⊛www.ledreborgslot.dk), a beautiful eighteenth-century castle with an imaginative French-style landscaped garden, often filled at weekends with Copenhageners soaking up the sun. The Holstein-Ledreborgs still live in the castle, but in the summer it's open to the public, and you can see the paintings, tapestries and furniture, in an interior left more or less as it was 250 years ago.

Central Zealand

South of Roskilde, Zealand becomes decidedly less industrial and features much less on the tourist trail, with a bucolic landscape typified by grassy plains, forests and lakes, and scattered with quaint towns. Among them, **Køge** has a well-preserved medieval centre and fine sandy beaches on the outskirts, while, further west, the settlement of **Ringsted** is one of Zealand's most enjoyable, with a stunning church filled with poignant reminders of the power and influence of the Danish royal court. The Viking ruins at **Trelleborg** are an important ethnographic testament to the fact that the Vikings were more than just marauding pillagers.

Køge

KØGE's medieval cobbled streets hold a laconic charm that make it a popular day-trip, just a 45-minute train ride from the capital, while its sweep of chalk-white beaches, which draw many a Copenhagener on weekends, stretch along the bay to the north and south of the town and are easily reached by bus from the town centre. Saturday is the best day to visit – a variety of free entertainment sweeps through the main streets in the morning, while from noon onwards the harbourside bars are at their liveliest. The hub of the action is the town square, **Torvet**; from the train station, walk along Jernbanegade and turn left into Nørregade. While on Nørregade, you might want to pop into **Køge Museum** at no. 4 (June–Aug Tues–Sun 11am–5pm; Sept–May Mon–Fri 1–5pm, Sat 11am–3pm, Sun 1–5pm; 30kr joint ticket with Køge Art Museum of Sketches), which contains remnants from the town's bloody past – it was a centre for witch burning in medieval times – not least the local executioner's sword, a beheading tool thought to have been wielded frequently on Torvet. Off here, pretty Kirkestræde, lined with sixteenth-century half-timbered houses, leads to **Skt Nikolai Kirke** (mid-June to Aug Mon–Fri 10am–4pm, Sun noon–4pm; Sept to mid-June Mon–Fri 10am–noon), where pirates captured in Køge Bay were hung from the **tower** – it's opened up every half an hour from July to mid-Aug Mon–Fri between 10am and 1.30pm (5kr). On a more aesthetic note, the intriguing **Køge Skitse Samlingen**, Nørregade 29 (Køge Art Museum of Sketches; Tues–Sun 10am–5pm; 30kr joint ticket with Køge Museum, free guided tour every Sun at 2pm; ⊛www.skitsesamlingen.dk), houses drawings, sculptures and models made by important Danish artists of the twentieth century, plus temporary exhibitions of works in progress by both local and international artists. The collection's highlight is Bjørn Nørrgård's colourful preparatory work for the queen's tapestries that liven up the Royal Reception Rooms in Copenhagen's Christiansborg Slot (see p.44).

Søndre Strand **beach** is a few minutes' walk from the train station and can be reached by heading south on Østre Banevej, while the larger beaches at Solrød and Greve offer watersport hire; they're just a few minutes' ride north on the S-Tog.

The **tourist office** (June–Aug Mon–Fri 9am–5pm, Sat 9am–2pm; Sept–May Mon–Fri 9am–5pm, Sat 10am–1pm; ☎56 67 60 01, ⊛www.koegeturist.dk) is on Torvet. If you fancy an overnight **stay**, head next door to the small and comfortable *Centralhotellet* (☎56 65 06 96; 670kr), at Vestergade 3. For a filling meal, *Christiansminde*, Brogade 7, serves tasty specialities such as ostrich and lobster from 138kr, while a few doors down, at no.19, *Hugos Vinkælder* offers libation both day and night in a cosy medieval cellar setting, with dozens of international stouts and bitters on tap, and warm *gløgg* in winter.

Ringsted

Though now little more than a small farming town, **RINGSTED**'s central location ensured it was one of the most important settlements in Zealand from the end of the Viking era until the Reformation, serving as the site of a regional *landsting*, the open-air court where prominent merchants and nobles made the administrative decisions for the province. For over eight hundred years, local life has centred on what is now the town's only significant tourist attraction, the massive and arresting **Skt Bendts Kirke** (May to mid-Sept Mon–Fri 10am–noon & 1–5pm; mid-Sept to April Mon–Fri 1–3pm). Erected in 1170 under the direction of Valdemar I, the church was the final resting place for all Danish monarchs until 1341. Many affluent Zealanders also had themselves buried here, presumably so that their souls could spend eternity in the very best of company. During the seventeenth century, a number of the coffins were opened and the finds are collected in the **Museum Chapel** within the church. Besides the lead slab taken from inside Valdemar I's coffin, there are plaster casts of the skulls of Queen Bengård and Queen Sofia, a collection of coins found in the church and a replica of the Dagmar Cross, discovered when Queen Dagmar's tomb was opened in 1697 – the original is in the Nationalmuseet in Copenhagen (see p.96).

Ringsted is a forty-minute train ride from Copenhagen. You can get a town map from the **tourist office**, at Skt Bendtsgade 6 (mid-June to Aug Mon–Fri 10am–5pm, Sat 9am–2pm; Sept to mid-June Mon–Fri 10am–5pm, Sat 10am–1pm; ☎57 62 66 00, ⊛www.visitringsted.dk). Should you need to **stay** over, you're best off going for one of the doubles (370kr) or dorms (118kr) at the local youth hostel (☎57 61 15 26, ⊛www.amtstuegaarden.dk), set smack in the town centre just across from the church. The tourist office can advise on other options including private rooms (from 150kr per person). For **food**, *Café Aspendos*, Møllegade 11, has late-morning brunches as well as burgers and pasta dishes, while *Café Guldbrand*, Tinggade 12, does specials such as salmon dishes from 60kr and serves food until midnight on weekends. In the evenings, *Løve*, Nørregade 12, once the town's apothecary, is now a lively, classy bar that hosts after-hours dance nights on weekends.

Trelleborg

Just one hour by train from Copenhagen, or thirty minutes from Roskilde, the Viking ruins at **TRELLEBORG** (April–Oct Mon–Thurs and Sat & Sun 10am–5pm; 50kr) are one of Scandinavia's most important historical sites, dating from 980 AD. Located between two rivers on a hilly, seventeen-acre headland, the circular compound of buildings – the most well-preserved of Denmark's four Viking ring fortresses – consisted of a main stronghold and an outer ring wall with four gates, and was intended as much for defence purposes as it was a centre of administration and trade. The sixteen residential longhouses that occupied the land inside the ring were home to four hundred or so Vikings and their families, the bodies of whom rest in the nearby burial grounds, alongside a mass grave containing the remains of some of their would-be attackers. On the way to the ring site from the car park, a large reconstructed longhouse with bulky wooden doors, supporting internal staved timbers and an oven for casting glass, provides a vague sense of what things might have looked like back then. For most of the grounds, however, you'll need to use your imagination: only the outline of the ring buildings' foundations are visible today since the eight thousand oak trunks used for the original stocky constructions and tall fortress walls have long rotted away. The excellent museum here has a scale model of the fortress alongside some of the findings from the site – swords, buckles and a sacrificial burial hole with the elfin skeletons of two children and a goat – with full documentation in English. During July, would-be Vikings from all over the country show up in full Dark Age regalia to take part in lively markets, jousting matches and even a full-on dramatisation of a historic battle scene. To **get there**, take the train to Slagelse, from where bus #312 (free with train ticket) leaves hourly for the ten-minute ride to Trelleborg.

Funen

Squeezed between Zealand and the Danish mainland, 118km west of Copenhagen, the island of **FUNEN** (*Fyn*) is connected to the capital and the rest of Zealand by a state-of-the-art combined bridge and tunnel that spans 18km across the Storebælt. Known as the "Garden of Denmark" for the lawn-like neatness of its fields and the immense amounts of fruit and vegetables that come from them, the landscape of Funen is barely punctuated by anything larger than a farmstead, except for **Odense**, the one sizeable town on the island, which stands out as a prime attraction for fairy-tale lovers from around the world.

Odense

Funen's sole industrial centre and one of the oldest settlements in the country, **ODENSE** – named after Odin, chief of the Norse gods – gained prominence in the early nineteenth century when the opening of the Odense canal linked the city to the sea and made it the major transit point for the produce of the island's farms. Nowadays, it's a pleasant provincial university town, with an **Old Town** housing some fine museums and – thanks to the resident students – a vigorous nightlife. Odense's main claim to fame, however, is as the birthplace of **Hans Christian Andersen**, a fact celebrated with two museums (one his childhood home), souvenir shops, and hotels catering for travellers lured by the prospect of a romantic Andersen experience. To the **south of town**, there are a few attractions of a rather different nature, from the reconstructed nineteenth-century buildings of **Funen Village** to the novel approach to the prehistoric era at the **Iron Age Village**.

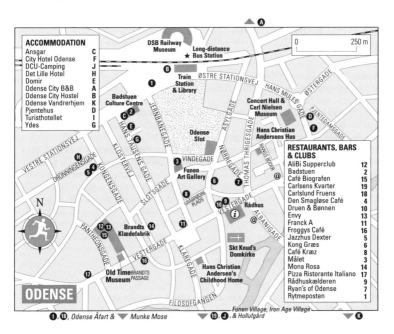

Arrival, information and city transport

The easiest and quickest way of reaching Odense is by the direct train that leaves half-hourly from Copenhagen's Central Station and takes roughly 1hr 15min; the **train station** is a ten-minute walk north of the city centre. In the centre, within the nineteenth-century Rådhus on Vestergade, you'll find the **tourist office** (mid-June to Aug Mon–Fri 9.30am–6pm, Sat & Sun 10am–3pm; rest of year Mon–Fri 9.30am–4.30pm, Sat 10am–1pm; ☎66 12 75 20, ⓦwww.visitodense.com). Local **buses** to outlying sights stop at various places in the centre, a major one being in front of the train station, another in front of the town hall on Albanigade; on Odense's bus system you pay 14kr to travel within the city limits: if you have to use more than one bus, ask the driver for a "change ticket" (*omstigning*) to use on the next bus. Better value if you're planning to see Odense's museums is the **Adventure Pass** (*Odense Eventyrpas*: one day for 120kr, two days 160kr), which gets you into most museums (and gives you a discount where it doesn't), along with reductions on the *Odense Åfart* boat and admission to the zoo (see p.152); it also allows unlimited travel on local buses. You can buy it from the tourist office and train station, as well as the youth hostel and most hotels. Odense is small enough to get around by bicycle: you can **rent a bike** from City Cykler, Vesterbro 27 (☎66 13 97 83, ⓦwww .citycykler.dk; from 99kr per day) or, next to the train station on Østre Stationsvej 33, from Rolsted (☎66 17 77 36, ⓦwww.rolstedodense.dk; 95kr per day).

Accommodation

Though Odense can easily be visited as a day-trip, **staying the night** offers the chance to see the place without the crowds and to enjoy the abundant nightlife that's more laid-back and less pretentious than it can be in the capital. Thanks to Hans Christian Andersen's popularity, the town has a plethora of pricey accommodation, although there are several affordable alternatives, including two central **B&Bs**, close to the Andersen museums, but often full during the summer. There are also a couple of **hostels** and a **campsite**.

Hotels

Ansgar Østre Stationsvej 32 ☎66 11 96 93, ⓦwww.hotel-ansgar.dk. A short walk from the train station, this beautifully renovated hotel offers spacious, fully equipped rooms and a good restaurant. 690kr.

City Hotel Odense Hans Mules Gade 5 ☎66 12 12 58, ⓦwww.city-hotel-odense.dk. Bright and sparkling upmarket option with a prominent yellow facade, just three minutes' walk from the train station. Rooms are cosy and come with en-suite bathrooms. 895kr.

Det Lille Hotel Dronningensgade 5 ☎66 12 28 21, ⓦwww.lillehotel.dk. The pick of the cheapies, this small hotel is run by a friendly proprietor who has done plenty of travelling himself. Rooms are adequate, with shared bathrooms. 450kr.

Domir Hans Tausens Gade 19 ☎66 12 14 27, ⓦwww.domir.dk. Bright, welcoming and of a slightly higher standard than sister hotel Ydes (see below) further down the street. The rooms are all sparkling clean and with

private baths, though as some are quite cramped, be sure to ask for one of the larger rooms. 595kr.

Odense City B&B Billesgade 9 ☎66 13 00 74, ⓦwww.odensecity-bedandbreakfast.dk. Good value, with smallish rooms and shared bathrooms. 695kr.

Pjentehus Pjentedamsgade 14 ☎66 12 15 55, ⓦwww.pjentehus.dk. Located in the heart of Odense's cobbled area, this beautifully renovated old house has a garden that guests can use; rooms are adequate, if on the small side. Breakfast costs 40kr extra. 350kr.

Turisthotellet Gerthasminde 64 ☎66 11 26 92, ⓦwww.turist-hotellet.dk. Cosy, Gothic-looking hotel – the small tower houses one of the rooms. Other rooms aren't as spacious, but they are pleasant enough, and the rates are reasonable. 600kr.

Ydes Hans Tausens Gade 11 ☎66 12 11 31, ⓦwww.ydes.dk. Cheaper and more basic than sister hotel *Domir* (see above); all rooms have private bathrooms. 550kr.

Hostels

Odense City Hostel Østre Stationsvej 31
ⓣ 63 11 04 25, ⓦ www.cityhostel.dk. Next
door to the train station, a friendly, brightly
decorated hostel with good doubles (two
including breakfast) as well as dorms
(200kr).

Odense Vandrerhjem Kragsbjergvej 121
ⓣ 66 13 04 25, ⓦ www.odense-danhostel.dk.
Offers slightly cheaper doubles (two
including breakfast) than its urban counterpart and is also much quieter. Dorm beds
are 200kr. Located just outside town in a
wood-beamed farmhouse; take bus #61 or
#62 from the train station or cathedral south
towards Tornbjerg or Fraugde and get out
along Munkebjergvej at the junction with
Vissenbjergvej. Open June–Sept.

Campsite

DCU-Camping Odensevej 102 ⓣ 66 11 47 02,
ⓦ www.camping-odense.dk. The only campsite
actually in Odense, near Funen Village, fully
equipped with excellent cooking facilities.
Take bus #21, #22 or #23 from the Rådhus
or train station towards Højby.

The Town

Save for three outlying museums, which are a bus ride away, Odense is easily
explored on foot. There's a lot to be said for simply wandering around the
compact **centre** with no particular destination in mind, but you shouldn't pass
up the chance to visit the **Hans Christian Andersen** museums – very much
what the town is known for – or fail to take in at least one of several absorbing
art collections. Two other **museums** provide more offbeat fare: one celebrates
composer Carl Nielsen – after Andersen, Odense's most famous son – and the
other eulogizes Danish railways. For up-to-date information on temporary
exhibitions and special events for all of the city's museums, check out ⓦ www
.museum.odense.dk.

Hans Christian Andersen museums and around

Odense's showpiece museum is the **Hans Christian Andersens Hus,** Bangs
Boder 29 (mid-June to mid-Aug daily 9am–6pm; mid-Aug to mid-June Tues–
Sun 10am–4pm; 55kr), set in the house where the writer was born and which
he described in *The Fairy Tale of My Life*. Oddly enough, Andersen was only
really accepted in his own country towards the end of his life; his real admirers
were abroad, which was perhaps why he travelled widely and left Odense at the
first opportunity. He wrote novels and a few (best-forgotten) plays, but since his
death it's his fairy tales that have gained most renown, partly autobiographical
stories (not least *The Ugly Duckling*) that were influenced by *The Arabian Nights*,
German folk stories, and the traditional Danish folk tales passed on by inmates
of the Odense workhouse, where his grandmother looked after the garden.

Few of the less-than-fairy-tale aspects of Andersen's life are touched upon in
the museum, which was founded in 1905 on the centenary of Andersen's birth
when Odense first began to cash in on its famous ex-citizen. The son of a hard-
up cobbler, Andersen's first home was a single room that doubled as a workshop
in what was then one of Odense's slum quarters. It was a rough **upbringing**:
Hans's ill-tempered mother was fifteen years older than his father, whom she
married when seven months pregnant with Hans (she also had an illegitimate
daughter by another man); his grandfather was insane; and descriptions of his
grandmother, often given charge of the young Hans, range from "mildly eccen-
tric" to "a pathological liar".

There's a nagging falseness about some aspects of **the collection**, but as
Andersen was a first-rate hoarder, it's stuffed with intriguing items: bits of school
reports, his certificate from Copenhagen University, early notes and manuscripts
of his books, chunks of furniture, his umbrella, and paraphernalia from his travels, including the piece of rope he carried to facilitate escape from hotel rooms

in the event of fire. A separate gallery contains a library of Andersen's works in seventy languages and headphones for listening to some of his best-known tales as read by the likes of Sir Laurence Olivier. Nearby is a very mixed collection of illustrations and other art inspired by his writing.

The area around the museum, all half-timbered houses and spotlessly clean, car-free cobbled streets, lacks much character; indeed, if Andersen were around he'd hardly recognize the neighbourhood, which is now one of Odense's most expensive. For more realistic local history, head to the **Møntergården City Museum** (Tues–Sun 10am–4pm; free), a few streets away at Overgade 48–50, where there's an engrossing assemblage of important archeological pieces found on Funen, plus an immense coin collection – from as long ago and as far afield as England under Danelaw and Danish rule in Estonia.

There's more, but not much, about Andersen in the tiny **Hans Christian Andersen's Childhood Home** at Munkemøllestræde 3–5 (mid-June to mid-Aug daily 10am–4pm; mid-Aug to mid-June Tues–Sun 11am–3pm; 25kr), the house where Andersen lived from 1807 to 1819 before moving to Copenhagen, where he spent the rest of his life. More interesting, though, is the nearby **Skt Knud's Domkirke** (April–Oct Mon–Sat 9am–5pm, Sun noon–5pm; Nov–March Mon–Sat 10am–4pm, Sun noon–5pm; ⓦwww.odense-domkirke .dk), whose crypt holds one of the most unusual and ancient finds Denmark has to offer: the **skeleton of Knud II**. Knud was slain in 1086 – by Jutish farmers, angry at the taxes he'd imposed on them – in the original Skt Albani Kirke, the barest ruins of which were found some years ago in the city park. The king was laid to rest in Skt Albani Kirke, but ten years of poor harvest following his death and reports of miracles in the king's tomb, resulted in his canonization as Knud the Holy in 1101, and his remains were subsequently moved to the present Domkirke. Close to Knud's is another coffin, thought to hold the remains of his brother Benedict (though some claim them to be St Alban, whose body was brought to Denmark by Knud), while displayed alongside is the fading, but impressive, Byzantine-style silk tapestry sent as a shroud by Knud's widow, Edele.

The rest of the cathedral itself is noteworthy, too. Mostly late thirteenth-century, it's the only example of pure Gothic church architecture in the country, set off by a finely detailed sixteenth-century wooden altarpiece that's rightly regarded as one of the greatest works of the Lübeck master-craftsman, Claus Berg.

Odense's art museums

The **Fyns Kunstmuseum** (Funen Art Gallery; Tues–Sun 10am–4pm; 30kr), a few minutes' walk from the cathedral at Jernbanegade 13, gives a good idea of the region's importance to Danish art during the late nineteenth century, when a number of Funen-based painters gave up creating portraits of the rich in favour of impressionistic landscapes and studies of the lives of the peasantry. The collection also contains some stirring works by many Nordic greats, among them Vilhelm Hammershøi, P.S. Krøyer, and Michael and Anne Ancher, but most striking of all is H.A. Brendekilde's enormously emotive *Udslidt* ("Worn Out"). The modern era isn't forgotten, with selections from Asger Jorn, Richard Mortensen and Egill Jacobsen, among many others, drawn from the museum's large collection.

For more modern art, walk along Vestergade and turn down Brandts Passage to reach **Brandts Klædefabrik** (ⓦwww.brandts.dk), a large former textile factory that's now given over to a number of cultural endeavours: three museums, a gallery, an art school, a music library and a cinema, along with cafés and restaurants. The **Kunsthallen** here (Art Exhibition Hall; July & Aug daily 10am–5pm, Sept–June Tues–Sun 10am–5pm; 30kr) is an increasingly prestigious spot for displays of work by high-flying new talent in art and design; close by are the varied displays of the **Museet for Fotokunst** (Museum of Photographic Art: same hours; 25kr), taken from the cream of modern (and some not so modern) art photography and almost always worth a look. There's also the more down-to-earth **Danmarks Mediemuseum** (Danish Museum of Printing; same hours; 25kr; ⓦwww.mediemuseum.dk), with its bulky machines and devices chronicling the development of printing, bookbinding and illustrating from the Middle Ages to the present day. You can buy a combined ticket for all three museums for 50kr. Further down Brandts Passage on the second floor of no. 29, the **Tidens Samling** (Old Time Museum; daily 10am–5pm; 30kr; ⓦwww.tidenssamling.dk) houses an interesting, if cluttered, collection of early twentieth-century fashion and house interiors.

Carl Nielsen and DSB Railway museums

The **Carl Nielsen Museum**, inside the concert hall at Claus Bergs Gade 11 (June–Aug Thurs & Fri 2–6pm, Sun noon–4pm; rest of year Thurs & Fri 4–8pm, Sun noon–4pm; 25kr), celebrates the life and work of Odense's second most famous son. Born in a village just outside Odense in 1865, Nielsen displayed prodigious musical abilities from an early age and joined the Odense military band as a cornet player when just 14 (wearing a specially shortened uniform). From there he left to study at the Copenhagen *conservatoire* and then on to gain worldwide acclaim as a composer, for his symphonies particularly, the musical cognoscenti in his own country regarding him as having salvaged Danish music from a period of decline. Despite his travels, and long period of residence in Copenhagen, Nielsen continually praised the inspirational qualities of Funen's nature and the island's tuneful dialect, even writing a somewhat sentimental essay romanticizing the landscape in which "even trees dream and talk in their sleep with a Funen lilt". If you've never heard of Nielsen, be assured that his music is nowhere near as half-baked as his prose: in the museum you can listen to some of his work on headphones, including excerpts from his major pieces and the polka he wrote when still a child. The actual **exhibits**, detailing Nielsen's life and achievements, are further enlivened by the accomplished sculptures of his wife, Anne Marie, many of them early studies for her equestrian statue of Christian IX that now stands outside the Royal Stables in Copenhagen.

The final museum in central Odense is hardly essential viewing unless you've been particularly impressed by the comfort and efficiency of modern Danish trains. The **Jernbanemuseum** (DSB Railway Museum; daily 10am–4pm; 48kr; ⓦwww.jernbanemuseum.dk), immediately behind the station, houses some of the state railway's most treasured artefacts, which include royal and double-decker carriages and the reconstruction of an entire early twentieth-century station, as well as a feast of otherwise forgotten facts pertaining to the rise of Danish railways.

Around Odense

A couple of kilometres south of the city centre on Sejerskovvej, the open-air **Funen Village** museum (April to mid-June & mid-Aug to Oct Tues–Sun 10am–5pm; Nov–March Sun only 11am–3pm; 40kr; mid-June to mid-Aug daily 10am–7pm; 55kr) comprises a reconstructed nineteenth-century country village that is lent an air of authenticity by its period gardens and wandering geese. From the farmhouse to the poorhouse, all the buildings are originals from other parts of Funen, their exteriors painstakingly reassembled and interiors carefully refurbished. In summer, the old trades are revived in the former workshops and crafthouses, and there are free shows at the open-air theatre. Though often crowded, the village is well worth a visit – look out, too, for the village-brewed beer, handed out free on special occasions. Bus #42 runs to the village from the city centre (get out at the Den Fynske Landsby sign), or do what the locals do and get here on the *Odense Åfart* **boat** (ⓦwww.aafart.dk; departs on the hour May to mid-Sept 10am–5pm; 35kr single, 55kr return), which runs along the canal from Munke Mose park in the city centre and terminates at Fruens Bøge, from where it's a short canalside walk to Funen Village. The boat also stops at the well-stocked **Odense Zoo** (April & Sept–Oct Mon–Fri 9am–5pm, Sat & Sun 9am–6pm; May–June & Aug Mon–Fri 9am–6pm, Sat & Sun 9am–7pm; July daily 9am–7pm; Nov–March daily 9am–4pm; 110kr; ⓦwww .odensezoo.dk) on the way – the chimpanzees are a highlight, and the zoo has a particularly large variety of tropical birdlife.

A fifteen-minute bus ride south of the centre (bus #82 towards Neder Holluf), but worth a special detour, is **Hollufgård**, a sixteenth-century manor house (not open to the public), whose enjoyable landscaped **gardens** (daily dawn–dusk; free) are decorated with sculptures by students from the Danish Academy of Fine Arts.

Also easily reached from the town centre (bus #91 towards Allesø), the **Iron Age Village**, some 5km southeast at Store Klaus 40 (July to mid-Aug Mon–Fri & Sun 10am–4pm; mid-Aug to June Mon–Thurs 8.30am–3.30pm, Fri 8.30am–2pm; 25kr; ⓦwww.jernalderlandsbyen.dk), is just one of many prehistoric collections in Denmark, but one that at least makes an effort to be different. There's a simulated TV news broadcast covering events in Bronze Age Denmark, alongside displays describing how ancient symbols are used in modern times.

Eating and drinking

Most of Odense's **restaurants** and **snack bars** are squeezed into the central part of town, which means there's a lot of competition and potentially some very good bargains during the day. If the weather is right for outdoor eating, pick up a freshly made sandwich from the in-house bakery at *Den Gyldne Ovn*, across the road from the tourist office, on Fisketorvet, and head down Albanigade to Odense Å, where there are plenty of benches.

Badstuen Østre Stationsvej 26. A stone's throw from the station, this inexpensive café on the upper floor of the Cultural Centre offers some of the best meal-deals in town. The dish of the day costs 35kr and is served promptly between 5pm and 7pm, while salads, sandwiches and burgers go for 15kr throughout the day.

Café Kræz Gråbrødre Plads 6. Just off Jernbanegade, serving simple, tasty salad, sandwich and soup café fare. Outdoor seating.

Carlslund Fruens Bøge Skov 7 ⓣ **65 91 11 25.** Near the Funen Village, this is a typical Danish restaurant (delicious smørrebrød) with the bonus of live jazz on summer Saturdays; call for info.

Druen & Bønnen Vestergade 15 ⓦ **www .druenogboennen.dk.** Odense's newest café-cum-wine bar has comfy decor with furry rawhide seats and serves great coffee and Scando-Mediterranean breakfast plates of pate, salmon and charcuterie. Open until midnight weekends, 10pm weekdays. Closed Sun.

Franck A Jernbanegade 4. Good, light snacks and decent full meals a short walk south of the train station. Outdoor seating during the summer, and busy most evenings for after-dinner drinking, occasionally accompanied by live music.

Froggys Café Vestergade 68. This pleasant spot for coffee and pie or a quick lunch platter sports a 1950s-era Hollywood decor

inside and a terrace out front that really livens up at night.
Mona Rosa Vintapperstræde 4 ☎65 91 49 13. Summer evenings at this well-priced Mexican restaurant are packed with families and couples spread across two terraces that give onto the cobbles of Vintapperstræde. Lunch

menu is 69kr; mains start at around 100kr.
Målet Jernbanegade 17. Reasonably priced Danish menu, and sports of every variety shown on its big screen.
Pizza Ristorante Italiano Vesterbro 9. Reliable pizzas and pasta at the best and oldest of the city's many pizzerias.

Nightlife and live music

Odense has a plethora of **late-opening cafés** that have usurped the role of nightclubs as evening hangouts. A good first stop is *Café Biografen* at Brandts Klædefabrik – enduringly fashionable and decorated with a dazzling display of movie posters; from there, try *Envy*, Brandts Passage 31, a trendy lounge-café where Odense's beautiful people sip expensive cocktails to drum and bass music. For unpretentious drinking, go for *Carlsens Kvarter*, Hunderupvej 19, south of the Hans Christian Andersen Childhood Home; *Ryan's of Odense*, just north of the Rådhus at Fisketorvet 12, an Irish pub with live Celtic music on weekends; or *Den Smagløse Café*, Vindegade 57, a divey, smoky rock pub packed with students.

The city's **live-music** scene is also worth investigating; pick up the leaflets found in most cafés, music shops and the tourist office for details of upcoming events. *Rytmeposten*, Østre Stationsvej 35 (☎66 13 60 20, ⓦwww.rytmeposten .dk), is Funen's prime live-music venue, where you'll often find heavy rock bands performing. Another busy spot is the radical Badstuen Cultural Centre, just opposite at Østre Stationsvej 26 (☎66 13 48 66, ⓦwww.badstuen.dk), which regularly hosts popular folk bands, while *Jazzhus Dexter*, Vindegade 65 (☎63 11 27 28, ⓦwww.dexter.dk), offers all types of **jazz** – entrance fee around 50kr. There's solid rock music several times a week at *Rådhuskælderen*, Vestergade 17 (☎66 12 58 08), while *AliBi Supperclub*, Brandts Passage 37 (ⓦwww .supperclub.dk) has the hottest **club scene** at weekends. Another good bet is *Kong Græs*, Asylgade 7–9, a spacious nightspot popular with twenty-somethings. For details on Odense's **gay and lesbian** scene, head for the Lambda organization's café at Vindegade 100 (☎40 89 62 49, ⓦwww.lambda.dk; Wed 8pm–midnight, Fri & Sat 10pm–2am).

Across to Sweden

Historically and culturally, Denmark and southern Sweden are closely linked. For centuries, Danish rule extended across the Øresund, and the connections continue today, most visibly in the splendid Øresunds Bridge, completed in 2000, that links the two countries. Historic **Malmö** – the main city of the area – is an easy day-trip from Copenhagen, and the journey across the **Øresunds Bridge** makes a spectacular start to the day: from the suburb of Kastrup, location of Copenhagen Airport, a four-kilometre tunnel brings you out onto the equally long artificial island of Peberholm, from where the eight-kilometre suspension bridge runs to the town of Lernacken, just south of Malmö. The bridge has two levels – the upper for a four-lane highway and the lower for two sets of train tracks – and comprises three sections: a one-kilometre-long central high bridge and approach bridges to either side, each over 3km long. All the way along the views of the Øresund are stunning.

△ Øresunds Bridge

Getting to Malmö is easy; though, at a prohibitive 470kr for a return ticket across the bridge, even if you have got a car, it's worth taking the **train** instead: Malmö is on the same line as Copenhagen Airport, so services from Central Station are frequent (3 per hour during the day), and the journey to Malmö Central, bang in the middle of town, takes just 35min.

Malmö

Founded in the late thirteenth century, **MALMÖ** rose to become Denmark's most important city after Copenhagen. Their interconnected histories mean that in many ways Malmö has more in common with Copenhagen than with the rest of Sweden, although most Swedes would profusely deny this. The Malmö dialect of Swedish is very similar to Danish and Danish kroner are accepted everywhere.

The high density of herring in the sea off the Malmö coast brought ambitious German merchants flocking to the city, an influence that can still be seen in the striking fourteenth-century St Petri kyrka. Erik of Pomerania gave Malmö its most significant medieval boost when, in the fifteenth century, he built the **castle** and mint, and gave the city its own flag – the gold-and-red griffin of his family crest. It wasn't until the Swedish king Karl X marched his armies across the frozen belt of water to within striking distance of Copenhagen in 1658 that the Danes were forced into handing back the southwestern counties to the Swedes. For Malmö, this meant a period of stagnation, cut off from nearby Copenhagen and too far from its own uninterested capital. Not until the full thrust of industrialization, triggered by the tobacco merchant Frans Suell's enlargement of the harbour in 1775, did Malmö begin its dramatic commercial recovery, and the city's fortunes remained buoyant over the following two centuries.

The 1990s saw a further commercial crisis after the city had invested heavily in the shipping industry (which had been in decline since the 1970s), but since the turn of the millennium the new university and the opening of the Øresunds Bridge have attracted an influx of investment and development that visitors can't fail to notice – particularly in the harbour area to the north of the station – helping to create an upbeat, energetic and thoroughly likeable atmosphere. The attractive medieval centre, delightful parks and the sweeping beach

MALMÖ

ACCOMMODATION
Baltzar F
Clarion G
Malmö Camping E
The Mayfair B
Radisson SAS Malmö A
Royal D
Scandic Hotel Kramer C
Villa Hilleröd H

RESTAURANTS, BARS,
CAFÉS & CLUBS
Årstiderna 3
Bageri Café 6
Buddha Lounge 5
Conditoria Hollandia 15
Espresso House 1
Grappa 11
Gustav Adolf 14
Johan P 10
Krua Thai 16
Mattssons Musikpub 2
Mello Yello 7
Moosehead 8
Rådhuskällaren 4
Schlagerbaren 12
Spot Restaurant 13
The Tunnel B
Victors 9

are all major draws, while the plentiful restaurants and bars and a lively nightlife serve as another inducement to stay awhile.

Information and discount cards

The **tourist office** (May & Sept Mon–Fri 9am–6pm, Sat 10am–3pm; June–Aug Mon–Fri 9am–7pm, Sat & Sun 10am–5pm; Oct–April Mon–Fri 9am–5pm, Sat & Sun 10am–3pm; ☎040/34 12 00, ⊛www.malmo.se), inside Central Station, offers a wealth of free information, including several good maps, the *Malmö Guide* and the *Malmö What's On* events brochure. You can also buy the very useful **Malmökortet** (Malmö Card; available for 1, 2 or 3 days for 130SEK, 160SEK or 190SEK respectively), which gives free public transport and free or discounted entrance to many of the city's sights. There are Forex **money exchanges** in Central Station (daily 7am–9pm), at Norra Vallgatan 60 (Mon–Fri 9am–7pm, Sat 9am–4pm) and at Gustav Adolfs Torg 47 (Mon–Fri 9am–7pm, Sat 9am–4pm) – you'll be better off getting some Swedish cash, especially if you're staying a couple of days, as even though you can use Danish kroner, the change paid back to you in Swedish kroner is often at a poor rate. Note that we have given all **prices in Swedish kroner** (SEK); at the time of writing, the rate of exchange was 1.24SEK to 1kr.

City transport and tours

The city centre is easy to walk around; should you need to make use of **buses**, an individual ticket will cost you 15SEK and is valid for an hour; a 200SEK magnetic card is also available and can be used by several people at the same time. A **taxi** for short distances in the city centre will cost you around 50–60SEK. In summer, **bicycle rental** is available from Rent-a-Bike, inside the tourist office (☎0707/49 94 22, ⊛www.rent-a-bike.se; 90SEK per day).

Between June and August, ninety-minute guided **sightseeing tours** by bus (daily; 100SEK, free with Malmö Card) leave at noon (mid-July to mid-Aug also at 1.30pm) from the tourist office. Alternatively, you can do your own tour on city bus #3, which leaves several times an hour from outside Central Station. The city's waterways offer another sightseeing option: leaving from the quay outside Central Station, the "Rundan" tourist **boat** (daily every hour on the hour: May to mid-June 22 11am–4pm; mid-June to end Aug 24–end Aug 11am–7pm; end Aug to mid-Sept 11am–3pm; mid-Sept to end Sept noon–2pm; 75SEK; ⊛www .rundan.se) winds its leisurely way along the lovely canals that encircle the old city and out into the harbour, taking in most of the main sights. The trip takes about fifty minutes, with commentary in English if requested.

Accommodation

Compared to Copenhagen, Malmö has some excellent and surprisingly afford-able **hotels**; being a city that attracts business travellers as well as tourists, competition can be fierce – prices plummet at the weekend (Fri & Sat) and most hotels have good summer-rate reductions, too. Note that booking via the tourist-office website (⊛www.malmo.se/hotel) can be cheaper than booking directly with the hotel. Malmö's new year-round **youth hostel**, *Villa Hilleröd*, is housed in a quaint old house just southwest of the city centre at Ängdalavägan 38 (☎040/26 56 26, ⊛www.villahillerod.se); dorm beds cost from 190SEK and there are also some private rooms; get there by bus #3 to the Mellanheden stop. The nearest **campsite**, *Malmö Camping* at Strandgatan 101 in Limhamn (☎040/15 51 65, ⊛www.camping.se/plats/m08), is in a picturesque spot, close to the Øresunds Bridge, and can be reached by bus #34.

When **telephoning** Sweden from Denmark you need to add the country code (46) and remove the first "0" in front of the Malmö area code (040), meaning that you would dial 0046 40/34 12 00 when calling the tourist office from Copenhagen. Prices given are for weekdays.

Baltzar Södergatan 20 ☎040/665 57 00, ⓦwww.baltzarhotel.se. Very central (between the two main squares), this is a swanky place done out with flourishes that owe more to British posh-hotel design than Swedish style. 1500SEK.

Clarion Engelbrektsgatan 16 ☎040/710 20, ⓦwww.choicehotels.se. Pleasant and characterful old hotel in a good central position; the price includes a buffet breakfast. 1890SEK.

Scandic Hotel Kramer Stortorget 7 ☎040/693 54 00, ⓦwww.scandic-hotels.com. Beautiful white-stuccoed, French-turreted hotel from the 1870s on the main square, once Malmö's top option and still very luxurious. 1200SEK.

Mayfair Adelgatan 4 ☎040/10 16 20, ⓦwww.mayfairtunneln.com. Very central

Danish-owned place and one of the finest of Malmö's more intimate hotels. Rooms are well furnished in cherry or Gustavian pastels. Good breakfasts and weekend discounts. 1395SEK.

Radisson SAS Malmö Östergatan 10 ☎040/698 40 00, ⓦwww.radissonsas.com. Just beyond the Caroli kyrka, this hotel's unimposing facade opens into a delightful interior. The rooms are large and stylish, and breakfast is eaten inside one of Malmö's oldest houses, cunningly incorporated into the 1960's building. 1495SEK.

Royal Norra Vallgatan 94 ☎040/664 25 00, ⓦwww.hotellroyal.com. Small, family-run hotel just up from the train station. Price includes breakfast, which is served in the garden in summer. 1295SEK.

The City

Standing outside the nineteenth-century train station, with its ornate red-brick arches and curly-topped pillars, the **canal** in front of you forms a rough rectangle encompassing the **Old Town** directly to the south and the moated castle, the **Malmöhus**, with its cluster of museums, to the west, surrounded by a series of attractive interconnecting parks. South down Hamngatan is the main square, Stortorget, heart of the old town; and further south the hub of multiethnic Malmö; to the west lies the appealing beach area; while to the north the rapidly redeveloping Western Harbour area, with its love-it or loathe-it landmark, the Turning Torso Skyscraper.

The Old Town

Stortorget, the city's main square, is home to a series of handsome, mostly nineteenth-century, buildings, amongst which the **Rådhuset** of 1546 draws most attention. A pageant of architectural fiddling and statuary, the building's original design was destroyed during remodelling in the nineteenth century, which left the present, finicky Dutch Renaissance exterior. The cellars, home to the *Rådhuskällaren* restaurant (see p.160), have been used as a tavern for more than four hundred years. The crumbling, step-gabled red-brick building on the opposite side of the square was once the home of sixteenth-century mayor and Master of the Danish Mint, Jørgen Kock; Danish coins were struck in Malmö on the site of the present Malmöhus, until irate local Swedes stormed the building and destroyed it in 1534. In the cellars here you'll find the *Årstiderna* (also known as *Kockska Krogan*, see p.160) restaurant, the only part of the building accessible to visitors. In the centre of the square, a statue of Karl X, high on his charger, presides over the city he liberated from centuries of Danish rule.

Head a block east, behind the Rådhus, to reach the Gothic **St Petri kyrka** on Göran Olsgatan (daily 10am–6pm), dark and forbidding on the outside, but light and airy within. The church has its roots in the fourteenth century and, although Baltic in inspiration, the final style owes much to German influences, for it was beneath its unusually lofty and elegantly vaulted roof that the German community came to pray. The ecclesiastical vandalism of whitewashing over medieval roof murals started early at St Petri – almost the whole interior turned white in 1553 – and consequently your eyes are drawn to the pulpit and four-tiered altarpiece, both of striking workmanship and elaborate embellishment. The only part of the church left with its original murals is a side chapel, the **Krämare Chapel** (Merchant's Chapel; from the entrance, turn left and left again). Added to the church in the late fifteenth century as a Lady Chapel, it was considered redundant at the Reformation and sealed off, thus protecting the paintings from the zealous brushes of the reformers. Best preserved are the paintings on the vaulted ceiling, mainly depicting New Testament figures.

Södergatan, Malmö's main pedestrianized shopping street, leads south of Stortorget down towards the southern canal via the pleasant Gustav Adolfs Torg; at the start of Södergatan, take a peak inside **Apoteket Lejonet** from the 1890s. Gargoyled and balconied on the outside, the pharmacy interior is a busy mix of inlaid wood, carvings and etched glass.

Despite the size of Stortorget, it still proved too small to suffice as the sole city square, so in the sixteenth century **Lilla Torg**, formerly marshland, was sewn on to the southwest corner. Looking like a film set, this little square with its creaky old half-timbered houses, flowerpots and cobbles, is everyone's favourite part of the city. During the day, people congregate here for a drink in one of the many cafés and to wander around the summer jewellery stalls. At night, Lilla Torg explodes in a frenzy of activity, with people from all over the city converging on the square to visit the bars. From the beginning of the twentieth century until the 1960s, the whole of Lilla Torg was a covered market; the sole vestige of those days is **Saluhallen**, to the right as you enter the square from Stortorget. A bustling collection of enticing food stalls – Greek, Italian, Japanese, Thai and seafood among others – it's a cool retreat on a hot afternoon and a great place to pick up lunch.

At the square's southeastern corner, walk through the gateway into the tiny, cobbled courtyard where, in addition to a handful of boutiques and craft shops, you'll find the stylish **Form Design Centre** (Tues, Wed & Fri 11am–5pm, Thurs 11am–6pm, Sat & Sun 11am–4pm; free; @www.formdesigncenter.com), housed in a seventeenth-century grain store and celebrating Swedish design in textiles, ceramics and furniture. It carries mostly temporary exhibitions, but the shop is a cornucopia of funky, designer kitchenware, toys and textiles, and there's a nice café, too.

A few streets away to the east, at Gasverksgatan 22, and well worth a visit if you're interested in contemporary art, is the **Rooseum** (Wed 2pm–8pm, Thurs–Sun noon–6pm; guided tours Wed 6pm, Thurs–Fri 4pm, Sat & Sun 2pm; 40SEK, free on Fri; @www.rooseum.se). Space is imaginatively used in this elaborate building from 1900, originally constructed to house the Malmö Electricity Company's steam turbines. The main turbine hall forms the central gallery, displaying experimental installations and interesting photographic works.

Malmöhus and around

Take any of the streets running west from Stortorget or Lilla Torg and you soon come up against the edge of **Kungsparken**, within striking distance of the fifteenth-century castle, **Malmöhus** (daily: June–Aug 10am–4pm; Sept–May noon–4pm; 50SEK, includes entry to Kommendanthuset and Teknista o Sjöfarts Museet; free guided tours in English Sat & Sun at 2pm; @www .malmo.se/museer), the largest Renaissance castle in Scandinavia. For a more dramatic approach, walk west (away from the station) up Citadellsvägen; from here the low castle with its grassy ramparts and two striking red circular keeps is straight ahead over the wide moat.

Originally Denmark's mint, Malmöhus was destroyed by the Swedes in 1534. Two years later, a new fortress was built on the site by the Danish king Christian III, only to be of unforeseen benefit to his enemies who, once back in control of Skåne, used it to repel an attacking Danish army in 1677. Serving as a prison for a time (the Earl of Bothwell, Mary Queen of Scots' third husband, was its most notable inmate), the castle's importance waned once back in Swedish hands, and it was used for grain storage until opening as a museum in 1937. It's now more of a **museum complex**, its diverse collections spread throughout the castle itself and a modern extension.

Arguably, the pick of the museums is the **Malmö Konstmuseum** (Art Museum), upstairs to the left, whose fine collection of paintings, furniture, ceramics and glassware is exhibited chronologically in a series of beautiful period interiors from the mid-sixteenth-century Renaissance through Baroque, Rococo, pastel-pale Gustavian and Neoclassical. A stylish *jugendstil* (Art Nouveau) interior is equally impressive, while other rooms feature Functionalist and post-Functionalist interiors. The collection is particularly strong on twenti-eth-century and contemporary Nordic art. Look out for the fine landscapes of the Swedish painter, **Carl Fredrik Hill**, his *Villa by the Seine* showing the influ-ence of the Barbizon school and French realism following a sojourn in Paris in 1873. There are also wonderful examples of modern **Scandinavian silverware** with luminaries such as Georg Jensen and Swedish designer Vivianna Toron Bülow-Hübe well represented. The museum is further bolstered by an excellent programme of temporary exhibitions.

On the ground floor, the **Naturmuseet** (Natural History Museum) features the usual taxidermal parade of the animal world, but the live section – the small aquarium, vivarium (lizards, snakes, frogs and the like) and nocturnal room brimming with bats and other night-time furry critters – is a real draw for the kids. The lack of English labels, plus old-fashioned displays of flints, bones, pots and chunks of medieval masonry, make the **Stadsmuseet** (Town Museum) a rather indigestible trawl through the area's history since the Stone Age. It's best skimmed through in favour of the more exciting **Power Over People** exhibi-tion, which traces the history of the castle through reconstructions (complete with mannequins, sound effects and so on) of what went on over time in the rooms you pass through; one, for instance, was where the Earl of Bothwell was held prisoner. Having fled Scotland after being accused of Mary Queen of Scots' second husband's murder, a storm brought his ship to Bergen in Norway, where he was recognized and taken to the castle.

A couple more museums (both same hours and ticket as Malmöhus) lie across the road on Malmöhusvagen; the pinky-red building is the **Kommendanthu-set** (Governor's House), with a funky café and changing photographic exhibi-tions upstairs. A little further west, the **Teknista o Sjöfarts Museet** (Science and Maritime Museum) is packed full of trams, cars, aircraft and engines and you can clamber around on a 1940s' U3 submarine. The science bit focuses on physics and chemistry with a great interactive centre for kids. Between the two sites, running off Malmöhusvagen, is a tiny road, **Banerkajen**, lined with higgledy-piggledy fishing shacks selling fresh and smoked fish in the morning.

Once you've had your fill of museums, the castle **grounds** are good for a stroll, peppered with small lakes and an old windmill. The paths lead all the way down to Regementsgatan – the Prime Minister lives at no. 10 – and the City Library in the southeastern corner of the park. You can continue walking through the greenery as far as Gustav Adolfs Torg by crossing Gamla Begravnings Platsen, a rather pretty graveyard.

The beach and Western Harbour

Formerly home to the Kockum shipyard, the redeveloped, high-tech **Western Harbour** district, a ten-minute walk north of the Malmöhus, or bus #2 from Central Station, is a popular spot for sunbathing and swimming, and for gazing across to the Öresunds Bridge from its marina-side cafés and restaurants. Towering over it all, and visible for miles around, is the quirky new 190m-high **Turning Torso Skyscraper**, designed by Spaniard Santiago Calatrava. This revolutionary residential tower, the highest building in Scandinavia, consists of nine stacked cubes that revolve through a ninety-degree twist from base to top.

From the Western Harbour, Malmö's sandy **beach** stretches several kilometres southwest of the city, fringed by Ribersborgs Park (bus #32 runs along the park). At the town end of the beach is the **Ribersborgs kallbadhuset** (mid-April to mid-Sept Mon–Fri 8.30am–7pm, Sat & Sun 8.30am–4pm; mid-Sept to mid-April Mon–Fri noon–7pm, Sat & Sun 9am–4pm; 35kr), a cold-water bathhouse with a sauna and café.

Eating

Most of Malmö's **eating places** are concentrated in and around its central squares, with Lilla Torg attracting the biggest crowds. If you want a change of scene, head south of the centre to Möllevångstorget, the heart of Malmö's immigrant community, for cheaper eats and a very un–Swedish atmosphere. Alternatively, to cut costs, stock up at the specialist food stalls within Saluhallen on Lilla Torg.

Årstiderna Suellsgatan 2, corner of Stortorget ℡040/23 09 10. This is a very fine – but rather pricey – old cellar-restaurant in the former home of Malmö's sixteenth-century mayor, Jörgen Kock. Daily lunch specials of traditional Swedish fare from 89SEK. Closed Sun.

Bageri Café Saluhallen, Lilla Torg. Excellent bagels, baguettes, pies and health foods – with outside seating, too. Closed Sun.

Conditoria Hollandia Södra Förstadsgatan 8. Traditional, pricey *konditori* south of the canal, with a window full of delicious chocolate fondants.

Espresso House Sundspromenaden, Western Harbour. An outlet of the coffeehouse chain serving excellent chocolate cake, muffins, ciabattas and Indian chai – milky tea with cardamom. All best enjoyed (weather permitting) on the lovely terrace sporting bridge views.

Grappa Lilla Torg 4 ℡040/12 50 65. Designer restaurant with a pleasant terrace, serving innovative Italian dishes from 110SEK.

Gustav Adolf Gustav Adolfs Torg 43. Long-established, slightly staid café-restaurant, but still a popular spot, in its grand,

white-stuccoed building with outside seating. Open late at weekends.

Johan P. Saluhallen, Lilla Torg ℡040/97 18 18, ℡www.johanp.nu. Great fish and seafood restaurant, centrally located, pricey, but perfect for a treat – lighter fare such as gravadlax, caviar or shrimp salad for 105SEK. mains will set you back around 200SEK. Also has a stall in Saluhallen. Closed Sun.

Krua Thai Möllevångtorget 12 ℡040/12 22 87. In the big square south of the city centre, this place serves the best Thai food in town, with an informal atmosphere that's more domestic than haute cuisine.

Rådhuskällaren Stortorget. Gloriously atmospheric setting beneath the town hall, with dishes at around 200SEK, though there's also a well-cooked and beautifully served daily economy meal for 65SEK and a lunchtime buffet for 85SEK. Outside seating in summer.

Spot Restaurant Stora Nygatan 33 ℡040/12 02 03. Great Italian daytime restaurant with attached charcuterie (all ingredients imported direct from Italy), serving delicious platters of antipasti and cold meats, salads and home-made pizza. Closed Sun.

Drinking, nightlife and entertainment

Most Malmöites head across the bridge to Copenhagen when looking for a good time out, but there are now corners of their home city worth exploring at night. The best place to head for an evening **drink** is Lilla Torg: the square buzzes with activity, the smell of beer wafts between the old, beamed houses, and music and chatter fill the air. It's a largely young crowd, and the atmosphere is like a summer carnival. It doesn't make a huge difference which of the ten or so bars you go for (expect to wait for a seat), but as a basic pointer, *Mello Yello* and *Victors* are for the 25-plus age group; *Moosehead* attracts a younger crowd.

A striking **nightlife** option is *The Tunnel*, in the same building as the *Mayfair* hotel at Adelgatan 4 (www.tunneln.com; first Fri of each month and every Sat; closed July; 100kr cover). Designed as a futuristic metallic tunnel by Argentinean Abelardo Gonzalez, it welcomes a wide age range and boasts a cellar bar with a wild dance floor of silver and mirrors. Just south of St Petri kyrka at Djäknegatan 9, the *Buddha Lounge* has a great lounge (unsurprisingly) and dancing area. For **live music**, head for *Mattssons Musikpub* (040/23 27 56), behind the Rådhus at Göran Olsgatan 1, which hosts a variety of Scandinavian R&B and rock bands every night.

9

OUT OF THE CITY | Malmö

Listings

Listings

Accommodation

A ccommodation in Copenhagen is varied but relatively expensive, with prices easily on a par with other Western European capitals. Most of the hotels in the city centre are aimed either at tour groups or business travellers – they generally have good service and amenities but can be a bit characterless, though a recent wave of new modern **designer and boutique hotels** has given the visitor more trendy and surprisingly good-value alternatives. Hotels in Copenhagen are awarded up to five stars by HORESTA, the Danish hotel association. The number of stars is an indication of the hotel's amenities – TV, minibar, restaurant, etc – rather than an indication of comfort, cleanliness or furnishings, and determines the price they can charge. **Room rates** are generally most expensive in summer, though in the majority of big hotels prices rise and fall on a daily basis according to demand. As a general rule, rates at business-oriented hotels fall at weekends; those at tourist-oriented hotels fall during winter (the Christmas period aside). It's always worth checking the **hotel websites** for **special rates** – particularly at weekends – and packages, and if you book in advance using the hotel's website, you can often get discounts of up to 35 percent. Rooms fill up quickly during the summer high season (July & Aug) and around Christmas. If you have a specific hotel in mind it's a good idea to book ahead during these times, but note that, if you're willing to take a chance, you can make great savings if you book via the hotel-booking service (see below) on the day of your arrival.

The tourist office also has a website (ⓦwww.bookcopenhagen.dk) and phone line (☏70 22 24 42; see "Basics", p.37) for you to book accommodation in advance (50kr booking fee). If you arrive without a reservation, the **hotel-booking service** at Wonderful Copenhangen's tourist office Copenhagen Right Now (see p.37) will find you a hotel room, although queues for this service can be lengthy during high season and the service costs 100kr. They have all the latest room rates, and in low season or when things are a bit quiet may be able to find you a really good deal. They also have several terminals with free Internet access for you to book a room for yourself via their website.

A more affordable guesthouse sector is slowly starting to develop, but numbers are presently low and rooms fill quickly in the busier summer months. Check ⓦwww.bedandbreakfast.dk for what's available and to book. Note that the price of a bed and breakfast in Denmark (from 300kr per night) doesn't actually include breakfast, and in some cases breakfast isn't even on offer. Another option is to contact the Wonderful Copenhagen Right Now tourist office or Use It (p.37) and ask about private rooms in local homes. Some of these are in as good a location as the best hotels, and prices are very reasonable – roughly 350kr to 400kr per double. If you're on a budget, there are a number of good hostels scattered around the city centre and suburbs. Finally, campsites provide an alternative if you're really watching the pennies.

If you're here for a **longer stay** of a couple of weeks or more, an apartment will be more cost effective than hotels. The efficient and friendly letting agency HAY4YOU, Vimmelskaftet 49 (☏33 33 08 05, ⓦwww.hay4you.dk) has a range of centrally located **apartments** for short or long-term stays.

The price given at the end of each listing is for the cost per night in that establishment of a **standard double room** mid-week in high season; as stated above, it's worth checking for reduced weekend and low-season rates. Unless stated, **breakfast** is included in the price.

Hotels

Copenhagen has experienced a hotel boom in recent years and new hotels – particularly at the high end – pop up constantly in all corners of the city. In the past, most of Copenhagen's classier hotels were concentrated in the desirable canalside area **around Kongens Nytorv** and **Nyhavn**, on the eastern side of Indre By, with a smattering around the Peblinge and Sortedams rampart lakes west of the city centre. These are now facing strong competition from a number of international chains that have rooted themselves firmly at the airport, around **Sydhavnen**, and also right in the city centre, as well as several new exciting **designer hotels** offering a more interesting hotel experience in great, central locations. Most of the **budget hotels** are just west of Central Station, in **Vesterbro**, with the majority clustered along the ever-so-slightly seedy (though rarely dangerous) streets of Helgolandsgade, Colbjørnsensgade and Istedgade. The area is also home to a number of mid-range hotels, and there are further mid-price options around Nyhavn canal, on the other side of Indre By, and out towards the suburbs of Nørrebro and Frederiksberg.

Indre By

Staying in Indre By has the major benefit of being close to all the action: some of the city's more unusual sites are squeezed in among the many historical buildings here, and good restaurants and bars can be found on almost every street corner. The locations of the following hotels are shown on the map on pp.54–55. **Copenhagen Strand Havnegade 37** ☏33 48 99 00, ⓦwww.copenhagenstrand.dk. **Bus #29.** Located on the waterfront behind Det Kongelige Teater, this long, narrow, converted red-brick warehouse features parquet flooring and heavy, dark mahogany furniture. Rooms are a bit on the small side but otherwise comfortable and neat. Popular with airline crews on a stopover, the restaurant only serves breakfast (included in the price). Rates are reduced substantially during weekends. 1635kr. **D'Angleterre Kongens Nytorv 34** ☏33 12 00 95, ⓦwww.remmen.dk. **Bus #1A, #15, #19, #26,**

#350S; Kongens Nytorv metro. Dating back to 1755, this prestigious and luxurious five-star is one of Europe's oldest hotels – guests have included Winston Churchill, Michael Jackson and Robbie Williams. The ultra-stylish classical rooms contain every conceivable amenity, and there's also a luxurious spa and fitness centre and two gourmet restaurants, though breakfast isn't included in the extravagant price, and parking costs extra, too. 2600kr.

Jørgensen Rømersgade 11 ☏33 13 81 86, ⓦwww.hoteljoergensen.dk. **Bus #5A, #14, #40, #42, #43 or #350S; Nørreport S-Tog/metro.** Within easy walking distance of the city centre, the friendly and relaxed *Jørgensen* has a range of good-value rooms with a mixture of en-suite and shared facilities. They're all comfortable, decent-sized and well furnished, and there's a good buffet breakfast included. There's also dorm-style accommodation (see p.172), which ensures an overall congenial mix of young travellers, families and tourists. 700kr, 575kr shared.

Opera Tordenskjoldsgade 7 ☎ 33 47 83 00, ⓦ www.hotelopera.dk. Bus #29; Kongens Nytorv metro. Slightly worn at the edges, with a restaurant reminiscent of Agatha Christie's *Orient Express*, this classy old hotel is full of character and appeal. Despite the misleading name – the opera has now moved to Christianshavn – it is convenient for Det Kongelige Teater, and the rooms here come with heavy drapes and carpeting and have an altogether very theatrical feel. Major reductions during weekends and summer. 1535kr.

Skt Petri Krystalgade 22 ☎ 33 45 91 00, ⓦ www.hotelsktpetri.com. Bus #6A. Located in a former discount department store slap bang in the centre, there is certainly nothing cut price about *Skt Petri*, proud to be the first and only designated designer hotel in Copenhagen (check ⓦ www.designhotel .com for details) and definitely a good place to head for if you're in town to be seen. Rooms are lush in the extreme (massive fluffy duvets and swanky colour-conscious decor), a fact that is very clearly reflected in the price. There's a posh café/restaurant next to the lobby, and if you're lucky you might get access to the downstairs bar/nightclub *Bar Rouge* (it tends to be invite only), although there's a strict dress code.1995kr.

Sømandshjemmet "Bethel" Nyhavn 22 ☎ 33 13 03 70, ⓦ www.hotel-bethel.dk. Bus #29; Kongens Nytorv metro. You don't have to be a sailor to stay at this seamen's hostel (although you get a 10% discount if you are), fantastically located on Nyhavn and with good rates to boot. The self-contained rooms are perfectly adequate and the corner rooms with fantastic views are worth paying a bit more for. There's a small breakfast restaurant that serves cakes and coffee throughout the day. 795kr.

Ibsens Vendersgade 23 ☎ 33 13 19 13, ⓦ www .ibsenshotel.dk. Bus #5A, #40 or #350S. Set between Nørreport station and the lakes, the cosy and welcoming three-star *Ibsens* has comfortable and attractively outfitted rooms – all dark wood, navy blue and gold furnishings. Each floor is themed – "romantic", "bohemian" and so on – and there's an Italian restaurant and a small Italian garden on the ground floor. 1220kr.

Kong Arthur Nørre Søgade 11 ☎ 33 11 12 12, ⓦ www.kongarthur.dk. Bus #5A or #350S. Located in a largely residential area by Peblinge Sø, this four-star is the more upmarket sister of *Ibsens* (see above), but with the same relaxed, friendly atmosphere. Choose from the country-manor-style old section with its comfy *Round Table* bar (open 24hr), or the newer, modern European-style wing. Rooms in both are well furnished though some are quite small. Breakfast is served in the courtyard in summer, and there's also a garden where you can play petanque. Free parking.1520kr.

Frederikstad

Situated in the city's old regal district, hotels in Frederikstad don't come cheap. The locations of the following hotels are shown on the map on pp.76–77.

Christian IV Dronningens Tværgade 45 ☎ 33 32 10 44, ⓦ www.hotelchristianiv.dk. Good-value hotel with comfortable rooms in a quiet neighbourhood halfway between Rosenborg and Amalienborg castles. Cheaper at weekends and in the winter. 1450kr.

Copenhagen Admiral Toldbodgade 24–28 ☎ 33 74 14 14, ⓦ www.admiralhotel.dk. Housed in a converted two-hundred-year-old granary in a great location right by the waterfront next to Nyhavn and the forthcoming play house, the six-storey brick building has kept its rustic maritime interior with vaulted ceilings and wooden beams throughout. Rooms are comfortable; half have great views of Inderhavnen and cost a bit more. Although the *Admiral* is geared mainly towards business travellers, rates don't tend to go down during weekends. Breakfast buffet (115kr) is not included. There's a classy restaurant, *Salt*, on the ground floor. 1540kr.

Comfort Hotel Esplanaden Bredgade 78 ☎ 33 48 10 00, ⓦ www.choicehotels.dk. Set in a nice location near Churchillparken and Kastellet, this pleasant hotel has decent en-suite rooms, with the choice of bath or shower. Breakfast (95kr) is not included. There's a good restaurant next door – *Sankt Petersborg* – and parking in the back yard (95kr). which must be booked in advance. Great offers during weekends and winter. 1445kr.

Front Skt Annæ Plads 21 ☎ 33 13 34 00, ⓦ www.front.dk. A Danish design team has beautifully transformed this former inexpensive hotel in Nyhavn, to become one of the classier hotels in town. With a range of en-suite rooms – showers only – each with a different colour scheme: orange, beige,

△ The Square

bordeaux, light grey or rose-pink – and thick fluffy carpets, staying here makes you feel like you're part of an Almodóvar movie. Breakfast (145kr) is not included; however, there's free access to the hotel's fully equipped gym. Prices go up 300kr for seaview. 1590kr.

Rådhuspladsen and around

Staying in this area will put you at the centre of things – close to Central Station, Tivoli, the shopping streets of Indre By and several major museums. As a result, hotels here tend to be pricey, though there are a couple of new, more affordable options. Note that most of the options below are on busy main roads; if you're a light sleeper, you might want to request a room away from the noise. The locations of the following hotels are shown on the map on p.90.

Hotel Alexandra HC Andersens Bld 8 ☎ 33 74 44 44, ⓦ www.hotel-alexandra.dk. Friendly and homely traditional hotel that prides itself on its ambience and attention to detail – lots of Danish furniture classics and paintings. Rooms are elegant and comfortable; a few have been furnished in the style of famous Danish designers such as Arne Jacobsen and Hans Wegner and feature some of their works, but to live with these icons of style you'll pay 500kr extra per night. 1565kr.

Cab-Inn City Mitchellsgade 14 ☎ 33 46 16 16, ⓦ www.cabinn.com. The only budget option in the area, offering a relatively cheap and reasonably comfortable place to bed down for the night in small, functional ferry-cabin-style rooms (suitable for 1–3 people). All rooms have own bathroom, TV, phone and kettle with free tea and coffee. 645kr (2-person occupancy). Breakfast 50kr. Two further branches in Frederiksberg, see p.171.

Hotel Fox Jarmers Plads 3 ☎ 33 95 77 55, ⓦ www.hotelfox.dk. Great-value, exciting, new hotel – the 61 rooms have been individually decorated and furnished by a team of young European designers, and though some may be a bit too garish or avant garde to live with for longer than a couple of days (1960s psychedelic movies inspired one, Manga cartoons another), they all use their space creatively and with a flair that makes even the small single rooms stylish and inviting. Doubles come in medium, large and extra large; some have showers, some baths, so give your preferences when booking. Breakfast – great coffee and pastries – is served on airplane-style compartmentalized trays in the bright and funky lobby with its low, moulded seating and soothing brown/blue/white decor.

There's a great restaurant, too (see "Eating", p.185). The lobby doubles as a cocktail bar Thursday to Saturday evenings, with DJs at weekends, so be warned that things do get lively. Bikes and rollerblades for hire. 1120kr.

Marriott Kalvebod Brygge 5 ☎ 88 33 99 00, Ⓦ www.marriott.com/cphdk. Bus #8. In a great harbourfront spot at the end of Bernstorffs-gade, the high-rise *Marriott* offers all the American-style swagger and amenities you could want – large, plush, well-equipped rooms (many with views over the harbour or city), restaurant, terrace café (summer only), bar, fitness room, sauna and solar-ium, and expensive shops. Prices vary considerably according to demand, and it's worth checking their website for special deals and weekend offers. Breakfast not included. 1295kr.

Radisson SAS Royal Hotel Hammerichsgade 1 ☎ 33 42 60 00, Ⓦ www.radissonsas.com. Bus #6 or #28; Central Station. Built in 1960, this five-star place bills itself as the first designer hotel in the world – the work of Danish architect/designer Arne Jacobsen, from the high-rise building itself down to the door handles. Several renovations later, it remains faithful to its original style and decor, a time capsule back to the jet-set glamour of the 1960s – the huge lobby has a glamor-ous sweeping staircase, and a classy bar that's perfect for a pre-dinner drink. The rooms aren't that big, but they are a model of tasteful, minimalist Danish design, with AJ furniture, pastel fabrics, maple-wood panelling and stylish lighting. The gourmet *Alberto K* restaurant on the twentieth floor adds to the luxurious ambience with its fine views over the city. For effortless style, slick service and sheer Scandinavian cool, this is still the one to beat. Rates signifi-cantly reduced at weekends. Breakfast not included. 1995kr.

Sofitel Plaza Bernstoffsgade 4 ☎ 33 14 92 62, Ⓦ www.sofitel.com. Central Station. The *Plaza*'s slightly worn exterior and position right next to Central Station might put some off, but inside it's a very friendly, welcoming hotel and an intriguing mixture of gentle-men's club – lots of dark wood panelling, heavy furniture and subdued elegance in the lobby and old-fashioned Library Bar – and, on the accommodation floors, light, modern murals based on Hans Christian Andersen's tales. Rooms are a good size and well furnished in stylish checks and pastels, but

some overlook the train tracks, so request the Tivoli side if possible. Breakfast not included. 2150kr.

🏃 **The Square Rådhuspladsen 14** ☎ 33 38 12 00, Ⓦ www.thesquare.dk. Great new addition to the city's hotels, slap-bang in the centre (hence no parking) and offering sig-nificant discounts (around twenty percent) at the weekends. Spacious, stylish modern lobby scattered with gorgeous, red Arne Jacobsen swan chairs; the minimalist look is carried through into the smartly decorated rooms. Those overlooking the square expe-rience some traffic noise, so if that's likely to keep you awake request a room further back. Breakfast (there's no restaurant) is served on the sixth floor with views over the city. 1635kr.

Vesterbro

The multicultural district of Vester-bro is packed with some of the city's most affordable hotel accom-modation. This, and its array of cheap ethnic eateries, make it an ideal area to head for if your budget is tight. The locations of the following hotels are shown on the map on pp.102–103.

Absalon Helgolandsgade 15 ☎ 33 24 22 11, Ⓦ www.absalon-hotel.dk. Bus #10; Central Station. On the corner of Istedgade, this large but friendly three-star family hotel with a one-star annex, offers a wide choice of rooms (some en suite), plus a number of deluxe doubles and suites. It's nothing special and the decor is rather dated, but it's reasonably priced, convenient and clean, and soundproofing keeps things nice and quiet. There's free Internet access in the lobby. 690–1150kr.

Ansgar Colbjørnsensgade 29 ☎ 33 21 21 96, Ⓦ www.ansgar-hotel.dk. Bus #10; Central Station. Former Danish Mission hotel at the far end of Colbjørnsensgade, near Halmtor-vet, with small, en-suite rooms kitted out in light Scandinavian style. There's a pleasant courtyard open in summer, and Internet access in the lobby 800kr.

Bertrams Hotel Guldsmeden Vesterbrogade 107 ☎ 33 25 04 05, Ⓦ www.hotelguldsmeden .dk. Bus #6A. As the latest member of the Danish Guldsmeden hotel chain, four-star *Bertrams* has been exquisitely done up in French colonial style with dark wooden interiors and fake furs lying around. Rooms are fairly large, bright and breezy, and come with the choice of shower or bath. Breakfast is sourced from *Emmery's* next door – in itself, reason enough to stay here. There's parking (50kr) just down the road at the Vesterbrogade 66 branch. 1495kr.

Centrum Helgolandsgade 14 ☏ 33 31 31 11, ⓦ www.dgi-byen.dk. Bus #10; Central Station. One of the trendier options in this area of town, the recently revamped *Centrum* has cool, modern decor – black leather sofas and cosy lighting in the lobby, tasteful whites, creams and pale wooden furniture in the modestly sized rooms (all en suite). Guests get free access to the DGI-byen swim centre. 1175kr.

DGI-byens Hotel Tietgensgade 65 ☏ 33 29 80 50, ⓦ www.dgi-byen.dk. Bus #1A; Central Station. Excellently located for sporty types, the *DGI-byens Hotel* is part of the sports centre of the same name and a beautiful example of minimalist Scandinavian design. Rooms are large and immaculate with light, pine wooden flooring, and guests have free access to the swim centre. 1295kr.

Grand Vesterbrogade 9 ☏ 33 27 69 00, ⓦ www .grandhotel.dk. Central Station. Popular with British travellers, trainspotters and businessmen, the big, old-fashioned *Grand*, at the Tivoli end of Vesterbrogade, is a bit overpriced, but its classic British decor and tastefully furnished rooms (all en suite) make it a comfortable stop right in the heart of the action. Prices drop at weekends. 1635kr.

Guldsmeden Vesterbrogade 66 ☏ 33 22 15 00, ⓦ www.hotelguldsmeden.dk. Bus #6A or #26. Almost opposite the Københavns Bymuseum, this is a small and charming hotel occupying a nineteenth-century building. All of the rooms are done out in French colonial style, with a laudable attention to detail, and some have small balconies, though the view isn't that enticing. Parking 50kr. 1395kr.

Hebron Helgolandsgade 4 ☏ 33 31 69 06, ⓦ www.hebron.dk. Bus #6A; Central Station. This three-star Best Western hotel at the quiet end of Helgolandsgade, near Vesterbrogade, is popular with Danish business travellers who don't mind the serviceable but bland decor. Rooms (all en suite) vary in size; some on the Helgolandsgade side have small balconies. Free tea and coffee in the lobby area.1050kr.

Ibis Triton Helgolandsgade 7–11 ☏ 33 31 32 66, ⓦ www.ibishotel.com. Bus #6A; Central Station. At the nice end of Colbjørnsensgade and

popular with business travellers, this recent addition to the chain has light and cheery public areas, including a bar, 24hr snack bar and courtyard. Rooms are large and en suite, but have had a style bypass, and some are a little worn around the edges. Breakfast not included. 625kr.

Løven Vesterbrogade 30 ☏ 33 79 67 20 ⓦ www .loeven.dk. Bus #6A or #26. There's no sign and the heavy steel door and scruffy entrance is a tad off-putting (ring the bell marked "1st floor Løven"), but this is one of central Copenhagen's real bargains, offering affordable, no-frills accommodation in plain but pleasantly decorated rooms sleeping up to four (mostly en suite). Breakfast isn't included, but there's a large and well-equipped kitchen and you can pop down to the great bakery next door for fresh bread and pastry. The major drawback is the noise – rooms facing the courtyard are quieter. 590kr.

Mayfair Helgolandsgade 3 ☏ 70 12 17 00, ⓦ www.choicehotels.dk. Bus #6A; Central Station. Part of the Choice hotel chain but one of the most characterful of the hotels in this street, with olde-English-style rooms complete with all mod cons – including minibar, and tea- and coffee-making facilities – plus carved wooden beds, leather armchairs and tasteful fabrics. There's also a cosy and plush lobby and bar area. Breakfast buffet (95kr) – not included in the price – is served outside in a courtyard during summer. 1530kr.

Missionshotellet Nebo Istedgade 6 ☏ 33 21 12 17, ⓦ www.nebo.dk. Central Station. Next door to Central Station – take the back exit – this well-run, recently renovated Danish Mission hotel is one of the best deals this close to the centre. Rooms – a mixture of en-suite and shared facilities – are simple but adequate and clean, and staff are friendly and relaxed. 690–860kr.

Saga Colbjørnsensgade 18–20 ☏ 33 24 49 44, ⓦ www.sagahotel.dk. Bus #10; Central Station. This friendly, laid-back family hotel at the grotty, but cheap, end of Colbjørnsensgade, is a good budget option. There are simple but pleasant rooms – mostly en suite – plus some bigger rooms with 3–4 beds, which are popular with families and backpackers. Free Internet access in the lobby. 650kr-950kr.

Scandic Hotel Webers Vesterbrogade 11b ☏ 33 31 14 32, ⓦ www.scandic-hotels.dk. Bus #6A,

#26; Central Station. Occupying a large, recently renovated, stately pink pile on busy Vesterbrogade, this place offers modern comforts – bar, fitness room and sauna – and nicely furnished rooms ranging from singles to suites. Ask for rooms facing the courtyard (open for drinks in summer) if you want to avoid street noise, though the soundproofing is good. Much cheaper at weekends and during the summer, but you'll need to book early. 1325kr.

Tiffany Colbjørnsensgade 28 ☎ 33 21 80 50, ⓦ www.hoteltiffany.dk. Bus #10; Central Station. Small, charming and welcoming hotel, a cut above most in the area and specially suited to those who want a more independent stay – the large, well-furnished double or family rooms all come equipped with mini-kitchens comprising a microwave, fridge and toaster, and continental breakfast is left in the fridge (with freshly baked rolls left at your door each morning). All rooms are non-smoking. 1145kr.

Frederiksberg

As a contrast to Vesterbro, Frederiksberg's tree-lined residential streets provide a calmer setting for somewhere to stay, though restaurants are thin on the ground. The locations of the following hotels are shown on the map on pp.102–103.

Avenue Åboulevard 29 ☎ 35 37 31 11, ⓦ www.avenuehotel.dk. Bus #67, #68, #250S; Forum metro. Comfortable and welcoming place on the border between Frederiksberg and Nørrebro – a ten-minute bus ride from the centre. Having recently undergone a thorough refurbishment the spacious rooms are stunning in their simple and stylish yet cosy design. There's a breakfast buffet (served outdoors in the summer) and free parking. Rates often fall at weekends. 1095kr.

Cab-Inn Copenhagen Express Danasvej 32–34 ☎ 33 21 04 00 and **Cab-Inn Scandinavia** Vodroffsvej 55 ☎ 35 36 11 11, ⓦ www.cabinn .com. Bus #29; Forum metro. The Cab-Inn concept was inspired by passenger cabins on the Oslo ferry, and the small rooms, flip-up tables and tiny showers certainly make you feel like a passenger on an overnight boat. But they're clean, very modern and safe, and the pleasant staff and unbeatably low price make this one of the top budget

hotels in town. The one on Danasvej is only open March to October. Both are wheelchair accessible. Breakfast buffet (50kr) not included. Parking 60kr per day. 645kr.

Euroglobe Niels Ebbesens Vej 20 ☎ 33 79 79 54, ⓦ www.hoteleuroglobe.dk. Bus #3A or #29. Basic but exceptionally good-value one-star hotel, on one of Frederiksberg's elegant and quiet streets (15min walk from the city centre). Rooms (no en suite) are a touch monastic – white walls, minimal furniture and a sink – but they're clean and bright. Those up in the eaves have a bit more character about them. There's also a kitchen for guests' use, and breakfast is included. No credit cards. 550kr.

Josty Pile Allé 14A ☎ 38 86 90 90, ⓦ www .josty.dk. Bus #18 or #26. Gorgeous hotel with just seven rooms (1 single, 4 doubles and 2 suites, so book well in advance) in a lovely position on the edge of Frederiksberg Have. Primarily used for weddings and large dinner functions (which can make it a bit noisy at weekends), *Josty* was built as a restaurant in 1813 by sculptor Agostino Taddei, and still preserves its original romantic Italian style. The elegant rooms are all en suite, and the beautiful location by the park makes it an ideal spot for a romantic break. A good out-of-season option. 900kr.

Memory Søndre Fasanvej 4 ☎ 38 87 13 42, ⓦ www.hotel-memory.dk. Bus #4A, #14 or #15. Small, reasonably priced hotel occupying a quaint old ochre villa with white shutters on the main road running along the western edge of Frederiksberg Have (15min by bus to the town centre). Only nine rooms – all cosy and well furnished – so book well ahead. Breakfast is served in your room. Cash and Visa only. 695kr.

Sct. Thomas Frederiksberg Allé 7 ☎ 33 21 64 64, ⓦ www.hotelsctthomas.dk. Bus #26. In a great location just past the junction with lively Vesterbrogade, this place is close to the delis and foodshops on Værnedamsvej and a 10min walk from Frederiksberg Have. The friendly owners, pleasantly decorated rooms (some cheaper with shared facilities) and easy-going atmosphere have made this hotel a runaway success, so be sure to book ahead (a couple of months in high season). Internet access, tea and coffee and buffet breakfast are included in the price, and in summer they rent out bikes (100kr/ day). Parking 50kr per day. Cash and Visa only. 795kr.

Nørrebro and Østerbro

There's not much available in these residential districts, which makes them appealing if you're looking for an insight into how Copenhageners live. The locations of the following hotels are shown on the map on pp.112–113.

Nora Nørrebrogade 18B, Nørrebro ☏35 37 20 21, ⓦwww.hotelnora.dk. Bus #5A or #350S. This excellent hotel is found in a residential apartment block and spans four floors. Rooms are spacious and comfortably decorated and come with fridge and tea- and coffee-making facilities; and there's a computer room with free Internet access. Popular with business travellers. Free parking in the back yard. 1200kr.

Rye Ryesgade 115, Østerbro ☏35 26 52 10, ⓦwww.hotelrye.dk. Bus #1A, #14 or #15. Near Fælledparken, Parken Stadium and busy Østerbrogade with its array of good places to eat and drink, *Rye* is a welcome home away from home. Located on the second and third floor of an old apartment block, which used to house a nursing home, the sixteen tastefully decorated rooms that all share bathing facilities – two rooms to a shower – come with slippers and housecoat. There is also a large breakfast buffet with home-made bread. 700kr.

The suburbs

Hilton Copenhagen Airport, Ellehammervej 20, Amager ☏32 50 15 01, ⓦwww.hilton.com. Copenhagen Airport station. See map, pp.120–121. One of Copenhagen's top hotels, the *Hilton* attracts celebrities and security-conscious politicians *en masse* to its twelve floors of absolute and beautifully decorated luxury. It's attached to the airport via internal walkways, and there's an emphasis on Viking themes throughout. As with Hiltons elsewhere, the hotel houses superb restaurants and a range of fitness facilities – at a price. Breakfast not included. 1800kr.

Hostels and sleep-ins

Copenhagen has a great selection of **hostels** and **sleep-ins** (often run by volunteer staff and geared towards backpackers, so some have age restrictions), which are ideal for those on a budget. They're mostly aimed at school groups and the hordes of young Swedes who descend on the city during the summer months looking for cheap alcohol and thrills, but some are more relaxed and quieter and have private rooms, which can work out good value if you're in a small group. **Prices** are roughly the same throughout the city (90–130kr for a dorm bed); sheets (you're generally not allowed to use sleeping bags) and breakfast cost around an extra 30kr each. **Availability** is only likely to be an issue in the peak summer months (June–August), when you should call ahead or turn up as early as possible on the day you want to stay. For the most up-to-date information, head for Use It (see p.37). Note that, at hostels run by Danhostel (the Danish branch of Hostelling International; ⓦwww.danhostel.dk), you'll also have to pay for temporary guest membership of HI if you're not already a member – 35kr per night, or 160kr for annual membership.

Indre By

The following place is shown on the map on pp.54–55.

Jørgensen Rømersgade 11 ☏33 13 81 86, ⓦwww.hoteljoergensen.dk. Bus #5A, #14, #40, #42, #43 or #350S; Nørreport S-Tog/metro. Great hostel-cum-hotel (see p.166) offering dormitory accommodation in three rooms of six to twelve beds, with a television in each room and breakfast included. You can rent sheets for 40kr if you don't have a sleeping bag. Very central, and popular with gay travellers. There's an age limit of 35. Open all year. 140kr per person.

Rådhuspladsen and around

The following place is shown on the map on p.90.

Danhostel Copenhagen City HC Andersens Bld 50 ☏33 11 85 85, ⓦwww.danhostel.dk. Central Station or bus #5A. Brand-new, trendy and bright HI "design" youth hostel in a multi-storey building overlooking the harbour and the green copper spires of the city.

With over one thousand beds (120kr) in four-to-six person rooms (all with en-suite bathroom), it prides itself on being the largest city-hostel in Europe and on its funky designer furniture. No curfew, and open all year.

Vesterbro

The following places are shown on the map on pp.102–103.

City Public Hostel Absalonsgade 8 ⓣ33 31 20 70, ⓦwww.city-public-hostel.dk. Bus #6A or #26. Easy-going and handily placed hostel, ten minutes' walk from Central Station next to the Københavns Bymuseum. There's a noisy 68-bed boy-only dorm on the lower floor, and less crowded 6- to 32-bed rooms on other levels – girls only in a 24-bed dorm – plus a kitchen and a barbecue out back. 24hr check-in and no curfew. Bed linen 35kr extra, breakfast 25kr, bed and breakfast 160kr. Open May–Aug. 140kr per person.

Sleep-In Fact Valdemarsgade 14 ⓣ33 79 67 79, ⓦwww.sleep-in-fact.dk. Bus #6A or #26. In the heart of Vesterbro, this is a sports centre out of season and has all sorts of sports facilities for hire when serving as a sleep-in. The eighty beds are divided between two large hall-type rooms, which can get very noisy at times. Reception open 7am–noon & 3pm–3am. Open July & Aug only. Sheets 30kr, small breakfast is included in the price. 120kr per person.

YMCA Inter Point Valdemarsgade 15 ⓣ33 31 15 74, ⓦwww.ymca-interpoint.dk. Bus #6A or #26. Run by the Danish YMCA/YWCA, with 28 cheap dorm beds, (4-, 6- and 10-bed rooms). There's a 12.30am curfew (check-in 7–11.30am, 3.30pm–12.30am). Sheets and blankets (15kr each) can be rented. Breakfast 25kr. Open July to mid-Aug. 95kr per person.

Nørrebro and Østerbro

The following places are shown on the map on pp.112–113.

Sleep-In Green Ravnsborggade 18, Nørrebro ⓣ35 37 77 77, ⓦwww.sleep-in-green.dk. Bus #5A or #350S. In the centre of hip Nørrebro, this place has bright rooms of 8, 20 and 38 beds, good all-volunteer staff, and organic snacks sold at the reception/chill-out room. Alcohol is not permitted on the premises. Extra charge for bedding (30kr) and organic breakfast (40kr). Max age 35. Open June–Oct. 100kr per person.

Sleep-In Heaven Struenseegade 7, Nørrebro ⓣ35 35 46 48, ⓦwww.sleepinheaven.com. Bus #250S. Popular hostel, next to Assistens Kirkegård, with two large dorms, subdivided into four- and eight-bed sections, plus two tiny self-contained "bridal suites" (though you still have to share a bathroom). Also has lockers, free Internet access, and takes credit cards. Sheets 30kr, breakfast 40kr. Max age 35. Open all year. 130kr per person.

The suburbs

The following places are shown on the map on pp.120–121.

Ajax Copenhagen Bavnehøj Alle 30, Sydhavnen ⓣ33 21 24 56, ⓕ33 25 24 56. Bus #1A, #3A or #10; Enghave or Sydhavnen stations. This hostel is in the clubhouse of Copenhagen's top handball club, in the twilight zone between Vesterbro and Sydhavnen, with three basic rooms, the largest with sixteen beds, and free access to a cooking area and outdoor grill. Open as the Roskilde Festival finishes (see p.231) and until mid-Aug. You can also rent tents here (70kr), and camping is possible in the garden. Breakfast costs 30kr and HI card is required. 110kr (3-bed dorm) and 80kr (16-bed dorm).

Belægningen Avedørelejren, Vester Kvartergade 22, Hvidovre ⓣ36 77 90 84, ⓦwww .belaegningen.dk. Bus #1A to Avedøre school; S-Tog to Avedøre station, then bus #133. Located in the old army barracks of Avedøre, next door to the Zentropa film production company (home to Von Trier and the Dogme concept, see p.211), this hostel has quiet and sparkling new two-, three-, four- and seven-bed rooms, a small kitchen and a restaurant, *Messen*, nearby. The only drawback is the distance from town. Breakfast is 55kr. Free Internet access and sheets included in the price. Bike rental 35kr per day. Open all year. Check-in Mon–Fri 2–8pm, Sat & Sun 2–6pm. 460kr for a self-contained double, 110kr for a dorm bed.

Danhostel Copenhagen Amager Vejlandsallé 200, Amager ⓣ32 52 27 08, ⓦwww .copenhagenyouthhostel.com. Bus #4A or #30; Bellacenter metro and a 500m walk. A three-star HI hostel on Amager, with cheap but basic two- and five-bed rooms, plus laundry and kitchen, *Amager* tends to be crowded and noisy, though there's no curfew. Reception is open 24hr, check-in daily 1–5pm. Breakfast 45kr, sheets 40kr. Closed Dec. HI members 110kr, non-members 145kr.

Danhostel Copenhagen Bellahøj Herbergvejen 8, Brønshøj ☎38 28 97 15, ⊛www.youth-hostel .dk. Bus #2A. More homely than its rivals, and situated in a residential part of the city – a 15min bus ride from the centre – *Bellahøj* has four-, six- and fourteen-bed rooms (sheets 40kr). There's a fully equipped kitchen and cheap laundry facilities, too. Reception is open 7am–8pm, check-in daily until 5pm, and there's no curfew, although there's a dormitory lockout from 10am–1pm. Breakfast 48kr. Closed Jan. HI members 110kr, non-members 145kr.

Danhostel Ishøj Strand Ishøj Strandvej 13, Ishøj ☎43 53 50 15, ⊛www.vandrerhjemmet.dk. Ishøj station then bus #300S. Out near Arken and some beautiful beaches, this five-star HI hostel has spacious four-person rooms and dorm beds, plus a decent restaurant, *Noah*. No curfew. Open all year, check-in daily 2—6pm. HI members 150kr, non-members 185kr.

Danhostel Lyngby-Tårbæk Rådvad 1, Lyngby ☎45 80 30 74, ⊛www.lyngbyhostel.dk. Lyngby station then bus #182 or #183. Beautifully located in the middle of Dyerhaven deer park and near Bakken (see p.119), 15km north of the city, this one-star HI hostel in a converted school has two- to eight-person dorms. Curfew 11pm. Open April–Oct. HI members 115kr, nonmembers 150kr.

Campsites

The Danes' love affair with camping is evident from the quality of their **campsites**, which are mostly very well run and have excellent facilities. Some of the campsites near Copenhagen are in peerless locations by beaches or in woods, whilst all are easily accessible by public transport. Most also have full hook-ups for trailers and camper vans, and some also have **cabins** – usually basic huts without bedding, though pleasant enough – but they're generally fully booked a year in advance. There's little difference in price among them (60–80kr per person per night, plus up to 40kr per tent), nor in facilities: all have laundries, kitchen areas with cookers, TV rooms, playgrounds and the like.

Some campsites may ask for a **Camping Card Scandinavia** (80kr), available at most sites and valid for a year. Alternatively, a transit pass costs 20kr per night. Prices quoted below are per person per night and not for the pitch. For locations of the following sites, see map pp.120–121.

Absalon Korsdalsvej 132, Rødovre ☎36 41 06 00, ⊛www.camping-absalon.dk. Bus #1A to Avedøre Havnevej, then a 10min walk. A friendly campsite about 9km to the west of the city (exit 24 on E47), *Absalon* has good facilities for campers or those with caravans, and pleasant cabins for rent (2–6 people). Open all year. 66kr.

Ajax Copenhagen Bavnehøj Alle 30, Sydhavnen ☎33 21 24 56, ⑤33 25 24 56. Bus #1A, #3A or #10; Enghave or Sydhavnen stations. In the gardens of the Ajax Copenhagen handball clubhouse and sharing facilities with the hostel housed here in the summer (see p.173), this is one of the most convenient campsites for the centre, but very basic and only open for a short period: after the Roskilde Festival (see p.231) until mid-Aug.

You can rent tents here for 70kr; otherwise, camping costs 45kr.

Bellahøj Hvidkildevej 66, Bellahøj ☎38 10 11 50, ⊛www.bellahoj-camping.dk. Bus #2A. One of the cheapest of Copenhagen's campsites, and near the city centre, *Bellahøj* is rather grim, with temporary facilities and little cover from the elements, but one plus point is its proximity to the excellent open-air Bellahøj public baths and the amazing view of the city from its hilltop location. Open June–Aug. 63kr.

Charlottenlund Fort Strandvejen 144, Charlottenlund ☎39 62 36 88, ⊛www .campingcopenhagen.dk. Bus #14. Situated in the old fort at beautiful Charlottenlund beach, this excellent campsite is the best within easy striking distance of the city centre (the bus stops right outside). There are also sites for camper vans and trailers. If you're camping, try to get a pitch around the back, where there's greater protection from the elements. Open mid-May to mid-Sept. 80kr.

City Camp Vasbygade ⓣ21 42 53 84, ⓦwww.citycamp.dk. Located close to the harbour, right behind the Fisketorvet shopping centre, *City Camp* offers safe parking for up to a hundred camper vans, and facilities such as showers and washing machines. You can also have breakfast delivered to your door. Open June–Aug. Check-in 8am–10pm. 35kr per camper and 75kr per person per day.

Nærum Ravnebakken, Nærum ⓣ45 80 19 57, ⓦwww.camping-naerum.dk. Jægersborg station, then private train to Nærum. Fifteen kilometres north of the city centre, in a pleasant setting beside some woods, this site is very family-oriented, with great play areas for the kids. Cabins are also available (390kr for up to 4 people). Open April to mid-Sept. 64kr.

Tangloppen Ishøj Havn, Ishøj ⓣ43 54 07 67, ⓦwww.fdmcamping.dk/tangloppen. Ishøj station, then bus #128. Right next door to Arken (see p.123), and facing onto a lagoon, *Tangloppen* is a wonderful place if you want a beach, modern art and not much else – shelter is minimal, and tents take a battering here in bad weather. There's also a cheap café selling grilled food, and a number of cabins (470kr for up to 4 people; 870kr for up to 8) and hook-up points for trailers and camper vans. Open April to mid-Oct. 70kr.

Eating

Copenhagen's **restaurant** scene has seen a dramatic increase in the quantity and variety of establishments over recent years and it continues to grow apace, covering the whole range from cheap ethnic eateries to Michelin-starred expense-account affairs. New designer places offering fancy fusion food and aimed at the city's young, trendy and wealthy open up on an almost monthly basis, though there's still a raft of old-fashioned eateries offering expensive but excellent Danish fare. As soon as summer arrives, the city is transformed as those cafés and restaurants that can, spill out onto the pavements – and for those less than balmy nights, most will turn on gas heaters or provide you with blankets to help along that *hygge* ("cosy") feeling. If your Danish is a bit rusty or nonexistent, it's good to know that most cafés and many restaurants in Copenhagen have English-language menus, though you may have to ask for one (see also p.263 for a glossary of food terms).

Traditionally, **Danish food** has been based on meat or fish plus two veg, though today it can encompass anything from delicious cuts of lean organic meat accompanied by wild mushrooms and berries to stodgy plates of gravy-soaked meatballs and mash. An affordable, if somewhat hit-and-miss way to sample traditional Danish food is to look for the chalk boards outside the city's *bodegas* ("bars") offering *dagens ret* ("meal of the day"), set lunches or dinners where the emphasis is on affordable and nourishing home cooking.

Whatever your tastes, don't miss the chance to sample the delicious and quintessentially Danish phenomenon of **smørrebrød**, or open sandwich – just as it sounds, a slice of delicious bread topped off with anything from herring to beef tartar to prawns, and always beautifully garnished. It's one of the highlights of a visit to the city, and better still when washed down with an invigorating shot or two of **snaps** (many restaurants have a snaps menu or card that will give you the lowdown on the different types available; failing that, just ask the waiter for advice on what goes best with what). Smørrebrød is best sampled in one of the many traditional smørrebrød restaurants, cosy and often packed cellar places open at lunchtime only and for which you're advised to book ahead. For a much less expensive option head for one of the many smørrebrød shops that, around lunchtime, sell readymade smørrebrød to go to the city's workforce. They're omnipresent throughout Copenhagen – look for the "smørrebrød" shop sign. A couple of good places include *Centrum Smørrebrød,* Vesterbrogade 6D near Central Station, and *Rådhus Smørrebrød* Vester Voldgade 90 near the Rådhus.

Of course, another speciality not to be missed is the famous **Danish pastry** – most cafés will serve reasonable versions, though they're best bought straight from the excellent and plentiful **konditorier** ("patisseries") and eaten on-the-move or in the *konditori*'s coffee bar.

Food
and drink

Sampling some of Copenhagen's traditional cuisine is a delight: the emphasis is on locally grown seasonal food, served in a simple yet effective manner; and a crispy, flaky pastry in the morning, followed by a heavily laden smørrebrød sandwich washed down with a glass of ice-cold beer, will set you up for the day. Not so long ago, eating out was a pastime enjoyed mainly by the city's rich, but nowadays lunchtime restaurants heave with Copenhageners piling an incredible variety of toppings onto their open sandwiches.

Bakeries and Danish pastries

Danes generally eat freshly made **bread** from the local bakers rather than sliced and packaged supermarket loaves. Try the *rundstykke* (literally "round piece"), a crispy bread roll baked with different combinations of seeds and grain, and eaten fresh at breakfast with butter and jam or cheese. Follow this with a piece of freshly made pastry and a cup of coffee and you have the traditional Danish breakfast.

Don't expect the **Danish pastries** to resemble those you'll find at home, however: they're less sweet and sticky, and much more flaky and crispy (in Denmark, Danish pastry is actually called *wienerbrød*, "Viennese bread", because the art of making flaking pastry was learnt from bakers in Vienna). Try the pristine *Hanekam* ("Rooster's comb"), a simple comb-shaped flaked pastry decorated with sugar and sliced almonds, or the aptly named *Bagerens dårlige øje* – the Baker's infected eye – flaky pastry adorned with a gooey splodge of sweet custard or jam in the middle.

Best bakeries

Bread- and pastry-making is a thriving business in Denmark, and you'll find a bakery around almost every corner in Copenhagen. The city's **top traditional bakeries** are Lagkagehuset at Torvegade 45, Christianshavn (see p.221), which produces amazing bread, baked in traditional stone ovens, plus great pastries and cakes, and *Rhein van Hauen*, Mikkels Bryggers Gade 8 (and other outlets), which has over 27 years of organic baking to its credit and serves up mouthwatering *rundstykker* and *wienerbrød*. More innovative bread – including spelt bread, and bread risen with sour dough rather than yeast (making it moister and more chewy) – is made at a Emmery's, a new bakery chain with city-centre branches at Vesterbrogade 34, Nørrebrogade 8, Østerbrogade 51 and Store Strandstræde 21. For more on bakeries, see "Shopping" on p.221. If you'd rather sit down and enjoy your pastry in comfort, try *Café Europa* (p.179), *Konditoriet* (p.180), *Rhein van Hauen* (see p.181), *La Glace* (p.180) and *Norden* (p.181).

Smørrebrød

The most characteristic, and perhaps the most appetizing, feature of Danish cuisine is the open sandwich, or **smørrebrød**. A quintessentially Danish concept – different in style and flavour, even, from the Swedish *smörgåsbord* – smørrebrød is eaten for lunch and finds its way into most Danish lunch packs. The concept is simple and the product scrumptious: a thin slice of **rye bread** (good for the digestion) is spread with **butter** (Danish butter, of course) or pork fat, layered with a selection of **fish** or sliced **meats**, and topped with a combination of thick **dressings** and raw or pickled **vegetables**, or, in a few cases, raw egg or caviar.

To the uninitiated, it can be a bit of a mystery deciding which spreads, slices and toppings go well together, but café and restaurant staff are only too happy to help – smørrebrød combinations are ingrained in the Danish psyche. Some of the combos even have names: **Dyrelægens Natmad** (Veterinarian's Midnight Snack) is liver pâté topped with a square of broth jelly, some cress

▲ A typical smørrebrød topping

and a slice of salted beef; **Sol over Gudhjem** (Sunset over Gudhjem) consists of smoked herring (preferably from Bornholm) covered with chives, radish slices and a raw egg yoke; while **Stjerneskud** (Starburst) is a piece of fried plaice topped with remoulade and prawns, and decorated with caviar and a slice of lemon.

Smørrebrød come in one of three forms: you can order your topping from a list of ingredients, construct your own sandwiches from a buffet, or have your smørrebrød served up ready made. At *Huset Med Det Grønne Træ* (p.179), *Told & Snaps* (p.182) and *Hansens Gamle Familiehave* (p.188), you'll be ordering from a **list of toppings**, while good restaurants for **ready-made smørrebrød** are *Kanal Cafeen* (p.186), *Slotskælderen Hos Gitte Kik* (p.181), *Café & Ølhalle "1892"* (p.178) and *Domhuskælderen* (p.178). For a much cheaper option, head for one of the city's many shops that, around lunchtime, sell ready-made smørrebrød to go to the city's workforce. A couple of good places include *Centrum Smørrebrød*, Vesterbrogade 6D, near Central Station, and *Rådhus Smørrebrød*, Vester Voldgade 90, near the Rådhus.

Beer

In recent years, the ubiquitous Carlsberg has had its monopoly somewhat threatened by microbreweries from both home and abroad. Small Danish breweries are experiencing a massive revival, with companies such as Thisted Bryghus, in West Jutland, and Bryggeriet Svaneke, on Bornholm, making major impressions on the Copenhagen beer market and attracting loyal followings. There are numerous beer halls, bars and pubs across the city, but below are our favourite five:

90eren (see p.197). A veritable Carlsberg temple serving the uncarbonated version of the Danish brew virtually straight from the barrel.

Bryggeriet Apollo (see p.196). Brewer's pub next to Tivoli, which produces a different type of beer – always organic, always delicious – every month.

Charlie's Bar (see p.194). Small, British-run place in the city centre whose outstanding selection of fresh, unpasteurized ales and ciders are pulled from a whooping eighteen taps.

Nørrebro Bryghus (see p.199). Microbrewery on Nørrebro, with a gourmet restaurant upstairs and a bar downstairs, serving award-winning home brews such as Stuykman Witt wheat beer, Czech pilsner, New York lager and the local Ravnsborg Rød.

Ølbaren (see p.199). Intimate place packed with bottles from all over the world, and with in-the-know bartenders, should you require anything special.

Copenhagen's abundant **cafés** are extremely versatile, serving coffee and cake, **brunch** (see box on p.179) and lunch for most of the day, and a generally more expensive evening menu, when many also double as bars. Filling sandwiches (not smørrebrød) are available in most as well as more substantial fare such as burgers and pasta and sundry international snack foods – tapas, nachos and the like. If you're really on a shoestring, there are dozens of takeaway **pizzerias**, most of a reasonable standard, along with the ubiquitous **pølser stands**, which offer a variety of surprisingly addictive hot dogs and burgers. There are also plenty of kebab joints and Chinese takeaways. Though not exactly cordon bleu, all of these can provide welcome pit stops on a long walk around the city.

Though Copenhagen is a long way behind London or Paris in terms of quality and diversity of **ethnic restaurants**, the immigrant community's impact is increasingly being felt, particularly in the Vesterbro and Nørrebro areas, with a large array of **Turkish** and **Indian** places – probably Copenhagen's cheapest eating-out options – along with a good selection of (slightly pricier) **Thai** restaurants and Japanese **sushi** joints. **Vegetarians** are reasonably well catered for in Copenhagen, with most restaurants offering at least a couple of meat-free dishes (see box on p.178 for a list of the best).

Eating out in Copenhagen's restaurants can be a very expensive affair, especially if you throw in a bottle of wine, which costs upwards of 175kr for something decent; it's best to stick to the all-day cafés or ethnic places if you don't want to break the bank, reserving that restaurant choice for a one-off special meal. That said, should some of the more pricey restaurants listed take your fancy, it's worth bearing in mind that many are open for lunch, too, with the daytime set menus offering a considerably more affordable way of sampling some of the city's finer, more adventurous cuisine. In the evening, dining out at any of the more formal restaurants will generally set you back at least 150–200kr for a main course, with a bottle of wine bringing things up to around 400kr. We've given phone numbers for restaurants in all cases where it's advisable to book in advance. Note that the **opening hours** given for each listing are for the venue's actual closing time; the **kitchen often closes** one or, in the case of café/bars, two hours earlier. Note also that many restaurants are closed Sunday or Monday – be sure to double-check before you set out. Our listings are broken down by area, largely corresponding to chapter divisions of the guide.

For more details, see the **Food and drink** colour section.

△ Park

Indre By has restaurants on virtually every street corner; as a general rule, they're small, cosy places with lots of history. The area's many offices and businesses also mean that most restaurants have an excellent lunch menu; indeed, for some, lunch is the busiest time of the day. For locations of the following places see the map on pp.54–55.

Atlas Bar Larsbjørnsstræde 18 ☏ 33 15 03 52. Mon–Sat noon–midnight. On trendy Larsbjørnstræde in the basement underneath *Flyvefisken* restaurant, the *Atlas Bar* features a globetrotting range of dishes (lunch 80kr plus, dinner 100kr plus) of an exotic – and generally spicy – nature such as Mexican chilli or Bali chicken. Portions are large, and the changing menu is chalked up on a bar blackboard daily – one side meat, the other fish and vegetarian. Always packed at lunchtime, when it's a good idea to book in advance.

Barbarellah Nørre Farigmagsgade 41. Mon–Wed & Sun 10am–midnight, Thurs–Sat 10am–2am. In spite of its Arabic sounding name, *Barbarellah* is actually the creation of three siblings from Chile who make a mean array of cocktails. On top of that, they also cook some pretty good and inexpensive food, mostly South American inspired, and serve brunch (one veggie, one meaty; 74kr) until 6pm. In the corner, Barbara – one of the three – sells her own design clothes.

Café & Ølhalle "1892" Rømersgade 22 ☏ 33 33 00 47. Daily 11.30am–4pm. In the basement of the Arbejdermuseet (see p.62), the atmospheric *Ølhalle* has been restored to its 1892 appearance, and specializes in food from the period, such as traditional Danish *bidesild* (strongly flavoured pickled herring) washed down with snaps. Booking advisable.

Cap Horn Nyhavn 21 ☏ 33 12 85 04. Daily 9am–1am. One of Nyhavn's most popular spots to soak up the quayside atmosphere. Cheaper lunch options include herrings galore, organic burgers or, if you're really hungry, "Sild & Bøf" – herrings followed by Argentinian beef for 159kr. The evening menu is just as good, with no-fuss fare such as leg of lamb or steak for 165kr, and there's always a vegetarian option (105kr) – save some room for the delectable homemade chocolate truffles. Service is friendly and efficient.

Dan Turéll Store Regnegade 3–5 ☏ 33 14 10 47. Mon–Wed 9.30am–midnight, Thurs 9.30am–midnight, Fri & Sat 9.30am–2am, Sun 10am–10pm (kitchen closes 10pm, Fri & Sat 11pm, Sun 8.30pm). Busy French-style café-bar devoted to the memory of author Dan Turéll. Renowned as one of the city's best, brunch until 1pm (weekdays 95kr, weekends 132kr) is packed with delicious homemade delicacies and is a lot more extensive at weekends. Sandwiches, pies and salads largely make up the lunchtime menu, while dinner features well-prepared fish and meat dishes (no veggie option) starting at 160kr. The big, tasty DT burger is available throughout the day. See also "Drinking", on p.194. Booking essential Fri & Sat evening. Jazz Festival venue.

Den Grønne Kælder Pilestræde 48 ☏ 33 93 01 40. Mon–Sat 11am–10pm. This busy but relaxed vegetarian cellar eatery offers a good selection of scrumptious seasonal dishes with wild mushroom lasagne one of the few constants on an ever-changing menu. Dinner here is relatively cheap, compared to other city-centre restaurants, starting at 95kr for generous portions. Also serves organic wines, beer and home-made bread.

Domhuskælderen Nytorv 5 ☏ 33 14 84 55. Daily 11am–10pm. This very popular traditional basement joint attracts a mix of tourists, shoppers and locals, with its large outdoor seating area on Nytorv. The lunch menu

Vegetarian Copenhagen

Most restaurants have at least a couple of vegetarian options on the menu. The following places are some of the best:

Atlas Bar (p.178)

Flow (p.185)

Den Grønne Kælder (p.178)

Morgenstedet (p.183)

Picnic (p.189)

Riz Raz (p.181)

Spiseloppen (p.183)

Copenhageners have taken to the concept of **brunch** with alacrity, and most cafés now offer a range of brunch options: from a restrained yoghurt, muesli and fruit combo to American-style blowouts. They're usually very good value at around 50–100kr and available until at least 2pm (sometimes all day), either plated up or as all-you-can-eat buffets. If you're on a budget, they're a good way to fill up. The following are some of the best brunch spots in the city:

Bastionen og Løven (p.183)

Dan Turéll (p.178)

Den Franske Café (p.190)

Det Gule Hus (p.187)

Klimt (p.180)

Marius (p.180)

Park Café (p.191)

Pussy Galore's Flying Circus (p.190)

Sebastopol (p.190)

Sommersko (p.182)

Thorvaldsens Hus (p.182)

Café Wilder (p.183)

---

is extensive, with a full range of generous smørrebrød (from 50kr a piece) and a filling smørrebrød platter for 138kr. Things get more expensive in the evening, with a hearty meat-and-veg menu that includes the likes of pork, guinea fowl and venison in the 150kr price range.

L'Education Nationale Larsbjørnsstræde 12 ☏ 33 91 53 60. Mon–Sat noon–midnight. Paris in Copenhagen: everything in this café comes from France – even the butter on the table – and the tipple of choice is French wine rather than the usual Danish beer. Lunchtime favourites such as Croque Monsieur/Madame (two sizes at 59kr/69kr) and moules frites (110kr) give way in the evening to hearty French country cooking in large portions of rabbit ragout, brochet lyonnaise or lamb casserole, all for 185kr.

Europa Amagertorv 1. Mon–Thurs 8am–midnight, Fri 8am–2am, Sat 9am–2am, Sun 9am–11pm. In a great spot, overlooking bustling Amagertorv, the large glass-fronted *Europa* is a welcome stop along Strøget for a cup of coffee, a superior slice of cake or a sandwich (99kr). Outdoor service on Amagertorv is very efficient, so if you're in a hurry, this is the place to go.

Extra Østergade 13 t35 26 09 52. Mon–Sat noon–11pm, Thurs-Sat lounge-bar open until 3am. Large, trendy new restaurant at the exclusive end of Strøget next door to Mulberry. Run by one of the city's top chefs, Extra's main focus is on tapas and more broadly on Spanish cuisine. Main courses start at 169kr with tapas between 16kr (oysters) and 395kr (caviar). There's

also a three-course lunch menu for 298kr. Fri & Sat the place converts into a nightclub at midnight (see p.203).

Flyvefisken Larsbjørnsstræde 18 ☏ 33 14 95 15. Mon–Sat 5.30pm–midnight. Upstairs from the equally popular *Atlas Bar* and with a good view of goings-on in trendy Larsbjørnsstræde, *Flyvefisken* is a great place to start off the evening in one of the city's liveliest quarters. Its excellent range of dishes from around the globe – added a not overly spicy Thai twist – start at 110kr and are served up amidst a stylish blend of modern, light Danish/Thai decor.

Hovedtelegrafen Købmagergade 37. Tues–Sat 11am–5pm, Sun noon–4pm, Wed open also 5.30–8pm. Most people bypass the exhibitions in the Post & Tele Museum and take the lift straight to this rooftop café. Cool, modern and light, with amazing views over the rooftops, it's a relaxing spot for some lunch – a mixture of posh open sandwiches starting at 42kr and cheesy omelettes (68k) and burger (89kr) – or just coffee and a piece of gorgeous cake.

Huset Med Det Grønne Træ Gammeltorv 20 ☏ 33 12 87 86. April–Aug Mon–Fri 11.30am–3.30pm; Sept–March Mon–Sat 11.30am–3.30pm. Frequented mostly by lawyers and solicitors from the nearby law courts, the old-fashioned "House with the Green Tree" offers some of the finer Danish lunches in the downtown area. The spread of smørrebrød leaves little to be desired; neither do the fourteen different types of snaps.

Ketchup Pilestraede 19 ☏ 33 32 30 30. Mon–Thurs noon–midnight, Fri noon–2am, Sat 11am–2am, Sun kitchen closed but bar open.

One of the most self-consciously stylish additions to the city's thriving café/restaurant/bar scene with a menu to match, mixing Danish fare with Asian influences ranging from club sandwich "Bali Style" (99kr) in the cheaper streetfront café to lobster a la ketchup priced at 1kr per gram in the back room and downstairs restaurant. Things get very lively when the food stops (around 10pm in the café, 11pm in the restaurant) and the bar kicks off with DJs on Friday and Saturday nights.

Klaptræet Kultorvet 13. Mon–Wed 10am–1am, Thurs 10am–3am, Fri & Sat 11am–5am, Sun 1pm–midnight. Frequented during the week by backgammon-playing locals and exhausted shoppers, *Klaptræet* transforms during weekends to a busy hangout for the local high-school kids. Breakfasts are cheap, and there are good-value sandwiches (57kr) and burgers (from 63kr) throughout the day.

Klimt Frederiksborggade 29. Mon–Thurs & Sun 10am–midnight, Fri & Sat 10am–2am. With a giant copy of a Klimt painting on the wall, and changing local artist exhibits, *Klimt's* main claim to fame is its great brunches (79–99kr) with a long list of side-order options, the fabulous Klimt burger (89kr) and the Cajun chicken (89kr). There's also a great range of sandwiches, omelettes and pasta dishes. High-quality fresh produce, at affordable prices, plus a large selection of choice teas, coffees, fruit juices and cognacs.

Kommandanten Ny Adelgade 7 ☎33 12 09 90. Mon–Sat 5.30–10pm. If your palate demands (and wallet permits) haute cuisine, then *Kommandanten* – with its Michelin star – won't disappoint. The menu is classic French with a Danish twist; the choice of three to four mains includes fish of the day starting at 320kr, or you may prefer the six-course option that will set you back a cool 790kr.

Konditoriet Amagertorv 6. Mon–Thurs 11am–5pm, Fri 11am–6pm, Sat 10am–4pm & summer only Sun noon–4pm. Once you've checked out the expensive wares in the Royal Copenhagen Porclain shop (see p.109), pop upstairs to *Konditoriet*, one of the best spots for a genteel cup of coffee or cocoa with a cream cake (starting at 32kr) or finger sandwich served up on the shop's own beautiful porcelain and silverware.

Kong Hans Kælder Vingårdsstræde 6 ☎33 11 68 68. Mon–Sat 6pm–midnight. With a Michelin star and a romantic setting in what was once King Hans' wine cellar, this is undoubtedly one of Denmark's best restaurants. For mouthwatering starters such as frothy parsley soup with Burgundy snails or Danish "Limfiord Oysters", and mains such as tournedos with morels, potato puree and sprouting onions, you can reckon on upwards of 895kr for a six-course meal.

Krasnapolsky Vestergade 10. Mon–Thurs 11am–midnight, Fri–Sat 10am–5am. Spacious café-bar off Strøget that caters for a broad range of customers, from suburban housewives on shopping sprees to hip techno freaks, with its almost round-the-clock service of French-style café food. Brunch (75–99kr) is served until 3pm, or try the excellent chilli con carne (75kr). See also "Drinking" p.195.

Krogs Fiskerestaurant Gammel Strand 38 ☎33 15 89 15. Mon–Sat 5.30pm–midnight. One of the city's oldest, best and most expensive fish restaurants, located where fisherwomen used to sell their catch. The interior oozes elegance, and is kept as it was when the restaurant first opened in 1910. If you can justify paying the mind-boggling prices, you'll get mouthwatering and beautifully presented dishes. The five-course *menu gastronomique* at 750kr is probably your best bet if you want more than one course (the Krogs bouillabaise costs a mere 420kr). Booking essential.

La Galette Larsbjørnsstræde 9. Mon–Sat noon–11pm, Sun 4–10pm. Tucked away in a backyard with outdoor seating in summer, this cosy, excellent-value and authentically Breton (the flour for the galettes is imported from Brittany) pancake joint offers the savoury and sweet buckwheat kind with a range of fillings, and you can wash it all down with a jug of equally authentic cider. Prices range from 25kr for a plain galette to 80kr for a galette with caviar and smoked salmon filling.

La Glace Skoubogade 20. Mon–Thurs 8.30am–5.30pm, Sat 9am–5pm, Sun 11am–5pm. Time seems to have stood still at the city's oldest patisserie, the unmissable *La Glace*, with primly dressed waitresses ministering to a genteel clientele who come for the beautifully sculpted, cream-heavy cakes and pots of real hot chocolate (48kr a pot). If all that sounds too much, you could just settle for a coffee and a Danish.

Marius Nørre Farimagsgade 55 ☎33 11 83 83. Tues–Wed noon–11pm, Thurs noon–1am,

Fri noon–2am, Sat 11am–2am, Sun 11am–4pm.
On the sunny side of Nørre Farimagsgade,
this Chicagoan corner café prides itself
on serving the "Best brunch in town", and
they're not far wrong. Weekends only (11am
to 3/4pm) two types of American brunch –
one including chorizo and potato pancakes
(99kr), the other bacon, hash browns and
buttermilk pancakes (95kr) – and an array
of side orders sets you up perfectly for the
day. The rest of the week freshly made
bagels, wraps, burgers and home-made
pasta set the tone for lunch and dinner.
Booking recommended for brunch.

Norden Østergade 61. Mon–Sat 9am–midnight,
Sun 9.30am–midnight. This Copenhagen café
stalwart is usually packed by virtue of its
great location. The café-style food – sandwiches, salads and soups – is nothing
special but fairly good value (around 100kr),
considering the location. The gorgeous
cakes, however, are to die for, freshly made
every day.

Nyhavns Færgekro Nyhavn 5 ☎ 33 15 15 88.
Daily 9am–1pm. Located on the sunny
side of Nyhavn, *Færgekro* (Ferry Inn) is a
good lunchtime option along this restau-
rant-heavy stretch, serving an amazing
lunchtime herring buffet with ten different
types of herring for 98kr. There's also the
filling Nyhavns platter with five heavily
laden pieces of smørrebrød for 159kr, or
you can try them individually starting at
49kr a piece. In the evening, the à la carte
restaurant upstairs does a two-course
menu for 195kr.

Paludan Fiolstræde. 10 Mon–Fri 8am–8pm, Sat
10am–6pm. In the heart of the Latin Quarter
and with a textbook-toting student clientele
to prove it, this pleasant bookshop-café is
a good spot to enjoy inexpensive coffee
and cake or a lunchtime sandwich (from
48kr) between browsing the bookshops on
Fiolstræde.

Pasta Basta Valkendorfsgade 22 ☎ 33 11 21
31. Mon–Thurs & Sun 11.30pm–3am, Fri & Sat
11.30am–5am. Big, very central and open
very late, *Pasta Basta* is a favourite final
stop for all-night groovers, and extremely
popular with young locals at all times. The
seasonal menu offers a good array of fish
and meat pasta dishes as well as several
heavier meat mains such as osso buco
(147kr plus 35kr for the pasta buffet) – or
you could simply just fill up on the all-day
buffet of pasta and salads for 79kr.

Peder Oxe Gråbrødretorv 11 ☎ 33 11 00 77.
Daily 11.30am–1am. Very popular French-
inspired steakhouse, with outdoor seating
on Gråbrødretorv in fine weather. Busy for
both lunch and dinner and serving up a
small menu of meat and fish mains and
rich desserts. The main attraction is the
juicy organic ox-burger made with finest
beef (115kr) – for an extra 35kr you can
also help yourself to the salad buffet.
The salad buffet on its own is 79kr. The
only drawback is the lack of elbow room
indoors.

Rhein van Hauen Mikkels Bryggers Gade 8.
Daily 9am–10pm. One of the acknowledged
masters of the Danish pastry, the Rhein van
Hauen bakery chain has several outlets in
the city; this one, down a side street leading south off Strøget, has the advantage of
a café where you can indulge in the flaky
wonders or a light snack.

Riz Raz Kompagnistræde 20. Daily 11.30am–
midnight. *Riz Raz*'s hot and cold Mediterranean veggie buffet is one of the city's
best (and healthiest) budget options – all
the fresh salads, pasta, falafel, rice and feta
cheese you can eat for 59kr (69kr in the
evening). There's also a menu with more
carnivorous fare, including kebabs and
steaks. As you'd expect, it's usually packed,
but turnover is high and there's outdoor
seating available. There's another branch at
Store Kannikestræde 19.

Roberts Coffee Larsbjørnsstræde 17. Mon–Thurs
10am–11pm, Fri 10am–1am, Sat 11am–
midnight, Sun noon–6pm. This popular addition to Copenhagen coffee-house culture
may be part of a successful Finnish chain
but it's a far cry from the bland homogene-
ity of Starbucks. The great range of coffees
and teas (as well as organic snacks and
sandwiches) can be sampled in the upstairs
bar or while sunk in a sofa in the candlelit
cellar area. There's occasional jazz, too.

Slotskælderen Hos Gitte Kik Fortunstræde 4.
Tues–Sat 11am–5pm. It may not look much
from the outside but this is one of the best
places in town to sample smørrebrød.
There's no menu – just walk up to the table,
presided over by Gitte herself, pick your
toppings from the heaped plates of delicacies, and the made-up smørrebrød will be
brought over to you. Prices start at 37kr for
a slice with herring.

Sommersko Kronprinsensgade 6. Mon–Wed
8am–midnight, Thurs 8am–1am, Fri 8am–4am,

Sat 9am–4am, Sun 10am–midnight. Excellent Parisian-style brasserie on a boutique street attracting a young and trendy clientele. Business starts with a breakfast of freshly made bread and a soft-boiled egg (45kr). Thereafter (10am–3pm), delectable brunch in three sizes (85–115kr) is overlapped by lunch and a fabulous array of sandwiches, burgers, soups and salads; this culminates in innovative pasta dishes, fish and meat mains in the evening till 11pm. Popular meeting spot during weekends. See also "Drinking", p.195.

Sporvejen Gråbrødretorv 17. Daily 11am–midnight. One of the city's more unusual eateries, *Sporvejen* is housed in the last of Copenhagen's old trams – the rest are now in Egypt – and dishes out some of the city's best-value burgers (omelettes for vegetarians) served up with egg and chips. There's outdoor seating in summer.

Sticks 'n' Sushi Nansensgade 59 ☎ 33 11 14 07. Mon–Thurs 6–10pm, Fri & Sat 6–11pm. This classy but pricey sushi bar on fashionable Nansensgade is among the city's favourite Japanese eateries. The menu changes according to season and there's an adventurous note to the sushi – duck breast in orange-teriyaki and goats cheese in pata negra ham make an appearance. Choose from several different set menus. There's a second branch *Sticks 'n' Sushi Take-away* (seating also available) further down Nansensgade at no. 47, which is also open during the day and offers a similar menu.

Thorvaldsens Hus Gammel Strand 34 ☎ 33 32 04 00. Mon–Thurs & Sun 10am–midnight, Fri & Sat 10am–2am. Popular canalside café/restaurant, serving up mostly Danish fare ranging from hearty brunch (daily 11am–3pm; 98kr), herring smørrebrød (from 65kr) to full-on meals (295kr for 3 courses). There's a great view of the colourful frescoes of Thorvaldsens Museum from the seats outside. Popular with business lunchers.

Told & Snaps Toldbodgade 2 ☎ 33 93 83 85. Mon–Sat 11.30am–4pm, closed Sun. Traditional lunchtime smørrebrød restaurant, focusing on high food quality rather than fashion, where you're handed a metre-long *smør-rebrødsseddel* – a list of possible toppings – to tick off your choice, before the waiter brings you the sandwiches one by one. Try the fresh fish meatballs with home-made remoulade and lemon (58kr); it's out of this world.

Tyvenkokkenhanskoneoghendeselsker Magstræde 16 ☎ 33 16 12 92. Mon–Sat 6pm–2am. Named after the Peter Greenaway film *The Cook, the Thief, his Wife and her Lover*, this cosy and charming restaurant pulls in discerning foodies with creative seasonal Danish/French fare – think seared foie gras with beetroot and fève beans and pigeon with oxheart cabbage. Only choice is the set menu of five courses for 550kr or the lobster menu at 695kr (min 2 servings). There's a great wine list, too, and service is excellent.

Vandkunsten Rådhusstræde 17. Mon–Fri 8am–5pm. Small Italian sandwich shop whose home-made focaccia and ciabatta, filled to bursting with pastrami, mozzarella, sun-dried tomato, avocado and the like, have a big reputation as one of the best sandwiches in town (25–38kr). They also do takeaway pastas and salads.

Christianshavn

Laid-back Christianshavn is a great spot to linger over lunch or dinner, which you can follow with a walk along the pretty Wilders Kanal; there's a wide range of eating options including the unique experience of eating out in the hippie haven of Christiania. For locations of the following, see map, p.67.

Bastionen og Løven Voldgade 50 ☎ 32 95 09 40, ⓦ www.bastionen-loven.dk. Summer daily 10am–midnight; winter Mon–Fri noon–midnight, Sat & Sun 10am–midnight. Set in the old miller's house next to Lille Mølle, up on the ramparts and with outside seating, this is a charming, relaxed spot for a bite of traditional Danish food. The lunchtime menu offers delicious soups, salads or smørrebrod from 60kr – try the delectable *kalveleverpostej* (calves' liver paté); in the evening, main courses start at 175kr. There's a large and very popular buffet brunch at weekends (10am–2pm) for 150kr; an unbeatable way to start your tour of Christianshavn.

Era Ora Overgaden Neden Vandet 33 ☎ 32 54 06 93, ⓦ www.eraora.dk. Mon–Sat noon–3pm (kitchen closes 2pm) & 7pm–1am (kitchen closes 10.30pm). In a lovely location by the Wilders Kanal and with a romantic courtyard for summer dining, *Era Ora* serves top-flight Italian cuisine – all of the ingredients are seasonal and most are sourced from Italy. You'll pay for the quality with lunchtime menus starting at 280kr and evening menus from 580kr, but for Italophiles looking for a special meal, it's hard to beat. Book well in advance.

Kanalen Wilders Plads 2 ☎ **32 95 13 30,** ⓦ**www.restaurant-kanalen.dk. Mon–Sat 11.30am–midnight.** Intimate, romantic and elegant canalside restaurant in a pink eighteenth-century building. The lunchtime menu consists of traditional Danish fare such as marinated herring (85kr) or fried plaice with remoulade (98kr); the evening set menu also focuses on local ingredients and costs from 358kr for three courses.

Lagkagehuset Torvegade 45. This fantastic bakery/café is awash with a mouthwatering array of Danish pastries, fruity muffins and cakes. A great place to pick up a sandwich, cake and coffee to eat by the canal. Also some counter seating.

Månefiskeren Fremtidsskoven, Christiania. Tues–Fri 10am–11pm, Sat & Sun 10am–1pm. Off to the left from Pusherstreet (look for the tall chimney), *Månefiskeren* is a predictably laid-back café renowned for its morning servings of eggs and bacon, followed later in the day by excellent sandwiches and home-made cakes. No alcohol.

Morgenstedet Langgaden, Christiania. Tues–Fri noon–9pm. Small and cosy Christiania favourite serving great-value vegetarian and vegan food from an organic kitchen – there are usually five dishes, along the lines of salads, stews, curry and ratatouille. No alcohol is served, but you can bring your own.

Noma Strandgade 93, ☎**32 96 32 97,** ⓦ**www .noma.dk.** For the gastronomically adventurous, *Noma*, a recent addition to the city's small Michelin-starred fraternity, is *the* place to go for a taste of modern, inventive and unusual Scandinavian cuisine. It's a quirky, ever-changing menu, relying totally on seasonal ingredients from the North Atlantic countries cooked by traditional methods, so there's a good deal of pickling, salting and drying. Regulars on the menu include such culinary delights as musk ox, lumpfish, Danish blood sausage, fungi and berries. Housed in a former warehouse that's also home to North Atlantic House, *Noma*'s decor is as modern and stylish as you'd expect – exposed brickwork, white paint-work, animal skins draped over expensive

chairs – and its location, overlooking the harbour, just completes the whole experience. With individual mains costing upwards of 295kr, the set menus, starting at around 350kr for three courses, are the way to go.

Spicey Kitchen Café Torvegade 56. Mon–Wed 2pm–midnight, Thurs–Sun noon–midnight. Good, cheap curries for around 65kr are the order of the day here – mostly chicken or lamb – though you may have to wait for a table in the rather cramped interior. They also do kebabs and a range of veggie dishes. Takeaway available; credit cards not accepted.

Spiseloppen The Loppe Building, Badmandss-traede 43, Christiania ☎**32 57 95 58,** ⓦ**www .spiseloppen.dk. Tues–Sun 5–10pm.** Upstairs from the music venue *Musikloppen*, this excellent restaurant has a reputation far beyond Christiania's borders for serving superb food from a changing but always imaginative menu of international dishes. Meat and fish mains start at 155kr; also has a good variety of vegetarian options. Very popular, so book ahead.

Café Wilder Wildersgade 56. Daily 9am–2am. Popular and relaxed locals' café, great for coffee and croissant, pasta or a range of salads, and usually packed on Sundays with brunch junkies tucking into the "Wilders Brunch" (90kr) – a generous helping of egg, bacon, sausage, yoghurt, cheese and fruit.

Rosenborg and Frederikstad

Restaurants in the Rosenborg and Frederiksstad area are generally slightly pricier than elsewhere in the rest of the city, reflecting the local clientele; this is where the royal family pop out for a bite to eat when they're home at Amalienborg. For locations of the following places see the map on pp.76–77.

Chico's Cantina Borgergade 2 ☎**33 11 41 08. Daily 11am–midnight.** Everything you would expect from a Mexican restaurant landed overseas, both menu- and decor-wise. The food is well prepared, and worth seeking out if you're missing your enchiladas (119kr). The 69kr lunch buffet has a large following.

Coffee Factory Gothersgade 21. Mon–Fri 7.30am–7pm, Sat 9am–6pm. Coffee for the *feinschmecker* (someone who can taste which estate a coffee comes from).

If you want to try the finest coffees from around the world, come here. If you're into something a bit more mainstream, try the Tofficino, a double espresso with toffee-flavoured milk, whipped cream and a sprinkle of hazelnut dust on top. There are also cakes, pastries and sandwiches.

Eastern Corner Sølvgade 85A ☎ 33 11 58 35. **Mon–Thurs & Sun 5–11pm, Fri & Sat 5pm–midnight.** *Eastern Corner* offers everything your heart could desire – if you like authentic Thai cooking, that is. Prices aren't hiked at dinner, and mains start at 80kr. The red and green curries are tasty and well spiced, and there's a small bar-café attached if you fancy a pre-dinner cocktail, or after-dinner coffee and cognac.

Gold Prag Gothersgade 39. **Mon–Sat 4pm–midnight.** Authentic Czech restaurant in a dark narrow room packed tight with tables, and richly decorated with plastic flowers and other knick-knacks. For the decidedly non-vegetarian, huge portions of goulash served with a hefty chunk of bread cost 75kr, other dishes include pork chops cooked in beer and Czech sausages. The fact that the beer is Czech, and cheap (30kr for 0.5l), is an added bonus.

Koriander Store Kongensgade 34 ☎ 33 15 03 15. **Mon–Sat 8–10pm.** Trendy new French/Indian gourmet restaurant decorated all in white with serious Michelin ambitions, as is evident from the price. Choice is limited but refined; try, for instance, the wadi mattar paneer with Norwegian lobster and cauliflower (285kr) or rhubarb halvah with coco and milk (110kr) for puds. Already very popular with expense-account dinners.

Kafferiet Esplanaden 44. **Mon–Fri 8am–6pm, Sat & Sun 10am–6pm.** On a cold winter's day, after having done Kastellet and the Little Mermaid, you can get warm again at *Kafferiet*. Choose between a vast number of coffees and an equally large selection of cakes and sandwiches. In summer, freshly squeezed fruit juices and smoothies may suffice.

O's American Breakfast & Dinner Gothersgade 15 ☎ 33 12 96 12. **Mon–Thurs 9.30am–10pm, Fri–Sun 3am–10pm; Øster Farimagsgade 27 ☎ 35 43 99 91. Daily 9am–3pm.** Full-on American diner-cum-steakhouse with a vast assortment of fry-ups that could satisfy your calorie count for an entire week. Especially recommended are the filling breakfast/brunches (from 69kr) that come with pancakes, hash

browns, sausages and eggs, and – at the Gothersgade branch – can be enjoyed as early as 3am during weekends. Dinner (only at Gothersgade branch) is soul food from "N'awllins", jambalaya and chicken gumbo among the two favourites.

Petersborg Bredgade 76 ☎ 33 12 60 16. **Mon–Fri 11.45am–10pm.** Danish cooking in a small unpretentious basement restaurant – one of the oldest in Copenhagen – popular with business lunchers in the know. The building used to house the Russian consulate, hence the name, and the old atmosphere still lingers. There's an extensive smørrebrød list and a large selection of traditional à la carte meals including a daily special from 80kr upwards.

Rebétiko Borgergade 134 ☎ 33 91 91 25. **Mon–Sat 5pm–midnight.** Modern Greek restaurant – no lyra in the corner – serving no-nonsense Greek food, prepared by the owner-cum-waiter-cum-chef, at very reasonable prices. You won't stumble across any major surprises on the menu, although the fish dishes come especially recommended. Cheapest main course 92kr.

Sult Vognmagergade 8B ☎ 33 74 34 17. **Tues–Sun 10am–10pm.** Part of Cinemateket (see p.210), this is a bright room with a harmonica wall at one end used to increase the size of the room when it's busy. Food here, from a global cuisine, cannot be faulted, nor can the friendly service. Throughout the day, well-prepared dishes leave the open kitchen, from the all-you-can-eat brunch buffet (Sat & Sun until 3pm; 150kr including coffee/tea and juice) and classic Danish lunch dishes (starting at 65kr for herring) to scrumptious evening meals such as halibut with gnocchi, mussels, mango nage and chorizo for 175kr. The obligatory coffee, burgers and salads are of course also available at any time.

Sushitarian Gothersgade 3 ☎ 33 93 30 54, **Mon–Wed noon–11pm, Thus–Sat noon–midnight, Sun 5.30–11pm.** Among the city's best sushi places, known for its Californian-style sushi as well as a few similarly inspired hot noodle dishes. Despite its diminutive size, there's seating in three areas; most authentic is the small upstairs section with cushions on the floor, but there are also regular table and chairs, and seating on bar stools by window counters. Prices vary enormously depending on the rarity of the fish you order:

most expensive is the three-course lobster sashimi at 635kr. Also takeaway.

Tapas Baren Dronningens Tværgade 22 ☎33 36 07 70. Mon–Wed 5–11pm, Thurs 5–11.30pm, Fri–Sat noon–11.30pm. Wonderful northern Spanish restaurant with a menu primarily of tapas. Try the delicious *espárragos rellenos con caviar oricios* – pickled white asparagus stuffed with sea-urchin caviar (105kr). For afters, there's a choice between Spanish cheeses and sweets, and, of course, a wide selection of Spanish wines.

Taste Store Kongensgade 80-82. Mon–Thurs 11am–4pm, Fri 11am–5.30pm. Small, exquisite deli near the Marmorkirken producing largely organic, vegetarian as well as meaty, salads, sandwiches (from 48kr), soups and cakes that cannot be bettered. The daily hot special (95kr, 60kr to go) is a bargain. You can either eat in at a small, stylish non-smoking seating area with Arne Jacobsen chairs or, on a sunny day, take your food to a bench in Amalieparken.

Traktørstet på Rosenborg Øster Voldgade 4A ☎33 15 76 20. Daily 11am–4pm, closed Mon Nov–May. By the gatehouse of Rosenborg Slot, *Traktørstet* focuses on modernized traditional Danish fare. Prices are fairly reasonable, considering the location, starting at 59kr for herring smørrebrød and from 75kr upwards for the likes of duck-breast salad, and chilli and lime marinated salmon. It's often crowded with tourists and it can be hard to find a seat, so book a table or, on a warm day, sit outside.

Umami Store Kongensgade 59 ☎33 38 75 00. Mon–Thurs noon–3pm & 6–10pm, Fri noon–3pm & 6–11pm, Sat 6–11pm, Sun 6–10pm. Funky new French/Japanese restaurant that has rightly blown away the critics with its fabulous food and sleek decor. With food ranging from the relatively inexpensive oxtail noodle soup (90kr) and culminating in the Omakase menu (485kr) – where the chef has a free reign to decide what's best for you – *Umami* caters for most budgets and should be experienced if only for its groovy decor. You'll find no other place like it.

Rådhuspladsen and around

The noisy, amusement-packed area around the Rådhus isn't that great for restaurants, tending more towards fast-food outlets, though there are a few gems to be searched out. For recommendations in Tivoli itself, see the box on p.186. For locations of the following places, see the map on p.90.

Café Bjørg's Vestervoldgade 19 ☎33 14 53 20. Mon–Thurs & Sun 10am–midnight, Fri & Sat 10am–2am. This busy, trendy café-bar on the edge of Indre By serves up good-value sandwiches, salads, burgers and brunch (10am–1pm, till 2pm on weekends; 89kr) by day and a more expensive menu (main courses 100kr upwards) by night.

Flow Gyldenløvesgade 10 ☎33 14 43 43. Daily 5–8pm. Organic vegetarian restaurant (with a takeaway next door) serving Ayurveda-inspired meals that should make you feel energetic, balanced and cheerful. The menu changes daily but can include dishes such as beetroot pie or cream-baked fennel, accompanied by home-made spelt (gluten-free) bread. No alcohol or smoking.

Fox Kitchen & Bar Jarmers Plads 3 ☎33 38 70 30, ⊛www.hotelfox.dk. Mon–Thurs & Sun 5pm–midnight, Fri & Sat 5pm–2am. Trendy yet relaxed with its curvy counter seating, cushioned banquettes and splatter-pattern murals, this is a hotel restaurant with a difference. The bar and kitchen work together recommending a special cocktail to suit each chosen course (limited to one shot per cocktail so you're still standing at the end of the meal), while the excellent food is modern Scandinavian and seasonal. Main courses such as sole in rye bread or lamb's leg poached in sheep's milk start at around 150kr; be sure to leave some space for the delectable desserts.

Glyptoteket Dantes Plads. Tues–Sun 10am–4pm. The Ny Carlsberg Glyptotek's café, set in the gallery's incomparable glass-domed, palm-filled Winter Gardens, makes for one of the best lunchtime settings in town. The food is excellent, too, with open sandwiches, salads, great home-made cakes and wonderful coffee; or you could fill up on the 145kr brunch before heading off to the galleries. Come on a Wednesday or Sunday and you won't have to pay the museum entrance fee.

Kanal Cafeen Frederiksholm Kanal 18 ☎33 11 57 70. Mon–Fri 11.30am–4pm. This rather cramped but cosy smørrebrød place dates back to 1852. The politicians' stable boys used to lunch here, now it's a

Whether you're eating in one of the thirty or so restaurants or grabbing a slice of pizza, stick of candy floss or ice-cream cone from one of the many fast-food stands, **eating in Tivoli** is all part of the experience, though be warned that you'll pay around twenty percent more for the privilege of eating in the park. If you'd rather spend that extra money on rides, bear in mind that you can always get your hand stamped and eat outside, returning for more fun and thrills later; see listings in "Radhuspladsen and around", p.185, for ideas on where to go nearby. Wallet permitting, you'll have no trouble finding something suitable, be it a hot dog, pasta, smørrebrød or gourmet cuisine. The following is a small selection of sit-down options to suit all budgets.

Viften On the eastern edge of the lake, tucked in a corner next to a small roller-coaster, this relaxed self-service café is great for a simple lunch (or just coffee and Danish pastry), dishing up rolls, pizzas, and steak or fish mains.

Grøften Next to the pantomime theatre, this country-cabin-style restaurant with red-and-white check tablecloths and rustic bonhomie is one of the oldest and most popular eateries in the gardens. It boasts an extensive smørrebrød selection (around 60kr upwards) – the tiny fjord shrimp are delicious.

Café Ketchup Next to *Groften*, close to the park entrance. ⓦwww.cafeketchup.dk. Great restaurant/grill standby serving excellent food at reasonable prices – meat and fish mains and salads from 100kr.

Fregatten Sct. George III ⓣ33 15 92 04, ⓦwww.fregatten-tivoli.dk. The setting may be a little cramped – on a replica eighteenth-century frigate on Tivoli lake – and it's expensive, but it's a sure-fire winner with kids and adults alike, and the food is delicious gourmet Danish fare, including heavenly desserts. Open for lunch, there are two-course kids' portions for 95kr and a three-course menu for adults for 375kr. Booking is essential, and tell them if you want to be above or below deck.

The Paul ⓣ33 75 07 75, ⓦwww.thepaul.dk. The most glamorous (and probably most expensive) dining spot in Tivoli, *The Paul* occupies part of the lovely Poul Henningsen designed "Glassalen" glass-dome building, built in the 1940s. This latest gourmet addition to Tivoli is presided over by English chef Paul Cunningham and has attracted a lot of well-deserved attention (winning a Michelin star in 2004) for its food, location and ambience. The menu, which changes daily, is largely French/Danish featuring the likes of grilled French rabbit or west-coast cod, all fresh, seasonal ingredients presented to perfection. Lunch menus from 450kr (three courses); dinner from 700kr (six courses). Booking essential.

haunt of the politicians themselves, munching their way through a selection of the 36 toppings on offer (English list available; from 35kr per topping). All the standards are here, while for the more adventurous there's pate of porkhead (winter only) or pressed belly of lamb. Booking essential.

Konditori & Café HC Andersen Rådhusarkaden, Vesterbrogade 1B. Mon–Thurs & Sat 8am–6pm, Fri 8am–7pm, Sun noon–6pm. The location may not be the most appealing – in the shopping centre next to Tivoli – but this place is very convenient if you're exploring the Tivoli area, and is usually packed with shoppers and sightseers tucking into sandwiches, rolls and salads, cakes and pastries, all made fresh on the premises.

Wagamama Tietgensgade 20. Mon–Thurs & Sun noon–11pm, Fri & Sat noon–midnight. Large, bright, new branch of the fast-growing London-based chain, dishing up unfailingly delicious steaming bowls of Asian soup, curries or noodles at very reasonable prices. Dishes, all in the 70–90kr price bracket, range from chilli chicken ramen to mandarin and sesame beef salad, with several good veggie options on offer, too.

Vesterbro

With its significant multicultural population, Vesterbro is your best bet if you fancy an ethnic meal, and is also the home to the city's largest range of more affordable eateries. For locations of the following options, see the map on pp.102–103.

Ankara Vesterbrogade 96. Mon–Sat noon–midnight. Sun 2pm–midnight. Whether you're on a budget or not, *Ankara*'s all-you-can-eat Turkish buffet for 49kr (69kr evenings) is a great filler – trays full of delicious meaty stews, rice and vegetables, accompanied by a variety of fresh salads. If you're not venturing this far up the street, there's another, bigger branch at Vesterbrogade 35.

Bang & Jensen Istedgade 130. Mon–Fri 8am–2am, Sat 10am–2am, Sun 10am–midnight (kitchen closes 10pm, 7.30pm on Sat). At the quieter end of Istedgade – no sex shops here – this popular café has a 8–10am breakfast buffet (50kr) and thereafter brunch until 4pm (75kr), featuring a wide range of unusual foods that you can combine as you wish – try the *ymer* (a mild, creamy yoghurt) with maple syrup. Sandwiches, pasta, tapas, tortillas and quiches are offered from lunch onwards. The place transforms into a popular cocktail bar Saturday evening (see "Drinking", p.196).

Det Gule Hus Istedgade 48. Mon–Thus 10am–midnight, Fri & Sat 10am–2am, Sun 10am–11pm. Unmissable yellow villa offering great breakfast and brunch. Choose between pancakes (21kr), three types of brunch (one vegetarian, one decidedly carnivorous, one French; all 69kr), or standard continental breakfast with bread fresh out of the oven (49kr). Also lunch and dinner with at least one veggie option, starting at 118kr.

Den Sorte Gryde Istedgade 108. Mon–Sat 4pm–midnight, Sun 2pm–midnight. It's meat, meat and more meat in this tiny takeaway joint (a few seats available), be it juicy burgers dripping with cheese and bacon, roast chicken, BBQ steak, beef stew or *flæskesteg* – fat slices of pork with crackling served in a sandwich or with potatoes, red cabbage and pickles. Fortifying, filling and delicious.

Estate Coffee Gammel Kongevej 1. Mon–Fri 8am–10pm, Sat & Sun 10am–10pm. Small coffee house at the southern edge of the lakes and with a full range of espressos, lattes and cappuccinos plus some more inventive options – great for a caffeine hit. Alternatively, there's crème Valrhona hot chocolate, and Valrhona Brownies and delicious banana and chocolate muffins available too.

Granola Værnedamsvej 4. Mon–Fri 9am–5pm, Sat 9am–4pm. Great little coffee bar/ice-cream parlour/chocolate shop tucked away in a small courtyard off Værnedamsvej, all done out in pretty pastels with authentic old coffee grinders and the like. Also does excellent fresh fruit smoothies.

Hackenbusch Vesterbrogade 124 ☎33 21 74 74. Mon–Wed 11am–2am, Thurs 11am–4am, Fri & Sat 11am–5am, Sun 11am–midnight (kitchen closes at 10pm, 9pm on Sun). Laid-back place serving three types of brunch (one veggie) until 2pm (from 75kr), and burgers and sandwiches, heaped with salad, in the café-bar at the front. The excellent Mediterranean-style restaurant at the back has steak and fish mains (braised shank of lamb for 119kr), with a daily special for 88kr and always one veggie option. Try the spicy and delicious "frog burger" (65kr) – its ingredients are a well-kept secret (don't worry: it's actually made of beef) – on offer on Tuesdays (35kr) in the restaurant.

Lê Lê Vesterbrogade 56. Mon & Wed–Sun 11.30am–11pm. Busy new Vietnamese restaurant opposite the Københavns Bymuseum (see p.104) with simple French colonial-style decor. Food is also simple but elegant and tasty. Lunch costs a fixed 75kr and you can choose between five dishes such as pho rice-noodle soup, cold rice-noodle salad, and stir-fried veggies in curry and coconut sauce. At dinner, the choices are more varied and prices max out at 135kr. Arrive early for dinner (they don't take bookings) or prepare for a long wait at the bar (which serves Vietnamese beer, of course).

Le Trois Cochons Værnedamsvej 10 ☎33 31 70 55. Mon–Sat noon–midnight, Sun 5.30pm–midnight. Popular French-style brasserie offering excellent-value three-course evening meals for 225kr. Starters and desserts are pre-set, and for mains you get to choose between beef, fish and veal – no veggie option – all freshly made and rustically presented. If there are two of you, you both have to pick the same mains. For lunch, there's a choice between six Danish and French classics such as the open potato sandwich (50kr) and moules frites (75kr). No smoking.

Riccos Butik & Kaffebar Istedgade 119. Daily 9am–11pm. One of the best coffee joints in town with a small seating area in the back room. The owner describes himself as a coffee nerd and if he's not working behind the counter, he's travelling the globe in search of the finest beans. Apart from coffee in various forms – hot as well as cold – there's also cakes and Italian ice cream.

Shezan Viktoriagade 22. Daily 11am–11pm. Denmark's first Pakistani restaurant, established in 1978, may be a bit shabby round the edges but it's still going strong. The fiery curries (from 52kr) come in mild, medium and strong – be warned, even medium burns your tongue off. Choose a table overlooking Istedgade if you want free entertainment watching the infamous red-light district.

Spicylicious Istedgade 27 ☎33 22 85 33. Daily 5pm–midnight. Great new Thai/Vietnamese restaurant overlooking the livelier end of Istedgade. The name says it all: the food is spicy and it's delicious, plus it's very affordable (mains between 85kr for beef noodle soup and105kr for prawn and squid noodle salad).

Sticks 'n' Sushi Istedgade 62 ☎33 23 73 04. Mon–Wed 11.30am–11pm, Thurs & Sat 11.30am–midnight, Fri 11.30am–2am, Sun 1–10pm. Fifth branch of this ubiquitous Japanese chain that has taken Vesterbro by storm. The menu changes according to season, and apart from the usual range of sushi and maki rolls there's also a selection of bento boxes (Japanese lunch boxes) with chopsticks and assorted accoutrements in separate compartments (from 124kr). This large branch also has a bar (opens at 10pm) with a good selection of Japanese beer.

Thai Esan Lille Istedgade 7 ☎33 24 98 54. Mon–Thurs & Sun noon–11pm, Fri & Sat noon–midnight. Taking advantage of fresh ingredients from the numerous Thai food shops in the area, the very popular and often crammed *Thai Esan* serves a wide range of cheap, hot food in a fairly authentic Thai atmosphere. Good choices are the chicken in oyster sauce for 85kr, or the Tom Yom shrimp soup for just 65kr.

Frederiksberg

The posh, residential Frederiksberg is hardly a fruitful hunting ground for restaurants, though there are several places worth taking dinner in after wandering the area's great parks and gardens. For locations of the following, see the map on pp.102–103.

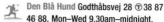 **Den Blå Hund Godthåbsvej 28 ☎38 87 46 88. Mon–Wed 9.30am–midnight, Thurs & Fri 9.30am–2am, Sat 10am–2am, Sun 10am–11pm (kitchen closes at 10pm).** Mediterranean-style café-restaurant featuring enormous sandwich platters and tapas, plus a fabulous brunch until 2pm (classic, vegetarian and deluxe; 79kr–89kr). Speciality main courses include grilled goats' cheese with crab tails (79kr) and chicken salad with bacon and cold curry sauce (73kr). During summer, tables are moved across the road to Axel Møllers Have and a small stage erected for live jazz used during the Jazz Festival (see p.232).

Det Indiske Spisehus Vesterfælledvej 8 ☎33 21 90 80. Daily; closed Tues 4–10pm. This small, no-frills place near the Carlsberg brewery serves up some of the city's best Indian food. Plenty of veggie options; try the vegetarian thali – dahl, pickles, vegetables, yoghurt, potatoes, chapati and rice for 91kr. Booking advisable at weekends.

Fiasco Gammel Kongevej 176 ☎33 31 74 87. Mon–Sat 5.30–10pm. Stylish, upmarket Italian restaurant a stone's throw from Frederiksberg Rådhus offering outstanding fare from Florence. Of special note is the antipasti platter – best described as a work of art. Otherwise, there's a choice of classic pasta dishes and salads or more full-on *primi* and *secondi* dishes in refined but relaxed, cream wood-panelled surroundings. The three-course set menus are good value at 255kr.

Hansens Gamle Familiehave Pile Allé 10–12 ☎36 30 92 57. Daily 11am–midnight. This historic outdoor restaurant (under a sliding roof during winter) dishes up some of the city's most stunning open sandwiches, with a fantastic spread of herring, cold meats and cheeses, all lavishly decorated with fresh salad, pickles, fried onions and other smørrebrød essentials. Beautifully prepared traditional hot meals, such as *biksemad* (80kr) and *flæskesteg* (142) are also on offer.

Sokkelund Smallegade 36 ☎38 10 64 00. Mon–Thurs & Sat 10am–11pm, Fri 10am–midnight, Sun 10am–9pm. French-style brasserie midway between the Royal Copenhagen Porcelain factory and Frederiksberg Rådhus and a convenient watering point after a tour at Royal Copenhagen or a visit to the Saturday flea market in the *rådhus* parking lot. The excellent brunch – book ahead at weekends – is served until 3pm and comes in three sizes from light (55kr) to large (120kr). There's also a selection of coffee, snacks and light meals, including good burgers.

Nørrebro

Possibly the hippest part of town, with a variety of venues tucked around Skt Hans Torv and Blågårdsgade; this is also a good area to grab brunch. For locations of the following, see map, pp.112–113.

Den Iranske Forening Blågårdsgade 4. Mon–Sat noon–9pm, Sun 1–9pm. Great-value Persian restaurant, on the first floor of an unobtrusive building housing the Iranian Cultural Society. There's no sign, so follow the noise and you'll suddenly find yourself dining on some delightful Persian classics such as the Special Kebab – skewered chicken and lamb served with saffron rice and a crispy salad (69kr). There's no alcohol, but they do an excellent mast sabzi – the Persian version of herbal lassi.

Floras Kaffebar Blågårdsgade 27. Mon–Wed 10am–midnight, Thurs–Sat 11am–1am, Sun 10am–11pm. Glitzy café on drab Blågårds Plads known predominantly as a coffee place with many exotic brands on offer, *Floras* also does an array of daily specials, plus soups, sandwiches and home-made cakes, all served in an easy-going atmosphere. Brunch is dished up daily until 3pm (89kr). Come back at night for cheap beer.

Front Page Sortedams Dosseringen 21 ☎35 37 38 29. Mon–Wed 11am–1am, Thurs 11am–2am, Fri & Sat 10am–2am, Sun 11am–1am. Corner café with outdoor lakeside seating, not to be confused with the restaurant next door. Apart from the usual array of sandwiches (59kr) and salads (69kr) try also the superb tapas – a plate for 95kr is enough for two. Also recommended is the daily brunch (until 3pm); for 79kr you get a plateful of bacon and eggs, chorizo, yoghurt, fruit, cheese and fresh bread.

Kaffesalonen Peblinge Dossering 6. Mon–Fri 8am–midnight, Sat & Sun 10am–midnight. Friendly neighbourhood coffee house, which also offers French-style dishes such as lightly grilled tuna steak, and vegetarian pasta (89kr). The excellent breakfast (until 11am; a bagel, cheese, ham and yoghurt; 49kr) and brunch (until 2pm; 85kr) draws in the crowds, too, and the superb location

makes it a great spot to enjoy a quiet couple of cool draught beers.

Kates Joint Blågårdsgade 12 ☎35 37 44 96. Daily 5.30–10.30pm. Small, intimate and somewhat grungy place, where you can find dishes from most corners of the world (the blackboard menu changes daily). Amongst the tasty offerings is the perennial favourite, Jamaican jerk chicken. Cheapest is tandoori chicken and rice for 62kr. Entertainment comes in the form of a huge stack of English-language magazines in the corner.

Nørrebro Bryghus Ryesgade 2 ☎35 30 05 30. Mon–Wed 11am–midnight, Thurs–Sat 11am–2am, Sun 11am–10pm. Super-hip brewery restaurant in a former factory building with restaurant upstairs and bar downstairs (see "Drinking", p.199). Food is made to accompany the beer – rather than the other way around – and the fixed menu changes monthly, leaving you only to choose between a three-, four- or five-course set menu for 315kr, 345kr and 398kr respectively. The curry sorbet with beer and white chocolate is quite unique.

Laundromat Café Elmegade 15. Mon–Thurs & Sun 8am–midnight, Fri & Sat 10am–2am. Icelandic café encompassing a marvellous new concept: café in the front, laundry out the back. While your clothes are being washed in the back room (32kr for a large load plus detergent, 1kr per min for tumble drier) you can wash down your brunch or light meal with mug-fuls of coffee or beer. Basic brunch starts at 65kr (95kr for a larger portion during weekends) and salads and sandwiches cost between 30kr and 95kr. The Icelandic chef's special is, naturally, fish soup (135kr).

Picnic Fælledvej 22B. Mon–Fri 11am–11pm, Sat & Sun noon–11pm. Tiny, friendly Turkish/Greek place serving only organic food – huge sandwiches and lots of vegetarian delicacies – and no alcohol. Not much seating, but it's great for takeouts, particularly if you're heading to Fælledparken for an afternoon's lazing.

Props Coffee Shop Blågårdsgade 5. Mon–Wed 11am–midnight, Thurs–Sat 11am–2am, Sun noon–11pm (kitchen closes at 8pm). Small, quirky place where everything is for sale (take a look at the price tags to see how much that comfy chair you're sitting in costs). It also does food – chilli con carne, tapas, sandwiches and salads – and every

Thursday during summer, burgers are grilled on a barbecue out front.

Pussy Galore's Flying Circus Skt Hans Torv 30 ⓣ 35 24 53 00. Mon–Fri 8am–2am, Sat & Sun 9am–2pm. Modern café-bar on trendy Skt Hans Torv, where the young and famous hang out. With its minimalist decor *Pussy's* – as it's known locally – is less pompous than its French neighbour *Sebastopol*. Food here is great throughout the day. First and foremost the infamous brunch pulls in a large crowd, while earlier still, the breakfast plate is good value at 25kr. Later in the day, the café-style sandwiches (from 70kr) and full-on meals (from 79kr) also come recommended, as does the extensive selection of beer, wine and alcohol (see "Drinking", p.199)

Sebastopol Skt Hans Torv 32 ⓣ 35 36 30 02. Mon–Wed 8am–1am, Thurs & Fri 8am–2am, Sat 9am–2am, Sun 9am–1am. Spacious brasserie with outdoor seating on hip Skt Hans Torv. Food here is predominantly French – apart from the omnipresent brunch – and prices fair (brunch starts at 54kr, sandwiches from 58kr). Mains include the likes of white wine steamed salmon, tagliatelle with beef, black truffles and wild mushrooms and grilled lamb (all around 130kr), and spinach lasagne as the veggie option (106kr). The burger with bacon, cheese and fries is also very popular.

Tibet Blågårds Plads 10 ⓣ 35 36 85 05. Tues–Sun 1–11pm. A unique Tibetan restaurant, next to the winter ice-skating rink, which doubles as an outdoor seating area during summer. Unusual dishes such as the traditional momo starter – steamed dumplings with either vegetable or meat fillings (35kr) – or thantuk – thin rice-noodle soup served with beef or vegetables (60kr) – make up the menu at both lunch and dinner.

Østerbro

Lacking the trendy appeal of neighbouring Nørrebro, Østerbro's restaurants are more glitzy, complementing the area's wealthier residents. For locations of the following, see map on pp.112–113.

Bopa Løgstørgade 8 ⓣ 35 43 05 66. Mon–Wed & Sun 10am–midnight, Thurs 10am–2am, Fri & Sat 10am–5am. More of a drinking and nightlife den (see p.199), *Bopa* is also good for some tasty salads, sandwiches and wraps

(all around 60kr), and filling Cajun chicken (99kr). There's live music or a DJ a couple of nights a week, grill evenings Wednesday to Saturday during summer, and petanque competitions on the square during summer.

Canteen Nordre Frihavnsgade 52 ⓣ 35 38 61 22. Tues–Sat 10am–midnight, Sun 10am–4pm. A friendly corner café, with light and delicious café meals prepared with the utmost attention to detail. If you want to try their popular brunch (until 3.30pm; 55–98kr), it's a good idea to book a table, as the place fills up quickly.

Circus Rosenvængets Allé 7 ⓣ 35 55 77 72. Mon–Thurs noon–midnight, Fri noon–2am, Sat 11am–2am, Sun 11am–6pm. Originally a butcher's shop, *Circus* has undergone many incarnations until finding its present form as part-café, part-restaurant. Food in both sections is French/Spanish/Italian-inspired, and delicious. If you're on a budget, try the daily pasta dish in the café section (85kr); if you're feeling flush try the flavour-packed Italian sushi (175kr) made with cold risotto topped by truffles, swordfish squid, figs and much more. Otherwise, a four-course Albino Latino menu will set you back 375kr.

Crazy Chicken Rosenvængets Allé 1 ⓣ 35 26 41 42. Daily 10am–10pm. On the corner of Østerbrogade, this small chicken joint is a great place to buy supplies for a picnic in Fælledparken. The chicken sandwich combos (from 30kr) are excellent as are the half (35kr) and whole (68kr) roasted chickens fresh off the spit. Also delicious is the counter full of different help-yourself salads (28kr). There are a few tables next to the counter if you'd rather eat in.

Dag H Dag Hammarskjolds Allé 36–40 ⓣ 35 25 35 35. Mon–Thurs 10am–11pm, Fri 10am–midnight, Sat 10am–11pm, Sun 10am–9pm. Parisian-style café with outdoor seating, near the American Embassy and a stone's throw from the lakes. Busy throughout the day, especially with young families (nappy-changing facilities in both ladies and gents), *Dag H* offers quality coffee and wonderful cakes, plus an eclectic mix of Danish and international sandwiches and burgers (109kr), light meals and dinners (from 158kr).

Den Franske Café Sortedam Dosseringen 101. Daily 10am–11pm. Despite its name, nothing here comes across as particularly French apart from the tranquil lakeside setting. Popular with families, you can try out standard Danish fare – such as *frik-adeller* (meatballs on rye bread with pickled red cabbage) – at very reasonable prices. Brunch (until 2pm at 83kr, weekends 105kr) is also popular.

Kulinaris Østerbrogade 98. Mon–Fri 11am–8pm, Sat 11am–4pm, Sun noon–8pm. Excellent little sandwich joint, convenient for Fælledparken and Parken Stadium, that specializes in organic Thai sandwiches – chicken or beef – topped with peanut sauce, chilli and cheese (small 38kr, large 56kr). There are many other delicious sandwich options and "sandwich meals" – sandwich, chips and soft drink – for 58kr and 73kr.

Le Saint-Jacques Skt Jakobs Plads 1 ☎35 42 77 07. Mon–Wed & Sun 11am–midnight, Thurs–Sat 11am–2am. French restaurant serving rustic country cooking, at a price. There's both indoor and outdoor seating during hot summer months, and apart from the recommended home-smoked salmon (lunch or evening starter; 95kr) and fish of the day mains (185kr), *Saint-Jacques* also does a popular brunch at weekends (115kr).

Park Østerbrogade 79 ☎35 42 62 48. Mon–Wed noon–midnight, Thurs–Fri from noon, Sat from 10am, Sun 10am–midnight (kitchen closes at 10pm). Classic two-storey café/restaurant with high stucco ceilings, crystal chandeliers and marble pillars. Divided through the middle – from the main entrance all the way up to the balcony – the left side is dressed up as a fine restaurant, while the right side is a café. Food is Italian/French-inspired with a global twist. Lunch consists of salads and sandwiches, plus a lunch platter (99kr) with a mix of hot and cold delicacies (Parma ham and the like). Evening mains start at 129kr for the daily special, and there's a three-course meal for 249kr. The café has a wide range of cocktails (see "Drinking", p.199), while *Park* is also a nightclub at weekends (p.204) with a relaxing roof-garden bar.

Paustian Kalkbrænderiløbskaj 2 ☎39 18 55 01. Mon–Sat noon–3pm & 6pm–midnight. *Paustian* is one of Copenhagen's most adventurous gourmet restaurants, scenically located overlooking the Kalkbrænderi harbour. Housed in the building also containing the exclusive Paustian designer furniture shop (see p.219), this is undoubtedly the restaurant of choice for the style-conscious and rich. The chef is famous for his unusual combinations (such as an

avocado, almond and caviar starter) and the two fixed menus – the surprise-laden "Alchemist" (700kr), and the vegan or vegetarian (depending on the diner) Chlorophyll (500kr) – come highly recommended.

Theodors Østerbrogade 106 ☎35 26 66 66. Mon–Wed 11am–midnight, Thurs–Sat 11am–2am, Sun 11am–8pm. Part café with outdoor seating, part posh French restaurant, both stylishly decorated with dark wooden panelling and Art Deco chandeliers. The restaurant serves delectable items such as pork tournedos served with Danish asparagus and crisp ham (188kr). The café excels in well-prepared salads and sandwiches for 70–90kr. Also a good weekend brunch spot (128kr).

The suburbs

Islands Bryggs Kulturhus Islands Brygge 18. Mon–Wed 11am–11pm, Thurs–Fri 11am–midnight, Sat 10am–midnight, Sun 10am–11pm. Next to the harbour pool on the banks of Inderhavnen, *Islands Bryggs Kulturhus* is a popular new cultural centre with live gigs four or five times a week and a waterfront café offering salads and sandwiches at very reasonable prices. After 4pm you can also, for 50kr, get a salad and steak that you cook yourself on the grill out front while enjoying great views across the harbour.

Jakobsen Strandvejen 449, Klampenborg ☎39 63 43 22. Mon–Fri noon–midnight, Sat 11am–midnight. Klampenborg station. Named after Danish design guru Arne Jacobsen (see *Danish Design* colour section), this restaurant couldn't possibly get any trendier. Furnished throughout with Jacobsen's designs, the place is often packed with foreign architects and designers checking out the decor while sampling the delightful selection of Mediterranean-inspired dishes such as braised lamb served with olive polenta and aubergine tartar for 190kr.

Jorden Rundt Standvejen 152, Charlottenlund. Daily 10am–10pm. Charlottenlund station and bus #14 and #166. Near the Danmarks Akvarium and the Charlottenlund beach and campsite, this popular circular café is housed in a beautiful old tram waiting room from 1939 where the old number 14 used to loop. It offers delicious sandwiches and salads (from 52kr) as well as a few hot meals (from 88kr for chilli con carne) and has a sought-after brunch (until 1pm; 88kr).

Krunch Øresundsvej 14. Tues–Fri 5–10pm, Sat & Sun 10am–10pm. Bus #2A and #12. Organic restaurant on Amager near the Amager Bio concert venue, with a delightful selection of seasonal buffet dishes (129kr) and daily specials such as steak with chilli-baked beetroot and new potatoes (95kr). The weekend brunch (until 4pm; 98kr) is very popular. *Krunch* also operates a popular beach tavern at Kastrup Fort (see p.125) on Amagerstrandvej 246 (May–Sept), selling fantastic sandwiches and hot and cold drinks, as well as food from a barbecue out front in the evening.

Peter Lieps Hus Dyrehaven 8 ☎39 64 07 86. Tues–Sun 10am–6pm, summer to 8pm. Klampenborg station. Originally a hunter's lodge, this thatched restaurant is the perfect spot to stop for a hot chocolate (28kr) and cake (28kr) after a stroll in Dyrehaven. *Peter Lieps* also does traditional Danish lunch (108kr), and two- or three-course dinner (209kr/239kr) from 5.30pm.

Sejlklubben Sundet Strandvænget 45 ☎39 29 30 35. May to mid-Oct Mon–Fri & Sun 5–11pm. A short walk from Svanemøllen S-Tog. Housed in an unobtrusive yellow wooden shack, the Sundet sailing club is one of the city's best inexpensive places to eat. With its beautiful harbourside setting and a range of top home cooking for less than 100kr, this can hardly be bettered. In summer, there's an outdoor grill and seating on wooden benches. In winter, the restaurant is only open in connection with the club's navigation courses.

⑫

Drinking

rinking is a favourite pastime for many Danes, with liberal licensing laws, a relaxed attitude to alcohol and the lowest prices in Scandinavia (a combination that has proved irresistible to the hundreds of thirsty Swedes who cross the Oresund each weekend and drink themselves senseless in Copenhagen's bars). Denmark's drinking holes come under a bewildering variety of names: a *vinstue* (literally "wine parlour") is an old and traditional venue, while a *værtshus* (a "hosting house") tends to be a small, dimly lit and smoke-filled den, populated with regulars playing dice and billiards. *Bodegas* are generally neighbourhood drinking places, while the French cafés aspire to the hip and fashionable – most also serve some kind of light food. The newest additions to the scene, British and Irish pubs, are mostly restricted to Indre By. The Danish *kaffebar* is the equivalent of the British greasy spoon, but serving beer instead of tea, and with less food on the menu. Bars are more neutral and cover just about everything not mentioned above. It's worth bearing in mind that the distinction between eating and drinking establishments is often blurred, and places that are worthy lunchtime pit stops can be equally good for a few cold beers the same evening.

The choice of drink has traditionally been quite limited, though this is gradually changing. Lager-style **beer** is still without doubt Denmark's staple drink. The two most common brands are Tuborg and the ubiquitous Carlsberg, usually sold by the bottle, less frequently in 250ml or 500ml draught measures – bottled beer is cheaper than draught (20–30kr per bottle; draught beer can cost up to 80kr for half a litre). The breweries also brew special "Christmas" and "Easter" beers – a bit stronger than normal to enhance the festive feel. The two days when they are released – "J-Day" and "P-Day" ("J" for *Jul* and "P" for *Påske* – Christmas and Easter respectively) see beer enthusiasts all around the country venturing out to taste the latest offerings. More choice is on offer at the handful of hip new microbars that feature lagers from local microbreweries and elsewhere in Europe. Guinness and draught British and Irish ales can generally only be found in British- and Irish-themed pubs, and are quite pricey. **Wine** is usually available in most bars, though in Denmark it's still predominantly drunk with meals and you won't usually have the same choice as in restaurants. **Cocktail bars** are also a colourful festive feature in Danish nightlife, and worth checking out for their eclectic menus.

Opening hours vary according to police licensing and the bar owner's inclination, though you'll be able to find somewhere to drink at any time of the day or night; it's generally possible to find a bar open within walking distance of your last venue, and most locals know of at least one so-called Death Route – an extensive pub-crawl – to ensure 24-hour drinking. As the evening moves

In the warm summer months, a cold *høker* beer – the generic name for any beer bought in a shop and drunk outside – can't be beaten. In Denmark, drinking al fresco – on beaches, parks or simply on a city bench – is seen as an appreciation of life and the great outdoors, so do what the locals do: stock up at a corner shop and find a spot you like.

on, people head to more lively dancing venues, often ending before breakfast in a traditional *værtshus* with billiards and a jukebox.

For a **glossary** of Danish drinks, see "Language", p.205.

Indre By

There's no shortage of bars in Indre By, most of them atmospheric joints with plenty of charm. There are also a few French café-style places, which are far more laid-back than their equivalents in trendy Nørrebro. For locations of the following places, see the map on pp.54–55.

Bankeråt Ahlefeldtsgade 29. Mon–Fri 9.30am–midnight, Sat & Sun 10.30am–midnight. On the corner of Nansensgade, this laid-back, lively café, usually packed with locals, is renowned for its quirky decor (an assortment of macabre mannequins sporting stuffed animal heads). Also does inexpensive light meals.

Bibendum Nansensgade 45. Mon–Sat 4pm–midnight. Small, crowded wine bar in a Nansensgade cellar, with a huge selection of wine, most of which is served by the glass. Also great tapas (140kr) to soak up the alcohol.

Bloomsday Bar Niels Hemmingsensgade 32. Daily noon to 2am. Irish bar named after the day in James Joyce's Ulysses when his "stream of consciousness" takes place. It's not a theme pub, though, and it has a good selection of ales and ciders – both of which make it especially popular with Copenhagen's large Irish population. Other attractions are a large-screen TV showing football, and pool tables and darts in a big room at the back. Sunday afternoons are known for their Irish music sessions.

Bo-Bi Bar Klareboderne 14. Daily 10am–2am. Home to Copenhagen's oldest bar counter – an idea first introduced to the city by a New York-returned sailor in 1917 – this small, atmospheric drinking hole is now patronized by inner-city professional types, artists and writers.

Charlie's Bar Pilestræde 33. Mon–Wed 2pm–2am, Thurs–Sat noon to 2am, Sun 2–11pm. Just around the corner from the Museum Erotica (see p.59), *Charlie's* is the only bar in Denmark that has been awarded the prestigious Cask Marque for its vast selection of high-quality real ales. If you want a seat, you have to arrive early.

Dan Turéll Store Regnegade 3–5. Mon–Thurs 9.30am–midnight, Fri & Sat 9.30am–2am, Sun 10am–10pm. Named after the popular Danish author, this swanky café-bar, covered in steel and mirrors, sports Turéll book covers on the wall and attracts an arty but sociable student crowd. In summer, the large front opens out onto the street. Also a popular brunch spot.

Café Floss Larsbjørnsstræde 10. Mon 2pm–2am Tues–Sat 1pm–2am. Trendy low-life bar, where artists and creative souls gather for full-on drinking sessions. To facilitate this, Guldøl (Tuborg's strong gold beer) and tequila are on special offer during Happy Hour between 10pm and 11pm. There's a pool table in the basement.

Globe Irish Pub Nørregade 45. Mon & Tues 1pm–1am, Wed 1pm–2am, Thurs 1pm–3am, Fri 1pm–5am, Sat noon–5am, Sun 2pm–midnight. Loud, flashy and spacious Irish pub, with lots of televised sports, although your fellow drinkers are more likely to be tourists or Danish theatre folk than expats from the Emerald Isle. Houses a good selection of Irish whiskey.

Heidi's Bier Bar Vestergade 18A. Mon–Wed & Sun 4pm–2am, Thurs 4pm–5am, Fri & Sat 2pm–5am. Fun new Austrian beer hall where braid-wearing waitresses in Tyrolean dresses practise handling half a dozen jugs of beer at once. Drinks on offer include ice-cold shots of Jägermeister and Paulaner Weissbier, and, should you get hungry, a plate of sausages and potato salad goes for 55kr.

Hviids Vinstue Kongens Nytorv 19. Mon–Thurs & Sun 10am–1am, Fri & Sat 10am–2am. Old-fashioned vinstue dating back to 1723 – Hans Christian Andersen was a regular, since he lived just around the corner – whose many crowded rooms are patrolled by uniformed and respectful waiters. There's a wide selection of Danish beers (27 at last count) and a great lunch deal – three pieces of smørrebrød and a Tuborg – for 55kr. Outdoor seating on Kongens Nytorv square in summer, and a popular place for gløgg in winter.

Krasnapolsky Vestergade 10. Mon–Thurs 11am–midnight, Fri & Sat 10am–5am. This once hip and trendsetting establishment has mellowed somewhat and now attracts a more mixed crowd of shoppers, tourists and serious partygoers. On Friday and Saturday, a visiting DJ delivers mainstream R&B, funk and disco-hits in the back-room dancing area (see p.203). The bartenders can be snooty, but don't let this put you off.

The Moose Sværtegade 5. Mon & Sun 1pm–3am, Tues & Wed 1pm–6am, Thurs–Sat 1pm–7am. Deceptively large bar in a long, narrow listed building and one of the cheapest places to get tanked up before hitting the clubs, especially Tuesday, Thursday and Saturday when it's Happy Hour from 9pm onwards.

Musen og Elefanten Vestergade 21. Mon–Thurs 3pm–2am, Fri 3pm–5am, Sat 1pm–5am, Sun 8pm–2am. Personable bar set up in homage to its owner's twin obsessions: Carlsberg Elephant Beer – one of the strongest in Denmark – and traditional rock music. Draught Elephant flows from a carved trunk at the first-floor bar, while rock fiends sit around discussing the trade and tapping their toes to the loud music.

Nyhavn 17 Nyhavn 17. Mon–Thurs & Sun 10am–2am, Fri & Sat 10am–3am. Located on fashionable Nyhavn, this is a cross between a British pub and a maritime museum, with old iron diving helmets, ships' figureheads, anchors and rudders scattered around the dimly lit interior – the gleaming brass bar fittings are the only bright feature. Popular among tourists and Danes alike, with moderately priced draught beers and ciders.

Sabines Cafeteria Teglgårdsstræde 4. Mon–Wed & Sun noon–1am, Thurs–Sat noon–2am. Small and bright café-bar where the city's young and good-looking begin their evening's drinking and flirting. During the day, a more sedate clientele comes here to drink coffee and read the newspapers.

Sommersko Kronprinsensgade 6. Mon–Wed 8am–midnight, Thurs 8am–1am, Fri 8am–4am, Sat 9am–4am, Sun 10am–midnight. Two-level, spacious French-style café (the first to appear in the townscape some thirty years ago), with bright-red plastic sofas and waiters with attitude. More of a meal place throughout the day – starting with a popular brunch – it transforms early evening into a popular spot to meet before hitting the clubs.

⑫

DRINKING | Indre By

Bars with outdoor seating

Alléenberg Al fresco drinking in a tranquil garden in smart Frederiksberg. See p.197.

Café Obelix Outdoor seating on cobbled Vesterbro Torv. See p.197.

Den Blå Hund Sit outside on Axel Møllers Have – you may catch one of the jazz concerts that are sometimes held here. See p.198.

Front Page and **Kaffesalonen** Enjoy a view of the waters of the rampart lakes with the city in the distance. See pp.198–199.

Hviids Vinstue Traditional old *vinstue* whose tables spill out onto busy Kongens Nytorv in good weather. See p.195.

Nemoland At the heart of the "Free City" of Christiania, and a good place to people-watch. See p.196.

Park Café Rooftop seating looking out over Fælledparken and busy Østerbrogade. See p.199.

Pavillonen I Fælledparken A tranquil spot in the centre of Fælledparken, with live music most weekends. See p.199.

Pussy Galore's Flying Circus and **Sebastopol** Right on trendy Skt Hans Torv – *the* place to be seen. See p.199.

Christianshavn

Nightlife on Christianshavn is dominated by Christiania, but a few places give a real flavour of Copenhagen's traditional drinking dens. For locations of the following places, see the map on p.67.

Eiffel Bar Wildersgade 58. Daily 9am–3am.
Next door to smart Café Wilder (see p.183), though this traditional drinking den couldn't be more different. Rumours of its shady past – featuring assorted sailors and can-can girls – add to the serious drinking atmosphere, while the old carved mirrors and the tricolour hanging outside take you back to Paris in the 1930s.

Fingerbøllet Wildersgade 39. Mon–Sat 11am–2am, Sun noon–2am. "The Thimble" is a real locals' hang-out where guys and gals of all ages drink beer and play billiards – old jeans and faded T-shirts seem to be the appropriate dress code.

Nemoland Christiania. Mon–Thurs & Sun 10am–2am, Fri & Sat 10am–3.30am.
One of Christiania's two main watering holes, and among Copenhagen's most popular open-air bars, with occasional live gigs during summer, when it's often packed with tourists and shoppers enjoying their purchases from nearby Pusherstreet. It's quieter during the winter, with regulars playing backgammon or billiards.

Woodstock Pusherstreet, Christiania. Daily 9am–5am. Housed in a former military barracks on Pusherstreet, chilled-out Woodstock is the place to enjoy a laid-back drink (and perhaps a smoke) in a ramshackle bar kitted out with old garden furniture and full of 1960s spirit.

Frederikstad and around

Bars are extremely thin on the ground in the Frederikstad area, possibly because the royals don't want too much night-time disturbance. For the location of the following places, see the map on pp.76–77.

Andy's Bar Gothersgade 33B. Daily 11pm–6am.
A so-called morning-pub, where the city's partygoers head when they can dance no more. Always crowded and noisy, with enough booze onboard that you'll soon be chatting to your bar companions like they're long-lost friends.

Kruts Karport Øster Farimagsgade 12. Mon 2pm–midnight, Tues–Thurs noon–midnight, Fri & Sat noon–2am, Sun noon–7pm. Closed August.
Small Parisian-style neighbourhood bar that prides itself on having Denmark's largest whisky selection (mainly Scotch single malts) and on for years being the only bar in Copenhagen selling Absinthe. Arranges whisky tastings and cigar evenings during the winter.

Rådhuspladsen and around

The bright lights of Rådhuspladsen set the tone for the area's nightlife. With a few exceptions, places here tend to be large, flashy and aimed at attracting tourists by the dozen. For locations of the following places, see the map on p.90.

Bryggeriet Apollo Vesterbrogade 3. Mon–Thurs 11.30am–1am, Fri & Sat 11.30am–2am, Sun 3pm–midnight. Close by Central Station, this place offers *Bryggeriet's* organic beer, freshly brewed on the premises and served up amidst gleaming vats, copper kettles and heavy wooden tables; food is available, too, in the bright upstairs section. If you want, you can have your beer served in a Belgian *kwak*, similar to a short-yard glass – be careful not to pour beer all over yourself. Not surprisingly, it's all a tad pricey, but fun.

O'Learys Central Station. Mon–Thurs 4–11pm, Fri 3–11pm, Sat & Sun noon–11pm. Large, glitzy chain pub at the train station, which shows non-stop sports on a large screen and serves basic American pub grub. A good meeting point, with plenty of seating and quaffable beer.

Zum Biergarten Axeltorv 12. Tues & Wed 4pm–11pm, Thurs 4pm–2am, Fri 2pm–3am, Sat 4pm–3am. Heaving new Bavarian bierstube housed in the old waterworks building in front of Palads cinema by Vesterport station, offering Oktoberfest atmosphere with long rackety wooden tables and huge litre-mugs of German microbrewery beer. When the weather allows, there's outdoor service, including food prepared on an open grill.

Vesterbro

Plenty of bars – especially cocktail bars – line Istedgade, from Central Station down to Enghave Plads, as well as along Vesterbrogade. For locations of the following places, see the map on pp.102–103.

Bang & Jensen Istedgade 130. Mon–Fri 8am–2am, Sat 10am–2am, Sun 10am–midnight. High stucco ceilings and a mahogany counter left over from its former incarnation as a pharmacy add to the character of this place, which is usually packed before concerts at Vega (see p.202) and on Saturday nights when Ingeborgs Cocktail Saloon takes over, and the in-house DJ sets the mood with some electronic jazz grooves. One of the pricier places in Vesterbro.

Boutique Lize Enghave Plads 6. Wed 8pm–midnight, Thurs 8pm–2am, Sat & Sun 8pm–4pm. Hugely popular cocktail bar across the square from Vega (see p.202) with a good selection of draught beer as well – both imported and from local microbreweries. Packed with people sipping drinks while deciding what to try next – the Tokyo Iced Tea comes especially recommended – and with reasonable prices – possibly because none of the cocktails are that strong.

Foley's Irish Pub Stenosgade 1. Daily 3pm–5am. Decorated as a replica of the owner's regular pub back home in Waterford. Guinness and Kilkenny flow continuously from the tap, as does Magner's cider, and during summer there's a courtyard bar. Often the final stop for Irish expats after a night of pub-crawling.

Ideal Bar Enghavevej 40. Wed 7pm–4am, Thurs–Sat 7pm–5am. Housed in the Vega music complex (see p.202), this stylish bar has a laid-back attitude and excellent cocktails. A relaxed post-gig atmosphere, with handy, large leather sofas, things don't really get started here until after midnight, when the dance tunes start playing.

Café Ludwigsen Sundesvedsgade 2. Mon–Wed noon–2am, Thurs noon–5am, Fri & Sat noon–6am, Sun 3pm–2am. Outrageously popular late-night bar (despite the "café" in the name, there's no food) where the young, free and desperate congregate en masse in the small hours.

Märkbar Vesterbrogade 106A. Mon–Wed 3pm–2am, Thurs–Sat 3pm–5am. Behind the decrepit facade alternative rock/punk is played in a dark, underground Berlinesque setting. There's good German weissbier on offer – which is enough of an attraction on its own for some.

Café Obelix Vesterbrogade 53. Daily 8.30am–2am. This winsome tribute to the large,

menhir-wielding Breton pulls in shoppers and locals alike, who drink amongst themed decorations based on the Gaulish cartoon village. During summer, tables are moved outside.

Pinden Reventlowsgade 4. Mon–Sat 2pm–2am, Sun 4pm–2am. Across the road from Central Station's back entrance, Pinden (The Stick) is a traditional, smoky drinking den where old-timers slump on worn-out furniture playing the odd game of dice – a much more entertaining meeting point than the station's cold platforms and shiny cafés.

Strassen Istedgade 128. Mon–Wed 11am–midnight, Thurs & Fri 11am–2am, Sat 10am–2am, Sun 10am–midnight. At the Enghavevej end of Istedgade and a popular place to meet up before gigs at Vega (p.202). *Strassen* is famous for its range of delicious cocktails, featuring both before-dinner and after-dinner drinks, plus the much needed Hangover Weekend Rescue drink. Also serves standard café fare.

Riesen Oehlenschlægersgade 36. Wed & Thurs 8am–2.30am, Fri & Sat 8pm–3.30am. Basic, no-frills student hangout with indie music playing in the background and an affordable selection of imported beer on offer, as well as the obligatory cocktail menu – this is Vesterbro after all.

Frederiksberg

Apart from the few exceptional places listed below, Frederiksberg isn't much of an area for nightlife. Allégade is the liveliest street, attracting the post-theatre crowd. For locations of the following places, see the map on pp.102–103.

90eren Gammel Kongevej 90. Mon–Wed 11am–1am, Thurs–Sat 11am–2am, Sun 1pm–1am. Famous for its painstakingly pulled draught beer, an operation that can take up to twelve minutes, *90eren* is the only bar in Copenhagen that serves uncarbonated Carlsberg beer (from the nearby brewery). The strong hops flavour is reminiscent of English real ale and – supposedly – very similar to the original Carlsberg beer produced in the mid-nineteenth century.

Alléenberg Allégade 4. Tues–Sat 10pm–6am. Decorated with Danish theatre memorabilia, this lively bar is the preferred watering hole of the local Frederiksberg theatre wannabes – they'll probably give you a tune on the piano at some point – and the last stop for the neighbourhood's high-school students after late nights on the town who, for reasons unknown to themselves, know the place fondly as "The Psychopath".

Den Blå Hund Godthåbsvej 28. Mon–Wed 9.30am–midnight, Thurs–Fri 9.30am–2am, Sat 10am–2am, Sun 10am–11pm. By day, people come here to drink coffee, read newspapers and chat. After sunset, the draught beer begins to flow and, on a few nights a week, there's live jazz. During summer, tables spread out across busy Godthåbsvej to Ael Møllers Have, where covered seating is available, serviced by tray-balancing white-aproned waiters. Good food, too (see p.188).

Café Svejk Smallegade 31. Mon–Sat noon–2am, Sun noon–midnight. Near Frederiksberg Have, in a red wooden townhouse extension, *Svejk*'s claim to fame is its Czech draught beer, Bohemia Regent, a refreshing change if you've had enough of Danish brands. There's also a large-screen TV showing football matches of any importance.

Nørrebro

People tend to head to Nørrebro if they want to be "seen"; the bars here are mostly trendy places where the clientele has thought long and hard about what to wear that night. For locations of the following places, see the map on pp.112–113.

Barcelona Fælledvej 21. Tues 11am–2am, Wed & Thurs 11am–4am, Fri & Sat 11am–5am, Sun 11am–5pm. Located close enough to Skt Hans Torv to be considered part of the hip Nørrebro café scene, this swanky, two-level hangout is a decent café-bar that draws the crowds in at weekends when the back-room dance floor becomes a sweaty cavern of funk and soul. The café prepares fabulous tapas – a tasty accompaniment to a vast array of drinks.

Café Blågård's Apotek Blågårds Plads 20. Daily 3pm–2am (in summer from noon). Homely bar, still patronized by some of the left-wing activists who used to clash on this square with the police during the 1970s. They're now joined by a less-committed crowd who come to sample the bar's many wines and Urquell draught beer. Gets jam-packed during weekends, when there's also live jazz, blues or rock.

Caféen Funke Blegdamsvej 2. Mon–Wed & Sun 2pm–2am, Thurs–Sat 2pm–5am. Even though *Funke* is located on hip Skt Hans Torv, it has nothing to do with the hype across the square. One of the oldest cafés here, it's still going strong, with cheap beer, a Tuesday-night backgammon tournament, and live music or stand-up comedy a couple of nights a week. Completely laid-back and

△ Ølbaren

low key. Reasonably priced food available, too.

Front Page Sortedams Dosseringen 21. Mon–Wed & Sun 11am–1am, Thurs 11am–2am, Fri & Sat 10am–2am. Attractive lakeside café-bar, especially popular in summer, when tables are moved outdoors and you can enjoy a relaxing drink while contemplating the city from afar. In winter, service moves inside to a cosy cellar.

Kaffesalonen Peblinge Dosseringen 6. Mon–Fri 8am–midnight, Sat & Sun 10am–midnight. Another popular lakeside café, worth seeking out in the summer when tables are moved out onto a floating dock and the outdoor draught beer pumps opened.

Nørrebro Bryghus Ryesgade 2. Mon–Wed 11am–Midnight, Thurs–Sat 11am–2am, Sun 11am–10pm. Immensely popular brewery pub housed in an old factory, with a range of homebrews that sell out quicker than they can be bottled. Pricey restaurant, too (see p.189).

Ølbaren Elmegade 2. Winter: Mon 9pm–1am, Tues–Thurs & Sat 4pm–1am, Fri 3pm–1am; summer: Mon 9pm–1am, Tues–Thurs & Sat 8pm–1am, Fri 3pm–1am. A small, crowded place frequented by beer enthusiasts, with an incredibly wide range of beer from all over Europe. Tell the bartender what flavours you like, and he'll find a beer to suit. Unfortunately, this personal service can be – endearingly – slow.

Props Coffee Shop Blågårdsgade 5. Mon–Wed 11am–midnight, Thurs–Sat 11am–2am, Sun noon–11pm. Small, laid-back bar-cum-secondhand wooden furniture shop, with price tags attached, should you suddenly decide that you can't live without the chair you've sat on all evening.

Pussy Galore's Flying Circus Skt Hans Torv 30. Mon–Fri 8am–2am, Sat & Sun 9am–2am. Named after the nubile heroine of the James Bond movie Goldfinger, you'll be stirred if not shaken by delicious cocktails, an extensive list of snaps, tasty sandwiches and outdoor seating on one of Nørrebro's hippest squares – definitely a place to be seen.

Sebastopol Skt Hans Torv 2. Mon–Wed 8am–1am, Thurs–Fri 8am–2am, Sat 9am–2am, Sun 9am–1am. Glitzy Parisian-style café, crowded at weekends with well-groomed professionals warming up for the night, that piles out onto the cobbles as the evening moves on.

Østerbro

Østerbro is mostly residential, with the few places listed below – at all of which you could easily while away a few hours – being the exception to the rule. For locations of the following places, see the map on pp.112–113.

Café Bopa Løgstørgade 8. Mon–Wed & Sun 10am–midnight, Thurs 10am–2am, Fri & Sat 10am–5am. Popular café-bar in a remote corner of Østerbro, offering all-day and late-night entertainment, especially in the summer when there's outdoor seating on Bopa square. Food, drink, live music and DJs all come together nicely, making it easy to spend full days here.

Park Café Østerbrogade 71. Mon–Wed noon–midnight, Thurs–Fri from noon onwards, Sat from 10am onwards, Sun 10am–midnight. One of Denmark's largest cafés, with a classical interior of high stucco ceilings, polished rotating doors, crystal chandeliers and marble pillars. Quiet in the day, it transforms by evening into a vibrant pick-up joint, while a drinks list as long as your arm, live music a couple of nights a week, and a disco from Thursday to Saturday all add to the party atmosphere. Expect queues at weekends.

Pavillonen i Fælledparken April–September: Mon–Thurs noon–10pm, Fri & Sat noon–5am, Sun 11am–10pm. Unusual small pavilion café in the middle of Fælledparken, serving French café food with outside benches ideal for enjoying the tranquil park while sipping some cool draught lager. The small, trailer-like stage to one side holds free world music sessions on Thursdays, and bands play for free Friday.

Theodors Østerbrogade 106. Mon–Wed 11am–midnight, Thurs–Sat 11am–2am, Sun 11am–8pm. Combined venue with a top-class, pricey French restaurant at the back and a cool, Art Deco-ish café-bar at the front. Quiet and sedate during the day, the clientele becomes younger and a lot louder at evenings and weekends, as it fills up with disillusioned revellers opting out of the hectic meat market across the road at *Park*.

12

DRINKING | Østerbro

Live music and clubs

T hough more subdued during the week, come the weekend, Copenhagen is Scandinavia's party town, with a range of nightlife to suit the widest – and wildest – tastes. The city's liberal drinking laws – the most relaxed in Scandinavia – pull in punters from across the region, particularly Swedes, who descend on the city in search of a good time. A wide range of **bars** (see pp.193–199) and **clubs** cater to fun lovers of all ages, with every sort of music from bebop to bhangra; entrance is usually around 30–70kr.

There's also a healthy raft of **live music** venues. Traditionally, the **jazz** scene has always been the city's liveliest – a legacy of the number of respected American jazz musicians such as Dexter Gordon and Ben Webster who lived here during the 1960s and 1970s – and the annual jazz festival is world renowned, whilst there are a number of other festivals worth keeping an eye out for, too (see p.230). There's also a decent local **rock** music scene, while many big-name international acts include Copenhagen on their tours (while many more turn up for the huge Roskilde Festival – see p.231). A number of the smaller venues double as cafés or restaurants during the day and bars in the evening, before becoming live music venues or nightclubs after midnight.

Many of the larger venues sell **tickets** through **Billetnet** (10am–9pm; ☎70 15 65 65, ⓦ www.billetnet.dk), at Vesterbrogade 3 (beside Tivoli's main entrance) and in all post offices (☎33 15 12; 10kr booking fee). You can also **book online** at many of the venues listed below – websites are given where they exist.

Check with the tourist office and see p.230 for details of free outdoor summer concerts and festivals at Fælledparken.

Live music

Indre By

For locations of the following places, see the map on pp.54–55.

Copenhagen Jazzhouse/Natklub Niels Hemmingsensgade 10 ☎33 15 26 00, ⓦ www .jazzhouse.dk. Mon–Wed & Sun 6pm–midnight, Thurs–Sat 6pm–5am. Copenhagen's premier jazz venue, this large, smart, two-level club is frequented by jazz lovers of all ages. Gigs start at 8.30pm weekdays and 9.30pm Friday and Saturday, with music ranging from traditional jazz and funkjazz, fusion and neobop to world music at its best. Thursdays to Saturdays the *Natklub* nightclub (see p.203) takes over at midnight (or whenever the gigs finish) and continues until the early hours of the morning. 120kr.

Drop Inn Kompagnistræde 34 ☎33 11 24 04. Mon–Thurs 11am–4am, Fri 11am–5am, Sat noon–5am, Sun 2pm–5am. A cosy café-cum-jazz bar that has live jazz, blues or folk music every night starting at 10pm – and often for free. In the summer, there's both indoor and outdoor seating, and sandwiches and light meals available throughout the day.

△ Copenhagen Jazzhouse

13

Huset Magstræde **Rådhusstræde 13** ☎ 33 69 32 00, ⓦ www.husetmagstraede.dk. **Mon & Tues 10am–11pm, Wed–Sat 10am–midnight, Sun 10am–5pm.** Located in the same building as Use It, through the courtyard in the first-floor café, jazz flows from Huset Magstræde's Jazzscenen up to seven days a week beginning at around 9pm. Prices start at 40kr, with big reductions for students.

Det Hvide Lam **Kultorvet 5** ☎ 33 32 07 38. **Mon 10am–midnight, Tues & Wed 10am–1am, Thurs–Sat 10am–2am, Sun noon–1am.** Traditional jazz gigs Tues–Sun 8.30pm to midnight. Small, dark basement bar with no stage but loads of atmosphere, and musicians giving it all they've got on the New Orleans jazz front most nights. During the day you're welcome to eat your packed lunch here as long as you buy drinks.

La Fontaine **Kompagnistræde 11** ☎ 23 44 97 77. **Daily 10pm–5am.** Frequented largely by up-and-coming Danish hopefuls, this is the place to come if you're into small smoky rooms and surprise appearances by the big boys of jazz when they're visiting the city. Later in the evening the stage is thrown open to aspiring performers in the audience.

Mojo **Løngangsstræde 21C** ☎ 33 11 64 53, ⓦ www.mojo.dk. **Daily 8pm–5am.** Live music nightly in this small venue with plenty of down-at-heel ambience, popular with blues

aficionados of all ages. Music starts around 10pm and is followed at weekends with a DJ until closing. Less-established local acts get things going before the big names come on stage. Happy Hour daily 8–10pm; large beer 25kr. Entrance fee from 60/120kr, discount with a student card.

The Rock **Skindergade 45–47** ☎ 33 91 39 13, ⓦ www.the-rock.dk. **Wed–Sat 9pm onwards.** The oppressive former law courts provide a perfect setting for the aggressive music played at this new live-music venue devoted to heavy metal and hardcore rock. Bands start at 9pm and are sometimes follow by a heavy-metal disco. From 40kr.

Christianshavn

For locations of the following places, see the map on p.67.

Loppen **Christiania** ☎ 32 57 84 22, ⓦ www .loppen.dk. **Tues–Sun 9pm–2am.** Most nights – around 11pm – this cool converted warehouse on the edge of Christiania hosts both established and experimental Danish rock, jazz and performance artists, and quite a few visiting British and American ones, too (some free, others 60–200kr).

Operæn **Christiania** ☎ 32 57 29 09, ⓦ www .operaen.net. Upstairs in one of Christiania's old warehouses on Pusherstreet, Operæn is a very laid-back venue with live gigs most nights except Tuesday (film night), ranging from blues to hip-hop. Sunday is Blues Day from 3–9pm.

Sofiekælderen Sofiegade 1, Christianshavn ☏33 57 77 01, ⊛www.sophiekaeldren.dk. **Mon–Wed & Sun noon–midnight, Thurs–Sat noon–3am.** The new owners of this old favourite among followers of Danish rock have made sure the tradition is kept alive as it transforms at weekends into a live-music and DJ venue. Music in the Latin, funk, soul, disco and jazz category starts at 10pm (some free, others 40–60kr).

Frederikstad

For locations of the following places, see the map on pp.76–77.

Jazzcup Gothersgade 107 ☏33 33 87 40. **Mon–Thurs 11.30am–5.30pm, Fri 11am–6.30pm, Sat 10am–5.30pm.** Ingenious arrival on the Copenhagen jazz scene, this original café-cum-CD-shop-cum-music-venue has live jazz every Friday and Saturday afternoon. Some of the best Danish and international musicians play here, including names from the world music circuit. 40–60kr.

Rådhuspladsen and around

For locations of the following places, see the map on p.90.

Pumpehuset Studiestræde 52 ☏33 93 19 09, ⊛www.pumpehuset.dk. The city's spacious former pumphouse is one of the city's best concert venues with a capacity of up to six hundred punters. A broad sweep of up-and-coming or fading international rock acts and big Danish names perform about eight times a month. 60–250kr.

Tivoli ☏33 15 10 01, ⊛www.tivoli.dk. Surprisingly good, sometimes even groundbreaking, live outdoor rock-pop every Friday night at 10pm from April to September – with a good crowd and decent weather it can be great fun. Entry is free with general Tivoli admittance.

Vesterbro

For locations of the following places, see the map on pp.102–103.

Vega Enghavevej 40 ☏33 25 70 11, ⊛www .vega.dk. In a former union hall, this top music venue retains its 1950s and 1960s decor while showcasing plenty of modern alternative rock. *Vega* houses two stages: Store Vega accommodating 1500 and used for international names; and Lille Vega with room for "only" 500 and used for smaller bands or when the big names want an intimate atmosphere, while in the weekends it becomes *Vega Nightclub*. Keep your eye out for local and visiting luminaries: Björk apparently loves the place. Up to 400kr.

Nørrebro and Østerbro

For locations of the following places, see the map on pp.112–113.

Café Blågård's Apotek Blågårds Plads 20, Nørrebro ☏35 37 24 42 ⊛www.kroteket.dk. **Daily 3pm–2am (in summer from noon).** Low-key place catering for a slightly older crowd that come here to listen to live jazz, blues, rock or world music every Monday, Friday and Saturday, when it gets packed. Monday is jazzjam and free, Friday and Saturday 20kr.

Café Rust Guldbergsgade 8, Nørrebro ☏35 24 52 00, ⊛www.rust.dk. **Wed–Sat 9pm–5am.** One of the best-known venues in town, this multifaceted place right on busy Skt Hans Torv hosts up-and-coming live indie rock, hiphop and electronic music acts on its main stage. Downstairs is the very hip *Rust Natklub* (see p.204) specializing in electro, hip-hop, house and cool, funky grooves. Age restriction after 11pm, only over-21s. Up to 120kr.

Stengade 30 Stengade 18, Nørrebro ☏35 36 09 36, ⊛www.stengade30.dk. **Tues & Wed 9pm–2am, Thurs 9pm–5am, Fri–Sat 10pm–5am.** Housed in a 1970s squat, *Stengade 30* is now recognized as the city's prime punk-rock-indie-metal venue. Every Tuesday, the Play It jam session is open for everyone, and the live acts are often followed by all-night dance parties with a mix of techno, indie and rock depending on the DJ. There's also the popular RubA'Dub Sundays club (see "Clubs", p.204) and *Café Stalingrad* bar upstairs. 50kr.

Pavillonen i Fælledparken Fælledparken, Østerbro ☏35 38 73 83, ⊛www.cafe -pavillonen.dk. **April to September Mon–Thurs noon–10pm, Fri & Sat noon–5am, Sun 11am–10pm.** Summer-only open-air venue at the romantic Pavillion in Fælledparken. Saturday to Wednesdays, it's an ordinary café, but Thursday and Friday there's live music on a trailer van next to the pavilion, featuring world music Thursdays and Danish rock bands Fridays. Music starts at 8pm. Free.

Amager

For locations of the following places, see the map on pp.120–121.

Islands Bryggge Kulturhus Islands Brygge 18. Mon–Weds 11am–11pm, Thurs–Fri 11am–midnight, Sat 10am–midnight, Sun 10am–11pm. A popular new cultural centre, next to the harbour pool on the banks of Interhavnen, with live jigs four or five times a week. Music, starting at around 9pm, ranges from

jazz, blues and world music to full-blown classical concerts. From 40kr upwards.
Femøren Amager Strandpark. June–August. Huge, inexpensive open-air rock concerts by top local bands and international acts on a big, temporary stage, a stone's throw from Amager beach. Check with Use It or the tourist office (p.37) about coming events.
Amager Bio Øresundsvej 6 ☏ 32 86 02 00, ⊛ www.amagerbio.dk. Converted cinema, now one of the city's largest and most popular live-music venues, hosting big names from the local and international music scene. Tickets start at 185kr.

Clubs

For map references to places covered in this section, refer to the relevant area under "Live music".

Indre By

Diskotek In Nørregade 1 ☏ 33 11 74 78, ⊛ www.discotekin.dk. Fri 11pm–8am, Sat 11pm–10am. Two nightclubs under one roof: *La Hacienda*, a Spanish-inspired club playing soul and R&B, and the more electronic *The Dance Floor*. Both are pretty mainstream – you can move freely between the two – catering for a young audience, and open until late into the following day. *Diskotek In* made a name for itself when it launched the free-bar concept a few years ago whereby you pay a fixed bar fee when you arrive (women pay about half what men do) and you can drink your fill of beer, wine and champagne all through the night. It's a wildly popular concept that still draws in the crowds. Entry 50kr, bar fees 25–100kr.
Club Mambo Vester Voldgade 85 ☏ 33 11 97 66, ⊛ www.saborlatino.dk. Thurs 9pm–3am, Fri & Sat 9am–5am. Salsa bar, long popular among the city's small South American community and now increasingly hip as Copenhagen discovers Latin fever. Free salsa and merengue classes every Thursday 9–10pm and Friday and Saturday between 10pm and 11pm. Thursday free, Friday and Saturday 60kr.
Extra Østergade 13 ☏ 35 26 09 52 ⊛ www .restaurant-extra.dk. Fri midnight–3am, Sat midnight–5am. Lounge-bar section of this large, trendy new restaurant at the exclusive end of Strøget next door to Mulburry. On Fridays and Saturdays, the place converts

into a heaving – and exclusive – nightclub at midnight. You have to be on the guest list to get in, to do that either phone or go on the website. 70kr.
Ketchup Pilestraede 19 ☏ 33 32 30 30. Fri noon–2am, Sat 11am–2am. One of the most self-consciously stylish additions to the city's thriving café/restaurant/bar scene where things get lively when the food stops (around 10pm in the café, 11pm in the restaurant) and the bar kicks off with DJs on Friday and Saturday nights. Free.
Krasnapolsky Vestergade 10 ☏ 33 32 88 00. Fri & Sat 10am–5am. This once ultra-cool cafe-bar (with a good selection of assorted cocktails) is now home to a free weekend disco where a visiting DJ plays mainstream R&B, funk and disco hits.
Natklub Niels Hemmingsensgade 10 ☏ 33 15 26 00, ⊛ www.jazzhouse.dk. Fri & Sat midnight–5am. When the live gigs are over at Copenhagen Jazzhouse (see p.200) *Natklub* takes over with in-house DJs serving up a mix of Latin, house, acid jazz, bossa nova, and old-school disco tunes to dance the night away. 60kr.
Woodstock Vestergade 12 ☏ 33 11 20 71, ⊛ www.woodstock.dk. Thurs–Sat 10pm–5am. Basically a large dance floor and not much else, *Woodstock* pulls in a large, fun-loving older crowd willing to bop to anything with a beat, though the music is predominantly retro, going all the way back to Elvis. Thursday 30kr (with free bar 100kr), Fri & Sat 50kr.

Rosenborg

Nasa/Kulørbar Boltens Gård ☎ 33 93 74 15, ⓦ www.nasa.dk. Nasa: Fri & Sat midnight–6am; Kulørbar: Thurs 10pm–5am, Fri–Sat 11pm–5am. You don't have to be rich and famous to come here, but it helps, and you'll certainly need to dress up to have any chance of getting in. *Nasa*, on the top floor, is the more exclusive – it's members only, but you might be able to talk your way in if you look the part – and is the haunt of Danish and visiting international movie and music stars. Downstairs, *Kulørbar* is marginally more relaxed and easier to get into, though you'll still need to slip on a posh party frock. *Kulørbar* 60kr.

Rådhuspladsen and around

Rosie McGee's Vesterbrogade 2A ☎ 33 32 19 23, ⓦ www.rosiemcgee.dk. Mon, Tues & Sun 11pm–3am, Wed & Thurs 11pm–4am, Fri 11pm–5am, Sat 11pm–6am. A stone's throw from Rådhuspladsen, Rosie McGee's pub-style venue attracts many Anglophone visitors. There's a restaurant and bar downstairs with occasional DJs and live gigs during the week, but it's the upstairs nightclub spanning two floors, and encompassing three dance floors and five bars, that gives life to the place, pumping out mainstream pop until dawn. Friday and Saturday after 10pm 60kr, rest of the week free.

Vesterbro and Frederiksberg

Kellerdirk Frederiksberg Allé 102, Frederiksberg ☎ 33 25 22 53, ⓦ www.kellerdirk.dk. Fri & Sat 11.30pm–4.30am. A restaurant and theatre café during the week, until it throws open its disco doors, featuring live "copy band" jam sessions until 2am followed by danceable pop/rock disco from the Eighties and Nineties. With very limited seating, the options are either to dance or stand by the bar; most choose to dance. Frequented by an "older" audience (25–40) that has opted to avoid the hassle of inner-city clubs. 50–100kr.

Vega Natklub Enghavevej 40, Vesterbro ☎ 33 25 70 11, ⓦ www.vega.dk. Fri & Sat 11pm–5am. One of the top clubs in the city, part of the immensely popular Vega (see p.202) and offering all you could possibly want for a fantastic night out. The actual club is based in Lille Vega and sees resident and internationally renowned guest DJs raising the roof with funky beats and soulful sounds. There's also an upstairs chill-out lounge with soothing tunes and fancy cocktails, and out front, *Ideal Bar* (see p.197). Gets very busy after 1am. 60kr after 1am.

Nørrebro and Østerbro

Café Bopa Løgstørgade 8, Østerbro ☎ 35 43 05 66, ⓦ www.cafebopa.dk. Thurs 11pm–2am, Fri & Sat 11.30pm–5am. Hugely popular café-bar in a remote corner of Østerbro, offering late-night boogying. Guest DJs play mostly mainstream dance tunes that appeal to the very mixed crowd. Free.

Park Nightclub Østerbrogade 79, Østerbro ☎ 35 42 62 48, ⓦ www.park.dk. Thurs 11pm–5am, Fri & Sat 11am–6pm. Housed in the ground floor of popular *Park* café (see p.191) – turn left as you enter – this Saturday Night Fever-style club offers R&B, soul, disco and house music at its most smooth, catering to a fun, diverse crowd, who ram the place, especially the open deck during summer. 50kr after 11pm.

Rust Natklub Guldbergsgade 8, Nørrebro ☎ 35 24 52 00, ⓦ www.rust.dk. Wed–Sat 11pm–5am. Crowded, multi-level venue named after Mathias Rust, who famously landed his small plane on Moscow's Red Square in 1987. His adventure resulted in the pan-Scandinavian peace initiative, the Next Stop Sovjet, which was based in this building. *Rust* subsequently began to host live bands and still has the occasional gig. Attractions today include the small basement nightclub, which focuses on serious underground electronic dance music selected by frequently changing in-house DJs. Upstairs, there's a laid-back, minimalist cocktail bar and a larger main stage and dance floor where guest DJs play hip-hop, house and cool, funky grooves. Age restriction after 11pm, only over-21s. 50kr.

Stengade 30 Stengade 18, Nørrebro ☎ 35 36 09 36, ⓦ www.stengade30.dk. Thurs–Sat 10pm–5am. Housed in a 1970s squat, *Stengade* 30 hosts all-night dance parties – after the live acts have finished playing – with a mix of techno, indie and rock depending on the DJ. There's also the popular RubA'Dub Sundays club. 50kr.

Classical music, theatre and cinema

n cultural terms, Copenhagen entered the new millennium at a crossroads. On the one hand, there were those who wanted to see the capital continue as a stronghold of conservative Danish traditions. On the other, many saw an opportunity to reinvent the city as a cosmopolitan regional hub, drawing on its burgeoning immigrant community and its new links via the Øresunds Bridge with Malmö in Sweden. The result is an increasingly vibrant mix of the traditional and alternative. While Copenhagen is still strong on "high" arts – **opera**, **classical music** and mainstream **theatre** receive most of the government's subsidies – an increasing number of more experimental ventures have managed to break through in the last decade and a half, particularly in the arena of alternative theatre and the **film** industry, made internationally famous with the work of the Dogme group (see box on p.211).

But even in the more traditional arts the city is undergoing something of a renaissance. Until recently, the Royal Opera, Royal Ballet and Royal Theatre all jostled for space in the grandiose **Det Kongelige Teater** on Kongens Nytorv; now the Royal Opera has its own state-of-the-art building, the fabulous Operæn (see p.73) on Holmen, while the Royal Theatre will move to its new showpiece home, currently under construction on the harbourfront, some time in 2008. They all still operate under the banner, however, of Det Kongelige Teater, which produces a *Kalendar*, available from the tourist office and the theatre itself, with details of all of the season's productions – opera, theatre, concerts and ballet – across its various venues. Alternatively, check out their website before you go at ⓦwww .kglteater.dk; you can buy tickets online, from their ticket hotline (ⓣ33 69 69 69; Mon–Sat 10am–8pm), or from the other sources mentioned below. If you don't mind leaving it till late, go in person to the box office at August Bournonvilles Passage 1, just off Kongens Nytorv. The theatre holds back around 25 tickets for that day's evening performance at Det Kongelige Teater and Operæn, which can be purchased on the day in person, while you can get some real bargains if you're willing to leave it to the last-minute – unsold tickets for that day's performances are sold off at the box office from 4pm onwards at a fifty percent discount.

Big-budget projects aside, the city has a plethora of smaller venues for music and drama – from churches and minor theatres to more quirky locations like the Rundetårn and the Teatermuseet. **Tickets** to many performances can be bought through **Billetnet** (ⓣ70 15 65 65, 10am–9pm; ⓦwww.billetnet.dk), at Vesterbrogade 3 beside Tivoli's main entrance, and in all post offices (ⓣ33 15

10 12; 10kr booking fee). **ARTE** (☏ 38 48 15 55 April–Sept daily 10am–10pm; Oct–March Mon–Fri 10am–7pm, Sat 10am–5pm) sell tickets, including same-day tickets at half price, for theatre performances and concerts through its outlet at the Tivoli ticket office on Vesterbrogade. For **listings** information, pick up a copy of the English-language *Copenhagen Post* (ⓦwww.cphpost .dk; 15kr) from the Wonderful Copenhagen tourist office on Vesterbrogade, or check their website; there are also English-language listings at ⓦwww.aok.dk and ⓦwww.kulturnaut.dk.

Classical music and opera

Copenhagen boasts a wide range of **classical music** and is home to a number of top-class ensembles – including the Zealand Symphony Orchestra, the Academic Orchestra and Choir, and the excellent Danish National Symphony Orchestra/DR and Danish National Choir (ⓦwww.dr.dk/dnso), set to move to their new premises in 2008 (see box below). There are also regular classical music concerts in many of Copenhagen's grandest **churches**, including Vor Frue Kirke, Vor Frelsers Kirke, Marmorkirken, Skt Petri Kirke and the church in Kastellet – a free quarterly programme listing all these concerts is available from the churches themselves or from the Wonderful Copenhagen tourist office; most are either free or very modestly priced. Look out, too, for concerts in the city's **museums** (including Ny Carlsberg Glyptotek, Louisiana, Arken, the Statens Museum for Kunst and the Nationalmuseet) and in the Queen's Hall of Den Sorte Diamant.

Opera in the city received a huge boost with the completion of the Operæn (see p.73) on Holmen, which kicked off with an ambitious production of Wagner's *Ring Cycle*, and although the familiar classics continue to predominate – works by Puccini, Mozart, Strauss, Verdi and Rossini – there's now the scope and space for more contemporary productions by modern composers. If your tastes run to the more experimental, the city's other opera company, Den Anden Opera, puts on altogether more avant-garde fare, in Indre By.

Copenhagen Koncerthuset

Not to be outdone by the other major players – opera, ballet and theatre all have new purpose-built premises – Copenhagen's classical music scene will soon get its own state-of-the-art, acoustic heaven in the form of the new **Copenhagen Koncerthuset**, currently under construction on the island of Amager (see p.124). Designed by French architect Jean Nouvel, the building will feature a huge external screen illuminated each evening with images from the events going on inside – to ensure musical perfection, all aspects of design are being overseen by Japanese acoustics expert, Yasuhisa Toyota. The Koncerthuset's main purpose is to house the Danish Broadcasting Corporation's (DR) music production division, though it will also, in its role as national concert hall, host non-DR concerts and eventually be the base for the Royal Danish Academy of Music. Big-name, crowd-pulling perform-ances – classical and otherwise – will be held in the main hall itself, but the musical smorgasbord will also include free jazz concerts in the foyer, small choir rooms for choral concerts, the specialized Orchestral Hall for concerts by the Danish National Symphony Orchestra/DR and other orchestras, plus a Rhythm Room for blues and rock. There'll also be audience studios for taped TV and radio, temporary exhibitions and the usual array of cafés and restaurants. Guided tours are planned – for develop-ments check out ⓦwww.dr.dk/koncerthuset.

CLASSICAL MUSIC, THEATRE AND CINEMA | Music and opera

The annual **Opera Festival**, which usually takes place at the end of May, is a fairly staid affair (see ⓦwww.aok.dk or ⓦwww.kglteater.dk for full programme). A more laid-back event for opera lovers is the one-off, free, open-air performance (generally a preview of the coming season at Det Kongelige Teater; see ⓦwww.kglteater.dk for details) staged mid-August in one of the city's green spaces. Arrive early to get a spot, and bring a picnic.

Thanks to subsidies, **tickets** are reasonably priced, though it depends on the production and, of course, where you want to sit – for the more popular classics, expect to pay 90–700kr.

Concert and opera venues

Den Anden Opera **Kronprinsensgade 7, Indre By** ☎33 32 55 56 (Mon–Fri 11am–3pm), ⓦwww .denandenopera.dk. An offbeat alternative to Det Kongelige Teater, Den Anden Opera (The Other Opera) stages small-scale new works by contemporary Danish composers.

Den Sorte Diamant Koncertsal **Christians Brygge 9, Slotsholmen** ☎33 47 47 47, ⓦwww.kb.dk. This stunning waterfront venue is a regular on the classical music scene and even has its own resident string quartet, which puts on regular performances. Tickets from Billetnet or at the entrance one hour before the concert begins.

Det Kongelige Teater **Kongens Nytorv, Indre By** ☎33 69 69 69 (Mon–Sat 10am–8pm), ⓦwww .kglteater.dk. Despite the arrival of the new opera house, Copenhagen's grandest theatre still stages a few fairly conservative operas and classical concerts. Prices rise according to the scale of the production (100–1200kr), and tickets for popular works sell out very fast. Tickets bought from the box office after 4pm on the day of performance are reduced by fifty percent.

Operæn **Holmen** ☎33 69 69 69, ⓦwww .kglteater.dk and ⓦwww.operaen.dk. The city's spanking new opera house has two stages – the opulent, maple-encased, gilt-ceilinged main stage "Store Scene", with seating for up to 1700, and the much more intimate "Takkelloftet" (Tackle Loft), used for more experimental productions. The Royal Ballet also uses the main stage for occasional performances.

Radiohusets Koncertsal (Studio 1) **Julius Thomsensgade 1, Frederiksberg** ☎35 20 62 62 (Mon–Fri 10am–6pm, Sat 10am–1pm). A classic of twentieth-century Danish architecture, Radiohuset is, however, also something of a white elephant, having been built ten metres shorter than originally planned due to lack of funds, a shortcut that drastically affected the hall's acoustics. However, the home of DR (Danish Radio), the Danish National Symphony Orchestra and Radio Choir, is set to move to swanky new purpose-built premises in Amager in 2008 (see box on p.206), but for now it hosts regular classical music performances (Sept–May) by its celebrated orchestra. Tickets are available from the box office or Billetnet and start at around 60kr;

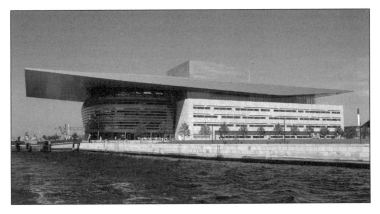

△ Operæn

unsold tickets sold on the door from ninety minutes before the performance.

Rundetårn Købmagergade, Indre By ⏀33 73 03 73, ⓦ**www.rundetaarn.dk.** Possibly the quirkiest venue in town, offering up regular chamber-music recitals (20–80kr), classical soloists and choral works. It also hosts the annual Copenhagen Guitar Festival in July/August.

Tivolis Koncertsal Tietgensgade 20, Indre By ⏀33 15 10 12, ⓦ**www.tivoli.dk.** Inside Tivoli, the garden's recently revamped concert hall – at the moment, the biggest in the city – stages a variety of classical performances and some opera, often featuring the major national orchestras.

Theatre and dance

Despite limited government funds for anything but the traditional ensembles, the Danish **theatre** scene is alive and kicking. In the past decade or so, several youthful and dynamic theatres and companies have appeared, though as many only stage Danish-language productions, they're unlikely to be of interest to most visitors. That said, if you're really keen for some of the more experimental performances where dialogue is sparse and not too integral to the experience, a lack of understanding shouldn't prove too much of a barrier to overall enjoyment. Alternatively, you could see whether there's anything playing by the **London Toast Theatre** (ⓦ www.londontoast.dk), a well-established English theatre company, based in Copenhagen, which performs English-language plays, comedies and musicals in the mainstream city theatres, including an ever-popular Christmas cabaret in Tivoli's Glassalen. Check the website for their full programme. There are also the English-language productions of **Hamlet**, staged during August in the appropriate setting of Kronborg Slot in Helsingør (ⓦ www.hamletsommer.dk; tickets go on sale early summer and cost around 235kr, contact Billetnet, see p.205). If you speak Danish, the listings below will point you in the direction of some of the better venues, and it's always worth checking if they are hosting any guest companies performing in English.

Copenhagen has a small but thriving **dance** scene – although there's only one venue, Dansescenen, specifically devoted to this, other theatres occasionally stage dance performances. For **ballet** lovers, there's the fairly traditional repertoire of the Royal Ballet, staged at Det Kongelige Teater and Operæn, as well as several performances in Tivoli during the summer and at Christmas. If you're in the city mid-August, you might try to catch the free open-air performance in the atmospheric surroundings of Kastellet (ⓦ www.kglteater.dk for details).

Ticket prices can be steep even for fringe performances: expect to pay at least 150kr, though seats may be cheaper if bought late on the day of performance. A free monthly programme, *Teater Kalenderen*, covering theatre and dance, is available at the theatres themselves and at the Wonderful Copenhagen and Use It tourist offices. Tickets to nearly all performances can be bought via Billetnet (see p.205).

Theatre and dance venues

Betty Nansen Teatret Frederiksberg Allé 57 ⏀33 21 14 90 (Mon–Fri 2–6pm, Sat 2–4pm) ⓦ**www.bettynansen.dk.** Grand old dame of Copenhagen theatre with a great reputation for award-winning plays – mostly in Danish – and in a beautiful building to boot.

CaféTeatret Skindergade 3, Indre By ⏀33 12 58 14 (Mon–Fri 3–6.30pm, Sat 1–3pm), ⓦwww .cafeteatret.dk. Part theatre, part trendy café (featuring its own programme of events) frequented by actors and arty types, CaféTeatret puts on a range of innovative performances – theatre, dance, cabaret – mostly in Danish.

Dansescenen Øster Fælled Torv 34, Østerbro ⏀35 43 20 21 (Mon–Fri 2–6pm), ⓦwww .dansescenen.dk. The only place in Copenhagen with regular performances of modern dance, showcasing top Scandinavian ensembles on its two stages plus the work of the current choreographer in residence. The Dansescenen programme (available from the Tivoli ticket office) has a section in English.

Det Kongelige Teater Kongens Nytorv, Indre By ⓣ 33 69 69 69 (Mon–Sat 10am–8pm), ⓦ www .kglteater.dk. Copenhagen's oldest – and finest – theatre provides all the gilt and velvet pomp you could ask for (see also p.207). Ballet – largely the Royal Ballet and their fairly traditional repertoire – is now split between three locations: the old stage, Gamle Scene; the 1930s extension, Stærekassen, at Tordenskoldsgade 5; and the new opera house on Holmen (see p.207). Most drama is now staged in the two more modern venues – Stærekassen and TurbineHallerne, a former turbine hall, at Adelgade 10. The permanent troupe performs a variety of mainstream contemporary and older plays. Tickets bought from the box office (August Bournonvilles Passage 7) after 4pm on the day of performance are reduced by fifty percent, and you can also book online up to seven days in advance.

Folketeatret Nørregade 39, Indre By ⓣ 33 12 18 45 (Mon–Fri 4.30–7pm, Sat & Sun 2–7pm), ⓦ www.folketeatret.dk. One of the oldest theatres in town. The main stage (Store Scene) tends to put on musicals and family-oriented stuff; the smaller Hippodromen shows more experimental work, as does the tiny stage, Boxen; Snoreloftet sticks to cabaret. The Christmas shows are always a hit.

Kanonhallen Øster Fælled Torv 37, Østerbro ⓣ 35 43 20 21 (Mon–Fri 2–6pm), ⓦ www .kanonhallen.net. One of the best venues in the city for contemporary Danish theatre and dance, with an excellent reputation for cutting-edge productions and as a venue for several annual festivals.

Østre Gasværk Nyborggade 17, Østerbro ⓣ 39 27 71 77 (Mon–Fri 2–6pm, Sat 2–3pm), ⓦ www .oestre-gasvaerk.dk. Set in an old gasworks, this is one of the hippest theatres in town, with new plays aimed largely at a younger audience – don't expect weighty classics. Also hosts modern dance shows from time to time. Occasional performances in English.

Film

The Danes' love affair with celluloid stretches back to the 1920s, when the country's thriving film studios looked for a time as though they would become Europe's answer to Hollywood. The success was spearheaded by internationally renowned director Carl Theodor Dreyer, with his series of dark, dramatic pieces such as *The Master of the House* (1925) and the French-produced *The Passion of Joan of Arc* (1928); he continued to make films until his death in the 1960s. Nowadays, the **Danish film industry** is booming again with a new set of film-makers achieving international critical acclaim, in particular the group originally associated with Dogme95 (see box, p.211), including its founder, Lars von Trier. Von Trier's controversial, yet high-profile films such as *Breaking the Waves* and *Dancer in the Dark* made his directorial name worldwide, and his star continues to rise as big Hollywood names, including Nicole Kidman, star of the recent *Dogville*, come on board, lured by the prospect of more challenging, non-Hollywood roles.

Danes are keen cinemagoers, and despite the inevitable predominance of mainstream Hollywood flicks in the city's **cinemas**, there's usually at least one Danish production on offer. Foreign-language films get good representation, too; most films are screened in their original language, with Danish subtitles. The city's arthouse cinemas, particularly Cinemateket at the **Filmhuset**, home to the Danish Film Institute (see also p.210) and Vester Vov Vov, always have a good selection of more offbeat offerings. Most cinemas offer cheaper **tickets** earlier in the day (before 6pm), with prices being staggered up to the most expensive evening and weekend screenings – from about 50–60kr to 60–80kr. At weekends, it's definitely worth booking ahead. Cinemas are not part of the Billetnet system.

In March, the city takes part in the **Night Film Festival** (ⓦ www.natfilm .dk; see also p.230) during which cinemas across the country screen large numbers of mostly foreign films (with English subtitles), which wouldn't otherwise be seen in Denmark, along with a few previews, and retrospectives showcasing the work of particular actors. In addition, the **Copenhagen International Film Festival**, inaugurated in 2003 and aiming to be the city's answer to Cannes, is held some time in autumn (Ⓦ www.copenhagenfilm festival.com for details; see also p.232), and focuses on European film and filmmaking, with an international jury bestowing awards, special screenings at a number of venues, events, seminars and interviews.

The weekly pamphlet *Film Kalenderen* (available in English on Ⓦ www.aok.dk) includes details of almost all of Copenhagen's movie offerings and is available free in most cinemas; the free city paper *metroXpress* also has a film calendar.

Cinemas

Cinemateket at Filmhuset Gothersgade 55, Indre By ☏ 33 74 34 12, Ⓦ www.dfi.dk. Closed Mon. Home of the Danish Film Institute, this three-screen, state-of-the-art cinema complex shows the best of Danish and international arthouse film – the more eagerly anticipated films sell out quickly, so bookings are advisable. The Benjamin theatre shows children's films and free documentaries, and the complex also houses a café, trendy restaurant, a decent film bookshop and fantastic cinematic archives (see p.79).

Cinemaxx Fisketorvet Kalvebod Brygge 57, Vesterbro ☏ 70 10 12 02, Ⓦ www.cinemaxx .dk/fisketorvet. Multi-screen complex in a mall showing the latest from Hollywood. Not worth a special trip unless you plan to go shopping beforehand.

Dagmar Teatret Jernbanegade 2, Indre By ☏ 33 14 32 22, Ⓦ www.dagmar.dk. Mostly mainstream movies in this popular cinema in the heart of Copenhagen containing five theatres and a bust of Carl Theodor Dreyer, the Danish director of the Oscar-winning *The Passion of Joan of Arc*, who was the cinema's manager for a short period.

Empire Bio Guldbergsgade 29F, Nørrebro ☏ 35 36 00 36, Ⓦ www.empirebio.dk. Very popular cinema with huge, comfy seats and a good selection of both Danish and international film.

Gloria Biografen Rådhuspladsen 59 ☏ 33 12 42 92, Ⓦ www.gloria.dk. Small cinema located right in the centre of the city, with an eclectic programme of some mainstream, some specially imported films and arthouse favourites. It also sells a range of arthouse films through its own video-distribution arm, some of which can be hard to find elsewhere. A cine buff's delight.

Grand Teatret Mikkel Bryggers Gade 8, Indre By ☏ 33 15 16 11. Very central cinema, in the heart of Indre By, and showing the best of mainstream international films.

Husets Biograf Magstræde 14, Indre By ☏ 33 32 40 77. Located on the second floor of the Huset building, this small cinema shows more esoteric, arthouse fare.

Imperial Ved Vesterport 4, Vesterbro ☏ 70 13 12 11. Copenhagen's largest cinema, and the usual site for gala openings and premieres. The enormous single screen – the biggest in Scandinavia – shows mainly middle-of-the-road Hollywood blockbusters, with reclining seats and a stunning sound system.

Palads Axeltorv 9, Indre By ☏ 70 13 12 11, Ⓦ www.biobooking.dk. One of the world's first multiplexes and probably the most colourful cinema on the planet, this Copenhagen landmark, with its famously gaudy exterior, shows the latest movies on its seventeen screens.

Park Bio Østerbrogade 79, Østerbro ☏ 35 38 33 62, Ⓦ www.parkbio-kbh.dk. One of the oldest in town, this atmospheric single-screen cinema tends to show a mixture of the better Hollywood offerings, and the more commercial arthouse films coming towards the end of their runs. It also has a decent café-bar.

Tycho Brahe Planetarium og Omnimaxteater Gammel Kongevej 10, Vesterbro ☏ 33 12 12 24, Ⓦ www.tycho.dk. Copenhagen's IMAX screen shows a mixture of non-fiction natural world and cosmic wonder films, although there's the odd 3D offering, too. You'll need to hire headphones for English translation. See p.94 for more details.

Vester Vov Vov Absalonsgade 5, Vesterbro ☏ 33 24 42 00, Ⓦ www.vestervovvov.dk. Three-screen arthouse cinema, with a decent bar and café for pre-flick nibbles. Also has a large and fairly comprehensive collection of film posters, some of them for sale.

Dogme 95 and Lars von Trier

Established in 1995 by Lars von Trier, the golden boy of Danish film, **Dogme 95** (® www.dogme95.dk) is perhaps the most distinctive European film movement of recent years. Founded in reaction to Hollywood domination with its reliance on special effects and massive budgets, Dogme 95 is basically a set of rules drawn up by von Trier and Thomas Vinterberg and dubbed "Vow of Chastity". This manifesto aimed to enhance cinematic realism by a series of rules – the film must be in colour, only hand-held cameras and natural lighting are allowed, shooting must be done on location with no props and sets, and no special costumes, special effects or extraneous soundtracks are permitted. Although the four main exponents of the movement – von Trier, Thomas Vinterberg, Søren Kragh Jacobsen and Kristian Levring – are all Danish, anyone can make a Dogme film if it follows the manifesto, and over thirty accredited Dogme films have been made, including ones from as far afield as Korea and Argentina. That said, the best-known Dogme films are Danish: *Idiots*, by von Trier himself, *Festen* by Thomas Vinterberg and *Mifune's Last Chance* by Søren Kragh Jacobsen. More recent successes have included the Copenhagen-set *Italian for Beginners* by Lone Scherfig.

Some commentators derided Dogme 95 as a cheap gimmick, but although at first it was largely ignored outside the European arthouse scene, it soon gained international recognition. Ironically, the Dogme Secretariat (responsible for accrediting films made in the Dogme mould) closed in 2002 for fear that Dogme was becoming too much of a genre in itself (one of the rules of the "Vow of Chastity" was no genre films), and claiming that it and the original founders had "moved on". Although the movement still exists, films no longer have to receive official accreditation to be called a Dogme film – they simply have to follow the manifesto.

The most famous member of the Dogme group, **Lars von Trier**, is now an internationally acclaimed director, with several Cannes Film Festival prizes under his belt and big Hollywood names like Nicole Kidman and Danny Glover headlining his projects. He continues to reject the technical artifices of film-making, filming his most recent productions – *Dogville* and *Mandalay* – on sound stages with no set, and encouraging more intense "method" performances from his actors by requiring them to stay in character for longer periods of time. Ever controversial, von Trier's current project is a trilogy, *USA – Land of Opportunities*, of which *Dogville* and *Mandalay* are the first two instalments (the third, *Wasington* [sic] is due out in 2008) – a gritty, uncompromisingly cynical look at what von Trier sees as "America's sins and hypocrisy".

⑭

Gay Copenhagen

Being the capital of a country where homosexuality has long been legal, and where gay and lesbian couples are allowed to marry, has led to Copenhagen becoming one of the world's **premier gay cities**. Heads don't generally turn if a gay or lesbian couple are seen kissing or holding hands, and many Copenhageners pride themselves on their liberal attitudes, although occasional cases of gay-bashing do take place. An example of the city's emancipated attitude is the way its main cruising spot, H.C. Ørstedsparken, has been equipped with "birdboxes" containing condoms and lubricating gel, while police patrols here don't chase out cottaging men, but protect them from homophobic violence.

Paradoxically, Copenhagen's liberal traditions mean that there are fewer specifically gay and lesbian venues than in less tolerant cities. For general **information**, the national organization for gays and lesbians, the Landforeningen for Bøsser og Lesbiske (LBL), at Teglgårdsstræde 13 (☏33 13 19 48, ⓦwww .lbl.dk), provides a very well-run advice service (Mon–Fri 11am–3pm) and is an excellent place to pick up news of any gay- or lesbian-oriented events in the city. Their first-floor library and reading room (Mon–Thurs 5–7pm) is packed with gay literature and magazines, but you have to be a member to take anything out. Alternatively, the telephone service (Thurs 6–8pm; ☏33 13 19 48) offers information on any aspect of the gay and lesbian scene in Denmark, and also runs a youth hotline (Tues 7–9pm; ☏33 36 00 80). LBL run a very useful gay guide website (ⓦwww.gayguide.dk) and publish a free monthly Danish-language *PAN Bladet* with dozens of handy listings – fairly easy to decipher even if you don't speak Danish – that you can pick up at all major gay hangouts. Also readily available is the monthly *Out and About* – mostly in Danish – published by Copenhagen Gay Life (ⓦwww.copenhagen-gay-life.dk), a network of gay and gay-friendly businesses and organizations that also produces a very useful *Gay Map of Copenhagen*.

The city's hugely popular annual gay-pride march – **Copenhagen Pride** – takes place in August. After parading through the street, the event ends with an all-night party. For further details, visit ⓦwww.copenhagenpride.dk.

Accommodation

Apart from the places listed opposite, you can also find rooms (from 350kr) in gay or gay-friendly private accommodation by contacting Enjoy Bed & Breakfast (☏70 22 02 25, ⓦwww.ebab.dk).

Carsten's Guest House **Bygge 28, 5th floor (ring the bell marked "Carsten Appel"), Indre By** ☎ 33 14 91 07, ⓦ www.carstensguesthouse.dk. **Bus #5A or #66; ten minutes' walk from Central Station or Rådhuspladsen.** This guesthouse has a very friendly and international atmosphere, though the rooms are a bit small and the walls thin. There's a great roof garden, a comfortable and attractive lounge, plus a kitchen for guests' use. Dorm beds 165kr. 550kr.

Copenhagen Rainbow Guesthouse **Frederiksberggade 25, Indre By** ☎ 33 14 10 20, ⓦ www.copenhagen-rainbow.dk. **Bus #2A, #5A, #6A, #10, #12, #14, #26, #29, #33, #66–69 or #250S.** *Rainbow* is a gay-only guesthouse in an excellent position on Strøget, just off Rådhuspladsen, with five different rooms, some en suite, and all with TV and tea- and coffee-making facilities. The rate includes a buffet breakfast, and there's free Internet access in reception. 750kr.

Hotel Windsor **Frederiksborggade 30, Indre By** ☎ 33 11 08 30, ⓦ www.hotelwindsor.dk. **Bus #5A; Nørreport station.** On the second and third floor of a residential apartment block, this long-established and unpretentious gay hotel has newly refurbished rooms – some ensuite, some sharing shower and toilets. Continental breakfast buffet included. 625kr.

Restaurants, bars and clubs

Can Can **Mikkel Bryggers Gade 11, Indre By. Rådhuspladsen or bus #6A, #12, #26, #29. Mon–Thurs & Sun 2pm–2am, Fri & Sat 2pm–5am.** Small and friendly bar during the day, alive and bustling at night when the place is mostly frequented by gay men. Cheap booze throughout the day.

Centralhjørnet **Kattesundet 18, Indre By** ⓦ www.centralhjornet.dk. **Rådhuspladsen or bus #6A, #12, #26, #29. Daily noon–2am.** Copenhagen's oldest gay bar frequented by predominantly older gay men: welcoming, unpretentious and very cheap, with a lively atmosphere and famous jukebox featuring a vast selection of kitsch pop. Live gigs most Thursday nights with fantastic drag queen performances.

Cosy Bar **Studiestræde 24, Indre By** ⓦ www.cosybar.dk. **Bus #5A or 6A. Mon–Thurs & Sun 10pm–6am, Fri & Sat 10pm–8am.** Popular dance and late-night/early-morning cruise venue (mostly gay men but a lot of straight people as well) for the partygoer with stamina. DJ Tues & Thurs–Sat.

Café Intime **Allégade 25, Frederiksberg** ⓦ www.cafeintime.dk. **Bus #14 or #15 or a short walk from Frederiksberg metro. Daily 6pm—2am.** Small, cosy piano bar frequented by a good mix of gay and straight people with a thing about musicals. Monday and Tuesday the floor is open for wannabe performers.

Jailhouse **Studiestræde 12, Indre By** ⓦ www.jailhousecph.dk. **Bus #5A, #14, #16 or #150S. Mon–Thurs & Sun 2pm–2am, Fri & Sat 2pm–5am.** Popular, basement bar designed as a jail with drinking "cells", handcuffs lying around, and waiters dressed up as jail wardens. On the first floor, there's a restaurant (open Thurs–Sat only) serving good-value daily specials.

Masken **Studiestræde 33, Indre By** ⓦ www.maskenbar.dk. **Bus #5A or 6A. Mon–Thurs 4pm–2am, Fri & Sat 4pm–5am, Sun 3pm–2am.** Nearly every segment of the city's gay and lesbian population makes it to this raucous bar at some point during the week, possibly because of the cheap beer. There's supposedly a "girls' night" in the basement section on Thursdays from 8pm, which seldom attracts the crowds, whilst Fridays are for young gays and lesbians and can be very cruisy.

Mens Bar **Teglgårdsstræde 3, Indre By. Bus #5A or #14 or ten minutes' walk from Nørreport station. Daily 3pm–2am.** The city's most macho bar, popular with leather-clad men and those who enjoy a walk on the butch side; you won't find any women or straights here – they're simply not let in. There's a popular Sunday brunch the first Sunday of every month.

Oscars **Rådhuspladsen 77, Indre By** ⓦ www.oscarbarcafe.dk. **Bus #6A, #12, #26 or #29. Daily noon–2am.** A traditional first port of call on a night out, the very popular *Oscars* serves good, classic Danish food as well as every kind of soft and alcoholic drink imaginable. Can get cruisy late in the evening.

PAN Bar & Disco **Knabrostræde 3, Indre By** ⓦ www.pan-cph.dk. **Bus #6A. Fri & Sat**

11pm–5am. Vibrant, loud and raunchy, *PAN* is Copenhagen's only permanent gay nightclub, though it attracts a straight crowd, too. It offers a variety of groovy beats for disco divas; and is a popular karaoke bar. 60kr.

Vela Gay Club **Viktoriagade 2-4, Vesterbro** Ⓦ**www.velagayclub.dk. Bus #6A or #26. Wed & Thurs 8pm–midnight, Fri & Sat 8pm—5am.** Predominantly lesbian venue with Happy Hour from 8–9pm. Busy during weekends when the party continues into the wee hours.

Shopping

S hopping is one of the highlights of a visit to Copenhagen, with an abundance of eclectic and original shops offering a refreshing alternative to the usual selection of chain stores. Quality is very high – as are prices. Exclusive handmade and luxury goods abound, often bearing witness to Denmark's fine traditions of innovative **design** (see *Danish design* colour section), something that can be seen in products as diverse as furniture, clothing, glassware and stereo equipment.

Most of the city's top shops – particularly fashion and design – are in Indre By, traversed by Strøget, the world's longest (and oldest) pedestrianized shopping street. With no real traffic to dodge or excessive distances to cover, shopping here is a real pleasure. For the best selection of **antique shops**, take a stroll down Kompagnistræde (in Indre By) or head out to Nørrebro, where, on Ravnsborggade, you'll find a raft of antique and secondhand shops, as well as several Danish designer clothes shops, making it an area to keep an eye on. When the weather is good, the city's outdoor Saturday **flea markets** are well worth a visit.

Opening hours for most shops are roughly Monday to Thursday 10am to 6pm, Friday 10am to 7pm, Saturday 9am to 4pm (5pm in summer), though be warned that many close around 2pm on Saturday. Hardly any shops are open late or on Sundays, though for food and basic supplies, a few central supermarkets (see p.221) are open later than normal and on Sundays. Failing that, the supermarket in Central Station is open daily 8am–midnight. We've only given opening hours in reviews if they differ greatly from those above. If you're shopping for wine or beer, note that shops aren't allowed to sell alcohol after 8pm.

Fashion

As far as **clothes** go, you can find pretty much whatever you want without leaving Indre By; designer boutiques, one-off independent outlets, secondhand shops, mainstream chains and department stores are all concentrated in this relatively small area, with plenty of cafés and bars to provide much-needed breaks. The main shopping thoroughfares of **Strøget** and **Købmagergade** are lined with international chains such as Benetton, Diesel, H&M, Zara and Esprit, though there's also a good smattering of quality Danish chains, including Noa Noa (see p.217), and cheaper discount outlets. The **Østergade** section of Strøget is the place to head for if your budget runs to the likes of Hermes, Prada, Louis Vuitton and Chanel.

Clothes and shoe sizes

Women's blouses and sweaters

American	6	8	10	12	14	16	18
British	30	32	34	36	38	40	42
Continental	40	42	44	46	48	50	52

Women's shoes

American	5	6	7	8	9	10	11
British	3	4	5	6	7	8	9
Continental	36	37	38	39	40	41	42

Men's suits

American	34	36	38	40	42	44	46	48
British	34	36	38	40	42	44	46	48
Continental	44	46	48	50	52	54	56	58

Men's shirts

American	14	15	15.5	16	16.5	17	17.5	18
British	14	15	15.5	16	16.5	17	17.5	18
Continental	36	38	39	41	42	43	44	45

Men's shoes

American	7	7.5	8	8.5	9.5	10	10.5	11	11.5
British	6	7	7.5	8	9	9.5	10	11	12
Continental	39	40	41	42	43	44	44	45	46

Kronsprinsensgade, off Købmagergade, is home to many of the best and most internationally recognized modern **Danish designer clothes** shops, such as Munthe plus Simonsen, Stig P and Bruuns Bazaar, though the streets stretching further east towards Gothersgade – Gammel Mont, Store Regnegade, Ny Østergade and Grønnegade – are also rich hunting grounds for trendy, up-and-coming labels. If your taste is for more vintage clothes, Larsbjørnsstræde, Studiestræde and Skt Peders Stræde, adjacent to the Latin Quarter, have the broadest selection of cheap **secondhand** and **ethnic clothes** shops. The area around **Nansensgade**, just north of Nørreport station, is also home to a good selection of small designer clothes shops, and branches of Danish designer boutiques have recently opened on Ravnsborggade in Nørrebro.

Designer clothes

Bruuns Bazaar Kronprinsensgade 8–9, Indre By ⓦ www.bruunsbazaar.com. Denmark's first fashion house, Bruuns has established itself as one of Europe's trendiest designer clothes shops, catering for both men and women, though it's as expensive and exclusive as you'd expect.

Casmose Nansensgade 35, Indre By ⓦ www .casmose.dk. Closed Mon. Casmose sells two floors' worth of its own exclusive (and expensive) range of practical but stylish clothes and shoes for women of all sizes. Their clothes have a Japanese slant, some made of *ramie* nettle fibre for a stylish crumpled look.

Dico Ravnsborggade 21, Nørrebro. Housed in one of Ravnsborggade's former antique shops, the Dico label (designed by the son of legendary Stig P, see p.216) is mainly found on trousers and suits, for both sexes. Classic, stylish and pricey.

Filippa K Store Ny Østergade 13, Indre By ⓦ www.filippa-k.com. Swedish designer with a penchant for simple stylish separates in cool, Scandinavian colours.

Hardware Pilestræde 17, Indre By. Trendy men's fashion with hot labels such as Duffer of St George and Marc Jacobs – mostly shirts and trousers.

Heartmade Pilestræde 45, Indre By. Tues–Fri 11am–5.30pm. Featuring sleek and simple clothes by Julie Fagerholdt, every item here is uniquely designed, with everyday garments alongside evening gowns and wedding dresses.

Kønrøg Teglgårdsstræde 4, Indre By. One-off, eye-catching new designs for men and women from this collective of ten young Danish designers.

Langelinie Outlets Langelinie Allé, Østerbro. Daily 11am–6pm. The likes of Diesel, Gucci and Kenzo all have factory outlets here, all sold at upwards of fifty percent discount.

Maxime Ravnsborggade 12, Nørrebro. Look for "L'Art" (that's what it says on the door) for womenswear imported in limited quantities from Paris and found nowhere else in the city. There's also a range of Danish labels and quirky items such as Brazilian flip-flops, extravagantly overpriced, but trendy nonetheless.

Munthe plus Simonsen Grønnegade 10, Indre By ⓦ www.muntheplussimonsen.com. Hot fashion to burn a hole in your pocket and reputedly a favourite with former supermodel Helena Christiansen. The clothes are by Danish designers Naja Munthe and Karen Simonsen, who have established an international reputation with garments that blend Far Eastern influences with Scandinavian simplicity.

Nørgaard på Strøget, Mads Nørgaard and Englebørn Amagertorv, Indre By. A family business with two generations of designers, each catering for a different group. Nørgaard på Strøget – the oldest shop – houses women's and teenage wear in all price brackets. Mads Nørgaard is geared towards the trendy man, whereas Englebørn is an exclusive kidswear shop with equally exclusive prices.

Noa Noa Købmagergade 5, Østergade 16, Larsbjørnsstræde 16, Indre By ⓦ www.noanoa.com. Popular Danish chain with a wide range of womenswear in natural fabrics – lots of cottons and linen separates in pastel and natural shades.

Pede & Stoffer Klosterstræde 15 & 19, Indre By. Casual, trendy gear for men (no. 15) and women (no. 19) featuring a range of up-and-coming designer labels.

Pisces Nansensgade 53, Indre By. Small boutique run by three women who produce their own clothes and jewellery. The light and comfortable clothes use unusual fabrics such as plastic and hemp; the simple jewellery is mostly silver, but also features copper, gold and a variety of semi-precious and precious stones. They also make clothes to order.

Stig P Kronprinsensgade 14, Indre By and Ravnsborggade 18, Nørrebro. The first designer shop to find its way to Kronprinsensgade in the 1970s and still going strong. A broad selection of designer labels as well as Stig P's own leatherwear. The Indre By branch is for women, whereas Ravnsborggade has a large men's section.

Secondhand clothes

KK Vintage Blågårdsgade 31C, Nørrebro. Wed–Fri noon–6pm, Sat 11am–3pm. Carefully selected vintage gear that's a cut above the usual fare sold in charity shops.

København K Studiestræde 32B, Indre By. Opens 11am. Down a small passage off Indre By's Studiestræde, this is the place to head for all the secondhand leather, velvet, suede, corduroy, denim and lace you could want.

The Second Way Studiestræde 15, Indre By. Another great place to hunt out quirky secondhand clothes and accessories.

Yo-Yo Skt Annæ Gade 31, Christianshavn. Wed–Fri 1–5.30pm. You can get some great designer bargains here, including Danish supermodel Helena Christiansen's cast-offs – her mother owns the shop.

Shoes, jewellery and accessories

In addition to a store dedicated to Denmark's internationally renowned jeweller, Georg Jensen, the city also offers many smaller shops selling beautifully crafted, highly individual designs.

Alli C Læderstræde 1, Indre By ⓦ www.alli-c.dk. Women's shoes and handbags – expensive but unusual one-off designs.

Anne Ammitzbøll Skt Annæ Plads 2, Christianshavn. Lovely jewellery shop selling old and new pieces.

Figaros Bryllup Store Regnegade 2, Indre By. Light, unpolished handmade jewellery using a variety of different metals including 22-carat gold, pink gold and platinum.

Georg Jensen Amagertorv 4, Indre By. Flagship store of the renowned silversmiths, selling a sophisticated mix of classics and more modern designs – beautifully worked brooches, solid rings and elegant watches.

Ilse Jacobsen Kronprinsensgade 11, Indre By. From glam stilettos to her trademark functional but stylish and colourful boots – all are designed by Jacobsen herself.

Louise Grønlykke Store Standstræde 19, Frederikstad. Beautiful handmade jewellery, mostly gold, inspired by Japanese and North African ornamental styles. Everything is created by Louise Grønlykke herself, a fully trained goldsmith.

Museums Kopi Smykker Grønnegade 6, Indre By. If you've been admiring the amazing Viking jewellery on display at the Nationalmuseet, this excellent, if pricey, shop produces outstanding handmade copies of these and other jewellery finds from the Bronze Age onwards.

Notabene Kronprinsensgade 10, Indre By. Great (mostly) Italian women's shoes at just-about-affordable prices.

Sanita Langelinie Promenaden Langelinie Allé 28, Østerbro ⓦ www.sanita.dk. Danish clogs of many colours and patterns from basic black to furry and pink plastic.

Design and interiors

Good **design**, be it lighting, furniture, candlesticks or corkscrews, is important to the Danes and, in line with the philosophy of design for the masses espoused by its founding fathers, not seen as the preserve of the rich; even relatively modest homes will have the odd Poul Henningsen light or Arne Jacobsen chair. Furthermore, in a country where going out to eat is an expensive treat, there's greater focus on entertaining at home, with the important art of table-setting crucial to the creation of a *hygge* ("cosy") atmosphere so integral to Danish social gatherings. This means you'll find a range of shops selling imaginative and stylish glassware, crockery, candlesticks, table linen and table decorations. The **Royal Copenhagen** shops (ⓦ www.royalcopenhagen.com) on Amagertorv showcase classic Danish design; there's also a cluster of smaller, cutting-edge design shops in the streets heading west off Østergade and, for admirers of Scandinavian furniture and lighting design, several specialist, high-end vintage and modern shops along the rather exclusive Bredgade in Frederikstad. However, for an all-under-one-roof style taster, you can't do better than the outstanding **Illum** (see opposite).

Bald & Bang aps Rømersgade 7, Indre By ⓦ www.bald-bang.com. Even if your suitcase space is limited, you can still take home a piece of Danish designer lighting from this place. Holger Strøm's self-assembly lampshades are formed of identical, interlocking quadrilaterals that can be made up into a range of shapes and sizes – a sort of Lego of the light world.

Bang & Olufsen Kongens Nytorv 26, Indre By ⓦ www.bang-olufsen.com. Check out the very latest in hi-fi equipment in the city's funky flagship store.

Bodum Home Store Østergade 10, Indre By ⓦ www.bodum.dk. Four floors of wares from the makers of the cafetiere, par excellence.

Casa Shop Store Regnegade 2, Indre By ⓦ www.casashop.dk. Classic and modern Danish and international design from furniture to watches. Arne Jacobsen icons are well represented, holding their own against the latest in spindly chairs, stylish sofas and funky lighting.

Dansk Design Center HC Andersens Boulevard, Indre By. A great place to acquire some chic but affordable Danish designs of everyday objects, including bags, T-shirts and pens. There's also a good selection of books and postcards.

Designer Zoo Vesterbrogade 137, Vesterbro. At the western end of Vesterbrogade, this large, bright gallery sells the glassware, ceramics and clothes made by the four young artists who have workshops out the back. They're happy to come and talk to you about their designs – all contemporary and individual.

Georg Jensen Amagertorv 4, Indre By. Famous the world over, Georg Jensen silversmiths, which features works by many craftsmen other than the great man himself, has been turning out simple yet stylish silverware – from jewellery and cutlery to candlesticks and tableware – for over a hundred years.

Georg Jensen Damask Ny Østergade 19, Indre By. The Danes make an art out of table dressing and this is about as good as it gets – classy tablecloths, napkins and the like to take home and impress your guests.

Holmegaard Amagertorv 8, Indre By. Stunning and exquisitely crafted glassware – wine glasses, vases, bowls and decanters – from

SHOPPING | Design and interiors

the Holmegaard glassworks, founded in 1825. There's a great blend of classic and modern designs, and a small Italian glass section.

House of Design Bredgade 21, Frederikstad Ⓦ www.houseofdesign.dk. This fabulous shop sells vintage twentieth-century Danish-designed furniture in tip-top condition – should you be smitten by a piece, they can arrange to ship it home for you (at extra cost, of course).

Illums Bolighus Amagertorv 10, Indre By. Four cool, elegant – and very Scandinavian – floors overflowing with an eye-catching assortment of Danish and international design, from fabulous kitchenware and glassware to slimline Poul Henningsen lamps and Arne Jacobsen furniture classics, though such quality and refinement doesn't come cheap.

Klassik Bredgade 3, Frederikstad Ⓦ www.klassik.dk. Original Scandinavian modern vintage furniture, lighting, ceramics, art and sculpture – ogle an original Poul Henningsen lamp, and furniture by such luminaries as Hans J. Wegner, Kaare Klint and Arne Jacobsen. With these prices that's about as far as most people get, though.

Kvindesmedien Christiania, Christianshavn Ⓦ www.kvindesmedien.dk. One of Christiania's many cottage industries: here you can watch the owners (all women) creating a variety of handmade and moderately priced steel and iron objects such as mirrors, candlesticks, tables and sculptures to their own unique designs. They also make pieces to order.

Paustian Kalkbrænderløbskaj 2, Østerbro Ⓦ www.paustian.dk. Stylish furniture shop designed by Danish architect Jørn Utzon (famous for the Sydney Opera House) beautifully situated on the Østerbro harbourfront. Expensive furniture and smaller must-have bits for your home, by local and internationally renowned designers. Also has a good in-house café.

△ Georg Jensen, Indre By

Royal Copenhagen Porcelain Amagertorv 6, Indre By. Even if you're not excited by the idea of china, it's worth a quick peep at one of Denmark's most famous exports, still being produced to centuries-old designs. Each piece is handmade and hand-painted, with the painter's signature as verification on the bottom – hence the extortionate prices. There's an equally refined café on the top floor, too (see p.180). Note that you can get it all considerably cheaper at the factory outlet in Frederiksberg (see p.108).

Something Special Løvstræde 10, Indre By. On a small side street by the Rundetårn, this sparkling den of old and new glassware, cocktail shakers, crystal decanters, lighting, jewellery and furniture (designed by the friendly owner) is a great place to find that special set of snaps glasses.

Bookshops

Central Copenhagen is well supplied with **book shops**, and many, especially the larger ones, have an excellent stock of English-language titles. Most of the big ones are found along Strøget and Købmagergade, though the Latin Quarter, particularly **Fiolstræde**, is a rich hunting ground for secondhand gems.

Arnold Busck Købmagergade 49, Indre By Ⓦ www.arnoldbusck.dk. Huge, central chain bookstore on three floors selling new titles and with a good English-language fiction section.

Arnold Busck Antikvariat **Fiolstræde 24, Indre By.** Cramped and slightly stuffy antiquarian and secondhand store with a sprinkling of English-language titles on everything from botany to clocks. If you feel like splashing out, there's a good selection of first editions of twentieth-century fiction classics.

The Booktrader Skindergade 23, Indre By. Situated on a quiet side street off Købmagergade, this rambling secondhand bookstore is filled with mostly Danish titles but has a good English-language fiction section (particularly crime) towards the back.

GAD Vimmelskaft 32, Indre By ⓦ www.GAD.dk. In a handy central location halfway down Strøget, this Danish chain bookstore has a wealth of new titles and a decent English-language fiction section. There are other branches at Central Station, Fiolstraede 31–33 and Falkoner Alle 21.

Nordisk Korthandel Studiestræde 26–30, Indre By ⓦ www.scanmaps.dk. Great guidebook and map store with friendly staff and an extensive range of travel guides to destinations worldwide, as well as a full range of Denmark maps, for walking, cycling and driving.

Politikens Boghandel Rådhuspladsen 37, Indre By. Large, mainstream bookstore right on the town-hall square, with possibly the best range of English-language fiction and non fiction in the city.

Vangsgaards Fiolstræde 34–36, Indre By ⓦ www.vangsgaards.dk. Three light and spacious floors of antiquarian and secondhand fiction and non fiction with English-language titles scattered throughout. It also sells old prints.

Department stores and shopping centres

Copenhagen is rather short on department stores, and almost devoid of multi-store shopping centres; the exception being the Fisketorvet shopping centre.

Fields Ørestaden, Amager ⓦ www.fields.dk. Gigantic shopping centre – the biggest in Scandinavia – housing, apart from hundreds of international and national chain stores, Denmark's largest cinema with 22 screens.

Illums Bolighus Amagertorv 10, Indre By. The city's most exclusive department store, with top-of-the-range consumer desirables – everything from men's underwear to quirky bottle openers – at equally top-of-the-range prices, also a delightful café on the top floor and a coffee shop, bakery, newsagent and hugely overpriced supermarket in the basement.

Magasin du Nord Kongens Nytorv 13, Indre By. Dating back to 1871, the redoubtable Magasin du Nord on fashionable Kongens Nytorv is the oldest department store in the city, running Illums Bolighus (see above) a close second in both exclusivity and price.

Fisketorvet Kalvebod Brygge 57, Vesterbro. With all you could really want in Indre By, there's no special reason to visit Fisketorvet unless you want it all under one roof. There's a cinema complex here, too (see p.210).

Music

Copenhagen hasn't got the range of music shops of say London or New York, but if you're after that special bit of vinyl or the latest in jazz, here are a few pointers – all centrally located.

Accord Vestergade 7, Indre By ⓦ www.accord.dk. All secondhand stuff, but with the whole first floor devoted to vinyl and lots of cheap CDs downstairs, it's great hunting ground for music aficionados.

Guf Vestergade 17, Indre By ⓦ www.gufmusik.dk. Mainstream pop and jazz are the specialities, with lots of discount CDs. There's another branch at Nørrebrogade 51.

Jazzcup Gothersgade 107, Indre By. New jazz CD store with a massive selection of both national and international names, as well as an in-house bar and frequent live-jazz gigs (see p.202).

Jazzkælderen Skindergade 19, Indre By ⓦ www.jazzmusic.dk. Speciality jazz store with a great selection of Danish and international jazz on CD, plus sheet music, videos and flyers for forthcoming gigs. The mellow café plays a selection of the goods on offer.

Soundstation Gammel Kongevej 94, Frederiksberg ⓦ www.soundstation.dk. Large collection of secondhand CDs, vinyl and DVDs – all genres covered from pop to rockabilly, punk to jazz. Also has some rare collectibles, memorabilia and posters.

Food and drink

Copenhagen has no shortage of delis and excellent bakeries where you can get the vital ingredients for a picnic or pick up something special to take home – jars of pickled and marinated herrings, cheeses, remoulade, rye bread and snaps or the bitter aperitif Gammel Dansk make good consumable souvenirs. Away from Indre By, the small street of Værnedamsvej, northwest of the Bymuseum in Vesterbro and lined with an array of delicatessens, bakeries and colourful fruit and veg shops, is the place to hunt out **gourmet food**. If you're self-catering, you'll find a good selection of centrally located **supermarkets** – opening hours are usually Monday to Friday 8 or 9am to 7pm, Saturday 8 or 9am to 4pm. Netto, the cheapest chain, has central branches at Nørre Voldgade 94, Fiolstræde 9 and Landemærket 11. Or there's the more upmarket Irma, in Rådhusarkaden, Vesterbrogade 1 and at Nørrebrogade 3 (also open Sun); Iso at Vesterbrogade 23; and Superbrugsen at Nørre Voldgade 15 and Halmtorvet 25 in Vesterbro. Copenhagen also has several good **health-food shops**. Three of the best are Naturpoteket, with branches at Teglgårdsstræde 6, Indre By and Torvegade 36, Christianshavn; and Solhatten, Istedgade 85, in Vesterbro.

Bakeries

You'll find good **bakeries** all over town selling delicious bread, sandwiches, cakes and, of course, Danish pastries. The following is a selection of those places worth seeking out.

Det Rene Brød Elmegade 6, Nørrebro. Homemade organic bread with a beautiful, flavour-packed texture that can't be bettered. Two more outlets in Østerbro on Rosenvængets Allé 17 and Ndr Frihavnsgade 54.

Emmerys Nørrebrogade 8, Nørrebro ⓦ www .emmerys.dk. Trendy bakery where the young, rich and health-conscious queue up every weekend for their organic non-dyed, non-yeast bread, though there are plenty of scrumptious cakes on offer, too. Also outlets on Østerbrogade 51, Vesterbro 34 and Store Standstræde 21.

Lagkagehuset Torvegade 45, Christianshavn. Right opposite the metro station and easily identifiable by the ever-present queue, this sumptuous bakery produces amazing bread baked in traditional stone ovens, plus great pastries and cakes. Grab a pastry or sandwich and sit by the canal. There's another branch in the Copenhagen Right Now tourist office on Vesterbrogade (see p.37).

Rhein van Hauen Mikkels Bryggers Gade 2–4 and Østergade 22, Indre By. The king of Danish bakeries, Reinh van Hauen has over 27 years of organic baking to its credit and serves up mouthwatering *rundstykker* (crispy bread rolls) and pastries.

Trianon Hyskenstræde 8, Indre By. Danish pastries that are as delicious and flaky as you'd expect of the purveyors to the queen.

Delis, speciality shops and wines

A.C. Perch's Thehandel Kronprinsensgade 5, Indre By. One of Europe's oldest teashops, founded in 1835, Perch's retains much of its delightful original wooden interior, around which waft the wonderful aromas of teas from across the globe.

Czar Købmagergade 32, Indre By. Follow the pungent odours emanating from Czar to discover Copenhagen's finest selection of cheeses from all over Europe; you're welcome to sample them, just take a ticket and wait to be served. There's also a good charcuterie, and a wine section at the back.

Elm Street Elmegade 8, Nørrebro. Delicious home cooking, including Danish meatballs, and a couple of Thai specialities as well. A few tables but mostly take-out.

Frederiksberg Chocolade Frederiksberg Allé 64, Frederiksberg. Mouthwatering homemade chocolates and truffles created without artificial colourings or preservatives.

Gammel Strand Ø log Vin Naboløs 6. Over two hundred different beers – Danish and international.

Granola **Værnedamsvej 4A, Frederiksberg.**
Chocolates, jams, coffees, teas and
ice cream are the specialities in this cute
little shop/café hidden away in a small
courtyard off Værnedamsvej.
Kana Vin Nansensgade 24, Indre By. A labour
of love for its friendly owners, this shop
offers a fantastic selection of Italian wines,
with most of that country's regions and
grapes represented. If you're lucky, you

may coincide with an impromptu free
wine-tasting session.
Sømods Bolcher Nørregade 24 & 36, Indre By.
Using century-old recipes – no chemical
additives – this shop makes a range of
tasty boiled sweets; you can also watch
the elaborate sweet-making process during which millimetre-thin strands of multi-
coloured mixture are coiled together to
make the rainbow-coloured candy.

Markets

You'll find plenty of opportunity to hunt for a piece of bargain Royal Copenhagen porcelain or Holmegaard glass at one of the city's several summer **flea
markets**, most of them centrally located and with nearby cafés. If you're here
at Christmas, especially with kids, don't miss the chance to check out one of
the Christmas markets.

**Christiania Christmas market Christiania,
Christianshavn. Second Mon in Dec until Dec
20: Mon–Fri 2–8pm, Sat & Sun noon–8pm.**
Held at Christiania's Grå Hal, this is where
Copenhagen's more alternative shoppers fill
up their Christmas stockings. You can find
some great stuff here, including many items
created in the Free City's workshops – cast-
iron candlesticks, colourful batik clothes and
much more.
**Det Blå Pakhus Holmbladsgade 113, Amager.
Sat & Sun 10am–5pm.** A year-round weekend fixture, Copenhagen's largest indoor
flea market boasts 4500 square metres of
uninhibited clutter, featuring objects of every
conceivable size, shape, form and value.
Entrance 15kr.
**Frederiksberg Rådhus Gammel Kongevej, Fre-
deriksberg. April–Oct Sat 8am–2pm.** Popular
trading place for locals of all ages, and,
thanks to this prosperous neighbourhood's
wealthier residents, you might turn up a few
better-than-usual wares.
**Gammel Strand flea market Gammel Strand,
Indre By. May–Sept Fri & Sat 8am–5pm.** The
most central flea market, situated by the
canal on Gammel Strand and selling the
usual range of old china, bric-a-brac, paintings and glassware.

**Israels Plads Israels Plads, Indre By. May–Oct
Sat 9am–3pm.** On the children's playground
behind the fruit and veg market just off Frederiksborggade, this Saturday flea market is
rumoured to be the place where Copenhagen's high-street shops get rid of stuff they
can't sell, and is a good spot to hunt out
unused clothes and jewellery.
**Kongens Nytorv Kongens Nytorv. May–Oct
Sat.** Seek out a bargain in this central flea
market then head across to Nyhavn for a
herring lunch.
**Nørrebro market Along the wall of Assistens
Kirkegård, Nørrebro. May–Sept Sat 7am–2pm.**
This is the city flea market where, if you
search patiently, you may unearth some real
bargains.
**Økologiske Torvegade Blågårds Plads, Nørrebro.
May–Sept Sat 11am–4pm.** Organic market
in the heart of trendy Nørrebro, offering a
wealth of vegetables, meat, bread, milk,
fish and some non-food products in a jovial
neighbourhood atmosphere.
**Tivoli Christmas market Tivoli Gardens. Central
Station. Mid-Nov to Dec 23 Sat.** During the
Christmas opening season, Tivoli's pathways are lined with over sixty stalls selling
Christmas decorations, gifts, Danish handi-
crafts, festive delicacies and warming gløgg.

Speciality shops

The following is a list of shops that don't fit into any of the categories above.

**Christiania Cykler Christiania, Christianshavn.
Mon–Fri 10am–5pm.** Next door to the

Månefiskeren music café and bar, the Christiania bicycle workshop is the home of the

SHOPPING | Markets • Speciality shops

well-known (at least to bicycle enthusiasts) Pedersen bike – an age-old design created to make cycling on cobbled streets more comfortable – which is produced and sold here.

Games Jorcks Passage, Indre By. All kinds of traditional board games and toys, ranging from functional pocket chess sets to suave Italian leather backgammon boards.

Sögreni of Copenhagen Skt Peders Stræde 30, Indre By. Beautiful, handmade bicycles, including ones made to your own specifications.

Tranhuset Strandgade 100, Christianshavn ⓦ www.tranhuset.dk. Adjacent to the Nordatlantens Brygge (see p.68), this unique shop is packed with traditional arts, crafts, clothes and food from Greenland, Iceland, the Faroe Islands and Denmark. All the seal-fur coats, sealskin bags, bone and tooth figurines, and woolly mittens you can handle, plus a freezer stocked with the likes of ox and reindeer, depending on what's in season.

16

SHOPPING | Speciality shops

Sport and outdoor activities

n terms of health and fitness, the Danes are a contradictory lot: the country has one of Europe's highest rates of smoking- and drinking-related deaths, yet also, thanks to massive government funding, boasts some of the best public sports facilities in the world. Far and away the country's most popular sport is **football**, an enthusiasm that has been nourished by some excellent performances from the national team during the past two decades. **Golf**, **badminton**, **squash** and **swimming** are also well catered for (**tennis** less so), while a glance at TV sports or sports pages of newspapers will show you that **handball** – particularly women's handball – and **ice hockey** (winter only) are popular spectator sports. If you're keen to catch a game of the former, contact Dansk Håndbold Forbund (☏43 26 24 00, ⓦwww.dhf.dk). Copenhagen's proximity to the sea means there are also plenty of opportunities for **water-based activities** such as windsurfing, kayaking and fishing, while, if you're here in summer, you shouldn't pass up the chance to swim in one of the open-air **harbour pools**. Back on land, the city's many parks and jogging paths offer the chance for **running**. All the venues listed below are within easy reach of the city centre.

DGI-byen (ⓦwww.dgi-byen.dk), the city's ultra-modern showpiece **sports centre** is right in the centre, behind Central Station, at Tietgensgade 65. There are usually a few people getting to grips with the climbing wall at the entrance, while inside you'll find a state-of-the-art swimming complex (see p.228), bowling alley and spa (though no gym), as well as a decent café and restaurant.

Fitness centres

Scandinavia's leading health-club chain, **SATS** (ⓦwww.sats.com), has several branches in the city – a day's membership costs 150kr and entitles you to use all the facilities. The most central branch is at Vesterbrogade 2E, fifth floor (☏33 32 10 02), in the Scala centre, just opposite Tivoli. Other branches include Vesterbrogade 97 (☏33 25 13 10), Gothersgade 8F (☏33 93 33 95) and Bragesgade 8, in Nørrebro (☏35 81 27 81).

Football

The 2006 World Cup aside, when they failed to qualify for the finals, the Danish national team has enjoyed a good degree of success over the last twenty years – European Championship winners in 1992 and previous qualifiers for the World Cups of 1998 and 2002 – and they're now fourteenth in the FIFA world rankings. This, together with the number of Danish players, including Peter Schmeichel, the Laudrup brothers and Jesper Grønkjær, who have played for Europe's largest clubs over the years, **football** has become the country's most popular sport. That said, the domestic game in Denmark is fairly low-key compared to the big European leagues – there were no professional clubs in the country until as recently as 1985 – and though there's plenty of football played in the Copenhagen area, don't expect big crowds or high-quality games unless you're going to a match involving the national side or the local derby between the city's two biggest teams, Brøndby and FC København (usually known as FCK), currently both in the professional **Superliga**. Matches are usually played on Sundays at 3pm, and the season lasts roughly from late July to early June, with a winter break from December to mid-March. **Tickets** for Brøndby, FCK and international games are available through Billetnet (see p.205) or at the respective stadiums. Danish football fans are noted for their relaxed and good-natured behaviour (see box below), and the laid-back atmosphere is enhanced by the availability of beer inside the stadium, as well as good hot dogs.

Founded in 1992, **FCK** (ⓦwww.fck.dk) is the country's richest club, thanks in part to the fact that they own their home ground (also the venue for international games), the enormous Parken stadium, which also rakes in cash from occasional rock concerts (see p.115 for more on Parken). FCK are now firmly established in the top flight of the Superliga, winning the league four times in the last six years. Games are well attended, with an average gate of about 15,000–20,000, though this still only half fills the 40,000-capacity stadium. If FCK are playing Brøndby during your visit, it's well worth going along to see the two rivals slug it out against a backdrop of noisy support. Tickets cost around 120kr; turn up on the day or buy them from post offices. If you want a more intimate atmosphere, try next door at Østerbro Stadium, where **B93** – a team in Denmark's semi-professional second division – play; tickets (90kr) are available on the gate.

FCK's main rivals, Brøndby (ⓦwww.brondby-if.dk), currently coached by Michael Laudrup, are from the working-class suburbs to the south of the city. Founded in 1964, they became the country's first professional football club

Roligans

During the 1986 World Cup in Mexico – the first the Danes had ever qualified for – the Danish football team's exemplary performances on the field were matched by the country's football fans off it. These supporters of the national team became known as the **Roligans** – a play on the words *rolig* ("relaxed") and "hooligan" – and their good humour, colourful hats and face paintings compared strikingly to the boorish behaviour of many rival fans. The Roligans' finest hour came during Denmark's victory at the 1992 European Championship, leading to the biggest street party ever seen in the country, and they still turn up in reasonable numbers to all Denmark's home games in Parken stadium, though you might find their antics a bit annoying if you've come to watch the football, rather than to Mexican wave. Check out their website at ⓦwww.roligan.dk, where you can purchase Viking hats decked out in the red and white of the national team.

when they turned pro in 1985. Brøndby have won the league several times since they turned pro, and have enjoyed successful campaigns in European competitions. Brøndby's smaller stadium has atmosphere, and even though the crowds have dwindled, numbers still rival FCK – a team Brøndby fans consider overpaid prima donnas with a middle-class following. Tickets cost from 100kr; take the S-Tog to Glostrup and then bus #131.

Golf

The gentle, rolling countryside surrounding the capital is perfect for golf, and the Copenhagen region is home to over thirty courses, with most clubs renting out equipment. The city boasts a wonderful eighteen-hole course at the **Copenhagen Golf Club**, 2 Dyrehaven, Lyngby (℡39 63 04 83, ⓦwww.kgkgolf.dk; Mon & Thurs 8am–2.45pm, Fri 11am until 30min before sunset, Sat & Sun 1pm until 30min before sunset; green fees 350kr Mon–Fri, 450kr at weekends, club hire 200kr per day; S-Tog or local train to Klampenborg station, then bus #388), set in the middle of a deer sanctuary, beautiful woodlands and meadows. It's the oldest club in Scandinavia, and has a friendly atmosphere, along with a restaurant and bar. **Copenhagen Pay & Play**, Skebjergvej 46, 2765 Smørum (℡44 97 01 11, ⓦwww.sgcgolf.dk; daily 9am–10pm), 2.5km from Ballerup, is open year round to everyone – green fees range from 60kr to 375kr depending on number of holes played (6-hole pitch-and-putt, 9-hole or 18-hole course) and your level. Among the facilities are a large, two-storey driving range and putting green.

During the colder winter months, you might prefer **Copenhagen Indoor Golf Centre**, the world's largest such centre, at Refshalevej 177, Christianshavn (℡32 66 11 00, ⓦwww.cigc.dk; mid-Oct to April Mon–Thurs 11am–10pm, Fri 11am–9pm, Sat & Sun 9am–7pm; May to mid-Oct Mon–Fri 4pm–9pm, Sat & Sun noon–5pm; 145kr per hour; bus #66), where there's a three-storey driving range, 27-hole pitch-and-putt course and a state-of-the-art golf simulator.

Ice skating and ice hockey

Come winter, temporary **outdoor skating rinks** pop up all over the city; most are free and offer skate hire for around 20kr. The most central are: Kongens Nytorv (Nov–March); Blågårds Plads, Nørrebro (Nov–Feb); and Frederiksberg Runddel (Dec–Feb), at the main entrance to Frederiksberg Have. There's also a winter-only **indoor** ice-skating rink, Østerbro Skøjtehal (Oct–March Mon, Wed & Fri noon–2.45pm, Tues noon–2.45pm & 9–11pm, Thurs noon–4.30pm, Sun 4–6.30pm, closed Sat), at Per Henrik Lings Allé 6, Østerbro (℡35 42 18 65; 20kr, kids 10kr, skate hire 25kr; bus #1, #6, #14 or #650S), next to Parken stadium (see p.115).

Ice hockey is an enormously popular spectator sport in Denmark, played at a national and international level. The two best teams in the Copenhagen area are Rødovre and Rungsted Cobras. If you're keen to catch a game, contact the Danish Ice Hockey Union (℡43 26 26 26, ⓦwww.ishockey.dk) for details of local matches.

Running

Apart from the obvious choices of the city's many parks, the paths bordering Copenhagen's lakes on the western edge of Indre By are great for scenic, relatively uncrowded **running**. Conveniently traversed by bridges at regular half-mile intervals or so, you can choose circuits of varying distances – a complete circuit of Skt Jørgen Sø, Peblinge Sø and Sortedams Sø is around four miles. Other popular, shorter, jogging paths are the route following the water's edge along the bastions of Christianshavn (see also p.70), southwest from Torvegade to Langebro; and along the Frederikstaden coast from Amaliehaven gardens at Amalienborg, north through Kastellet (or an extra mile if you go round it), and on to the Little Mermaid.

On the third Sunday of May, many of the prettiest areas of Copenhagen are cordoned off to make way for the **Copenhagen Marathon** (Ⓦwww.copenhagenmarathon.dk) during which around six thousand participants of all ages and abilities, from professional athletes to fun-runners, take over the streets, cheered by more than twice that number of spectators. If you're fit enough and want to give it a try, contact Sparta (Ⓦwww.sparta.dk).

Swimming and beaches

Copenhagen has plentiful and well-maintained public **swimming pools**. Some also have saunas, and others form part of sports centres offering a range of different activities; most rent towels and swimming costumes for a small fee. If you're here in summer, you might prefer a more exciting and refreshing dip in the harbour itself – part of the ongoing harbourfront makeover has seen the recent introduction of two open-air **harbour pools**, one at Islands Brygge (June–Aug Mon–Fri 7am–7pm, Sat & Sun 11am–7pm; see p.24), which offers an adult pool, children's pool and diving pool; and one at Havneholmen, next to Fisketorvet shopping centre (June–Aug daily 11am–7pm; bus #1A, #30, #65E or Dybbølsbro S-Tog), which also has the mocked-up sandy "Copencabana" beach, complete with volleyball and other sports activities. Both are free.

In addition, there are numerous great **beaches** within striking distance of the capital. The water is generally pretty cold, although it can get as high as 20°C in summer. The most popular beaches are **Bellevue** (p.119) and **Charlottenlund**

(17)

△ Playing volleyball on Bellevue beach

(p.118) to the north of the city, and **Amager** (p.124), on the island of Amager, to the east.

Two types of **flag systems** operate on Danish beaches. A blue-and-white FEE (Foundation for Environmental Education) flag indicates that a beach is environmentally sound with good water quality and clean toilet facilities available. A green-and-red flag system operates at the busiest beaches with lifeguards on watch. Red means danger and no swimming; green means it's safe to swim. Going topless is commonplace everywhere; if you want to swim in the nude, find a quiet spot or go to a designated nudist bathing spot; there's one at Helgoland bathing pier (p.125), and another at Charlottenlund Søbad (p.119).

Swimming pools

Bellahøj 1–3 Bellahøjvej, Bellahøj ☎ 38 60 16 66. Open third week of May to third week of Aug Mon–Fri 7.30am–5.30pm, Sat & Sun 10am–6pm; 22kr. Bus #5A, #250S or #350S. Only fifteen minutes' bus ride from the city centre, this pleasant outdoor complex has five heated pools, including two for children and one for babies.

DGI-byen Vandkulturhuset Tietgensgade 65, Vesterbro ☎ 33 29 80 00. June–Aug Mon, Tues, Thurs & Fri 6.30am–7pm, Wed 6.30am–9pm, Sat & Sun 9am–5pm; Sept–May Mon–Thurs 6.30am–midnight, Fri 6.30am–7pm, Sat & Sun 9am–5pm. Right in the heart of the city, set in a state-of-the-art complex, this place features a gorgeous elliptical pool, children's pool and diving and climbing area. Entry is 52kr; swimsuit hire costs 25kr with a deposit of 150kr or photo ID. If you really want pampering, visit the spa (kurbadet), where 245kr buys you access to a sauna, steam rooms, plunge pools and the swim centre;

a variety of treatments are also available (at extra cost) by prior appointment (call ☎ 33 29 81 00 to book).

Fælledbadet Fælledparken, 50 Borgmester Jensens Allé, just off Nørre Alle, Østerbro ☎ 35 39 08 04. June–Aug Mon & Wed 7am–5pm, Tues 7am–8pm, Thurs 10am–5pm, Fri–Sun 10am–4pm; 28kr. Buses #184, #185 or #150S. Outdoor paddling pool (summer only) for kids, set in the huge park.

Øbre-Hallen 3 Gunnar Nu Hansens Plads, Østerbro ☎ 35 25 70 60. Mon, Tues, Thurs & Fri 7am–7pm, Wed 10am–7pm, Sat & Sun 8am–2pm; 28kr. Bus #6 or #14. Beautifully renovated swimming baths dating from the 1930s, complete with sauna and steam bath.

Vesterbro Swimming Baths Angelgade 4, Vesterbro ☎ 33 22 05 00. Mon 10am–7pm, Tues–Thurs 7am–7pm, Fri 7am–2.30pm, Sat & Sun 8am–1pm; 28kr. Bus #1A or Enghave S-Tog. Located up near the Carlsberg brewery, this complex includes a 25-metre indoor pool, diving area, sauna and solarium.

Tennis, squash and badminton

Copenhagen's one notable **tennis** tournament, the indoor ATP **Copenhagen Open** takes place at KB Hallen on Peter Bangsvej in Frederiksberg (Peter Bangsvej S-Tog or bus #1) in the last week of February. Unfortunately, few of the really big names in the game turn up but that doesn't stop it being a major event for the Danes, who avidly watch to see whether Danish players – notably Kenneth Carlsen – can make it just a little bit further than they did last year. KB Hallen's beautiful interior provides the perfect surroundings. **Tickets** (150kr upwards depending on the stage of the tournament) are available at any post office, through Billetnet (p.205) or at the ticket office at KB Hallen (☎ 38 71 14 18).

Playing tennis is prohibitively expensive and courts aren't easy to come by – there are no public tennis courts in central Copenhagen and non-members of the various centres and clubs will often find themselves paying a surcharge of around 100kr per person on top of the 100kr-plus court fee. Note, too, that you will always have to book in advance due to high demand. Options include the indoor and outdoor courts at the B93 tennis club at Svanemølleanlægget 10, Østerbro (☎ 39 27 18 90; bus #1A, #14 or Svanemøllen S-Tog; bring rackets

17

and balls), the outdoor courts at the *Hotel Mercur*, 17 Vester Farimagsgade (☎33 12 57 11; Vesterport S-Tog; rackets for hire), or the courts at KB Hallen itself.

Badminton is a far more widely played – and cheaper – sport than tennis in Denmark, and the country has produced a couple of world champions in recent years. Courts are available at Nørrebrohallen, Bragesgade 5, Nørrebro (Ⓦwww .noerrebrohallen.dk; Nørrebro S-Tog or bus #5 or #16), for around 60kr per hour (racket hire 15kr). You can't book over the phone but call ahead (☎35 31 05 50) for availability. **Squash** courts are also available at Nørrebrohallen for 80kr per hour.

Watersports and fishing

With its strong links with the sea, Copenhagen should be an excellent place to indulge in **watersports**, though unfortunately the waters around the city have more than their fair share of crazed speedboaters and kamikaze jet-skiers; coupled with a complete absence of policing, this makes the whole harbour area feel like an accident waiting to happen. If you want to take a trip in a small craft such as a kayak or dinghy, it's best to go with a guide.

Copenhagen Adventure Tours (☎40 50 40 06, Ⓦwww.kajakole.dk) runs excellent and affordable guided **kayak** tours around the canals and harbour area on unsinkable, easy-to-use individual kayaks with intercom equipment. The guides' local knowledge is excellent, and they offer both group and individual tours of one-and-a-half to three hours' duration (165–210kr per person), including drinks stops along the way. They can also organize seal-spotting and fishing trips. The Surf and Snowboard School (June–Oct Mon–Fri 5–7pm; ☎26 73 39 38, Ⓦwww.surfsnowboard.dk) at Amager Beach rents out everything you need for **windsurfing**, a very popular activity in Denmark; prices start at 80kr per hour for equipment hire, and beginners' lessons are also available. If you really want to get out to sea, Baltic, at Kalkbrænderihavnen, Lautrupkaj, Østerbro (☎33 22 00 25 or ☎30 27 53 09; bus #29 or Nordhavn S-Tog), organizes day-long (8am–3pm) **fishing trips** (160–220kr, tackle 50kr) out into the Øresund; you need to book a few days in advance (one week if you want to hire tackle) and remember to bring warm, waterproof clothing, as the weather can be fierce even during summer. Food and drink is available on board at extra cost.

⑰

Festivals and events

Copenhagen has a good offering of **festivals** and **events**, particularly in summer, though you're only likely to have heard of Roskilde and the Copenhagen Jazz Festival, both big events with an international reputation. As well as the listings below, which represent some of the best-attended and more popular events, there's a host of smaller, more specialized happenings, as well as temporary exhibitions – check ⓦwww.woco .dk or ⓦwww.kulturnaut.dk or ask at the tourist office. The comprehensive free monthly publication *Copenhagen This Week* – available from the tourist office and many of the bigger hotels – is also a good source of information. Dates given below are a rough indication; always consult the festival websites for exact dates, as they can vary considerably from year to year.

March/April

Night Film Festival ⓦwww.natfilm.dk. Well-established festival showing a wide range of Danish and international films, including re-runs of old classics and cult films, foreign films in their original language, and previews of films yet to have their cinema premieres.
Copenhagen Fashion & Design Festival ☎33 55 74 81. One week during March or April, well-known and up-and-coming Danish (and some international) fashion designers showcase their work in an extravaganza of exhibitions and shows in Skt Nikolaj Kirke (see p.63) and the city's major shops and department stores.

April

Queen Margrethe II's birthday April 16. Catch a glimpse of Danish royalty as the queen greets the crowds (well, waves from the balcony anyway) at Amalienborg at midday, accompanied by a suitable display of pomp from the Royal Guards.

May

May Day May 1. Trade unions march through

the city to the open spaces of Fælledparken (see p.115), where there's a rock-concert-cum-political-rally. Most Danish political parties are represented, and although the speeches go on forever, it's all kept fun and lively with stalls selling ethnic delicacies, Danish bands performing between speeches and, naturally, enormous quantities of beer.

May–September

International Theatre Sommerscene ⓦwww .kit.dk. Summer-long programme of modern dance, theatre, kids' activities and exhibitions at several venues across, and within striking distance of, the city. Tickets cost 30–165kr and are available from Billetnet (see p.205).

June

Whitsun Carnival (Karneval) ⓦwww.karneval .dk. Whitsun weekend. Copenhagen's answer to a Brazilian carnival, this weekend-long sequin-and-feather extravaganza attracts crowds of around one hundred thousand with its salsa, samba and African rhythms and skimpy, offbeat costumes, which wearers optimistically liken to those found in Rio. The main parade takes place on Saturday with a procession along Strøget, continuing up Øster Alle to Fælledparken (see p.115) with several themed dance and music stages and a Rio-style "Sambadrome" where the samba parades finish up. The market area has lots of stalls selling delicious exotic food, clothing and trinkets.

Sankt Hans Aften (St Hans Night) June 23. The Danes at their patriotic best with an overdose of *hygge* ("cosiness") and bonhomie in towns and villages across the country. An ancient tradition celebrating the longest day of summer, it's a beer-fuelled evening of music, dancing, eating, bonfires and the burning of witch effigies, originally instigated to keep bad forces at bay for the summer. The best places in the city to head for are Fælledparken, the rampart lakes and the Christianshavn fortifications (near the Torvegade bridge to Amager). It usually starts with the communal singing of Danish folksongs (the most famous, honouring Sankt Hans, was written by Carl Nielsen; see p.151), followed by local bands and a few speeches by city dignitaries.

June/July

Roskilde Festival ☎ 46 36 66 13, ⓦ www .roskilde-festival.dk. **Last week of June to first weekend in July.** Held in fields outside the town of Roskilde (see p.141) over four days and nights (with a pre-festival "warm-up" period of another four days), the Glastonbury-style Roskilde Festival is one of Europe's largest rock events, attracting over 75,000 people. The diverse line-up – rock, jazz, indie, hip-hop and more – features a mixture of new and established Danish and international bands and DJs but usually offers at least five big-name acts (recent years have seen Arctic Monkeys, Franz Ferdinand, Placebo, Coldplay and Massive Attack) plus the odd legend like Bob Dylan and Morrissey. You can camp (check the website for details), and there's the usual horde of stalls selling food, clothes, jewellery and other festival paraphernalia, as well as an Internet café, cinema and dance hall. The festival is a massive boost to the local economy and all profits go to community projects.

Tickets go on sale from December 1 (via Billetnet ☎ 70 15 65 65, wwww.billetnet .dk; or check the festival website for ticket venues in your country of origin) and usually sell out around two weeks before the festival. If there are any left, they are sold at the entrances. A ticket for all four days (or eight if you want to attend the warm-up events) will set you back around 1350kr; one-day tickets (for the last Sunday only) cost 550kr. For details of getting to Roskilde, see p.143.

△ Roskilde Festival

Copenhagen Jazz Festival

Whatever time of year you visit you'll usually stumble across some jazz somewhere in the city but for ten days from the first Friday in July, it seems the city thinks of little else, as its stages, large venues, museums, cafés, clubs, squares and canals are taken over by around eight hundred events, from big band to experimental, that make up the **Copenhagen Jazz Festival**, attracting music lovers from all over the world. The festival showcases a handful of jazz legends – Herbie Hancock, Sonny Rollins and Keith Jarrett are regulars – as well as new kids on the block like Jamie Cullum, but for many shows the term "jazz" is used in the loosest sense possible, as international musicians come to perform everything from classic bebop to experimental electronica and spoken-word poetry, with popular acts such as Gotan Project and Salif Keita complementing dozens of cutting-edge Scandinavian groups. The largest **venues** are the Det Kergelige Teater, Tivoli and the Copenhagen Jazzhouse, but the most exciting performances are often the impromptu ones that get going well after midnight: La Fontaine, at Kompagnistræde 11, and the Børneteatret, in Christiania, are the best bets for late-night, ad-hoc jam sessions – intimate, foot-stomping affairs that seat you just inches away from some of Denmark's hottest musical talents. The festival **programme** is usually published in May and is posted on the website (see below) in English. Tickets usually range anywhere in price from 50kr for lesser-known ensembles to 300kr for larger venues (the latter of these usually sell out a few days before the concert), though many concerts are free. Tickets for all but the largest shows can be purchased at the door. For more information and online ticket sales, visit ⓦ www.jazzfestival.dk.

August

Kulturhavn ⓦ www.kulturhavn.dk. First weekend in August. Making the most of the revamped harbourfront, Kulturhavn (Cultural Harbour) is a four-day annual festival of dance, music, theatre and sports, offering a chance to try activities as diverse as sailing, trampolining, kayak polo or flamenco dancing. All activities are free.

Copenhagen Pride ⓦ www.copenhagenpride.dk. **Third week in August.** The city's gay, lesbian, bisexual and transsexual inhabitants strut their colourful stuff in a flamboyant parade of outlandish frocks, spandex, Lycra and whatever else takes their fancy. The parade route follows Nørrebrogade across the bridge to Nørreport and on to Rådhuspladsen.

Copenhagen Cooking ⓦ www.copenhagen cooking.com. **Last week of August.** New but very successful gastronomic festival aimed at highlighting Nordic and Danish cuisine with the city's squares and streets given over to the likes of crayfish parties, food tents, ice-cream tastings, and novelty events such as a waiter's relay-race on Nyhavn and posh chefs in the city's best restaurants cooking up feasts for half the price. Check the website for this year's events and locations.

Copenhagen International Ballet Festival ⓦ www.copenhageninternationalballet.com. Founded by dancer Alexander Kølpin, the festival runs for two weeks at the Arne Jacobsen-designed Bellevue theatre in Klampenborg (see p.119), just north of the city, as well as at a few other venues. Featuring choreographers and dancers from companies around the world, the modern programme provides ballet lovers with an alternative to the city's mostly traditional performances. Tickets are available from ⓦ www.billetnet.dk.

August–September

Images of the World ⓦ www.images.org. **Mid-August to mid-September.** A triennial festival (next event will be in 2009) put on by the Danish Centre for Culture and Development, which aims to promote understanding and knowledge of non-Western cultures with a programme of exhibitions, film nights, open-air markets, concerts and lectures.

August–October

Copenhagen International Film Festival (CIFF) ⓦ www.copenhagenfilmfestival.com. One for film buffs, this week-long festival (usually some time in August, September or October), begun in 2003, has grand aims to be in the same league as Berlin, Cannes and Venice and is already attracting big-name directors, producers and actors. The international jury dishes out Golden Swan awards for Best European Feature Film, and there's a programme of lectures, workshops and special screenings at Cinemateket (see p.210) and other major cinemas in the city.

September

Golden Days in Copenhagen ☎ 35 42 14 32, Ⓦ www.goldendays.dk. Biennial festival (next one is in 2008) that showcases Copenhagen's cultural history with a three-week programme of concerts, exhibitions, theatre and lectures focusing on a period of Danish history – usually the Danish Golden Age (see p.247).

October

Copenhagen Gay & Lesbian Film Festival (CGLFF) Ⓦ www.cglff.dk. CGLFF has been going for around twenty years, bringing short films, feature films and documentaries to Copenhagen's cinemas, and attracting straight and gay devotees.

Culture Night ☎ 33 25 74 00, Ⓦ www .kulturnatten.dk. Mid-October. Over three hundred venues, including the city's museums, galleries, libraries, churches and cultural institutions, throw open their doors for an evening (6pm–midnight) of culture, giving the public a chance to see behind the scenes and hosting a wide range of musical, artistic and literary events. Ticket prices vary; a total-access ticket covering all events (and including free public transport within the city) costs around 70kr and is available from mid-September from S-Tog stations, the tourist office and participating

venues. See the website for a full programme and latest prices.

Halloween at Tivoli Ⓦ www.tivoli.dk. One for the kids, Tivoli is transformed during autumn half term (usually third week of October but check website for exact timing) into a ghoulish wonderland with all manner of scary decorations and festive treats on offer. (See p.93 for Tivoli ticket prices.)

October/November

Copenhagen Autumn Jazz Ⓦ www.festival.jazz .dk. This week-long jazz fest – offspring of the main jazz festival in July (see p.232) – is held in thirty or so of the city's top music venues, offering everything from mainstream bebop to traditional swing.

November/December

Christmas A great time to be in the city, as the Danes do Christmas with consummate taste. Tivoli (fourth week of November to December 23) steps up a gear, with markets selling all sorts of seasonal goodies, as well as Christmas-themed performances on its many stages. There are also open-air ice-skating rinks (see p.226) scattered around town to get you in the festive spirit, and a parade (usually the last Saturday in November) through town featuring Santa Claus. Christmas fairs spring up across the city (check with the tourist office for details) and, not to be outdone, the "Free City" of Christiania (see p.71) also puts on a great bash, with an excellent market open to all and a party for the homeless.

New Year's Eve Copenhageners celebrate the New Year with an all-night party throughout the city, kicking off with a massive fireworks fest on Rådhuspladsen at midnight, attended by revellers in their thousands. Bring your own champagne, and keep your eyes open for stray crackers.

Kids' Copenhagen

C openhagen is a child-friendly city, and places without facilities for children are few and far between – even the more exclusive cafés and restaurants now have highchairs and children's menus. The low level of traffic, pedestrianized shopping streets, decent quota of child-centred attractions and scattering of large, rambling parks make the city easy and relaxing to explore with kids, while if your children are into cycling, there are dedicated lanes throughout the capital, and it's generally very safe (see p.30 for a list of bike-hire places). Boat trips around the harbour and canal (see p.27) are also a sure-fire hit. Furthermore, unlike most European capitals, Copenhagen is close to several **beaches**, both in the suburbs to the north of the city (see p.119) and on Amager (see p.124), where a string of sandy stretches and a wonderful nature reserve make the city seem miles away. Finally, two **amusement parks**, Tivoli (see p.92) and the lesser known but just as entertaining, Bakken (see p.119), are fun days out.

Most of Copenhagen's larger **museums** cater for children in some way, so travelling with kids doesn't mean you have to miss out on the city's cultural side. Some, such as the Nationalmuseet (see p.96), have made a special effort to involve children and make sure they have a memorable experience. A number of galleries, such as Louisiana (p.130) and the Statens Museum for Kunst (p.80), also have well-equipped and imaginative children's sections where you can unload your little ones while you go off and do your own exploring.

The city is blessed with some fine **parks** – **Fælledparken** (see p.115) is especially popular with kids, and its wide, open areas are ideal for relaxing and letting them expend all that energy. A scent garden in the southeastern corner of the park is aimed especially at young visitors, giving them the opportunity to smell and touch plants and rocks. **Kongens Have** (see p.79) is also very child-friendly, staging free puppet shows every summer (June–Aug Tues–Sun 2pm & 3pm) on the Kronprinsessegade side of the park; on the other side, by the Hercules Pavilion, there's a novel children's play area complete with dragons for clambering on. Spacious **Frederiksberg Have** (see p.108) and Søndermarken are also two great, open spaces. In summer, football and kite-flying are the two main activities here, or you can rent a rowing boat for the afternoon and experience the park from the old hand-dug canals. During winter, **ice skating** is a favourite pastime for the city's children – there are free temporary outdoor rinks at Kongens Nytorv, Blågårds Plads, and Frederiksberg Runddel at the entrance to Frederiksberg Have (skates can be rented for 20kr/hour). There are also some good hills for sledding at Frederiksberg Have.

Finally, two fun climbs are the internal ramps of **Rundetårn** (see p.60) and the outer stairs spiralling the church tower of **Vor Frelsers Kirke** (see p.70).

For more detailed information on any of the following attractions, including location and transport, see the main account in the relevant guide section of the book.

Attractions and sights

Copenhagen Zoo Roskildevej 32, Frederiksberg Ⓦwww.zoo.dk. March Mon–Fri 9am–4pm, Sat & Sun 9am–5pm; April, May & Sept Mon–Fri 9am–5pm, Sat & Sun 9am–6pm; June–Aug daily 9am–6pm; Oct daily 9am–5pm; Nov–Feb daily 9am–4pm; 100kr, children 3–11 years 60kr. One of the oldest and largest in Europe, with over 3300 animals ranging from elephants to apes to polar bears, the Copenhagen Zoo has an excellent Children's Zoo, where they can touch several of the more domesticated inhabitants, as well as pony rides, adventure trails and a playground if they get fed up with animals. *Café K*, as you'd expect, has plenty of children's options; alternatively, there are hot dog stands and numerous picnic areas.

Changing of the guard at Amalienborg Daily at noon; free. The changing of the guard at Amalienborg is always a big pull for children, as one set of splendidly costumed guards marches off and another arrives, sometimes to the accompaniment of a band. At other times, kids can have fun trying to outstare the mannequin-like guards as they stand to attention outside the palace.

Danmarks Akvarium Kavalergården 1, Charlottenlund Ⓦwww.danmarks-akvarium.dk.

May–Aug 10am–6pm, Feb–April & Sept–Oct 10am–5pm, Nov–Jan 10am–4pm; 85kr, children 3–11 years 45kr. Apart from the aquarium's vast display of colourful and exotic marine animals, there's also a designated children's area (weekends and holidays 10.30am–4pm) with three touch-pools containing hermit crabs, plaice, shrimp and sea anemones. Marine biology students are happy to answer any questions you may have about the animals' habitats and ecology.

DGI-byen Tietgensgade 65, Vesterbro Ⓦwww.dgi-byen.dk. June–Aug Mon, Tues, Thurs & Fri 6.30am–7pm Wed 6.30am–9pm, Sat & Sun 9am–5pm; Sept–May Mon–Thurs 6.30am–midnight, Fri 6.30am–7pm, Sat & Sun 9am–5pm; 52kr, children 2–14 years 32kr; swimsuit hire 25kr, with a deposit of 150kr or photo ID. The city's flashest swimming complex, with pleasantly warm water, geysers, bubble columns, wave machines and diving platforms spread around three unusually shaped pools.

Rosenborg Østervoldgade 4A, Indre By Ⓦwww.rosenborg-slot.dk. June–Aug daily 10am–5pm; May, Sept & Oct daily 10am–4pm; Nov–April Tues–Sun 11am–2pm; 65kr, children 0–17 free. A fabulous Dutch Renaissance

△ Children's Zoo at Copenhagen Zoo

seventeenth-century fairy-tale castle with the Treasury in the basement, where the Queen's precious crown jewels are displayed – a sparkling dream-come-true for many would-be princesses.

Tycho Brahe Planetarium Gammel Kongevej 10, Vesterbro ⓦ www.tycho.dk. Mon–Fri 9.30am–9pm, Sat & Sun 10.30am–9pm. IMAX film: 95kr, children under 13 years 65kr. 3D film: 105kr, children under 13 years 75kr. (Note: children under 3 are not admitted to the films.)

Exhibition only: 25kr, children under 13 years 15kr. Kids will love the push-button displays on the Mysterious World of Astronomy and Space Travel, and the shop full of all things space oriented. The Space Theatre shows thrilling hourly IMAX or 3D films (you'll need to rent headphones with English translations; 15kr) usually about deep-sea exploration, the natural world, history or space travel.

Museums and galleries

Children's Museum at the Nationalmuseet Ny Vestergade 10, Indre By ⓦ www.natmus .dk. Tues–Sun 10am–5pm; free. This place, spread over several large rooms on the ground floor, is aimed specifically at children between 6 and 12, though there's plenty of interest for toddlers upwards. Kids can clamber on the Viking ship; play hide-and-seek and point cannons in the small medieval castle; wander onto the rooftop of a traditional Pakistani house; draw pictures; play with crowns, coins and assorted trinkets; or dress up in a variety of costumes.

Cirkus Museum Avedørelejren, Avedøre ⓦ www .cirkusmuseum.dk. Mon, Tues & Sun 10am–3pm; 25kr, children 15kr. Spanning two floors in the old commandant headquarters of the Avedøre military camp, this small museum is a delight for children passionate about the circus and all things magical. The first of three sections is dedicated to clowns and has a number of their richly decorated costumes and gadgets on display. The second is devoted to the late Truxas, a once famous Danish magician. The theme of the third room is the thrilling life of Chinese trapeze artist Wong Ko Lian, who worked and lived in Denmark during the last century. There's also a playroom where children can dress up in fabulous costumes, and a small stage where they can practise performing.

Experimentarium Tuborg Havnevej 7, Østerbro ⓦ www.experimentarium.dk. Mon & Wed–Fri 9.30am–5pm, Tues 9.30am–9pm, Sat & Sun 11am–5pm; 120kr, children 3–11 years 75kr. This fascinating, hands-on science centre lets children explore the laws of nature by performing their own experiments. There are over three hundred interactive exhibits, using easy-to-follow guidelines – helpful instructors are on hand if you get stuck

– and covering topics such as magnetism, aerodynamics, anatomy, astronomy and environmental science. Regular demonstrations are given throughout the day, and there's a special kids' pavilion for 3 to 6 year olds.

Louisiana Humlebæk ⓦ www.louisiana.dk. Daily 10am–5pm, Wed 10am–10pm; 80kr, children under 18 free. Taking as a starting point different pieces of art from the collections, the Children's Wing of the fantastic modern-art museum is full of artistic materials for kids aged 3 upwards to get creative and get their hands messy. It opens onto the lovely Lake Garden with tiny wooden houses for them to explore.

Frilandsmuseet Kongevejen 100, Lyngby ⓦ www.natmus.dk. Mid-April to Sept Tues–Sun 10am–5pm; free. A wonderful mixture of heritage park, city farm and woodland retreat, and an eldorado for kids, with horse-carriage rides, sheep shearing and wool dyeing, to name just a few of the many activities.

Post and Tele Museum Købmagergade 37, Indre By ⓦ www.ptt-museum.dk. Tues & Thurs–Sat 10am–5pm, Wed 10am–8pm, Sun noon–4pm; 30kr, under-12s free, free on Wed. The children's section of this informative museum has old postal uniforms for kids to dress up in, and telegraph equipment and bits of other antiquated telecommunications equipment for them to play with, including a morse-code transmitter. For older children, the museum's "B@lkony" section is dedicated to computers and the Internet, with lots of fun programmes to fiddle around with.

Statens Museum for Kunst Sølvgade 48–50 ⓦ www.smk.dk. Tues & Thurs–Sun 10am–5pm, Wed 10am–8pm; free. The Children's Art Museum section of the National Gallery spans three floors and has a cinema,

Places to eat with kids

Aside from the cafés and restaurants you'll find in most of the attractions and museums listed above, which all have highchairs and are child-friendly, there are a few places that are particularly welcoming to children or have good novelty value to keep them amused for a while.

Bastionen og Løven (see p.182)

Den Franske Café (see p.190)

Dag H (see p.190)

Fregatten Sct. Georg III (see box on p.186)

Islands Brygges Kulturhus (see p.191)

Krunch at Kastrup Fort (p.192)

Peder Oxe (see p.181).

Peter Lieps Hus (p.192)

Sporvejen (see p.182)

Sult (see p.184)

workshop and special child-oriented art exhibitions featuring real exhibits (though they obviously can't touch them!). Aimed mostly at 6–12 year olds, there are family guided tours of the Children's Art Museum at the weekends with the opportunity to get hands-on in the workshop afterwards. Zoologisk Museum Universitetsparken 15, Østerbro ⓦ www.zoologiskmuseum.dk.

Tues–Sun 11am–5pm; 50kr, children 3–16 years 15kr. One of the city's most popular museums with school kids, featuring traditional displays of stuffed animals in their reconstructed natural habitats – kids will love the immense Greenland whale skeleton that takes up the entire hallway, and the mammoth.

Amusement parks and playgrounds

Bakken ⓦ www.bakken.dk. July to mid-Aug daily noon–midnight; late March to June & mid-Aug to mid-Sept Mon–Fri 2pm–midnight, Sat 1pm–midnight, Sun noon–midnight. Pass for all 35 rides 199kr; free entrance. The world's oldest amusement park, Bakken's attractions include Denmark's longest and highest Big Dipper, assorted merry-go-rounds and many other fun and breathtaking rides, including a ghost train and a waltzer. There's also a free children's play park with see-saws and swings. Bakken is located at the edge of Dyrehaven, which is fun to explore by horse-drawn carriage and also a great picnic site.

City playgrounds The city council produces a map of all of the playgrounds in the greater Copenhagen area; you can get it from the office next to the bus depot in Rådhuspladsen. The most central options include Nikolaj Plads in Indre By, Gammel

Vagt 5 in Frederikstad, Skt Annæ Plads, two in Ørstedsparken, and Christianshavns Voldgade 36 on Christianshavn. For further locations, see ⓦ www.kk.dk/legeplads.
Tivoli ⓦ www.tivoli.dk. See p.92 for opening hours; 75kr, children 3–11 years 35kr; multi-ride ticket 200kr/150kr. An absolute must for families with children, this magical amusement park offers everything a child could ever want: 26 fun rides from tame to stomach churning, candy floss, ice cream and all manner of tasty treats, spectacular fireworks at midnight, pantomimes and plenty of opportunities to win colourful and completely useless plastic gadgets or furry toys. Transformed into a winter wonderland over the Christmas period and now with a new Halloween theme during half term in October. There's also a wonderful saltwater aquarium in the basement of the Concert Hall.

Shops

Bambam Strandvejen 117, Hellerup @www .bambam.dk. Wooden and allergy-friendly kids' furniture and equipment – such as see-through bathtubs on stilts – but on the expensive side.

Build-a-Bear workshop Vesterbrogade 3, at Tivoli main entrance. @www.buildabear.dk. Kids can pick a bear and make it their own, dressing it up to their heart's content.

De Små Øjne Prinsessegade 50, Christianshavn. Closed Sun & Mon. Great but expensive kids' clothing from 0 to 10 years.

Enfant Terrible Strandvejen 189, Hellerup. Quality children's clothing – 0 to 14 years – with a great selection of designer and Danish brand names.

Fætter BR Frederiksberggade 11; Fisketorvet shopping centre (see p.220); Nørrebrogade 34; Vesterbrogade 73; and Østerbrogade 39–41. Denmark's main toy-store chain selling a wide selection of games and toys, both local and international makes.

Kaj & Zitta Fælledvej 18, Nørrebro. Small children's clothing store with some in-house designs as well as a selection of soft toys.

Krea Vestergade 4–6, Indre By @www.krea.dk. A treasure trove of beautifully made wooden toys.

Lego Shoppen Fisketorvet shopping centre (see p.220), Vesterbro. Mon–Fri 10am–8pm, Sat 10am–5pm. The latest offerings from the ever-popular brand, with a play area to test it out in.

Pif Paf Strandboulevarden 108, Østerbro. Huge baby and child store selling goodies such as towels made of organic cotton and beautifully designed wooden beds and playpens, mostly produced by Pif Paf themselves. There's a second Pif Paf store, selling only toys, on Nordre Frihavnsgade.

Sømods Bolscher Nørregade 24 & 36, Indre By. Candy-loving kids will enjoy a visit to this famous sweet shop, where you can watch the skilful process of traditional sweet-making before sampling the scrumptious, rainbow-coloured end products.

Contexts

Contexts

History

S pend much time in Denmark and you'll soon realize that its history is entirely disproportionate to its size. Nowadays a small – and often overlooked – nation, Denmark and the long line of monarchs who have lived in its capital city, Copenhagen, have nonetheless played an important role in key periods of European history, firstly as the home of the Vikings, and later as a medieval superpower. What follows is a necessarily brief outline of major events that have shaped the city and the nation. For a fuller account of the country's history, see the further references in "Books" on p.254.

Beginnings

Although a few tools found in what is now Denmark suggest *Homo sapiens* was present around 200,000 years ago, these cannot be precisely dated and the earliest reliable archeological evidence of **human activity** dates to 80,000 years ago with the remains of a meal eaten near a lake in central Jutland – deer bones prized open for marrow. However, it's likely that settlements of this time were only temporary, as much of the land was still covered by ice. From 14,000 BC, the climate started to warm up, ushering in the end of the Ice Age, and by 11,000 BC the ice had completely melted away from Denmark, leaving vast forests and tundra populated by herds of reindeer. Around this time, tribes from the more southerly parts of Europe arrived during the summer to hunt the reindeer for their meat and antlers, which provided raw material for axes and other tools. The hunters established the first permanent settlements and, as the climate gradually warmed and the reindeer headed north, a **Stone Age village culture** developed. A further significant shift occurred around 4000 BC with the cultivation of land and keeping of livestock, and before long, agricultural communities covered the country. With this came a more organized approach to society and religion – the farmers buried their dead in dolmens or megalithic graves, and sacrifices, in the form of flint tools, axes, amber beads and pots containing food, were made to the gods responsible for farming. Many of these objects have survived, preserved in the peat bogs where they were offered up to the deities.

The earliest metal and bronze finds are from 1800 BC, the result of trade with southern Europe. During the **Bronze Age**, foreign trade flourished, with bronze objects becoming a particularly popular commodity; the richness of some pieces, such as the bronze sun chariot dating to 1400 BC (on display in the Nationalmuseet), provides evidence that even at this early date there was contact between Denmark and the Mediterranean cultures of Crete and Mycenae. From this period also come the famous Danish *lurs*, curved metal horns that were blown to call villagers to meetings – a statue of two *lurs*-blowers stands outside Copenhagen's Rådhus – and the excavated coffin of Egtved girl.

After 500 BC, iron gradually replaced bronze as the main material for tools, helped by a ready supply of the raw material in the form of bog ore. Around this time, too, it seems that conflicts between various communities were common, as villages formed alliances to obtain more territory or plunder others' land. However, it was the threat of the advancing Roman Empire – which launched an offensive into northern Germany in 5 AD – that galvanized these hitherto ad hoc fighting units into something more along the lines of mini-armies, equipped with horsemen, archers, soldiers and more sophisticated weaponry. The need to fight didn't arise, as the Romans were beaten back to the areas around the Rhine before they could reach Jutland, but military organization among the various Jutland communities had already made important strides – developments that were then utilized for fighting each other.

The Viking era

Battles for control over individual areas in Scandinavia saw the emergence of a ruling warrior class, and, around 500 AD, a tribe from southern Sweden calling themselves **Danes**, part of a group of peoples who collectively became known as the **Vikings**, migrated southwards and took control of what was known as **Danmark**. The Vikings were seamen, warriors and peasants who quickly grew notorious for their opportunistic raids on surrounding countries – at their peak, they travelled as far as North America and the Caspian Sea. In Denmark itself, the majority of people were farmers: the less wealthy paid taxes to the king, and those who owned large tracts of land provided the monarch with military forces. In time, a **noble class** emerged, expecting and receiving privileges from the king in return for their support, while law-making became the responsibility of the *ting*, a type of council consisting of district noblemen. Above the district *ting* there was a provincial *ting*, charged with the election of the king. The successful candidate could be any member of the royal family, which led to a high level of feuding and bloodshed.

The **first Danish state** – established by the Viking Godfred, King of Jutland – emerged some time around 800 AD, encompassing most of the Jutland peninsula. A century later, the Norwegian chieftain Hardegon conquered the peninsula and began to expand eastwards over the rest of Denmark, establishing the foundations of the modern Danish nation, the oldest in Europe – the present Danish monarchy can be traced back to his son, Gorm the Old. Shortly afterwards, **Christianity** became the national religion. Benedictine monks had started arriving in Denmark in 826, but it wasn't until the baptism in 961 of Gorm the Old's son, **Harald** ("**Bluetooth**"), that Christianity became Denmark's state religion – even if his reasons for doing so (to make peace with the Franks to the south) were not entirely spiritual. Harald gave permission to a Frankish monk, **Ansgar**, to build the **first Danish church**, and Ansgar went on to take control of missionary activity throughout Scandinavia. Harald was succeeded by his pagan son **Sweyn I** ("**Forkbeard**"), who tolerated Christianity, despite suspecting the missionaries of bringing a German influence to bear in Danish affairs. From 990, Sweyn relaunched attacks on England (Viking attacks on the English had been intermittent since the late eighth century) for what seems to be primarily economic motives; a severe reduction in the availability of silver from Arabia saw a shift in focus to England as a potential source of income through exaction of tribute. By the time of Sweyn's death in 1014, Ethelred's England was all but under Danish rule, though continued resistance and struggle meant that it took a further two years for Sweyn's son Knud (Canute) to be accepted as English king, marrying Ethelred's widow into the bargain. By 1033, the Danes controlled most of southern Sweden, the whole of England and Normandy, and dominated trade in the Baltic. This was the zenith of Viking power, and it's from this period that we get the first historical record of the small fishing village of **Havn** (literally "Haven" or "Harbour", and later to become København or

Copenhagen), when it was mentioned in 1043, after the Norwegian King Magnus sought refuge there following his defeat in a sea battle in the Øresund.

The Middle Ages

A century of violent **internal struggles**, not only between different would-be rulers but also among the Church, nobility and monarchy, weakened Viking power in Denmark, and it wasn't until the accession of Valdemar the Great in 1157 that the country was once again united and free of factional fighting. Valdemar strengthened the crown by ending the elective function of the *ting*, and shifting the power of choosing the monarch to the Church. Technically, the *ting* still influenced the choice of king, but in practice hereditary succession became the rule.

One of Valdemar's key supporters, his foster brother **Bishop Absalon**, became Archbishop of Denmark and was given the village of Havn, strategically located on the **Øresund** – the narrow sea channel that divides Denmark from Sweden, and the main entrance to the Baltic – which was soon to become one of the main trading routes of medieval Europe.

Within a decade, Absalon had built a castle on the small island (today's Slotsholmen) opposite Havn, from where he countered the Wendish pirates, based in eastern Germany, who had previously raided the coast with impunity. Besides being a zealous churchman, Absalon possessed a sharp military mind and came to dominate Valdemar the Great and his successor, Knud IV. During this period, Denmark saw some of its best years, expanding to the south and east, taking advantage of internal strife within Germany. Havn itself developed rapidly following the castle's construction. In 1209, Vor Frue Kirke – later to become the city's cathedral – was consecrated by Bishop Absalon's successor (Absalon had died in 1201), and in 1238, the city's first monastery was established on Gråbrødretorv; by 1254 the town had acquired its modern name, **København** (Merchants' Harbour), a fortified market town with full municipal rights.

Thirty years later, following a German invasion of Jutland, the Danish nobles seized the opportunity to curb the powers of the monarch, forcing Erik V (in 1282) to sign a charter under which he agreed to rule together with the nobles of the **Council of the Danish Realm**, an institution that was to survive as a major influence in Danish government until 1660. Almost a century of civil war followed, as the nobles fought against the king and one another, during which Copenhagen was passed back and forth between the warring factions. In 1369, the city fell to Hanseatic forces, and stonemasons from the city of Lübeck proceeded to dismantle Bishop Absalon's castle brick by brick, with the intention of ending Danish control of the Øresund once and for all.

The Kalmar Union

Despite the temporary loss of its castle, however, Copenhagen's fortunes continued to prosper. Following the death of her son, King Olav – for whom she had reigned as regent for much of his life – **Margrethe I**, one of Denmark's shrewdest rulers, ascended the throne. Her moment of glory came in 1397 when she formed the **Kalmar Union**, an alliance between Denmark, Norway and Sweden aimed at countering the Hanseatic League's influence on regional trade. It became evident that Denmark was to be the dominant partner within the union, however, when Margrethe placed Danish nobles in civic positions in Norway and Sweden but failed to reciprocate with Swedes and Norwegians in Denmark. Margrethe promptly saw to it that her grandnephew, Erik of Pomerania, was crowned king, though, as he was only 15, she continued to play a major role in the affairs of the country till her death in 1412. Under Erik, a new fort to replace Absalon's dismantled castle was completed in 1417, becoming the main residence of the royal family. Erik also ensured Copenhagen's further growth by imposing the **Sound Toll** tax on all vessels passing through the Øresund, an endless source of income that would underpin the city's fortunes for the next four centuries. Revenues from the toll allowed an increasingly self-confident Copenhagen to seize growing amounts of trade from the declining ports of the Hanseatic League and to establish itself as the Baltic's principal harbour.

In 1443, Copenhagen was made the **capital of Denmark** by Erik's nephew, Christoffer III, decisively shifting the national balance of power away from the former capital and ecclesiastical centre of Roskilde. Thirty years later, the first **university** in Scandinavia was founded in Copenhagen by Christian I, helping to establish the city as the nation's cultural as well as administrative hub. At the same time, **Kronborg Slot**, just north of Copenhagen at Helsingør, was built to control the Øresund and enforce payment of the Sound Toll, further entrenching Copenhagen's pre-eminent position in the region.

The Reformation to the Thirty Years' War

At the time of **Frederik I**'s acquisition of the crown in 1522 there was a growing unease with the role of the Catholic Church in Denmark, especially with the power – and wealth – of its bishops. Frederik, though a Catholic, refused to take sides in religious disputes and did nothing to prevent the destruction of churches, being well aware of the groundswell of peasant support for Lutheranism. When he died in 1533 the fate of the Danish **Reformation** hinged on which of his two sons would succeed him. The elder and more obvious choice was Christian, but his open support for Lutheranism set the bishops and nobles against him, while the younger son Hans, just 12 years old, was favoured by the Church and aristocracy. **Civil war** ensued – peasant uprisings spread across the country, and Hanseatic Lübeck sent mercenaries to Copenhagen, where they sided with the city's anti-clerical merchants. A year-long siege of the city followed, and though Copenhagen's defensive ramparts held up, many of its citizens starved to death or died during the epidemics that ravaged the city. The capital finally surrendered in the summer of 1536, signalling the end of the war, and, after the dust had settled, the nobles found themselves back in control, but obliged to accept religious reform. With Christian III on the throne, the new **Danish Lutheran Church** was established, with a constitution placing the king at its head, and Lutheranism became the official state religion.

Following the travails of the Reformation, Copenhagen experienced a period of relative peace and prosperity. The city was now home to the Danish navy – during the fifteenth and sixteenth centuries the largest in northern Europe – and the Sound Toll provided a continuous source of revenue for Danish coffers. It was in this atmosphere of wealth and stability that **Christian IV** became king. Ruling from 1588 (when he was 10) until 1648, he became the Danish monarch who made the most lasting contribution to Copenhagen's skyline, ordering the creation of buildings including the Rundetårn and Rosenborg Slot, along with the district of Nyboder and the fortress of Kastellet. In addition, he almost doubled the city's size by moving the defensive fortifications outwards to include Frederikstad and Nyboder to the north and the newly reclaimed island of Christianshavn to the east.

Unfortunately, Christian IV's architectural vision was not matched by his political skill. As Denmark's arch-rival Sweden became increasingly powerful, Danish military prowess steadily declined. In 1625, Christian IV took Denmark into the disastrous **Thirty Years' War** – Danish defeat was total, and the king was widely condemned for his lack of foresight. The war led to increased taxes, inflation became rampant, and a number of merchants displayed their anger by petitioning the king over tax exemptions and other privileges enjoyed by nobles.

In 1657, during the reign of **Frederik III**, Sweden occupied Jutland, and soon after marched across the frozen sea to Funen island with the intention of continuing to Zealand and the capital. Hostilities ceased with the signing of the **Treaty of Roskilde**, under which Denmark finally lost all Swedish provinces. Sweden, however, was still suspicious of possible Danish involvement in Germany, and broke the terms of the treaty, commencing an advance through Zealand towards Copenhagen. The Dutch, to whom the Swedes had been allied, regarded this as a precursor to total Swedish control of commercial traffic through the Sound and sent a fleet to protect Copenhagen. This, plus a number of local uprisings within Denmark and attacks by Polish and Brandenburg forces on their troops, halted the Swedes' advance and forced them to seek peace. The **Treaty of Copenhagen**, signed in 1660, acknowledged Swedish defeat but allowed the country to retain the Sound provinces acquired under the Treaty of Roskilde, so preventing either country from monopolizing trade through the Sound.

Absolute monarchy

The conflict with Sweden and the loss of former territory left Denmark heavily in debt, and, to make matters worse, the nobles of the Council of the Danish Realm were reluctant to impose the taxes needed to rescue the state's finances. In response, in 1660 Frederik III compelled the nobles to sign a charter reinstating the king as absolute monarch, removing all powers from the Council. The king proceeded to rule, aided by a Privy Council in which seats were drawn mainly from the top posts within the civil service. The aristocracy's influence on royal decision-making had been drastically cut and Copenhagen was made a free city, with commoners accorded the same privileges as nobles. Frederik III started rebuilding the military, and, following three minor wars with Sweden, a peaceful coexistence was finally achieved.

Christian V, king from 1670, instigated a broad system of royal honours, creating a new class of landowners, who enjoyed exemptions from tax, and whose lack of concern for their tenants led Danish peasants into virtual serfdom. In 1699, **Frederik IV** set about creating a Danish militia to make the country less dependent on foreign mercenaries. While Sweden turned its allegiances towards Britain and Holland, Denmark re-established relations with the French, a situation which, in 1709, led to Danish involvement in the **Great Northern War**. The end of the conflict saw the emergence of Russia as a dominant force in the region, while Denmark held a strong position in Schleswig, and Sweden's exemption from paying the Sound Toll was ended.

The two decades of peace that followed saw the arrival of **Pietism**, a form of Lutheranism that strove to renew the devotional ideal. Frederik embraced the doctrine towards the end of his life, and it was adopted in full by his son, **Christian VI**, who took the throne in 1730. He prohibited entertainment on Sunday, closed down the Royal Theatre, and made court life a sombre affair: attendance at church on Sundays became compulsory and confirmation obligatory.

Meanwhile, in 1711, bubonic plague wiped out a third of Copenhagen's population, while two devastating **fires** in 1728 and 1795 forced the reconstruction of most of the city, during which the basis of the present-day street plan was established.

The Enlightenment in Copenhagen

Despite Christian VI's beliefs, Pietism was never widely popular, and by the 1740s its influence had waned considerably. The reign of **Frederik V** (1746–1766), saw a great cultural awakening in Copenhagen, as the new royal district of Frederikstad, with the grand royal palaces of Amalienborg and the Marmorkirken church, were erected (though the latter wasn't finished until 1894), and there was a new flourishing of the arts. The king, perhaps as a reaction to the puritanism of his father, devoted himself to a life of pleasure and allowed control of the nation effectively to pass to the civil service. Political life enjoyed a period of relative stability, and, with their international influence significantly reduced by the ravages of the Great Northern War, the Danes adopted a position of **neutrality** – a decision that saw the economy benefit as a consequence.

In 1766, **Christian VII** took the crown, but, with his mental state unstable and his moods ranging from deep lethargy to rage and drunkenness, by 1771 he had become incapable of carrying out even the minimum of official duties. Decision-making became dominated by a German court physician, **Johann Friedrich Struensee**, who spoke no Danish (German was the court language) and had no interest in Danish traditions, and was sympathetic to many of the Enlightenment ideas then fashionable elsewhere in Europe – during his short period of power a number of sweeping **reforms** were enacted, including the dissolution of the Privy Council, the abolition of the death penalty and the relaxation of press censorship. However, these reforms invited opposition from several quarters: merchants complained about the freeing of trade, and the burghers of Copenhagen were unhappy about their city losing its autonomy. In addition, there were well-founded rumours about the relationship between Struensee and the queen. Since nothing was known outside the court of the king's mental state, it was assumed that the monarch was being held prisoner, and Struensee was forced to reintroduce censorship of the press as their editorials began to mount attacks on him. Eventually, a coup in 1772 by Frederik V's second wife, Juliane Marie of Brunswick, and her son, Frederik, saw Struensee arrested, tried and, soon afterwards, beheaded, while the dazed king was paraded before his cheering subjects. Anyone who had been appointed to office by

Struensee was dismissed, Danish became the language of command in the army – and later the court language – and in 1776 it was declared that no foreigner should be given a position in royal office. In the wider sphere, the country prospered through dealings in the Far East, and Copenhagen consolidated its role as the new centre of Baltic trade.

The Napoleonic Wars

Despite its improving domestic position, Denmark found itself once again embroiled in the mire of international power struggles with the outbreak of the **Napoleonic Wars** (1796–1815). Under the leadership of Crown Prince Frederik (his father, the unstable Christian VII, had been stripped of all authority since 1784), Denmark at first reluctantly sided with the League of Armed Neutrality – Russia, Sweden and Prussia – in an attempt to stay out of the conflict between expansionist Britain and revolutionary France. However, the British, considering the treaty potentially hostile, sent a fleet under admirals Nelson and Parker to Copenhagen in 1801, damaging the powerful Danish navy and forcing them to withdraw from the agreement. In 1807, the British returned, worried that Napoleon's advancing armies would take over the newly rebuilt Danish fleet if they didn't, and demanded Danish surrender. When Frederik refused, the British blockaded the city, subjecting it to a murderous three-day bombardment that saw many of its finest buildings damaged, before towing away what was left of the Danish fleet. Denmark understandably rejected the subsequent British offer of an alliance, siding instead with France. With the eventual defeat of Napoleon, however, the luckless Danes were left bankrupt and without allies, and Norway had to be handed over to Sweden as payment for war debts.

The Golden Age and the coming of Liberalism

Despite this terrible beginning to the century, by the 1830s Copenhagen had become the centre of the Danish **Golden Age**. For two decades the nation's arts flourished as never before (or since): Hans Christian Andersen charmed the world with his colourful fairy tales, while **Søren Kierkegaard** (see p.105) scandalized it with his philosophical works. At the same time, the nation's visual arts reached new heights under the auspices of sculptor **Bertel Thorvaldsen** (see p.48), and C.W. Eckersberg, who led the emergence of the first specifically Danish school of painting. From this period date many of the city's most notable Neoclassical buildings, such as Christiansborg Slotskirke, the Domhus (Law Courts) and Vor Frue Kirke. Social changes were in the air, too. In the early nineteenth century, the theologian **N.F.S. Grundtvig** (see p.123) developed a new form of Christianity that aimed to draw its strength and inspiration from the people.

On the political front, however, there was trouble brewing in the duchies of Danish-speaking **Schleswig** and German-speaking **Holstein**, which, in response to the wave of nationalism in France and Germany, were demanding their independence. The issue became inextricably linked with the call for constitutional reform when a group of scholars in Copenhagen suggested that

Schleswig be brought closer to Danish affairs and, to pursue their aim, formed the Liberal Party and began pressing for a new liberal constitution. As the government wavered in its response, the movement grew, and its first newspaper, *Fædrelandet* (*The Fatherland*), appeared in 1834.

In 1839, **Christian VIII** came to the throne. Despite introducing a liberal constitution during his brief tenure in power in Norway during its short transition phase from Danish to Swedish rule, the new king didn't agree to a similar constitution back home. By 1848, when Christian was succeeded by his son **Frederik VII**, the liberals had organized themselves into the **National Liberal Party**, and Frederik signed a **new constitution** that made Denmark the most democratic country in Europe, guaranteeing freedom of speech, freedom of religious worship and many civil liberties. Legislation was to be put in the hands of a Rigsdag elected by popular vote and consisting of two chambers: the lower Folketing and upper Landsting. The king gave up the powers of an absolute monarch, though he could still select his own ministers and his signature was required before bills approved by the Rigsdag became law.

Continuing strife over the duchies of Schleswig and Holstein saw a series of small wars; eventually, Denmark ceded both to Germany during the reign of **Christian IX**, leaving the country smaller than it had been for centuries. The blame for this territorial loss was laid firmly on the National Liberals, and the new government, appointed by the king and drawn from the country's affluent landowners, saw its initial task as replacing the constitution with one far less liberal in content. The landowners worked in limited cooperation with the National Liberals and the Centre Party (a more conservative version of the National Liberals). In opposition, a number of interests encompassing everything from leftist radicals to followers of Grundtvig were shortly combined into the **United Left**, which put forward the first political manifesto seen in Denmark. It called for equal taxation, universal suffrage in local elections, more freedom for the farmers, and contained a vague demand for closer links with the other Scandinavian countries. The United Left became the majority within the Folketing in 1872.

The ideas of **revolutionary socialism** had begun percolating through the country in 1871 via a series of pamphlets edited by Louis Pio, who attempted to organize a Danish Internationale. Following a major strike, the government banned the organization, but the workers banded instead into trade unions and workers' associations, while the intellectual left also became active. A series of lectures delivered by Georg Brandes in Copenhagen cited Danish culture, in particular its literature, as dull and lifeless compared to that of other countries. He called for fresh works that questioned and examined society, instigating a bout of literary attacks on institutions such as marriage, chastity and the family, and starting a conservative backlash as groups in the government formed themselves into the **United Right**. The fortunes of the two sides fluctuated until the end of the century, when the left reasserted its dominance.

Meanwhile, the city itself had been undergoing something of a transformation. In 1851, Copenhagen's fortifications were demolished, finally allowing the cramped city to expand beyond its medieval limits and sowing the seeds for the new industrial era. Railways, factories and shipyards began to change the face of the city, and Copenhagen gradually developed into a thriving manufacturing centre, while the new working-class districts of Nørrebro and Vesterbro were flung up, with Copenhagen's workers packed into slum tenements that would subsequently become hotbeds of left-wing politics. The second half of the nineteenth century also saw the establishment of the **Carlsberg Brewery**, the rapid growth of the **Royal copenhagen Porcelain** factory, and the founding of a number of recreational possibilities for the city's aspiring bourgeoisie, from the city's two main department stores, the Magasin du Nord and Illums Bolighus, to Det Kongelige Teater and the city zoo.

Parliamentary democracy and World War I

The elections of 1901, under the new conditions of a secret ballot, saw the right reduced to the smallest group within the Folketing and heralded the beginning of **parliamentary democracy**.

The government of 1901 was the first real democratic administration, assembled with the intention of balancing differing political tendencies – and it brought in a number of reforms. Income tax was introduced on a sliding scale, and free schooling beyond the primary level began. As the years went by, Social Democrat support increased, while the left, such as it was, became increasingly conservative. In 1905, a breakaway group formed the **Radical Left** (*Det Radikale Venstre*), politically similar to the English Liberals, calling for the reduction of the armed forces to the status of coastal and border guards, greater social equality and votes for women.

Denmark had enjoyed good trading relations with both Germany and Britain in the years preceding **World War I**, and was keen not to be seen to favour either side when hostilities broke out in 1914. On the announcement of the German mobilization, the now Radical-led cabinet, with the support of all the other parties, issued a **statement of neutrality** and was able to remain clear of direct involvement in the conflict. At the conclusion of the war, under the **Treaty of Versailles**, a new German–Danish border was drawn up just north of Flensburg.

In 1920, a change in the electoral system towards greater proportional representation was agreed in the Folketing, but the prime minister, **Carl Theodore Zahle**, whose Radicals stood to lose support through the change, refused to implement it. The king, Christian X, responded by dismissing him and asking **Otto Liebe** to form a caretaker government to oversee the changes. The (technically legal) royal intervention incensed the Social Democrats and the trade unions, who were already facing a national lockout by employers in response to demands for improved pay rates. Perceiving the threat of a right-wing coup, the unions began organizing a general strike to begin after the Easter holiday, and there was a large republican demonstration outside Amalienborg.

On Easter Saturday, urgent negotiations between the king and the existing government concluded with an agreement that a mutually acceptable caretaker government would oversee the electoral change and a fresh election would immediately follow. Employers, fearful of the power the workers had shown, met many of the demands for higher wages.

The next government was dominated by the Radical Left. They fortified existing social policies and increased state contributions to union unemployment funds. But a general economic depression continued, and there was widespread industrial unrest as the krone declined in value and living standards fell. A month-long **general strike** followed, and a workers' demonstration in Randers was subdued by the army.

Venstre (the "Left", though the party was originally Liberal in ideology), formed in 1872 to represent the significant agricultural lobby, and the Social Democrats jostled for position over the next decade, though under the new electoral system no one party could achieve enough power to undertake major reform. The economy did improve, however, and state influence spread further through Danish society than ever before. Enlightened reforms were put on the agenda, too, making a deliberately clean break with the moral standpoints of the past – notably on abortion and illegitimacy.

World War II

When **World War II** broke out, Denmark again tried to remain neutral, this time unsuccessfully. At 4am on April 9, 1940, the German ambassador in Copenhagen informed Prime Minister Stauning that German troops were preparing to cross the Danish border, and issued the ultimatum that unless Denmark agreed that the country could be used as a German military base – keeping control of its own affairs – Copenhagen would be bombed. To reject the demand was considered a postponement of the inevitable, and to save Danish bloodshed the government acquiesced at 6am. "They took us by telephone," said a Danish minister. German troops marched up Nordre Frihavnsgade to the royal palaces at Amalienborg and took power the same day. The Danish parliament was left to operate purely as an administrative body, and the economy was geared towards German war needs. At first, the Danes could do little other than comply, but growing resistance made life difficult for the Nazi forces. Passive non-cooperation gradually turned to armed struggle, and by the war's end, thousands of citizens had fought (and many died) for the Danish resistance, whose crowning moment came with the smuggling of 7000 Jews to Sweden to avoid their deportation to concentration camps (see box on p.51). In Copenhagen, the effect of the war was felt mainly in food and fuel rationing, and, apart from the occasional air raid, the city largely escaped the devastation visited on other European cities – its finest moment came when a British air raid on the Nazi headquarters on Rådhuspladsen allowed most of the captured members of the Danish Resistance to escape.

The modern era

While Copenhagen and the country as a whole had been spared the devastation seen elsewhere in Europe, it still found itself with massive economic problems following World War II, and it soon became apparent that the newly elected liberation government – consisting largely of former leaders of the Resistance – could not function. In the ensuing election there was a swing to the Communists, and a minority Venstre government was formed. Domestic issues soon came to be overshadowed by the **international situation** as the Cold War began. Denmark had unreservedly joined the United Nations in 1945, and had signed up to the IMF and World Bank to gain financial help in restoring its economy. In 1947, Marshall Plan aid from the United States brought further assistance. As world politics became polarized between East and West, the Danish government at first tried to remain impartial, but in 1947 agreed to join NATO – a total break with the established concept of Danish neutrality.

The years after the war were marked by much political manoeuvring among the Radicals, Social Democrats and Conservatives, resulting in many hastily called elections and a number of ineffectual compromise coalitions, notable mainly for their infighting. Working-class support for the Social Democrats steadily eroded, and support for the Communists was largely transferred to the new, more revisionist, **Socialist People's Party**.

In spite of political wrangling, Denmark succeeded in creating one of the world's most successful **welfare states**, with a comprehensive programme of cradle-to-grave benefits, and a quality of life that soon ranked among the highest in the world. Social reforms continued apace, not least in the **1960s**, with the abandoning of all forms of censorship and the institution of free abortion on demand. A referendum held in 1972 to determine whether Denmark should join the EC resulted in a substantial majority in favour, making Denmark the first Scandinavian member of the community.

Copenhagen itself became the centre of attention when, in 1971, the old military base on the eastern side of Christianshavn was taken over by squatters, who created the "Free City" of **Christiania**. Initial, unsuccessful attempts by the police to clear the squatters were followed by a twelve-year trial period, after which the city was legally recognized, even to the point where "Pusherstreet" is now marked on official maps. Perhaps the biggest change in the 1970s, however, was the foundation – and subsequent influence – of the new **Progress Party** (*Fremskridtspartiet*), initially headed by Mogens Glistrup, who claimed to have an income of over a million kroner but to be paying no income tax through manipulation of the tax laws. The party stood on a ticket of immigration curbs and drastic tax cuts, and Glistrup went on to compare tax avoidance with the sabotaging of Nazi railway lines during the war. He was eventually imprisoned after an investigation by the Danish tax office; released in 1985, he set himself up as a tax consultant.

The success of the Progress Party pointed to dissatisfaction with both the economy and the established parties' strategies for dealing with its problems. In September 1982, **Poul Schlüter** became the country's first Conservative prime minister of the twentieth century, leading the widest-ranging coalition yet seen – including Conservatives, the Venstre, Centre Democrats and Christian People's Party. In keeping with the prevailing political climate in the rest of Europe, the prescription for Denmark's economic malaise was seen to be spending cuts and an extension of taxation into areas such as pension funds. These policies continued until the snap election of 1987, which resulted in a significant swing to the left. Nevertheless, Schlüter was asked to form a new government, which he did in conjunction with the Progress Party in order to gain a single-seat working majority. A further election, in May 1988, largely served to affirm the new Schlüter-led government, if only, perhaps, because of the apparent lack of any workable alternative.

The 1980s and 1990s also saw further huge changes to the city's fabric, as attempts were made to clean up the derelict areas of **Nørrebro** and **Vesterbro**. In Nørrebro, the result was disastrous, with blocks of ramshackle but characterful buildings being torn down and replaced by concrete housing estates until mass protests forced the city to desist. The remaining buildings in Nørrebro – and most of Vesterbro – were restored rather than demolished, with the result that housing in these areas increased enormously in value. The negative side of this gentrification, however, was the forcing out of many of the original inhabitants, with waves of Copenhagen yuppies taking the places of the districts' formerly working-class inhabitants.

Changes in the city's physical make-up have been mirrored in arguments about its culture and character. The arrival since the 1960s of substantial numbers of immigrants – the so-called **new Danes** – continues to raise questions about the future identity of Copenhagen (see p.252). Immigrants, mainly from Yugoslavia and Turkey, brought in during the boom years of the 1960s to fill the city's menial jobs, became suddenly less welcome in the 1970s, as unemployment rates began to rise and the ugly face of racism raised its head. Tensions continued to simmer, reaching boiling point in 1999 with riots in Nørrebro, protesting against the extradition of a second-generation Turkish immigrant. Though nothing along these lines has occurred since, whether the city's ethnic communities – often faced with overweening pressure to conform to the Danish way of life – will succeed in bringing true cultural diversity to the city remains to be seen.

Into the millennium

From the 1970s to the present day, the major barometer of national feeling in Denmark has been the way in which people have seen the country's role in Europe. Despite being members of the **European Union** for over thirty years, the Danish people have in recent years constantly rocked the European boat. A 1992 referendum saw them reject the Maastricht Treaty, and it took a second referendum in 1993, backed by massive state propaganda, to establish the necessary majority for the treaty's implementation. This result so inflamed popular opinion in parts of Copenhagen that it led to a riot in Nørrebro during which eleven people were shot and injured. At a third referendum, in late 2000, the Danes again shocked fellow EU member states by choosing to opt out of the third stage of EU monetary union (adopting the euro), as right-wing politicians stirred up nationalist emotions, claiming that giving up the Danish krone was equivalent to relinquishing national sovereignty (the fact that the krone was already linked to the Deutschmark was conveniently overlooked).

Poul Nyrup Rasmussen's Social Democratic government retained the largest share of the vote in the 1998 elections, and, as the new millennium dawned, the country enjoyed a relatively strong position compared to other European countries, in terms of environmental awareness, healthcare costs and low poverty and unemployment.

At the same time, Copenhagen and its environs received the most significant change to its landscape for centuries – the opening in 2000 of the **Øresunds Bridge**, a road-and-rail link connecting Copenhagen with Sweden. As well as significantly enhancing Copenhagen's connections with the rest of Scandinavia, the bridge brought the nearby Swedish city of Malmö within thirty minutes of central Copenhagen, adding at a stroke half a million people to the city's catchment area and establishing it as a major regional hub capable of attracting serious foreign investment.

Copenhagen today

Copenhagen today is a city facing an identity crisis as it struggles to maintain its much cherished individuality and independence in the face of an ever-expanding Europe and the pull of **European monetary union**. A Danish referendum on the adoption of the EU constitution, scheduled for September 2006, was cancelled in the wake of "no" results in France and Holland, but it's pretty much accepted that the Danish result would have gone the same way. In the meantime, the city's ties with the rest of Scandinavia, particularly Sweden, are undergoing a period of frenetic activity. The Øresunds Bridge itself may have proved something of a flop – steep tolls have kept the number of cars using the bridge way below expected figures – but the Øresund region in general is booming, with a network of Danish and Swedish universities, cross-border migration and an influx of biotech, medical and food companies employing nearly thirty thousand people.

It's not all positive, though; **immigration and asylum** issues have, over the past decade or so, risen to the forefront of the political agenda. As a result, the last two general elections (in 2001 and 2005) have seen the ousting of the once-dominant Social Democrats in favour of the centre-right party **Venstre**, led by Anders Fogh Rasmussen, with its hard-line stance on immigration. Over the past five years, the government – a coalition of Venstre and the Conservative People's Party – has passed a series of laws (the most stringent in Europe), aimed at curbing non-EU immigration and severely limiting asylum applications, answering its numerous critics by saying that it believes Denmark to be at capacity, even though the country, with an ageing population and expensive welfare state to maintain, is in need of the kind of boost to the workforce and young population that immigration can bring. The degree of public unease on issues of immigration is also evident in the rise in popularity of the right-wing, anti-immigration Danish People's Party (DFP), which gained more than thirteen percent of the vote in the last election and continues to successfully lobby the government into taking an even harder line. The peaceful coexistence and mutual tolerance of the Danish people and its 150,000 Muslim immigrants was seriously challenged with the highly controversial printing of twelve **cartoons** featuring the prophet Mohammed (some depicting him as a terrorist) in the daily broadsheet, *Jyllands-Posten*, in 2005. The cartoons brought condemnation and violent protests from Muslims around the world and death threats to newspaper staff and the cartoonists; in Denmark, five thousand Muslim immigrants took to the streets in protest and radical Danish *imams* demanded an apology from the newspaper. The newspaper stood firm, backed by the prime minister, and defended its democratic right to freedom of expression. The incident has now largely blown over and Denmark, and its largely moderate Muslim population, many of whom took a reasoned stance and distanced themselves from more radical elements, have made their peace.

Immigration policies aside, the government has also shown itself to be hardline on many issues: anti-environment (with massive cuts in energy-saving initiatives); anti-development (cuts in overseas aid); anti-culture (slashing financial support to alternative types of entertainment); and, on a subject dear to Copenhageners' hearts, anti-Christiania (see p.71).

But, putting to one side national politics, the city itself is undergoing something of a rejuvenation, at its most visible in the new metro system and renovated harbourfront, increasingly dominated by revamped warehouses housing cultural institutions and prestigious new buildings such as Den Sorte Diamant library extension, the opera house on Holmen and the new play-house theatre. The city, in general, seems in the grip of prosperity, with burgeoning numbers of trendy restaurants, bars and shops aimed at the young and cash-rich. And, with a new addition to the royal family, the young Prince Christian, coming hot on the heels of the royal wedding of the popular Crown Prince Frederik in 2005, even the monarchy is getting in on the act.

Though the issues of European integration, immigration and an ageing population are likely to dominate the city's and country's political agenda for some time to come, a trip to Copenhagen is a visit to a proudly patriotic city, confident in its heritage and individuality and rather reluctant to sacrifice either.

Books

T here are relatively few English-language books on Copenhagen and it's especially difficult to find an English history of the city or, for that matter, the country; the sheer volume of books on the Vikings leaves you with the impression that historians consider it the only period worth writing about. The list below represents a fairly comprehensive selection of what's available, either on the city itself, or Danish history, culture and literature in general. All those below are very readable, but those marked with 🏃 are particularly recommended. Out-of-print titles are marked "o/p".

History and philosophy

Robert Bretall *A Kirkegaard Anthology* (Princeton University Press). An excellent cross-section of Kirkegaard's work, reflecting all the major themes of his proto-existential philosophy.

Jane Chamberlain & Jonathan Ree (eds) *The Kirkegaard Reader* (Blackwell). An expensive hardback but by far the best and most accessible introduction to this notoriously difficult philosopher and writer, with an excellent introductory essay and plentiful extracts from his most famous works.

Inga Dahlsgård *Women in Denmark, Yesterday and Today* (o/p). A refreshing presentation of Danish history from the point of view of its women.

T.K.Derry *A History of Scandinavia* (Minnesota Press). Authoritative history of the Scandinavian countries from the Stone Age to the 1990s. Rather dense and scholarly, but one of the only works on the topic in paperback.

Ole Feldbæk *The Battle of Copenhagen 1801* (Pen and Sword Books Ltd). Accessible examination by the leading Danish authority on the period of the events surrounding the great sea battle that saw Nelson deliberately disobeying his superior in the fight to crush the Danish Navy during the Napoleonic Wars.

🏃 **Tony Griffiths** *Scandinavia: At War with Trolls* (Hurst & Co.). A concise and witty cultural history of Scandinavia and the contributions of its great thinkers, artists and musicians from the eighteenth century to today. One of the best contemporary histories available.

John Haywood *Penguin Historical Atlas of the Vikings* (Penguin). A pithy, map-laden summary of the plundering voyages that brought the Vikings into contact with the rest of the world.

Stig Hornshøj-Møller *A Short History of Denmark* (Aschehoug Dansk Forlag A/S). This 72-page romp through Danish history is the perfect, lightweight companion to sightseeing, giving succinct information on the key periods and figures you'll encounter along the way. Available from the shops of the major historical museums, castles and palaces.

🏃 **Knud J.V. Jespersen** *A History of Denmark* (Palgrave). Thoroughly readable and accessible history of Denmark since the Reformation, examining the way the modern Danish state evolved through its numerous territorial wars and providing interesting insights into the Danish identity and psyche.

Gwyn Jones *A History of the Vikings* (Oxford Paperbacks). Probably the best book on the subject: a superb, thoughtful and thoroughly researched account of the Viking period.

W. Glyn Jones *Denmark: A Modern History* (o/p). A valuable account of the twentieth century (up until 1984), with a commendable outline of pre-twentieth-century Danish history, too. Strong on politics, useful on social history and the arts, but disappointingly brief on recent grassroots movements.

Søren Kirkegaard *Either/Or* (Penguin). Kirkegaard's most important work, packed with wry and wise musings on love, life and death in nineteenth-century Danish society, including the (in)famous "Seducer's Diary". If you can take more, his next book *Fear and Trembling* treats the subject of faith via a discussion of the biblical account of Abraham; or there's equally light reading with *The Sickness Unto Death*, focusing on man's despair and its relationship to his weakness and sins.

Else Roesdahl *The Vikings* (Penguin). A lucid, introductory account of the three-hundred-year reign of Scandinavia's most famous (and most misunderstood) cultural ambassadors, covering all aspects of their society, including religion, dress, language and politics.

Emmy E. Werner *A Conspiracy of Decency* (Westview). A short, well-written account detailing how the Danish people were able to rescue nearly all of the country's Jews from deportation and death by hiding them and helping them escape to neutral Sweden. The first-hand accounts of eyewitnesses make for compelling reading.

Literature and biography

Hans Christian Andersen *Hans Christian Andersen's Fairy Tales* (Penguin Classics). Andersen's fairy tales are so widely translated and read that the full clout of their allegorical content is often overlooked: interestingly, his first collection of such tales (published in 1835) was condemned for its "violence and questionable morals". *A Visit to Germany, Italy and Malta, 1840–1841* (o/p) is the most enduring of his travel works, while his autobiography, *The Fairy Tale of My Life* (Cooper Square Press) is a fine alternative to the numerous sycophantic portraits that have appeared since.

Karen Blixen (Isak Dinesen) *Out of Africa* (Vintage); *Letters from Africa* (University of Chicago); *Seven Gothic Tales* (Vintage). *Out of Africa*, the account of Blixen's attempts to run a coffee farm in Kenya after divorce from her husband, is a lyrical and moving tale. But it's in *Seven Gothic Tales* that Blixen's fiction is at its zenith: a flawlessly executed, weird, emotive work, full of twists in plot and strange, ambiguous characterization.

Elias Bredsdorff *Hans Christian Andersen*. One of the better biographies out of a huge raft of works on the life and times of the great fairy-tale writer.

Stig Dalager *Journey in Blue: A novel about Hans Christian Andersen* (Peter Owen). Dalager, one of the most renowned Scandinavian authors of recent decades, imagines the musings and words of Andersen through experiences and events of his life, providing insight into what caused the writer's sense of alienation and how this drove him to search for literary validation in the world that shunned him.

Tove Ditlevsen *Early Spring* (o/p). An autobiographical novel of growing up in the working-class Vesterbro district of Copenhagen during the 1930s. A captivating evocation of childhood and early adulthood.

Per Olov Enquist *The Royal Physician's Visit* (Simon & Schuster). Gripping, racy, historical novel of eighteenth-century court intrigue, charting the power struggles of the various weasly courtiers manipulating the young and mentally unstable King Christian VII, including his German doctor, Johann Struensee, who took the queen as his mistress.

Michael Frayn *Copenhagen* (Methuen). Frayn's excellent play re-examines the reasons and tensions behind the mysterious visit in 1941 by the German atomic physicist, Werner Heisenberg, to see his counterpart Niels Bohr in Nazi-occupied Copenhagen, formerly a close colleague and friend, now working for the opposite side in the race to develop the atomic bomb.

Joakim Garff *Søren Kirkegaard: A Biography* (Princeton University Press). The most comprehensive book on Kirkegaard's life to date, this eight-hundred-page tome is surprisingly readable, offering an insight into the tortured world of a great thinker through the minutiae of his life.

Martin A. Hansen *The Liar* (o/p). An engaging novel, showing why Hansen was one of Denmark's most perceptive – and popular – authors during the postwar period. Set in the 1950s, the story examines the inner thoughts of a lonely schoolteacher living on a small Danish island.

Peter Høeg *Miss Smilla's Feeling for Snow; A History of Danish Dreams; The Woman and the Ape; Tales of the Night* (Harvill Press). Probably Denmark's most famous modern author, with the worldwide best-seller, *Miss Smilla's Feeling for Snow* – a compelling thriller dealing with Danish colonialism in Greenland and the issue of cultural identity – his best-known work.

Christian Jungersen *The Exception* (Weidenfeld & Nicholson). A real page-turner, this thrilling bestseller follows the fictional lives of four women who receive threatening emails at the Centre for Genocide Studies where they work. It delves deeply into the issues of moral ambiguity as the women confront the ethical dilemmas that face them.

Thomas E. Kennedy *Kerrigan's Copenhagen: A Love Story* (Wynkin deWorde). The city co-stars in this witty, Joyce-style tale of an American writer attempting to come to terms with his past with the help of Copenhagen's many bars. Each chapter is devoted to a different bar, with the loveable if frustrating hero meeting a host of characters and musing on life, the city, beer, books, jazz, sex, cigars and architecture, among other things.

Dea Trier Mørch *Winter's Child* (o/p). A wonderfully lucid sketch of modern Denmark as seen through the eyes of several women in the maternity ward of a Copenhagen hospital. See also *Evening Star*, which deals with the effect of old age and death on a Danish family.

Martin Andersen Nexø *Pelle the Conqueror* (Mondial). Made into an Academy Award-winning film in 1989, by Bille August, this moving tale about life as an immigrant has been a classic in Denmark for years.

Hans Scherfig *Stolen Spring* (Fjord Press). A group of Copenhagen youths studying for their high-school exams feel they're missing out on the most important spring of their lives. A classic novel, mandatory reading for all Danish high-school students.

🏃 **Judith Thurman** *Isak Dinesen: The Life of Karen Blixen* (Picador). The most penetrating biography of Blixen, elucidating details of the farm period not found in the two "Africa" books.

🏃 **Rose Tremain** *Music and Silence* (Vintage). Captivating novel that follows the lives of Christian IV, his consort, his English lutenist and their lovers. Life in the many castles around Copenhagen is brilliantly described, and the novel provides a delightful insight into Danish aspirations and superstitions during the period.

Jackie Wullschlager *Hans Christian Andersen: The Life of a Storyteller* (Penguin). This finely documented and insightful work examines the misery of Andersen's childhood, his subsequent rapid success and his troubled sexuality, arguing that it was the shock and power of these experiences that fuelled many of his mournful fairy tales.

Architecture and design

Christian Datz & C. Kullmann (eds) *Copenhagen: Architecture and Design* (teNeues Publishing Ltd). Great little glossy featuring the city's and suburbs' modern architectural masterpieces.

Charlotte Fiell and Peter Fiell *Scandinavian Design* (Taschen). Beautiful, photo-driven history of Scandinavian design from 1900 to the present day, covering all of the major designers and the whole range of crafts – from glass to furniture to jewellery – with ample coverage of more modern design phenomena such as Ikea and Lego.

Takako Murakami and Noritsugu Oda *Danish Chairs* (Chronicle Books). If you've been bitten by the bug, this book will tell you all you need to know about the illustrious history of chair design in Denmark, featuring timeless classics from the likes of Kaare Klint and Arne Jacobsen, as well as more up-to-the-minute designs.

Anja L. Oriol (ed) *New Scandinavian Design* (teNeues Publishing Ltd). The most up-to-date assessment of recent trends in Scandinavian architecture, furniture and product design.

Bradley Quinn *Scandinavian Style* (Conran Octopus). Bright, sumptuous, coffee-table book combining ample coverage of contemporary design and interiors with useful overviews of twentieth-century movements from Functionalism to Danish Modernism.

C

Travel, cooking and film

Tom Cunliffe *Topsail and Battleaxe: A Voyage in the Wake of the Vikings* (Seafarer Books). The intertwined stories of the tenth-century Vikings who sailed from Norway, past the Faroes and Iceland to North America, and the author's parallel trip in 1983 – made in a 75-year-old pilot cutter. Enthusiastically written, and illustrated with good photos.

Christer Elfving and Petra de Hamer *New Scandinavian Cooking: A Culinary Journey through Scandinavia* (Mo'media). A cook's tour through Scandinavia's capital cities, mixing history, culinary trends and tips on the hottest chefs and restaurants with delicious modern recipes.

Richard Kelly *The Name of this Book is Dogme 95* (Faber & Faber).

Offering excellent insights into the whole Dogme movement, this diary-style account of the making of a documentary on the Dogme group features interviews with the founders, and an in-depth look at some of the films.

Ben Nimmo *In Forkbeard's Wake: Coasting Around Scandinavia* (HarperCollins). Light and lively account of the author's sailing trip around Scandinavia, brimming with sailing mishaps and encounters with Nordic types – divers, fishermen, archeologists and a drunk Swedish dentist. An all-too-rare modern travel book on the area.

Jack Stevenson *Dogme Uncut: Lars von Trier, Thomas Vinterberg and the Gang that took on Hollywood* (Santa Monica Press). Accessible, jargon-free and in-depth history of the Dogme movement, focusing on its origins and development and influence on current film-making.

Mary Wollstonecraft *A Short Residence in Sweden* (Penguin). A searching account of Wollstonecraft's three-month solo journey through southern Scandinavia in 1795. Part travelogue, part history, part love story – a remarkable trip for a woman of that era, albeit from the author of one of the first truly feminist works, *A Vindication of the Rights of Woman*.

Language

Language

Language

T hough similar to German in some respects, **Danish** has significant differences in pronunciation, with Danes tending to swallow the ending of many words and leaving certain letters silent. In general, English is widely understood throughout Denmark, as is German, and young people especially often speak both fluently. However, even with little need to resort to Danish, learning a few phrases will surprise and delight any Danes you meet. If you can speak Swedish or Norwegian, then you should have little problem making yourself understood – all three languages share the same root.

The language section below will equip you with the bare essentials, but if you want something more comprehensive, the *Berlitz Danish–English Dictionary* and *Berlitz Danish Phrase Book* are good reference guides. If you're planning to really get to grips with the language, the best teach-yourself book is *Colloquial Danish* (W. Glyn Jones and Kirsten Gade). For serious students of the language, the *Danish Dictionary* (Anna Garde and W. Glyn Jones, eds) is excellent; while for grammar, you can't do better than *Danish: A Comprehensive Grammar* (Philip Holmes, Robin Allan and Tom Lundskær-Nielsen).

Words and phrases

Basics

Danish pronunciation is a confusing affair, so for the phrases below we've explained in brackets how to pronounce them.

Taler de engelsk? (tayla dee ENgellsg)	Do you speak English?	Hvor er? (voa ea?)	Where is?
Ja (ya)	Yes	Hvor meget? (voa maYETH?)	How much?
Nej (nye)	No		
Jeg forstår det ikke (yai fusTO day igge)	I don't understand	Hvad koster det? (vath kosta day?)	How much does it cost?
		Jeg vil gerne ha... (yai vay GERna ha)	I'd like...
Værså venlig (verso venli)	Please	Hvor er toiletterne ? (voa ea toaLETTaneh?)	Where are the toilets?
Tak (tagg)	Thank you		
Undskyld (unsgul)	Excuse me	Et bord til ... (et boa te...)	A table for...
Hi (hye)	Hello/Hi		
Godmorgen (goMORN)	Good morning	Må jeg bede om regningen? (moah yai beyde uhm RYningan?)	Can I have the bill/ check, please?
Goddag (goDA)	Good afternoon		
Godnat (goNAD)	Goodnight		
Farvel (faVELL)	Goodbye	Billet (billed)	Ticket

Numbers

Nul	0	Atten	18
En	1	Nitten	19
To	2	Tyve	20
Tre	3	Enogtyve	21
Fire	4	Tredive	30
Fem	5	Fyrre	40
Seks	6	Halvtreds	50
Syv	7	Tres	60
Otte	8	Halvfjerds	70
Ni	9	Firs	80
Ti	10	Halvfems	90
Elleve	11	Hundrede	100
Tolv	12	Hundrede og et	101
Tretten	13	Hundrede og enoghalvtreds	151
Fjorten	14		
Femten	15	To hundrede	200
Seksten	16	Tusind	1000
Sytten	17		

Days and months

Mandag	Monday	Marts	March
Tirsdag	Tuesday	April	April
Onsdag	Wednesday	Maj	May
Torsdag	Thursday	Juni	June
Fredag	Friday	Juli	July
Lørdag	Saturday	August	August
Søndag	Sunday	September	September
		Oktober	October
Januar	January	November	November
Februar	February	December	December

Some signs

Indgang	Entrance	Lukket	Closed
Udgang	Exit	Ankomst	Arrival
Skub/træk	Push/pull	Afgang	Departure
Fare	Danger	Politi	Police
Herrer	Gentlemen	Rygning forbudt/ Ikke rygere	No smoking
Damer	Ladies		
Åben	Open	Ingen adgang	No entry

Food and drink

Basics

Kniv	Knife	Det kolde bord	Help-yourself cold buffet
Gaffel	Fork	Is	Ice cream
Ske	Spoon	Kiks	Biscuits
Tallerken	Plate	Nudler	Noodles
Kop	Cup	Ostebord	Cheese board
Glas	Glass	Pølser	Frankfurters/sausages
Salt	Salt	Ris	Rice
Peber	Pepper	Sildebord	A selection of spiced and pickled herring
Brød	Bread		
Bøfsandwich	Hamburger	Smørrebrød	Open sandwiches
Skummetmælk	Skimmed milk	Sukker	Sugar
Smør	Butter	Wienerbrød	"Danish" pastry

Egg (Æg) dishes

Kogt æg	Boiled egg	Røræg	Scrambled eggs
Omelet	Omelette	Spejlæg	Fried eggs

Fish (Fisk)

Ål	Eel	Rejer	Shrimp
Forel	Trout	Rogn	Roe
Gedde	Pike	Rødspætte	Plaice
Helleflynder	Halibut	Røget Sild	Kipper
Hummer	Lobster	Sardiner	Sardines
Karpe	Carp	Sild	Herring
Klipfisk	Salt cod	Søtunge	Sole
Krabbe	Crab	Stør	Sturgeon
Krebs	Crayfish	Store rejer	Prawns
Laks	Salmon	Torsk	Cod
Makrel	Mackerel		

Meat (Kød)

And(ung)	Duck(ling)	Kylling	Chicken
Oksekød	Beef	Lammekød	Lamb
Dyresteg	Venison	Lever	Liver
Fasan	Pheasant	Rensdyr	Reindeer
Gås	Goose	Skinke	Ham
Hare	Hare	Svinekød	Pork
Kalkun	Turkey	Vildt	Venison
Kanin	Rabbit		

Vegetables (Grøntsager)

Ærter	Peas	Løg	Onions
Agurk	Cucumber	Majs	Sweetcorn
Artiskokker	Artichokes	Majskolbe	Corn on the cob
Asparges	Asparagus	Peberfrugt	Peppers
Blomkål	Cauliflower	Persille	Parsley
Bønner	Beans	Porrer	Leeks
Champignoner	Mushrooms	Rødbeder	Beetroot
Grønne bønner	Runner beans	Rødkål	Red cabbage
Gulerødder	Carrots	Rosenkål	Brussels sprouts
Brune bønner	Kidney beans	Salat	Lettuce, salad
Hvidløg	Garlic	Selleri	Celery
Julesalat	Chicory	Spinat	Spinach
Kål	Cabbage	Turnips	Turnips
Kartofler	Potatoes		
Linser	Lentils		

Fruit (Frugt)

Æbler	Apples	Hyldebær	Elderberries
Abrikoser	Apricots	Jordbær	Strawberries
Ananas	Pineapple	Kirsebær	Cherries
Appelsiner	Oranges	Mandariner	Tangerines
Bananer	Bananas	Melon	Melon
Blommer	Plums	Pærer	Pears
Blåbær	Blueberries	Rabarber	Rhubarb
Brombær	Blackberries	Rosiner	Raisins
Citron	Lemon	Solbær	Blackcurrants
Ferskner	Peaches	Stikkelsbær	Gooseberries
Grapefrugt	Grapefruit	Svesker	Prunes
Hindbær	Raspberries	Vindruer	Grapes

Danish specialities

Æbleflæsk	Smoked bacon with onions and sautéed apple rings	Flæskesteg	A hunk of pork with red cabbage, potatoes and brown sauce
Æggekage	Scrambled eggs with onions, chives, potatoes and bacon pieces	Frikadeller	Pork rissoles
		Grillstegt kylling	Grilled chicken
Ålesuppe	Sweet-and-sour eel soup	Hakkebøf	Thick minced-beef burgers fried with onions
Boller i karry	Meatballs in curry sauce served with rice	Kalvebryst i frikasseé	Veal boiled with vegetables and served in a white

	sauce with peas and carrots		boiled eggs in a cream sauce, spiced with fish mustard and served with rye bread, garnished with sliced bacon and chives
Kogt torsk	Poached cod in mustard sauce with boiled potatoes		
Medisterpølse	A spiced pork sausage, usually served with boiled potatoes or stewed vegetables	Skipper labskovs	Danish stew: small squares of beef boiled with potatoes, peppercorns and bay leaves
Røget sild	Smoked herring on rye bread, garnished with a raw egg yolk, radishes and chives	Stegt ål med stuvede kartofler	Fried eel with diced potatoes and white sauce
Sild i karry	Herring in curry sauce		
Skidne æg	Poached or hard-		

Drink (Drikke)

Vand	Water	Citronvand	Lemonade
Kaffe (med fløde)	Coffee (with cream)	Eksport-Øl	Export beer (very strong lager)
Te	Tea		
Chokolade (varm)	Chocolate (hot)	Øl	Beer
Mælk	Milk	Fadøl	Draught beer
Sødmælk	Full-fat milk	Guldøl	Strong beer
Letmælk	Semi-skimmed milk	Vin	Wine
Kærnemælk	Buttermilk	Husets vin	House wine
Appelsinjuice	Orange juice	Hvidvin	White wine
Æblemost	Apple juice	Rødvin	Red wine
Tomatjuice	Tomato juice	Gløgg	Mulled wine
Appelsinvand	Orangeade	Mineralvand	Soda water

Glossary

Båd	Boat	Kanal	Canal
Bakke	Hill	Kirke	Church
Bro	Bridge	Kongens	King's, royal
By	Town	Lille	Little, small
-et/-en	suffixes denoting "the"	Museet	Museum
		Nørre	Northern
Fælled	Common	Ny	New
Folketing	Danish Parliament	Ø	Island
Gade	Street	Øster	Eastern
Gammel	Old	Plads	Square
Gård	Yard	Port	Gate
Have	Garden	Rådhus	Town Hall
Havn	Harbour	Sankt(Skt)	Saint
Hus	House	Slot	Castle

Sø	Lake, sea	Tårn	Tower
Sønder	Southern	Tog	Train
Stor	Big	Torv	Square
Stræde	Street	Vej	Road
Strand	Beach, shore	Vester	Western

Travel store

D: Rough Guide
DIRECTIONS for
short breaks

Available from all good bookstores

ROUGH GUIDES

Complete Listing

Visit us online

www.roughguides.com

Information on over 25,000 destinations around the world

- **Read** Rough Guides' trusted travel info
- **Access** exclusive articles from Rough Guides authors
- **Update** yourself on new books, maps, CDs and other products
- **Enter** our competitions and win travel prizes
- **Share** ideas, journals, photos & travel advice with other users
- **Earn** points every time you contribute to the Rough Guide community and get rewards

BROADEN YOUR HORIZONS

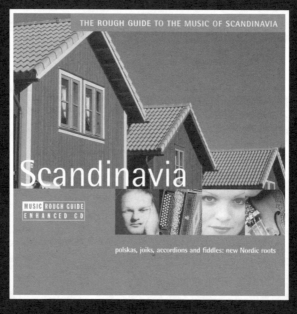

Small print and

Index

A Rough Guide to Rough Guides

Published in 1982, the first Rough Guide – to Greece – was a student scheme that became a publishing phenomenon. Mark Ellingham, a recent graduate in English from Bristol University, had been travelling in Greece the previous summer and couldn't find the right guidebook. With a small group of friends he wrote his own guide, combining a highly contemporary, journalistic style with a thoroughly practical approach to travellers' needs.

The immediate success of the book spawned a series that rapidly covered dozens of destinations. And, in addition to impecunious backpackers, Rough Guides soon acquired a much broader and older readership that relished the guides' wit and inquisitiveness as much as their enthusiastic, critical approach and value-for-money ethos.

These days, Rough Guides include recommendations from shoestring to luxury and cover more than 200 destinations around the globe, including almost every country in the Americas and Europe, more than half of Africa and most of Asia and Australasia. Our ever-growing team of authors and photographers is spread all over the world, particularly in Europe, the USA and Australia.

In the early 1990s, Rough Guides branched out of travel, with the publication of Rough Guides to World Music, Classical Music and the Internet. All three have become benchmark titles in their fields, spearheading the publication of a wide range of books under the Rough Guide name.

Including the travel series, Rough Guides now number more than 350 titles, covering: phrasebooks, waterproof maps, music guides from Opera to Heavy Metal, reference works as diverse as Conspiracy Theories and Shakespeare, and popular culture books from iPods to Poker. Rough Guides also produce a series of more than 120 World Music CDs in partnership with World Music Network.

Visit www.roughguides.com to see our latest publications.

Rough Guide travel images are available for commercial licensing at www.roughguidespictures.com

Rough Guide credits

Text editor: Keith Drew
Layout: Ajay Verma
Cartography: Alakananda Bhattacharya
Picture editor: Mark Thomas
Production: Katherine Owers
Proofreader: Martin Moore
Cover design: Chloë Roberts
Photographer: Helena Smith
Editorial: **London** Kate Berens, Claire Saunders, Geoff Howard, Ruth Blackmore, Polly Thomas, Richard Lim, Alison Murchie, Karoline Densley, Andy Turner, Edward Aves, Nikki Birrell, Helen Marsden, Alice Park, Sarah Eno, Joe Staines, Duncan Clark, Peter Buckley, Matthew Milton, Tracy Hopkins, David Paul, Lucy White, Ruth Tidball; **New York** Andrew Rosenberg, Steven Horak, April Isaacs, AnneLise Sorensen, Amy Hegarty, Sean Mahoney, Ella Steim
Design & Pictures: **London** Simon Bracken, Dan May, Diana Jarvis, Jj Luck, Harriet Mills; **Delhi** Madhvi Singh, Umesh Aggarwal, Jessica Subramanian, Ankur Guha, Pradeep Thapliyal, Sachin Tanwar, Anita Singh

Production: Sophie Hewat, Aimee Hampson
Cartography: **London** Maxine Repath, Ed Wright, Katie Lloyd-Jones; **Delhi** Rajesh Chhibber, Jai Prakash Mishra, Ashutosh Bharti, Rajesh Mishra, Animesh Pathak, Jasbir Sandhu, Karobi Gogoi, Amod Singh
Online: **New York** Jennifer Gold, Suzanne Welles, Kristin Mingrone; **Delhi** Manik Chauhan, Narender Kumar, Shekhar Jha, Rakesh Kumar, Amit Verma, Amit Kumar, Rahul Kumar
Marketing & Publicity: **London** Richard Trillo, Niki Hanmer, Louise Maher, Jess Carter; **New York** Geoff Colquitt, Megan Kennedy, Katy Ball; **Delhi** Reem Khokhar
Custom publishing and foreign rights: Philippa Hopkins
Manager India: Punita Singh
Series editor: Mark Ellingham
Reference Director: Andrew Lockett
PA to Managing and Publishing Directors: Megan McIntyre
Publishing Director: Martin Dunford

Publishing information

This third edition published January 2007 by **Rough Guides Ltd**,
80 Strand, London WC2R 0RL
345 Hudson St, 4th Floor,
New York, NY 10014, USA
14 Local Shopping Centre, Panchsheel Park, New Delhi 110017, India
Distributed by the Penguin Group
Penguin Books Ltd,
80 Strand, London WC2R 0RL
Penguin Putnam, Inc.
375 Hudson Street, NY 10014, USA
Penguin Group (Australia)
250 Camberwell Road, Camberwell, Victoria 3124, Australia
Penguin Books Canada Ltd,
10 Alcorn Avenue, Toronto, Ontario, Canada M4V 1E4
Penguin Group (NZ)
67 Apollo Drive, Mairangi Bay, Auckland 1310, New Zealand
Cover concept by Peter Dyer.

Typeset in Bembo and Helvetica to an original design by Henry Iles.
Printed in China

288pp includes index
A catalogue record for this book is available from the British Library
ISBN 1-84353-756-7
ISBN 13: 9-78184-353-756-4

The publishers and authors have done their best to ensure the accuracy and currency of all the information in **The Rough Guide to Copenhagen**, however, they can accept no responsibility for any loss, injury, or inconvenience sustained by any traveller as a result of information or advice contained in the guide.

1   3   5   7   9   8   6   4   2

Help us update

We've gone to a lot of effort to ensure that the third edition of **The Rough Guide to Copenhagen** is accurate and up to date. However, things change – places get "discovered", opening hours are notoriously fickle, restaurants and rooms raise prices or lower standards. If you feel we've got it wrong or left something out, we'd like to know, and if you can remember the address, the price, the time, the phone number, so much the better.
We'll credit all contributions, and send a copy of the next edition (or any other Rough Guide if you prefer) for the best letters. Everyone who writes to us and isn't already a subscriber will receive a copy of our full-colour thrice-yearly newsletter. Please mark letters: "**Rough Guide Copenhagen Update**" and send to: Rough Guides, 80 Strand, London WC2R 0RL, or Rough Guides, 4th Floor, 345 Hudson St, New York, NY 10014. Or send an email to **mail@roughguides.com**
Have your questions answered and tell others about your trip at
www.roughguides.atinfopop.com

Acknowledgements

From **Caroline**, thanks to: Roy and Lise for making this book a possibility in the first place, Martin and Daisy for being wonderful research companions, Roger Norum for additional contributions, and Keith Drew for his calm and supportive editorial presence throughout.

From **Lone**, thanks yet again to: Henrik Thierlein of Wonderful Copenhagen for his invaluable ideas and support, Tina Schneider for a roof over her head, and Knud for some wild nights on the town.

Readers' letters

Thanks to all the readers who have taken the time to write in with comments and suggestions (and apologies if we've inadvertently omitted anyone's name):

Gitta Bechshøft; Cindy Chen; Cyril J Davies; Christian Holm Donatzky; G Goldsmith; Ian Hankinson; Edith L Hull; Richard Karpen; Klavs at Copenhagen Rainbow; Anne T S Nielsen, Yizhar Regev; Edward and Christine Thomas; Patricia Wright

SMALL PRINT

Photo credits

Index

Map entries are in colour.

INDEX

Map symbols

maps are listed in the full index using coloured text

---	Chapter boundary	⊞	Hospital
▬▬	Expressway	@	Internet access
═══	Major road	ⓘ	Information office
═══	Minor road	⊠	Post office
▬▬	Pedestrianized street	ⵜ	Fountain/gardens
⬚⬚⬚	Steps	⊙	Statue
‿	Bridge	■	Toilets
- - - - -	Path/cycle route	✡	Synagogue
▬●▬	Railway	Ⓜ	Metro station
———	Coastline/river	Ⓢ	S-Tog station
✈	Airport	★	Bus stop
✦	Point of interest	⊠—⊠	Gate/entrance
♯	Castle/fort	▬	Building
🏛	Stately home/palace	⊞	Church
♦	Museum	⬭	Stadium
🛉	Windmill	⊡	Cemetery
⛢	Campsite	▦	Park

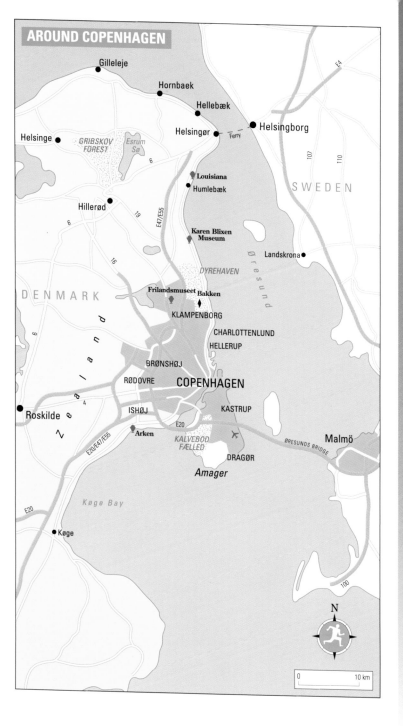

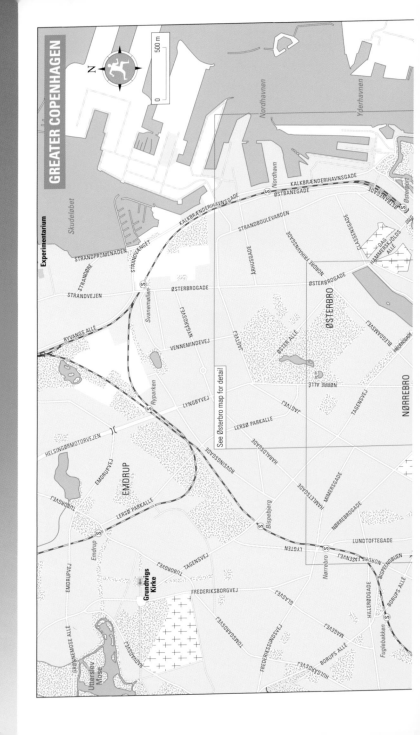

GREATER COPENHAGEN

N

0   500 m

Experimentarium

Skudeløbet

Nordhavnen

Yderhavnen

STRANDPROMENADEN

STRANDØRE

STRANDVEJEN

STRANDVÆNGET

KALKBRÆNDERIHAVNSGADE

STRANDBOULEVARDEN

KALKBRÆNDERIHAVNSGADE

ØSTBANEGADE

Nordhavn

CLASSENSGADE

DAG HAMMERSKJÖLDS ALLÉ

Østerport

ØSTBANEGADE

Svanemøllen

ØSTERBROGADE

ÅRHUSGADE

NORDRE FRIHAVNSGADE

ØSTERBROGADE

NYGÅRDSVEJ

ØSTERBRO

RYVANGS ALLÉ

VENNEMINDEVEJ

JAGTVEJ

ØSTER ALLÉ

BLEGDAMSVEJ

RYESGADE

Ryparken

LYNGBYVEJ

NØRRE ALLÉ

JAGTVEJ

TAGENSVEJ

NØRREBRO

See Østerbro map for detail

LERSØ PARKALLÉ

HELSINGØRMOTORVEJEN

ROVSINGSGADE

HARALDSGADE

HAMLETSGADE

MIMERSGADE

NØRREBROGADE

EMDRUPVEJ

EMDRUP

TUBORGVEJ

LERSØ PARKALLÉ

Bispebjerg

LUNDTOFTEGADE

Emdrup

EMDRUPVEJ

TAGENSVEJ

TUBORGVEJ

Nørrebro

NORDRE FASANVEJ

LYGTEN

Grundtvigs Kirke

FREDERIKSBORGVEJ

GLASVEJ

HILLERØDGADE

BISPEENGBUEN

GRØNNEMOSE ALLÉ

RÅDVADSVEJ

FREDERIKSSUNDSVEJ

TOMSGÅRDSVEJ

GLASVEJ

MÅGEVEJ

BORUPS ALLÉ

Fuglebakken

Utterslev Mose

HULGÅRDSVEJ

BORUPS ALLÉ

BORUPS ALLÉ

FASANVEJ

Nordhavnen

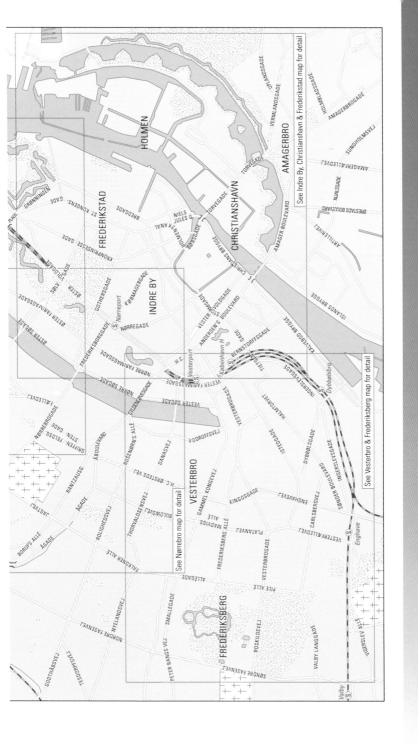

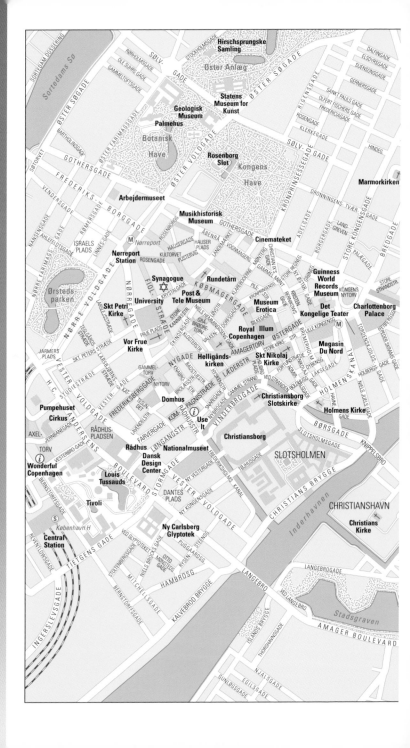

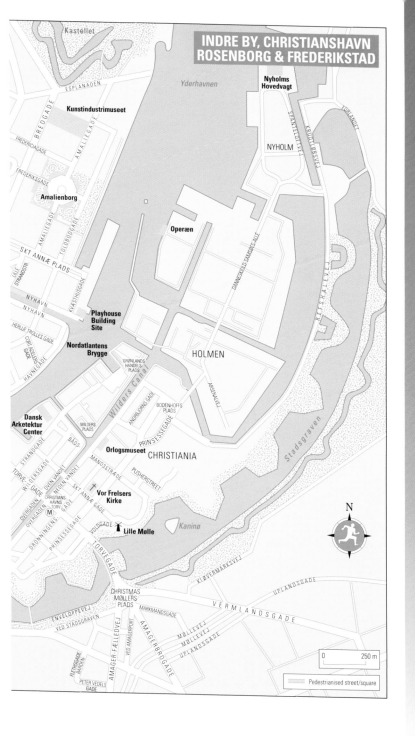

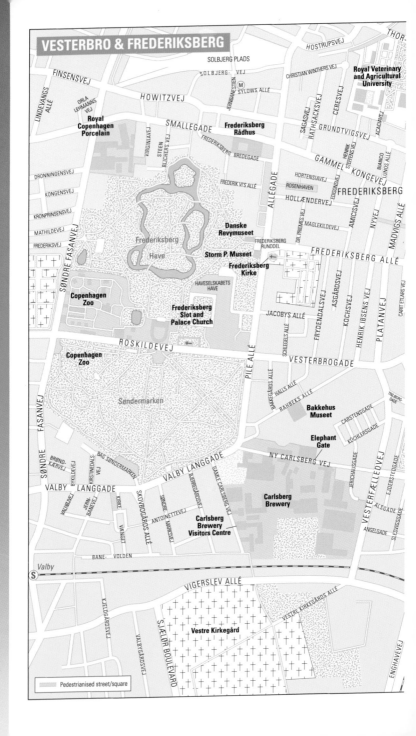

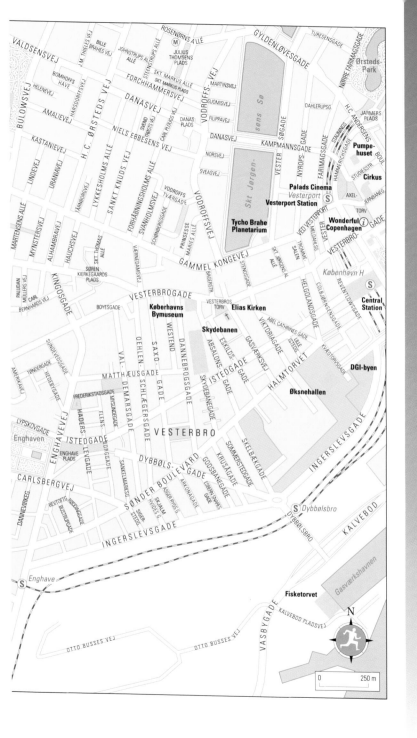

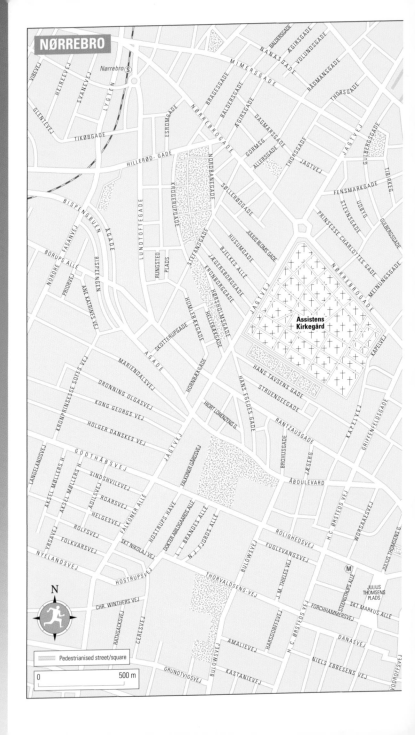

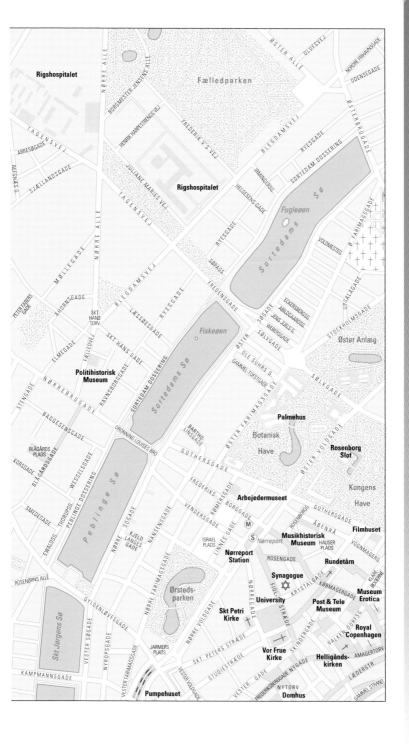

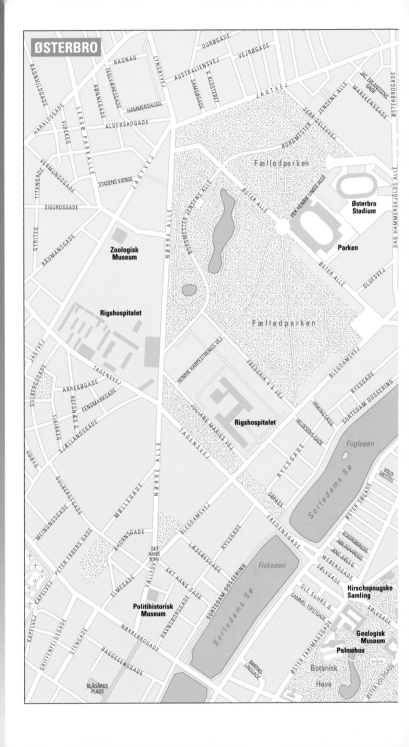

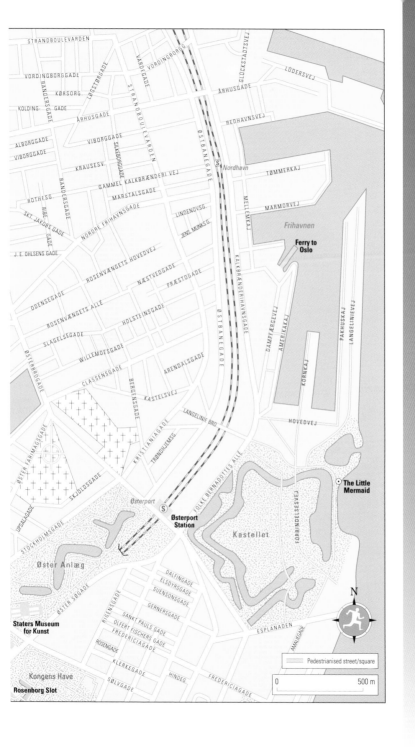

COPENHAGEN TRANSPORT

Gilleleje Øst
Stæremosen
Søborg
Firhøj
Dronningmølle
Kildekrog
Hornbæk Sand
Hornbæk
Karinebæk
Saunte
Skibstrup

Ålsgårde
Hellebæk
Højstrup
Marienlyst

Gilleleje
Fjellenstrup
Pårup
Græsted
Græsted Syd

Tisvildeleje
Godhavn
Holløse
Vejby
Ørby

Saltrup
Mårum

Grønholt
Fredensborg
Langerød
Kvistgård
Mørdrup

Grønnehave
Helsingør
Snekkersten
Espergærde
Humlebæk
Nivå
Kokkedal
Rungsted Kyst
Vedbæk
Skodsborg
Klampenborg
Ordrup
Charlottenlund

Kagerup
Gribsø
Slotspavillonen

Hillerød
Allerød
Birkerød
Holte
Virum
Sorgenfri
Lyngby

Hundested Havn
Hundested
Østerbjerg
Dyssekilde
Melby
Hanehoved
Frederiksværk
Lille Kregme
Kregme
Ølsted
Grimstrup

Vilbelius
Lodrup
Lausø
Helsinge
Duemose

Skævinge
Borupgård
Gørløse
Bredeskov

Gentofte
Bernstorffsvej

Nærum
Ravnholm
Brede
Ørholm
Fuglevad
Anker Engelunds Vej
Jægersborg

Hellerup

Farum
Værløse
Hareskov
Skovbrynet
Bagsværd
Stengården
Buddinge
Kildebakke
Vangede
Dyssegård
Emdrup
Ryparken

Svanemøllen
Nordhavn
Østerport
Nørreport
Kongens Nytorv
Christianshavn
Lergravsparken

Frederikssund
Ølstykke
Gl. Toftegård
Stenløse
Veksø
Kildedal
Måløv
Ballerup
Malmparken
Skovlunde
Herlev
Husum
Islev
Jyllingevej
Vanløse
Flintholm

Bispebjerg
Nørrebro
Fuglebakken
Grøndal

Lindevang
Solbjerg
Frederiksberg
Forum

Vesterport
København H
Islands Brygge
Universitetet
Sundby
Bella Center

KB Hallen
Ålholm

Peter Bangs Vej
Langgade

Dybbølsbro
Enghave
Valby

Amagerbro

Mod Kalundborg

Hvalsø
Lejre
Roskilde
Trekroner
Hedehusene
Høje Taastrup
Taastrup
Albertslund
Glostrup
Brøndbyøster
Rødovre
Hvidovre
Danshøj

Vigerslev Allé

Ørestad
Vestamager

Tårnby
Københavns Lufthavn, Kastrup

Mod Malmö

Mod Fyn og Jylland
Nykøbing F

Viby Sjælland
Borup

Gadstrup
Havdrup
Lille Skensved

Ny Ellebjerg

Sydhavn
Sjælør
Ellebjerg
Amarken
Friheden
Avedøre
Brøndby Strand
Vallensbæk

Herfølge
Tureby

Hvidovre

Karlslunde
Greve
Hundige
Jersie
Solrød Strand
Ølby
Køge

Egøje
Vallø
Grubberholm
Himlingøje
Hårlev
Varpelev

Mod Næstved

Lille-Linde

Mod Fakse Ladeplads   Mod Rødvig

Mod Rødvig

Metro
S-Tog
Regionaltog
Lokalbaner

DSB S M HUR Trafik